ANALYTIC VERSUS CONTINENTAL

ANALYTIC VERSUS CONTINENTAL

ARGUMENTS ON THE METHODS AND VALUE OF PHILOSOPHY

JAMES CHASE AND JACK REYNOLDS

McGill-Queen's University Press
Montreal & Kingston • Ithaca

© James Chase and Jack Reynolds 2010

ISBN 978-0-7735-3807-8 (bound)
ISBN 978-0-7735-3808-5 (pbk.)

Legal deposit fourth quarter 2010
Bibliothèque nationale du Québec

Published simultaneously outside North America
by Acumen Publishing Limited

McGill-Queen's University Press acknowledges the financial support of the Government of Canada through the Canada Book Fund for its activities.

Library and Archives Canada Cataloguing in Publication

Chase, James, 1969-
    Analytic versus continental : arguments on the methods and value of philosophy / James Chase and Jack Reynolds.

Includes bibliographical references and index.
ISBN 978-0-7735-3807-8 (bound).--ISBN 978-0-7735-3808-5 (pbk.)

    1. Analysis (Philosophy). 2. Continental philosophy. 3. Philosophy, Modern--History. I. Reynolds, Jack, 1976- II. Title.

B808.5.C53 2010   146'.4   C2010-906329-5

Printed in the UK by MPG Books Group.

CONTENTS

ACKNOWLEDGEMENTS

Trust is perhaps a necessary but not sufficient condition for friendship, and it is also a necessary but not sufficient condition for any dialogue worthy of the name (along with some scepticism and "trust-busting", but we get this for free on account of our respective philosophical orientations!). It is trust that has allowed this dialogue between two philosophers with rather different investments and interests to take place, despite the histories of animosity between analytic and continental philosophers over the years. Of course, the trust that makes this project possible also carries with it certain associated risks, notably that we have fashioned in an ecumenical spirit a harmony that belies the complexity of the issues at stake. If we have been successful in avoiding this potential problem, and that is up to the reader to decide, it is because we have involved other philosophers in this project throughout its duration. In that respect, we are grateful to everybody who has been party to this dialogue with us. We should mention at minimum: our postgraduate students (Sherah Bloor and Ricky Sebold, whose very different projects have themselves been philosophically illuminative); the co-investigators on the Australian Research Council grant of which this book is a part, and who have offered invaluable feedback on the penultimate draft of this book (George Duke, Edwin Mares and James Williams); colleagues at our respective universities with whom we have had innumerable discussions and some of whom have also responded to parts of this book (at La Trobe University: Andrew Brennan, Brian Ellis, John Fox, Frank Jackson, Norva Lo, Toula Nicolacopoulos, Tim Oakley, Philipa Rothfield, Janna Thompson, George Vassilacopoulos, Robert Young and Edoardo Zamuner; at the University of Tasmania: David Coady, Richard Corry, Ingo Farin, Jeff Malpas and Graham Wood). In the broader philosophical community, important and helpful comments have been made on this project by Andrew Benjamin, Chris Cordner, Andrew Cutrofello, Jay Garfield, Simon Glendinning, Douglas Lackey, Martyn Lloyd, Paul Patton, Jon Roffe, Hugh Silverman, Robert Sinnerbrink, Marion Tapper, Nick Trakakis,

James Watt, Ashley Woodward and Søren Overgaard, and C. G. Prado (who reviewed the manuscript for Acumen), as well as everyone who attended and presented at the workshops and conferences on this theme that were conducted in 2008 and 2009. Thanks are also due to the Australian Research Council for funding this research project, as well as the following journals and their editors for permission to republish material here, albeit in usually quite different forms: *International Journal of Philosophical Studies*, *Philosophy Compass*, *Philosophical Forum*, *Theory and Event* and *Parrhesia*. Thanks are also due to Continuum for allowing us to reuse the chapter "The Fate of Transcendental Reasoning in Contemporary Philosophy" from our co-edited collection (with Williams and Mares), *Postanalytic and Metacontinental: Crossing Philosophical Divides*. Our editor at Acumen, Tristan Palmer, has, as usual, been of great assistance in helping to frame this project and bring it to completion, as has Kate Williams and the rest of the Acumen team. Finally, we are most indebted to our families: Emily, Ada and Max; Jo, Rosa and Penelope. Thanks for your patience.

INTRODUCTION
ANALYTIC VERSUS CONTINENTAL
ARGUMENTS ON THE METHODS
AND VALUE OF PHILOSOPHY

Anyone who works within academic philosophy is familiar with the (claimed) distinction between analytic or Anglo-American philosophy and its so-called continental or European counterpart. On the standard view, a divergence has been under way since at least since the late nineteenth or early twentieth century, emphasized by differing interests, specializations and attitudes to the common philosophical heritage. Indeed, many would agree with Michael Dummett's assessment that "we have reached a point at which it's as if we're working in different subjects" (1993: 193).

Yet what does the distinction actually amount to? It is occasionally given a geographical tilt (analytic philosophy as a creation of the English-speaking countries; continental philosophy as a creation of France, Germany, Italy and other non-English-speaking countries) but this, at least, is a grotesque oversimplification. Some of the early influences on analytic philosophy are to be found in Austria and Germany: consider, for instance, Ernst Mach's positivism, Einstein's invocation of questions of meaning in his 1905 paper on special relativity, the philosophical logic of Bernard Bolzano's *Wissenschaftslehre*, the mathematical work of Kurt Weierstrass, Georg Cantor and Richard Dedekind, and Franz Brentano's conception of intentionality. Many of the heroes of early analytic philosophy were themselves Austrian or German (most notably Gottlob Frege, Ludwig Wittgenstein, Moritz Schlick and Rudolf Carnap). These connections are extremely well known, but they tend to be viewed through the filter of the subsequent migration to the anglophone world of many of the philosophers involved, and/or the first translation of their work into English. Dummett goes so far as to claim:

> The sources of analytical philosophy were the writings of philosophers who wrote, principally or exclusively, in the German language; and this would have remained obvious to everyone had it

> not been for the plague of Nazism which drove so many German-
> speaking philosophers across the Atlantic.   (*Ibid.*: ix)

We can add to Dummett's claims about origins. Early-twentieth-century analytic philosophy was also influenced by Polish logic, mathematics and associated philosophical work (consider Stanislaw Leśniewski, Alfred Tarski and Jan Łukaciewicz), and by ongoing developments in logic and the philosophy of mathematics in the German-speaking world (an enormous group, including among others David Hilbert, Kurt Gödel and Tarski again); by the mid-twentieth century Scandinavian analytic philosophers were also influential (consider Eino Kaila, Georg Henrik von Wright and Jaakko Hintikka). In the other direction, much early-twentieth-century anglophone philosophy in the United States and United Kingdom fell outside the analytic movement, was openly hostile to it, and indeed was straightforwardly Kantian or Hegelian in inspiration. The analytic dominance in the United Kingdom and the United States after the Second World War is far too easily read back into the earlier-twentieth-century philosophical history of both countries, filtering what we notice in the journals, appointments and monographs of the time.

Without geography to help us, is the distinction simply a spurious case of cross-classification? Certainly, it is a little disquieting that the "analytic–continental" distinction apparently opposes a method to a geographical location. As Bernard Williams puts it, it is "as though one divided cars into front-wheel drive and Japanese" (1996: 25). But this is a little too quick. Apparently empty descriptions may, like "the Holy Roman Empire", be entirely successful at picking out real entities; similarly, not too much weight should be placed on the preferred idiom here.[1] We think that meaningful philosophical differences can be found between the two traditions and so we use the conventional names for convenience, leaving aside any prescriptive implications they inevitably have for the ways in which philosophy ought (or ought not) to be done. But there are plenty of further potential snares here. Following common usage in this way does not magically make the distinction one that matters; it is at least an open possibility that the philosophical differences here are part of a larger story, in which one or both "traditions" are seen as heterogeneous entities. For instance, it might be that the "continental" tradition is something of a fiction; an opposing straw man invented by analytic philosophers. There are, after all, many ways to be non-analytic, as Simon Glendinning (2007) points out: consider pragmatism, the various forms of Asian philosophy, traditional philosophy (with a largely exegetical interest in the history of the tradition), feminism, and so on. Again, there could be a scale question here. Even if each of analytic and continental philosophy is in some sense a *genuine* tradition, it is not immediately clear that we are comparing species to species, rather than species to genus or family.

In the literature on the divide, there are two opposing positions that appear fairly regularly. On the one hand, there is something of an essentialism about the differences between these two traditions that, by implication, denies the possibility of any meaningful rapprochement. On the other hand, there is a deflationary response that calls into question any value that this distinction, and these terms, might have. It seems to us that both the essentialist and deflationary responses are misleading and unhelpful.

Innumerable essentialist accounts have been proffered by analytic and continental philosophers, often dropping out of a general or programmatic conception of philosophy as a whole (we shall see this illustrated in Part I). If philosophy has to engage in a critique of modernity, or has to embrace its historicity, then it is tempting to reject analytic philosophy as a faux-neutral and ahistorical game. If philosophy has to adopt norms of argument discourse constrained by formal logic or probability theory, or has to be continuous with the natural sciences, then it is equally tempting to reject continental philosophy as nonsense, mysticism or literature. Such claims are natural enough, given the tribal allegiances involved here, but they obviously need close examination and are, at best, contestable. Moreover, such meta-philosophies *are* contested, each within the very camp that the essentialist is championing. Analytic philosophers, for instance, vigorously debate the role of logic, the relations between philosophy and science, the worth of standard analytic techniques and so on among themselves, and these are not peripheral debates carried out in minor journals by obscure philosophers, but rather major debates that mark serious divides within analytic philosophy, obvious to all participants. Even if one prefers to keep essentialist walls up, they simply do not quite run where the essentialist wants them to. And, of course, there is evidence that actual philosophical practice can undermine the walls in any case. There are places (such as ethics and feminist philosophy, and perhaps some parts of the philosophy of mind) where the two traditions come closer and even perhaps sometimes overlap, and there are topical areas where significant rapprochements and helpful dialogue have been achieved. Essentialism thus ignores the internal diversity of each tradition, rather too quickly rules out all potential for engagement between them, and is blind to the places where this is already under way. Finally, essentialism is to some extent risky. By describing philosophy's "divided house" in an essentialist manner, one runs the risk of performatively making it more real and oppressive than it is or needs to be – it is in this sense that appeals to the idea of the "divide" can be said to partake in what Glendinning describes as the "rotten contemporary scene" (*ibid.*: 7), rather than merely to neutrally describe it.

Deflationary responses hold that we are all simply doing philosophy, a more or less continuous practice, and that we should ignore the so-called analytic and continental distinction. Those who argue that style is the main difference between the traditions tend to be deflationary, in that they usually take there to be no significant problem with the translation of the issues and problems that concern the one group to the language of the other, beyond the difficulties brought about by stylistic difference. Bernard Williams (2002: 4) suggests that appeals to the idea of a "divide" involve positing a distinction without a difference, and he intimates that it largely comes down to matters concerning style; Hilary Putnam asks "why can we not just be philosophers without an adjective?" (1997: 203).[2] This may be an effective way to do comparative philosophy between the traditions on particular occasions (indeed, we think that the deflationist spirit can be extremely useful here), but something is missing as well. Strict deflationism does not offer an *explanation* for the very real disdain (which has a philosophical component to it, whatever else is involved) that many analytic philosophers feel for continental philosophy and that many continental philosophers feel for analytic philosophy.

The divide is an immediately apparent feature in the lives of many or most contemporary philosophers in the West. Academic philosophers, journals, conferences, publication series and even entire publishing houses very often live entirely within one or the other tradition. In some cases, the result is that continental philosophers (or those, like Richard Rorty, who take steps in that direction) are consigned to or move to other disciplines, such as comparative literature; occasionally analytic philosophers have had the same treatment, being sorted into the technical academies well away from traditional philosophical strongholds (as has happened in France). More usually, philosophers simply inhabit their own tradition without really attending to the other, perhaps looking at or attending occasional papers from the other side out of collegial politeness or personal loyalty (and often regretting it when they do). All the signs are there that many people on each side of the divide simply have nothing to say to each other. The divide has also, notoriously, ramified throughout the social sciences and humanities. It is familiar wherever a confirmation theorist meets a constructivist, or a poststructuralist meets a positivist, in myriad debates about the significance of Michel Foucault's work or the scope of covering law explanation (or indeed in the careful avoiding of such encounters). Arguably, the analytic–continental divide has underwritten methodological incomprehension and rejection between different camps in sociology, history, anthropology, literary theory, archaeology and many other fields.

The social fact of division is, it seems to us, unarguable, but we would also contend that there is a philosophical dimension to it as well. This is easiest to bring out if we concentrate on the analytic side of the fence. There is a kind of interactivity between analytic philosophers that is not extended to philosophical outsiders (including members of the putative continental tradition).

Characterizations of analytic philosophy in terms of patterns of influence and communication are not at all uncommon in the literature, if only as part of a fuller account.[3] The claims about influence and communication that are made in this way are usually causal, but we believe that there is a normative aspect to such connectivity as well. One of us (Chase 2010) has previously argued that contemporary analytic philosophy can be seen as a common dialogic enterprise characterized by a degree of internal interactivity and responsiveness, which aims to promote a certain kind of "inferential connectivity" without employing the kinds of structuring devices that are found in the sciences (such as explicitly hierarchical authority relations based purely on area of expertise, or explicit research agendas). If this is right, analytic philosophers are not merely influenced by past members of the tradition, and are not just communicating to other analytic philosophers of their time; rather, their communications are in part designed to bring out the inferential connections between pieces of philosophical work produced by different philosophers. Hence, for example, the ubiquity, within analytic philosophy, of devices of common reference: stock examples and thought experiments, standard patterns of argument, deliberately abstracted model or toy views such as "vanilla" Bayesianism, placeholder concepts, and so forth. A *ceteris paribus* concern for common reference lets more be wrung out of the connection-making practices of the analytic tradition; real debate on local matters is furthered by defeasible agreement on starting places, it becomes possible to "join" different pieces of work to draw further inferences from them, and so on.

The point behind such invocations is that analytic philosophical work of this kind by and large references other analytic work. Figures thought of as paradigmatically continental (Edmund Husserl, Martin Heidegger, Jacques Derrida and so on) are rarely referred to in analytic work, and appear to have had very little influence within that tradition (except in the sense of helping to confirm the identity of analytic philosophy by reference to what it is not), and analytic philosophers generally do not seek to bring out inferential connections with their writings. Figures within analytic philosophy who are interested in liaisons with the continental tradition do exist, but their work of particular continental interest is itself rarely referred to in analytic work, appears to have had little influence in that tradition, and is not generally inferentially integrated with analytic discussions.[4] Bluntly, the early Donald Davidson is a major presence in the analytic tradition and the late Davidson is not. This pattern ramifies. If one collects what analytic literature there is on the late Davidson, and compares it to the non-analytic literature on the same work, it is apparent that the two proceed in parallel without much interconnection or overlap. There is hardly a bridge between the traditions here. From the point of view of the analytic philosophical tradition itself, the lack of influence, lack of communication and lack of joint work on display here is itself enough to make out the case that there is a philosophical aspect to the divide.

METHOD AS A MIDDLE WAY: BETWEEN ESSENTIALISM AND DEFLATIONISM ABOUT THE "DIVIDE"

Dummett suggests that only by going back to the roots of the divide can we now hope to establish communication between the traditions. Although this is evidently a project of interest in itself, we see no reason to think that this is the *only* way for those with such hopes to approach the divide. Our own preference is to seek an informed understanding of the limits and possibilities of the methods employed in each tradition, and that is what we attempt here. While facts about the divide, the general lack of trust on either side of it, and the reality or unreality of various alleged bridges across it can be discussed from the above perspective, to address possible rapprochements between the traditions and to make judgements about the desirability of this situation requires us to take more of an internal stance, so to speak.

Part I provides some required background, in the form of a short history of the interactions between the traditions that have become celebrated on one or the other side. In Part II we consider some of the core methodological differences between the traditions as well as the meta-philosophical justifications bound up with them. By elaborating in Part III on the topical consequences of these methodological preferences, we think we can steer a middle way between essentialism and deflationism in outlining the current state of the divide. A broad theme of the book is that there is a quasi-unity undergirding each tradition (even the "motley crew" that is continental philosophy), in terms of the methodological norms each has adopted, which makes it difficult for those in each tradition to take seriously the work carried out in the other. In the face of such entrenched methodological difference, it can be tempting to simply accept the usual non-mutual practices in which each tradition ignores the other and concerns itself only with criticism from within. Certainly, this seems more realistic than to look for a thoroughly implausible mutual coherence, in which the contested understanding of the role and value of philosophy somehow fades into the background, and critical discussion somehow leads to methodological agreement. But there is a middle ground here as well. It can be enlightening to look at the ways in which representatives of each tradition can (by the lights of that tradition) legitimately respond to methodological criticism from the other. Such responses are very unlikely to satisfy those in the other tradition, but that is not the only goal one can have here.[5]

Since we are, in effect, seeking to partially explicate the divide by considering method, our project might seem to take issue with a number of recent meta-philosophical works in which methodological accounts of one or other tradition are put into question.[6] But we are not engaged in the game of coming up with a "necessary and sufficient conditions" characterization of each tradition in purely methodological terms; it is clear enough that not all analytic philosophers place a high value on explicit argument (nor respect science, etc.), and not all non-analytic philosophers ignore such desiderata. The approach here is more exemplary, and allows for the possibility of figures standing in both traditions, or indeed for there being regions of philosophy in which the traditions somewhat overlap. Analytic and continental philosophers frequently employ distinct methods, and disagree as to their worth and proper field of application. Each tradition exhibits distinct stylistic preferences, norms of engagement and discussion, and harbours distinctly different attitudes as to what are the more significant philosophical issues and questions. We seek here to engage each tradition's respective philosophical "other" (whether analytic or continental) by looking at some of the methods that are particularly prevalent in one tradition and rare in the other, and by then considering the way these methodological preferences tilt the discussion of particular topics that both traditions have engaged with.

In fact, our approach seems to us fairly close to the family resemblance account of philosophical traditions, in which they are seen as united by networks of overlapping but discontinuous features. A prominent example of this is Hans-Johann Glock's *What is Analytic Philosophy?* (2008: 212–18), in which it is argued that the analytic tradition is united by a chain of causal influences across time (analytics read Russell, Carnap, Quine and so on), but also by varying but overlapping commitments to the linguistic turn, the rejection of metaphysics, the claim that philosophy is continuous with science, a reductive approach to analysis, the employment of formal logic, a focus on argument and a concern for clarity. Many of these indicia are also methodologically suggestive; indeed, in characterizing *contemporary* analytic philosophy, one might just as readily look for the use of thought experiments, the direct appeal to intuition, the reliance on reflective equilibrium, the preparedness to use a range of naturalizing devices and so on. These are all clearly methodological commitments, and just as clearly markers of contemporary analytic philosophy. Moreover, in similar spirit we could add to Glock's own list a number of other apparent indicators of analyticity in the earlier tradition that are also methodological, such as the injunction to minimize one's departure from empiricist respectability, or to place some weight on the deliverances of common sense. The family resemblance strategy has been less common in discussions of continental philosophy, possibly because it is felt to be more difficult to provide such overlapping indicia. We think this is a difference in degree rather than a difference in kind. Part of the burden of this book will be to show that there is a loose philosophical unity to continental philosophy, despite the quite radical differences between existentialists, structuralists, poststructuralists, critical theorists, phenomenologists and so on, and despite the fact that the term "continental philosophy" was bestowed from without in much the same manner as the English idea of a "continental breakfast". Indeed, indicia of the continental tradition appear to us to include such matters as: a wariness about aligning philosophical method with common sense; a "temporal turn" that encompasses both ontological issues and an emphasis on the historical presuppositions of concepts and theoretical frameworks; an interest in thematizing intersubjectivity; an anti-representationalism about the mind; an investment in transcendental arguments and, more generally, transcendental reasoning; a concern with the relation between style and content; a critical and non-deferential (or transformative) attitude to science; and an "anti-theoretical" attitude to ethico-political matters. Some of these are rather more negative than positive features, but they are features of the tradition nonetheless, and there are few continental philosophers in whose work many or most of these features cannot be found. In addition, of course, the continental tradition, like the analytic tradition, exhibits patterns of influence over time (in this case, Kant, Nietzsche, Husserl and Heidegger, among others, are the key figures). For these reasons, it seems to us that the claim that there is a distinctive tradition of continental philosophy is not significantly less plausible than the corresponding claim for analytic philosophy.

Our main aim, here, however, is not to affirm any given identity of either analytic or continental philosophy. Rather, examining the methodological preferences of the respective traditions is intended to help in understanding what is at stake in this distinction and the limits and possibilities of the methods employed in each tradition. In the preface to his *The Philosophy of Philosophy*, Timothy Williamson remarks that his book grew "out of a sense that contemporary [analytic] philosophy lacks a self-image that does it justice" (2008: ix), and he points to places where analytic practice is not backed up by a well-developed understanding of the legitimate scope of analytic methods. On the other side, many continental philosophers have an *a priori* concern about the very idea of philosophical methods that it is difficult to justify writ large. Although it makes for a lively meta-philosophical dialogue, it is certainly not evident that the widespread continental suspicion and rejection of characteristically analytic devices is much more informed, or that continental practices are better off for largely side-stepping analytic concerns. Modest pluralist benefits can follow on both sides from being forced to look at one's own presuppositions through sceptical eyes. Of course, this is a contingent claim. The history of twentieth-century philosophy attests to the fact that interaction between the traditions can instead lead to antagonism (and on a personal level, we have found that this project *annoys* some of our colleagues). We would not go so far as to claim that one cannot understand either analytic or continental philosophy without its "other", but we would suggest that for those with a meta-philosophical interest in understanding their own tradition, the eyes of the "other" are worth attending to.

PART I

FORMATIVE ENCOUNTERS

A SHORT HISTORY OF THE "DIVIDE"

The origins and early years of the divide have been explored from several angles (e.g. Ansell-Pearson 2002; Beaney 2007; Cobb-Stevens 1990; Dummett 1993; Friedman 2000); here our concern is simply to provide an overview of some of the main performative encounters between (what are now thought to be) canonical representatives of analytic and continental philosophy, which also have some historical resonance at present. In roughly chronological order, we shall focus here on the encounters between: Husserl and Frege; Henri Bergson and Bertrand Russell; Heidegger and Carnap; Max Horkheimer against logical positivism; Karl Popper and several major targets of his thought – Sigmund Freud, Karl Marx and Theodor Adorno (in relation to the "Positivist Dispute" of the 1960s); the 1958 Royaumont discussions, including Maurice Merleau-Ponty, A. J. Ayer, W. V. Quine and Gilbert Ryle; and the sometimes vitriolic debate between Derrida and John Searle in the 1970s.

While this selection is obviously not all-encompassing, these encounters were historically important in laying the groundwork for (and in reinforcing) the analytic–continental distinction. Throughout the period we examine, it becomes increasingly less common for members of the analytic movement to enter discussions or contestations with philosophers from rival camps, if only because it becomes easier to talk directly to analytic philosophers alone. In late 1933, the journal *Analysis* was launched, edited by A. E. Duncan-Jones with the help of, among others, Ryle (at that time firmly a proponent of the linguistic turn) and Susan Stebbing (who had an explicit interest in the differing methods of analysis of the Vienna Circle and Cambridge). The first issue opened with a "Statement of Policy", which noted "there is a considerable number of philosophers a great part or the whole of whose philosophical interests is in discovering the precise constitution of particular facts or specific types of fact" (Duncan-Jones 1933: 1). In effect, this is the first English-language journal that a philosopher could open confident in the knowledge that it contained *nothing but* analytic philosophy; perhaps it is not accidental

11

that the phrase "analytic philosophy" itself dates from around this time.[1] Around 1950, the positivist émigré community in the United States took further steps in this direction, and Herbert Feigl and Wilfrid Sellars published an influential collection of readings in philosophical analysis in 1949, based on a survey of ninety "teachers of philosophy" in the United States and United Kingdom (Feigl & Sellars 1949: 85–102), and then launched and edited the standard-bearing *Philosophical Studies* (subtitled "an international journal for philosophy in the analytic tradition") in 1950. There is no statement of policy here, although the first paper in the first volume is concerned to establish the claim that "a great deal of the contemporary analytic movement is a genuine continuation of the analytic traditions long established in Western philosophy" (Weitz 1950: 2). Something of a determined marking out of a tradition seems to be going on here; at the very least, the Feigl and Sellars collection, like influential anthologies in other fields, served to identify a canon for teaching purposes. By contrast, anglophone continental philosophy seems to have been a little more ecumenical. *Philosophy and Phenomenological Research* was launched in 1940, and the first editor, Marvin Farber, contributed as the first article an appreciation of Husserl, which predicted that "the period of Husserl's international effectiveness on a large scale has now begun, as shown by the systematically organized interest of scholars all over the world in the understanding and development of his philosophy" (1940: 20). Despite these words, Farber accepted work from all traditions in the journal, and he maintained a philosophical correspondence with philosophers from both traditions, including Roderick Chisholm, Carnap, Sellars and Russell.

What follows from this? For a start, in an environment where philosophers from the two traditions encountered each other on fewer occasions (notwithstanding Farber's attitude), well-known brushes between prominent members of the traditions could take on a significance that they simply would not have if communication were more common. Frege's critique of Husserl's psychologism and subjectivism has echoed throughout the twentieth century in the analytic attitude to phenomenology. Likewise, Carnap's dismissal of Heidegger as a bad metaphysician whose philosophy of Being rested on nothing more than a linguistic confusion has been subsequently repeated in influential books by Ayer and Quine, and has something of the same status (as the analysis of grammatical confusion about existence in a metaphysical argument) as Kant's objection to the ontological argument. Following Russell's attacks on his work (and at least partly as a consequence of them), Bergson went from being one of the most famous living philosophers in the world at the start of the twentieth century to being almost totally neglected in Anglo-American countries for most of the twentieth century (Bergson also suffered a corresponding fall from esteem in France, for different reasons, arguably until Deleuze reawakened interest in him in the mid 1960s). And, given that twentieth-century continental philosophy is heavily indebted to what Paul Ricoeur called the "masters of suspicion" – Marx, Nietzsche and Freud – Popper's criticism of two of this triumvirate, along with psycho-analysis and Marxism more generally, has also been significant. Whatever one thinks of Popper's own analytic credentials, he played a major role in placing Freud and Marx beyond the pale of professional philosophy in anglo-phone countries. In general then, our reconstruction and deconstruction of this history hopes to illuminate philosophical options that were foreclosed by these key encounters, and to renew some important debates that remain live today concerning reason, clarity, the value and role of "first philosophy" and transcendental argumentation more generally, as well as to frame some of the methodological and topical discussions that follow in later chapters.

It is also difficult to deny that the antagonistic analytic "versus" contin-ental framework here has been largely (but not exclusively) promulgated by analytic philosophers. The polemical debates that we shall examine were on many occasions intended to be demonstrations that the methods of analysis have an antibacterial function in exposing error. There is arguably nothing particularly distinctive about this in the history of philosophy as a whole; indeed, in continental philosophy each generation seeks to distinguish itself from prior influences in a similarly pugnacious manner. But, of course, con-tinental philosophies often contained implicit or explicit criticism of analysis that fuelled such episodes. The dialectical philosophies of Hegel and Marx contain much anti-analytic material in embryo; for instance, the theme that only a synthetic approach, considering unities as wholes, could attain to gen-uine philosophical truth. Continental projects concerned with a reworked first philosophy often clear the ground with a wholesale rejection of other philosophical traditions or ideas, perhaps most notably philosophies that make formal logic central; despite the centrality his early work accords to philosophical logic, consider Husserl's declaration that only phenomenology provides a "presuppositionless" philosophy. Bergson's evolutionist philoso-phy is directed against analysis in metaphysics. More explicitly, critical theor-ists such as Horkheimer and Adorno offered early and influential criticisms of logical positivism, and a highly critical attitude to logic is a common trope in the tradition. It is evident in Heidegger's work, and also in Deleuze and Félix Guattari's dismissive writings on logic in *What is Philosophy?*, where there is a whole chapter on the confusion introduced by the conflation of philosophy and science that logic is for them.

Our strategy of focusing on these moments of dialogic disputation between representatives of (what has come to be called) analytic and con-tinental philosophy does not, of course, mean that we dismiss prior historical influences that were pivotal to the instantiation of the divide. There are many such pre-schisms. One is the simple contrast between British empiricism and continental rationalism. Yet even this well-worn contrast is itself to some extent imposed on the history of philosophy by those who have an eye on the analytic–continental divide, rather than something that is found in the work of Descartes, Spinoza, Leibniz, Locke, Berkeley and Hume. Ayer remarks – only exaggerating slightly – that English *analytic* philosophers did not read any French philosopher after Descartes, and that every French philosopher that he knew (quite a few) thought that British empiricism was an unmitigated disaster (1986: 24). But this was hardly the dominant attitude within either French or English philosophy (let alone German and Austrian philosophy) in the eighteenth and nineteenth centuries. A second pre-schism that is sometimes pointed to is the divide between the Romantic and scientific inheritances of the Enlightenment, something that in the case of philosophy is itself bound up with divergent historical receptions of Kant. On the one hand, Kant's larger philosophical and aesthetic enterprise and concern with subjectivity are stressed; on the other, his status is that of an anti-sceptical epistemologist and debunker of the claims of dogmatic metaphysics.[2] A related pre-schism is simply that between Hegelian idealism and some kind of realism; certainly, the conventional account of early analytic philosophy is as something of a revolt against the British Idealists (F. H. Bradley, T. H. Green, J. M. E. McTaggart, etc.). Finally, and bringing in themes from all of the above schisms, one might point to the positivist inheritance of analytic philosophy from late-nineteenth-century empiricism (Mach, Karl Pearson, Pierre Duhem, etc.), and its opposition to scientific projects in the *Naturphilosophie* tradition (an explicitly idealist heritage), to the explanatory positing of entities such as *élan vital*, to the use of the methods of *Verstehen* (or hermeneutic understanding), and so on.

Again, in focusing on philosophical engagements, it would be foolish to ignore wider historical patterns that have arisen since the birth of the analytic movement. The rise of Nazism and the Second World War have undoubtedly influenced the divide. Nearly all of the prominent British analytic philosophers were involved in the war effort, and they gave up their philosophical work to be so. It is hence unsurprising that many of the criticisms of continental philosophy in this period have a distinctly political register, seeing fascism, for example, as the logical outcome of certain tendencies in continental philosophy from the nineteenth century on (especially Romanticism and German idealism). Popper targeted Hegel and Marx as forerunners of totalitarian thinking in *The Open Society and its Enemies*, a view that Russell repeats in *A History of Western Philosophy*; elsewhere Russell also suggests that the work of Fichte and Nietzsche culminates in Hitler (Akehurst 2008: 550). Other eminent British analytic philosophers of the time – Isaiah Berlin, Anthony Quinton, Stuart Hampshire, R. M. Hare, Ayer and Ryle – offered similar, if less strident, sentiments. Ayer, for example, suggests that Nazism is Romanticism gone wrong, and that the philosophy of Nietzsche, although no doubt misappropriated by the Nazis, "seems to me to represent a kind of woolly romantic thinking which made Nazism possible" (quoted in *ibid.*: 551). French existentialism during and after the war was seen as a continuation of this Romantic-cum-fascist trajectory, although, of course, most of the philosophers associated with existentialism were members of the French resistance. Thomas Akehurst is hence right to say that this was never simply a philosophical quarrel, but also to some extent a political and ideological one (*ibid.*: 557).

We shall start with two philosophers who are significant parts of the inherited canon of each tradition (even the "founders" for some) and remain vital to the self-conception and identity of contemporary analytic and continental philosophers: Frege and Husserl.

1. FREGE AND HUSSERL

Recall Dummett's suggestion that contemporary communication between analytic and continental philosophers requires a revisiting of the work of Husserl and Frege. Husserl and Frege are both remarkably influential in their respective traditions at present, but the point behind Dummett's remark is that, in the period from about 1884 to 1896 (i.e. between the publication of Frege's *Foundations of Arithmetic* and Husserl's first version of the "Prolegomena to Pure Logic") the two are to some extent on the same philosophical page. They communicate both privately and publicly; they do not always disagree when they do so; and when they do disagree they nonetheless hold to sufficiently common argumentative standards to allow for shifts of position in the face of objection and counter-argument. We can see some important similarities in their philosophies, and yet the differences between them have nonetheless set in place much of what we come to associate with analytic and continental philosophy.

It is worth flagging at the outset the curious place of Frege within the analytic pantheon. Whether or not he is regarded as its founder, Russell is often seen as the most vigorous promoter of the analytic movement at the turn of the nineteenth and twentieth centuries. The story is told in detail in Russell's own autobiography, and in later biographies of himself and Alfred North Whitehead. Russell's embrace of the method of analysis followed an earlier (Hegelian) commitment to the methods of synthesis and dialectic in philosophy (he appears to have been unusually alive to questions of philosophical method at this time).[1] In both his dialectical and analytical phases, Russell's guiding concern came from the philosophy of mathematics. His preference for dialectic synthesis over analysis originated in the conviction that mathematical difficulties with the nature of continuity and the infinite were the expression of underlying philosophical antinomies, and his change of mind in 1898 came upon encountering symbolic logic in Book II of Whitehead's *Treatise on Universal Algebra* (and thence appreciating

Dedekind's achievement in taming such matters; Lowe 1985: 230–31). Moore's 1899 essay "The Nature of Judgment" then gave Russell a conception of metaphysics in which the central role was played by the "proposition", an entity that "positively cries out to be broken up into its constituent parts" (Monk 1996: 117). This is a problem landscape for which the tools of logical analysis are perfectly suited, and so, in bringing Moore and the mathematicians together, Russell sets analytic philosophy on its path.

To contemporary philosophical audiences, the absence of Frege is striking here; his role as the logico-mathematical influence on Russell appears to have been entirely usurped by Whitehead. Yet none of the details above are untrue. Russell acknowledges in the preface to *The Principles of Mathematics* (1903) that he only came to realize that Frege had in many ways anticipated him when he absorbed the contents of the first volume of Frege's *Grundgesetze der Arithmetik* (*The Basic Laws of Arithmetic*) in that year. In the period to his death in 1925, Frege's *only* direct influence on analytic philosophers other than Russell and Wittgenstein was in his contributions to logic and the analysis of mathematical concepts (and even here he is often read at second hand through Russell). Frege's crucial shift to the sense–reference account of meaning – not one of the features in which Russell had unwittingly followed him – is most clearly set out in his 1891–92 articles (those usually rendered in English as "Function and Concept", "On Concept and Object" and "On Sense and Reference"), but those early analytic philosophers who encountered the view at all did so in the rather more rarefied environment of his *Grundgesetze*. As a result, and despite the enormous influence of Russell's "On Denoting", much that we think of as the analytic inheritance from Frege barely appears in the pre-war literature. Frege's specifically philosophical work was first translated into English in the late 1940s, partly explaining and explained by his lack of earlier influence in the anglophone philosophy of language;[2] but the same pattern of neglect also holds with respect to German-speaking analytics. For instance, Carnap's 1934 *Logische Syntax der Sprache* (*The Logical Syntax of Language*), most certainly a work concerned with the application of philosophical logic to language, uses Frege's mathematical and logical work, but makes no mention of his work in the philosophy of language.

What has occurred here is a kind of projection backwards, which also inevitably affects the way in which we see the Frege–Husserl debate. In the post-war period, Frege's sense–reference distinction very rapidly became a central feature of analytic philosophy of language, and, since the interpretative work of Dummett in particular, Frege has been considered an analytic philosopher *par excellence*. Yet to some extent this genuine fact about his late influence makes it difficult to see that Frege has retrospectively been enrolled in a tradition with which he had only sporadic relations at the time. Certainly, in the *early* twentieth century, the Frege–Husserl dispute did not have any special significance for most in the analytic tradition; psychologizing charges directed against phenomenology are not to be laid to this particular door. Indeed, Frege's 1894 review of Husserl was only partially excerpted in the standard Geach–Black translation of his work, and the translators avoided most of the more polemical parts of the review.[3] The symbolic significance of the Frege–Husserl exchange for the analytic tradition more lately is largely due to Dagfinn Føllesdal (1958), who argues that Frege's 1894 review of Husserl's *Philosophy of Arithmetic* may have influenced Husserl not only in abandoning psychologism, but in developing an account of meaning that is in many respects very similar to Frege's own. Føllesdal's claim has since come under attack, and evidence has been adduced that Husserl quite independently arrived at the relevant theses; one aspect of this reaction has been the development, in turn, of something of a defence of the early Husserl against the continental tradition's tendency to regard his work in this period as immature and pre-phenomenological.[4] Both of these developments within the analytic literature do something to bring the early Husserl within the tradition.

The episode begins with Frege, and his ambition, following his development of modern logic in 1879, to put mathematical proof on as sound a footing as possible by demonstrating that arithmetic is a subset of logic. In the *Foundations of Arithmetic*, Frege goes part-way to this conclusion by making a case for regarding arithmetical statements as analytic. Beginning with a highly influential reshaping of Kant's notion of analyticity (as that which is true by logic and definitions alone), Frege launches an attack on subjectivist or psychological accounts of mathematical entities, and instead identifies number statements as statements about objective concepts:

> While looking at one and the same external phenomenon, I can say with equal truth both "It is a copse" and "It is five trees", or both "Here are four companies" and "Here are 500 men". Now what changes here from one judgement to the other is neither any individual object, nor the whole, the agglomeration of them, but rather my terminology. But that is itself only a sign that one concept has been substituted for another. This suggests ... that the content of a statement of number is an assertion about a concept. This is perhaps clearest with the number 0. If I say "Venus has 0 moons", there simply does not exist any moon or agglomeration of moons for anything to be asserted of; but what happens is that a property is assigned to the *concept* "moon of Venus", namely that of including nothing under it. If I say "the King's carriage is drawn by four horses", then I assign the number four to the concept "horse that draws the King's carriage".   (Frege 1953: §46 at 59e)

From this point on, the major contribution of the *Foundations* to Frege's overall logicist project is in the definition of number that Frege gives. Very roughly, Frege defines the number belonging to a concept *F* in the following way. Call a set of things "equinumerous with *F*" if the objects in the set can be put into one-to-one correspondence with the set of objects for which *F* holds (*ibid.*: §68 at 79e; §72 at 85e). (For example, the set of arms on Plato's body is equinumerous with the set of eyes on his face.) Then the number belonging to *F* is defined as the extension of the concept "equinumerous with *F*". (That is, it is the set of sets, each of which is equinumerous with *F* – in the previous example, the number of Plato's eyes is a set consisting of the set of Plato's arms, the set of Plato's legs, the set of Socrates' legs, etc.) Definitions are then given of zero (as the number belonging, in the way we have just defined, to the concept "not identical to itself") and the successor relation (the relation that holds between one integer and the next), and Frege demonstrates that the ordinary properties of the natural numbers obtain from these definitions.[5] Notice that the whole of this project has been carried out without relying on psychological entities (given Frege's metaphysics of concepts and extensions).

Husserl's *Philosophy of Arithmetic* of 1891 takes issue with all this. His general view in this work is that much of our work with numbers concerns only *symbols* of them; we engage in a formal rule-bound activity in which numbers themselves are absent. Numbers are only given to us when a psychological achievement is possible, in which we collect objects and consider them as wholes or aggregates under the aspect of plurality. Very obviously, this is a psychologistic account. Husserl therefore rejects Frege's anti-psychologism. In particular, he objects to Frege's conception of *non*-stipulative definition within an analytic project; definition, that is, which is at once informative and yet somehow only recognitional. As Dummett (1996: 24–8) points out, Husserl here appears to hit on a version of the "paradox of analysis", a puzzle usually attributed to G. E. Moore.

The paradox of analysis raises questions about the method of analysis as a whole: if a piece of conceptual analysis (say) is successful, then it must have hit on an analytic truth – it must have found a meaning equivalence between the definiens and the definiendum. However, if it has done this, it appears neither to genuinely give us new information nor to be the kind of thing the correctness of which could be possibly in doubt, so the whole point of the analysis is put into question. This is a major issue within analytic philosophy. Michael Beaney suggests that what is distinctive about analytic philosophy is not simply the use of analysis, since all philosophers have done and continue to do analysis of some kind, but instead the use of what he calls "transformational analysis", in which everyday language is translated into an ideal language (often with the help of logic) before one undertakes analysis of some other kind, commonly decompositional. Nothing like this takes place within continental philosophy of language; when cognate problems (such as the learning paradox of the *Meno*) are discussed, say in Merleau-Ponty or Heidegger, they are typically resolved not by refinement of the notion of analysis but by attention to background presuppositions and the inevitability of a certain hermeneutic circle.

Husserl's concern is expressed in psychologistic terms, so he does not approach Frege's project directly on Frege's terms, as it were, but Dummett identifies this as something of a parting of the ways:

> Husserl had clearly faced the paradox of analysis, and had come to the conclusion that it is irresoluble, and hence that analysis is impossible. Frege, in his review, rejects the paradox, and, with it, the demand that the definition of a term should be analytic in the sense of his 1914 lectures [that is, an equivalence of senses].
>
> (*Ibid.*: 24–5)

Of course, this is at best a one-sided parting, in that, even if the Husserlian attitude to the paradox of analysis is somehow replicated through the continental tradition, Frege's reply is by no means the main line of analytic response to the paradox.

Husserl has other objections to Frege's project. For instance, he presents an extended critique of the idea of equinumerosity (and related approaches in mathematicians other than Frege), in effect on psychologistic grounds; the idea is that the notion only has the logical force it appears to when we are able to perform the psychological act of one-to-one correlation. He also takes issue with Frege's discussion of identity, holding that Frege has confused equality and identity. Finally, he responds to a number of Frege's statements that cause theoretical difficulties for Husserl's project. For example, on Husserl's own account, the numbers are all the potential determinations of the notion of plurality. Since a plurality requires more than one object within the whole aggregate, neither zero nor one can be a number. Husserl accepts this conclusion.

Later in 1891, Husserl sent Frege a copy of his work and some other related papers. The tone of the subsequent correspondence is generally courteous. As Mohanty (1977) points out, one of the papers Husserl sends to Frege (a review of E. Schröder's *Algebra of Logic*) contains clear indications that at that point Husserl had already formulated a near-relative of Frege's sense–reference distinction independently of Frege's own work on that subject (which also appeared in 1891); moreover, Husserl's discussion draws a divide between the (objective) sense of a name and the (subjective) presentation of it for the agent. The matter here is contested, but at any rate it is not easy to maintain the claim that Frege's later review was the *only* cause of Husserl's move to anti-psychologism, or indeed to claim that phenomenology owes its foundations to Frege.

Frege's review of Husserl's *Philosophy of Arithmetic* is not pleasant reading, although this is to some extent because his criticism of others is generally unsparingly sarcastic and biting. Throughout the review, Frege makes a series of points against the Husserlian critique; some of these are straightforward corrections of errors on Husserl's part (as in the claim that Frege has confused equality and identity), and Frege is acute in following up the implications of Husserl's admission that zero and one are not for him numbers. But the major thrust of the review is that Husserl's psychologism itself is disastrous (for instance, in compelling the view that a number is a property of an aggregate), and that as a result Husserl regularly equivocates between a psychological and a non-psychological approach to number. After laying out his case, Frege comments:

> In reading this work, I was able to gauge the devastation caused by the influx of psychology into logic; and I have here made it my task to present this damage in a clear light. The mistakes which I thought it my duty to show reflect less upon the author than they are the result of a widespread philosophical disease. My own, radically different, position makes it difficult for me to do justice to his achievements, which I presume to lie in the area of psychology.
>
> (Frege 1972: 337)

Husserl's direct published response is straightforward, if minimal: in *Logical Investigations* he acknowledges in a footnote within the "Prolegomena to Pure Logic" (2001: 318) that he no longer approves of the criticisms of Frege's anti-psychologism set out in his earlier book, and he associates himself with Frege's remarks on psychologism in the *Foundations of Arithmetic* and the preface to volume one of the *Grundgesetze*. Although it is sometimes noted that his *mea culpa* here is partial, not withdrawing all criticisms contained in the earlier work, the concession comes at the tail of six chapters devoted to psychologism, in the course of which a range of criticisms of the view are advanced. Husserl's retraction did not amount to an endorsement of Frege's own logicist programme, and he would later criticize the philosophical employment of logic that did not "understand itself", but the "Prolegomena" itself is, like the *Philosophy of Arithmetic*, a point of at least some agreement with the analytic tradition, both in the critique of psychologism and in those aspects of the foundations of phenomenology that are reminiscent of Fregean ideas about sense. However, given the very patchy absorption of the *Logical Investigations* in the early analytic world, it is not at all clear that this potential agreement was actually taken up to any degree at the time. Mohanty (1982) suggests that, although direct communication between the early phenomenological and analytic traditions was lacking, the problems and opportunities afforded by the common reflection on logic by Frege, Husserl and Russell ensured that at least some independently done work would have suggestive conceptual connections; perhaps the more recent analytic literature on Frege and Husserl (or indeed the realist phenomenology discussed in Chapter 11) in some ways acts as a model of what might have been. If so, this first interaction between the traditions is a missed opportunity as much as the deepening of a divide.

2. RUSSELL VERSUS BERGSON

As we have noted, Russell is central to the advertisement of early analytic philosophy; his "On Denoting" and *Our Knowledge of the External World* are shop windows in which the new methods are publicly put through their paces. He was also willing to enter into contention with philosophers from other schools in a way that Frege, Moore or Wittgenstein were not, and especially to attack philosophies that he himself had abandoned (such as Hegelianism and Meinongian realism). Perhaps inevitably, he thereby also played a highly significant role in "othering" much of the contemporaneous philosophical work being done in France, Germany and the United Kingdom. Indeed, despite his own merits as a philosopher, Russell can be a problematic reader of other philosophers, perhaps especially early continental philosophers (Hegel, Nietzsche, etc.), although he has almost nothing to say about Husserl and Heidegger throughout his career.

The Russell–Bergson encounters have been considerably less discussed in the recent literature than either the Frege–Husserl or the Carnap–Heidegger encounters, despite being perhaps equally significant in the development of the divide; both Russell and Bergson were at the time of the debate well-known public intellectuals, unlike Frege, Husserl, Carnap and Heidegger (at the time of their relevant debates). For a period, from around 1903 until after the First World War, Russell was indeed arguably the most famous philosopher in the world; Bergson's most well-known work, *Creative Evolution* (1907), very rapidly brought him a public fame that increased with the publication in 1911 of an English translation that saw him feted on a visit to England that year (Monk 1996: 232–3). This encounter begins with that work.

Bergson's philosophy stands in a broadly evolutionary tradition that includes Herbert Spencer and some pragmatists (such as William James); within that tradition Bergson is especially notable as an early practitioner of a process philosophy. Change and becoming is the ultimate reality; fixity an illusion, brought about by reliance on the intelligence instead of instinct (Bergson

1944: 1–6). Bergson concedes, of course, that it is instrumentally useful to perform intellectual acts such as decompositional analysis (science, medicine and so on are predicated on it), in which we break concepts down and classify the component attributes, and then through synthesis arrive back at a general concept of the thing. But these capacities are inevitably guided by instrumental and evolutionary needs; hence they are oriented to a utilitarian counting and sorting. If one does metaphysics in this manner, Bergson contends, one will inevitably foist separations on a reality that is foreign to them; intelligence is at heart "the faculty of relating one point of space to another, one material object to another; it applies to all things, but remains outside them; and of a deep cause it perceives only the effects spread out side to side" (*ibid*.: 185). Moreover, since the choice of the manner in which nature is cleaved at the joints is essentially perspectival, analysis can give us only relative knowledge of things (*ibid*.: 160–61).

Bergson's solution to this predicament is to appeal to our intuition, a form of instinct that is "disinterested, self-conscious, capable of reflecting upon its object and of enlarging it indefinitely" (*ibid*.: 176). In intuition we enter the thing rather than survey it from outside; this at once allows the intellect to realize its own limitations (in particular those attending to the understanding of life) and gives us the possibility of absolute knowledge of things. For Bergson, contrary to Husserlian phenomenology, it is not that a unified consciousness attends with intuition to a given multiplicity. Rather, intuition shows us the multiplicity that we ourselves are, and this is related to a non-measurable lived time (*durée*) that is also said to be the proper medium of thinking. The spatial (intelligence) and temporal (instinct) opposition is stressed.

Russell's encounter with Bergson began with the visit of 1911, at which the two clashed in discussion after a paper Russell gave to the Aristotelian Society.[1] In 1912 Russell's "The Philosophy of Bergson" was published in *Monist* (Russell 1912a), attracting a great deal of comment; Bergson also receives lengthy treatment in Russell's 1914 *Our Knowledge of the External World*; and the two were participants at a conference with Einstein in 1922 at the Collège de France (expressing some disdain for each other's views). Although particular objections to Bergson's work, taken as philosophy, are certainly advanced in his writings, Russell's general conclusion is that in some sense such detailed criticism misses the point; Bergson's work could only be understood as literature rather than philosophy (see Russell 2007: 790). This is a comment that has since been bestowed on many of those working in continental philosophy, and it suggests a difference in style that is quickly apparent to any contemporary reader of their work. However, it is also interesting to see that, beyond stylistic issues, Russell raises as issues a number of the other conventional markers of analytic philosophy.

24

First, Russell expresses the concern that Bergson does not pursue or value argument, understood as a matter of assembling premises to deductively back a conclusion, or a matter of careful analysis.[2] Of course, this is not a mere oversight on Bergson's behalf. Bergson wants to proffer a methodological *critique* of analysis as a tool for thinking, as part of a return to a metaphysics based on speculative thinking, and in order to not lose sight of the value and complexity of life. Bergson's valorization of intuition is an obvious ground for Russell's concern: he remarks at one point that "intuition is at its best in bats, bees, and Bergson" (1912a: 331). Bergsonian intuition is understood by Russell to be equivalent to mere instinct, which is not quite true; it develops from instinct, but is not reducible to it. Certainly Bergson does not think the instinctive abilities of bats and bees, say, allow them to do metaphysics. Nonetheless, it is fair to say that there is a strongly anti-intellectualist spirit in the work of Bergson (and one that can be discerned in parts of twentieth-century continental thought thereafter) that the analytic and Russellian projects do not share. While it is paradoxical for philosophers to take positions that seem anti-intellectualist, to many in the continental tradition this is a needed corrective to the philosophical intellectualism that has dominated much of the history of Western philosophy and, to invoke Nietzsche, is a consequence of the particular psychologies and dispositions of those who practise it.

A second resonant theme here comes out in Russell's declaration that Bergson's philosophy of intuition rests on a "complete condemnation of all the pretended knowledge derived from science and common sense" (1917a: 14). Whether Bergson's work involves a condemnation of science and common sense is not entirely clear, although they are certainly transformed. Of course, both science and common sense remain significant methodological touchstones for analytic philosophy throughout the history of the twentieth century. From the outset, Moore and, to a lesser extent, Russell allied the emergent analytic movement with the goal of examining and so reaffirming common sense, and many analytic philosophers have accepted that view. On the question of precisely what role common sense (or related datum such as folk psychology, trust in pre-theoretic/intuitive judgements, etc.) should have in reining in the possible excesses of our philosophical methods, it seems to us that the continental answer to this question, for most philosophers, would be "as little as possible". While this difference at the level of both rhetoric and meta-philosophy is sometimes problematized by the actual philosophical practices of representative philosophers of either tradition, this norm (and its absence) nonetheless arguably continues to play an important role in the methodological preferences of each tradition, as we discuss in Part II.

Finally, differing analytic and continental attitudes to time are also on display in this exchange. What, Russell asks, does our experience of time (*durée*) tell us about time *per se*, real or objective time? This issue regarding the relation between philosophical accounts of time (or psychological for most analytic philosophers) and those proffered by physicists and mathematicians persists. Although various attempts have been made to reconcile these two accounts of time, perhaps most notably by Sellars, in his lifelong attempts to reconcile a Kantian, experiential conception of time with the scientific image of time, the separation has generally persisted. Ayer's influential book *Philosophy in the Twentieth Century*, for example, contains a fairly thorough chapter on Merleau-Ponty and a somewhat hastier dismissal of Heidegger. The charge of psychologism is apparent against both, and he says of Merleau-Ponty's understanding of time:

> Time itself is said to be "a setting to which one can gain access and which one can understand only by occupying a situation in it" ... This need not be true if it is possible to conceive of time as the domain of the relation which holds between events when one is earlier than another. On the other hand, if the concepts of past, present, and future are taken as fundamental then, since the present is captured in this schema only by use of the demonstrative "now", all citing of events in time will contain at least a tacit indication of the temporal position of the speakers. Merleau-Ponty takes the second course, but pursues it in such a way that he is led into a thicket of idealism. (1982: 224)

Ayer adds, if we go Merleau-Ponty's way "we put ourselves in the awkward position, of seeming to contradict the well-established scientific hypotheses". In regard to Heidegger's influential studies on time, Ayer says "we have found an echo of this treatment in Merleau-Ponty, but it is obvious that any such attempt to extract temporal predicates out of psychological or metaphysical ones must be circular at best" (*ibid.*: 228).

3. CARNAP VERSUS HEIDEGGER

Throughout the 1920s, the divide between analytic and continental philosophy became more entrenched, but also more complicated. An illuminating episode that was fundamental to the perpetuation of the idea of philosophy being a "divided house" is the analytic reaction to the phenomenologist/ontologist Heidegger's *Being and Time* (1927) and his text "What is Metaphysics?", his inaugural lecture at the University of Freiburg in 1929 (see Heidegger 1996a). In the course of this work, Heidegger develops a substantive nothing (given a definite article as "the Nothing"), and has it act (it "noths", or "nihilates"). Unsurprisingly, this is something of a natural target for an analyst who views misuse of language as a path to metaphysical confusion, and Heidegger's work is used as an example in Carnap's 1932 positivist manifesto, "The Elimination of Metaphysics Through Logical Analysis of Language". The introductory remarks make it clear that Heidegger is standing in for a tradition here:

> Let us now take a look at some examples of metaphysical pseudo-statements of a kind where the violation of logical syntax is especially obvious, though they accord with historical-grammatical syntax …. We select a few sentences from that metaphysical school which at present exerts the strongest influence in Germany.
>
> (Carnap 1996: 19)

Carnap then presents a table of different grammatical constructions in Heidegger, detailing Heidegger's usages of "Nothing" in comparison with acceptable ordinary sentences with the same surface grammar and acceptable semi-logical sentences with a different underlying grammar. Throughout, the point is that Heidegger has failed to attend to the quantificational structure of sentences containing "nothing" (the familiar post-Fregean analysis of sentences of the form "Nothing is F" as "It is not the case that there exists an F", rather than as the subject–predicate sentences they appear to be). This is an elementary point about logical grammar; Carnap's charge of meaninglessness therefore is not *directly* dependent on his verificationist criterion of meaning, although the criticism is meant to be part of a larger survey of metaphysical meaninglessness, and this survey does on occasion make use of that criterion. Moreover, as we will see, verificationism does play a role in the explanation of this episode. Carnap ends his essay with praise of Nietzsche, because he fundamentally remains an artist, but is highly critical of Heidegger, whose metaphysics purports to be serious philosophy.

Heidegger's own reply to Carnap can be found in *Pathmarks,* where he essentially repeats Husserl's insistence that rigour and exactitude are not the same thing (cf. Heidegger 1998b: 83, 96, 235, 263). This is a little gnomic, but can be opened out into the counter that things are not as clear as Carnap is prepared to allow here. In *Being and Time*, Heidegger draws a famous distinction between beings and Being that is sometimes referred to as the ontico-ontological difference. On Heidegger's view, ontic beings such as objects and entities of the world have Being in common (that which allows entities to be, their condition of possibility), but there remains an ontological difference between all of these various beings and Being: despite beings partaking in Being, they are not the same thing. The Being of entities is not itself an entity. In "What is Metaphysics?", Heidegger hence argues that Being is necessarily non-being in that it cannot be located in the world as beings can. He suggests that the Western philosophical tradition has ignored this lack, this "nothingness" that is Being, and has struggled to free itself of the implications ever since. From this point of view, Carnap is being somewhat tone-deaf to a problem of expression, much like the problems of expression Wittgenstein wrestles with in his *Tractatus Logico-Philosophicus.* The language employed in discussing Nothing is associated with Heidegger's expressive problems *vis-à-vis* Being. He cannot himself *say* what Being is or *define* it, since this would be to treat it as an entity; he would himself be forgetting the ontological difference. At one stage Heidegger tries writing under erasure (B̶e̶i̶n̶g̶). Similarly, he works language beyond a boundary in "What is Metaphysics?", when he (in)famously states that the "nothing noths", or "the nothing itself nihilates". Apparently anticipating some of the objections to such statements that were soon to come, Heidegger also noted that any primacy accorded to logic and the law of non-contradiction also involved a forgetting of the question of Being: "the commonly cited ground of all thinking, the proposition that contradiction is to be avoided, universal 'logic' itself, lays low this question" (1996a: 99). Heidegger eventually came to the view that philosophy cannot successfully perform such indirect expression, and he thereafter aligned genuine thinking more with poetry than philosophy.

On Carnap's part, things are also a little more nuanced than they might seem. For one thing, Carnap is well aware of claims that the framework of meaning entails that philosophy sometimes has to find ways of communicating other than direct expression. This is, of course, Wittgenstein's own view in the *Tractatus*. Moreover, Wittenstein himself was prepared to cut Heidegger much the same slack as he required:

> To be sure, I can imagine what Heidegger means by being and anxiety. Man feels the urge to run up against the limits of language. Think for example of the astonishment that anything at all exists. This astonishment cannot be expressed in the form of a question, and there is also no answer whatsoever. Anything we might say is a priori bound to be mere nonsense. Nevertheless we do run up against the limits of language.[1]

Many other analytic philosophers were rather more sceptical of such claims (in Ramsey's words, in response to a related claim by Wittgenstein, "What we can't say we can't say, and we can't whistle it either" [1990: 146]). The Carnap–Heidegger episode acquires special resonance only when this divide within analytic philosophy is overlooked (whether by continental or analytic philosophers), and so Carnap appears to be taking on the continental tradition rather more than he is. Carnap explicitly rejected Wittgenstein's own claims of this kind (Carnap 1934: 282–4), on grounds he would regard as carrying over to Heidegger as well, and he moved to a view on which such "limits of expression" concerns were better seen as "external" questions about the appropriate choice of language (see Carnap [1947] 1988). Moreover, Carnap refused to take advantage of the covert appeal to the limits of expression when, with many other logical positivists, he eventually entirely abandoned the verifiability criterion on the grounds of its own unverifiability.

Prima facie, this seems like a clear case of a debate that never really got started, but appearances may be somewhat deceptive. Heidegger and Carnap shared certain philosophical convictions in common, despite the appearance of incommensurability. Both were coming from a neo-Kantian orientation that opposed metaphysics, and were responding in different ways to the tension between life philosophy (Romanticism) and rationalistically oriented neo-Kantianism. Indeed, in *A Parting of the Ways*, Michael Friedman traces the historical emergence of analytic and continental philosophy out of the neo-Kantian split between the Marburg School and the Southwest German school, and so provides a context in which this episode has rather more significance. As James Luchte summarizes the position:

> Cohen, Cassirer, and Carnap set forth an epistemological interpretation of Kant which set out from the "fact of science" as the primary datum, and saw the task of philosophy to trace the

foundations of this fact... The latter school, including Rickert and Heidegger, appropriated the work of Kant with a distinct focus on the human sciences which sought to reintegrate the theoretical expression of the natural sciences into a broader concern for the lifeworld of human existence. (2007: 243)

The priority of the life-world is a refrain that we shall return to, since it is arguably a central *leitmotif* not only for German philosophy but also for other important trajectories in continental philosophy, including French existentialism. Friedman further sees Ernst Cassirer as a kind of middle way closed off by Nazism, a missed opportunity that could potentially have brought the separating analytic and continental traditions in the German-speaking world into closer relation.

4. THE FRANKFURT SCHOOL, THE POSITIVISTS AND POPPER

Of course, the formative years of the emergence of a divide weren't one-sidedly characterised by analytic philosophers projecting certain despised characteristics onto their continental philosophical "others". In different ways, both Bergson and Heidegger targeted calculative thinking and logicism (as Hegel had done before them), and often with more than a nod in the direction of the emerging analytic movement. Soon after *Being and Time*, Horkheimer was appointed director of the Institute for Social Research in Frankfurt, and in the early 1930s he put forward his own critique of logical positivism, while also attacking *Lebensphilosophie* and early forms of existentialism. For Horkheimer, it is not just the positivist fetishism of facts that is objectionable, but also the reliance on formal logic. He suggests, in essays collected in *Critical Theory*, that to see logic and mathematics as privileged disclosers of truth reduces both to a series of tautologies with no real meaning in the historical world. Moreover, Horkheimer claims that logical positivism remains securely bound to metaphysics despite its attempts to leave it behind, since the absolutizing of facts also entailed a reification of the existing order (1975: 140). Indeed, the bald claim is made that logical positivism is connected to the existence of totalitarian states. In regard to the positivist deference to science, Horkheimer also brings in the charge of conservatism:

> With respect to the future, the characteristic activity of science is not construction but induction. The more often something has occurred in the past, the more certain that it will in all the future. Knowledge relates solely to what is and to its recurrence. New forms of being, especially those arising from the historical activity of men, lie beyond empiricist theory. (*Ibid.*: 144)

Such criticisms are later echoed in Herbert Marcuse's *One Dimensional Man* (see Marcuse 1991: ch. 7). For Horkheimer and then Marcuse, dialectical thinking contrasts favourably with this empiricist conception of knowledge. It does not confound rational thinking with calculative thinking or with instrumental reason, a supposition that Horkheimer alleges "solidifies the monadological isolation of the individual engendered by the present form of economy" (*ibid.*: 180). Finally, the positivist disentangling of facts from values – roughly Hume's is–ought gap – was also a particular target of the Frankfurt School. In this respect we might sum up their position as follows: when meaning constituting acts are rendered redundant to the issue of knowledge or truth, and when knowledge and truth are understood in a manner that subtracts them from the condition of their pursuit or production, we have a not unpredictable response of the bourgeoisie. Reason and philosophy are also thus radically diminished on this view.

In this barrage, the theme that has most persisted in the continental tradition is that of the political conservatism of analytic philosophy. This is something that is subsequently unambiguously argued by John McCumber in *Time in the Ditch* (2001); his claim is that there is a complicity in the United States between the McCarthy era witch-hunts for communists between the late 1940s and the late 1950s, and the increasing dominance of the apparently politically neutral analytic philosophy. A related accusation, pressed by many (including Jürgen Habermas and Rorty), is that by giving too much attention to linguistic and conceptual analysis, analytic philosophy has engaged in a kind of retreat from reality, and so is rendered irrelevant in regard to the key issues of our time. On the whole, analytic philosophers have generally only engaged with such concerns in ethics (putting aside some replies in metaphilosophical works[1]).

The early 1930s also saw the philosophical emergence of Popper as something of an internal opponent of the positivist movement. Popper is not a positivist. He rejects entirely the verifiability thesis about meaning, according to which sentences are senseless unless there exist procedures for their verification or refutation, and presents arguments against the kind of empiricism adopted by the positivists. On the whole he is also extremely sceptical about the characteristically linguistic turn taken by the positivists, and – most famously – he completely rejects the positivist idea that induction plays a role in rational scientific theory choice. However, although very few analytic philosophers indeed are Popperians, many think that close analogues of the concept of falsifiability can play some kind of role in rational deliberation; for instance, on Quine's completely different "theoretical virtues" account of science, falsifiability (or at any rate, a related notion shorn of Popper's own conventionalism) is a virtue that theories can possess, to be balanced up against many others. As a result, Popper's critique of Marx and Freud on the basis of their unfalsifiability was on the right grounds, as it were, to be influential in the analytic tradition,[2] giving an added impetus to a certain sidelining there of the "masters of suspicion".

Popper's first attack on Marx occurs in *The Open Society and its Enemies* (1945), which rails against Marxism and Hegelianism, and is hostile to dialectical and holistic thinking. For Popper, dialectical thinking either involves banal truths (things change in interaction with opposing forces and movement) or contravenes the law of non-contradiction and hence should be dismissed. These are the kinds of charges that have produced continental reaction; Adorno, for instance, claims that without dialectics argumentation "deteriorioates into the technique of conceptless specialists amid the concept, as it is now spreading academically in the so-called analytical philosophy, which robots can learn and copy" (2000: 76). However, this is not an aspect of Popper's work that has especially resonated within analytic philosophy. The attack on Freud and Marx that is most well known is in his essay "Science: Conjectures and Refutations", originally given as an address in 1953, but drawing on work originally done in the 1920s and 1930s.

In *Conjectures and Refutations*, Popper frames his guiding question as one of distinguishing between science and pseudo-science (2002b: 33–41). He argues that a pseudo-science may well have a scientifically respectable past, but that it will have gone wrong either by introducing *ad hoc* auxiliary theories on occasions to avoid falsifying events, or by making unclear, imprecise claims, which are never clearly testable and so never run the risk of falsification in the first place. In either of these situations, the theorists involved are breaching what Popper takes to be a basic norm of science: the determination to prefer theories on the basis of their falsifiability. The norm will be breached even if, to all appearances, the pseudo-science is in the best of confirmatory health, in that its proponents can offer copious positive proof for their claims or provide explanations of seemingly great power and range. All of this is irrelevant; they have abandoned the falsificationist spirit of real science, which is an inherently critical enterprise. Popper points out that Marx's original theory of history entailed falsifiable predictions (the revolution is imminent; it will happen in England first), and was thus quite respectable as a candidate scientific theory. When these predictions were falsified, however, Marxists added various *ad hoc* auxiliary theories to explain the failure, rather than rejecting it and seeking another. By the mid-twentieth century, Popper thought that Marxism (in the hands of those such as the Frankfurt School) had an answer for everything. It had become completely unfalsifiable, and thus lost all connection to science. Freudian psychoanalysis is subjected to harsher criticism, as it appears never to have been a candidate scientific theory by these lights; however an individual behaves, whatever dream they may have, psychoanalysis can account for this in terms of the unconscious. Popper thinks that it is precisely this all-encompassing explanatory power of psychoanalysis that precludes it being genuinely scientific. There is no possible evidence that would count against psychoanalysis, and this means that, while it cannot be proved false, it also makes no sense to claim that it is empirically true.

This Popperian critique has had an unusually robust life, given the difficulties that the falsificationist standard itself was seen to give rise to. Many analytic objections to Popperianism in effect point out that perfectly good scientific work fails the test of falsifiability (see e.g. Putnam 1974). For instance, any scientific theory such as Newtonian dynamics that involves *ceteris paribus* clauses is unfalsifiable, as is any theory that has the "all–some" quantificational structure ("For any *F* there is a *G* such that ..."), as is any theory (such as Pauli's postulation of the neutrino) that makes existence claims without specifying a procedure to locate the posited object, as is any statistical theory claiming that an event occurs with non-extremal probability. In the face of these objections, it is difficult to see why unfalsifiability is felt to be a *special* problem for Marx or Freud. Perhaps it is best to see Popper's critique in a wider focus, as one of several ways in which analytic philosophers of science sought to express what they found suspiciously glib about Marxism and psychoanalysis; a related (and also very influential) objection from the same period is Carl Hempel's claim that the two theories fail the standards required for a good scientific explanation (see Hempel 1965). From this point of view, the Popperian critique of Marx and Freud does fit into a wider pattern of positivist policing of the boundaries of science.

Some of these issues returned in a debate between Adorno and Popper (joined along the way by various German sociologists and philosophers). The debate went from 1961 to 1969 and some of the most important contributions are collected in a book entitled *The Positivist Dispute in German Sociology* (Adorno *et al.* 1976). The title is provocative – and this aspect of the debate accordingly bizarre – to analytic philosophers, given Popper's long career of loud opposition to the positivist movement. The original exchange happened in 1961, when Popper was invited to address the German Sociological Association with the expectation that Adorno would reply. Adorno did not respond point for point to Popper's presentation, saying precisely where he agreed and disagreed; as Steve Fuller notes, the "point of rupture between Popper and Adorno was adumbrated in their manner of expression" (2006: 190). The subject for discussion in the debate was, as before, the rational status of Adorno's theories; evidently they were neither verifiable nor falsifiable. In later rounds of the debate Hans Albert and Habermas became more involved. Habermas insisted that Popper's straight-talking approach was politically and intellectually naive, and he maintained that the Frankfurt School's dialectical critique was superior to Popperian critical rationalism. On the other hand, Popper and his followers seem to have concluded that the Frankfurt School members were irrationalists (see Adorno *et al.* 1976: 297).

5. ROYAUMONT: RYLE AND HARE VERSUS FRENCH AND GERMAN PHILOSOPHY

In *The Idea of Continental Philosophy* (2007), Simon Glendinning makes a strong case for the 1950s as the decade in which the divide became truly substantial. In 1958,[1] in an attempt to institute a British–French philosophical dialogue, Ayer, Ryle, Quine, J. L. Austin, Hare, Peter Strawson, Bernard Williams and J. O. Urmson were invited to a joint conference at Royaumont, with French philosophers such as Jean Wahl, Maurice Merleau-Ponty and H. L. Van Breda (a Husserlian) in the audience. The conference was described by all involved as a failure, a sterile set-piece affair. It has therefore acquired a certain significance as a symbol of the sheer pointlessness of debate between the traditions, although some have suggested that the appearance of radical difference between the phenomenologists and the ordinary-language philosophers is misleading and, in fact, ultimately not the case.[2]

Perhaps the most polemical of the papers presented at Royaumont was Ryle's, subsequently published as "Phenomenology vs. *The Concept of Mind*". Ryle had previously taught on Husserl and published a review of Heidegger's *Being and Time*; his engagement, although critical, was extremely unusual in pre-war British analytic circles. However, at Royaumont, as Glock remarks, "Ryle seemed interested less in establishing whether there was a wide gulf between analytic and 'continental' philosophy than in ensuring that there would be" (2008: 63). The burden of Ryle's paper is that there is a chasm between phenomenology and analytic philosophy, which is attributable to the development of logical theory (including non-formal matters, and perhaps the general theory of meaning) on the one hand, and its neglect on the other. Husserl comes in for some remarkably crude stereotyping: "Claims to *Fuehrership* vanish when postprandial joking begins. Husserl wrote as if he had never met a scientist – or a joke .... We [the British] have not worried our heads over the question Which philosopher ought to be *Fuehrer*?" (Ryle 1971: 181–2).

Around the same time, R. M. Hare's visit to Germany yielded an equally dismissive tract. While avoiding naming any single German philosopher, Hare notes that they produce "verbiage disguised as serious metaphysical inquiry", "build monstrous philosophical edifices" and turn philosophy into "mysticism", and that their work is characterized by "ambiguities, evasions, and rhetoric ... the mark of a philosopher who has not learnt his craft" (1960: 110–15). Both philosophers seem to have decided in advance, perhaps unconsciously, that no genuine communication was possible, and their uncharacteristic lack of rigour might be interpreted symptomatically. According to Glendinning, the threat that is constitutive of all philosophy (failure, verbosity, meaninglessness) is thus projected onto the "other" located on the other side of the channel, and (claimed to be) secured against by the methodological rigours of analytic philosophy: "the personification of an internal possibility as an external (and literally) foreign body gave analytic philosophy the false assurance that it was, in principle, healthy philosophy" (2007: 83). It is perhaps no coincidence that shortly after this period the analytic–continental divide receives its full name; Maurice Mandelbaum is, as far as we can tell, the first to explicitly use the analytic–continental distinction, in an American Philosophy Association presidential address (see Mandelbaum 1962). Around this period of time, the French existentialist philosopher and theologian Gabriel Marcel, having had some experience as a visiting professor at Harvard and Aberdeen universities, also noted that there had been a major parting of the ways:

> Experience shows us undeniably that in most of the Anglo-Saxon world the word "philosophy" is taken in an absolutely different sense than it is where phenomenology, proceeding from Husserl and Scheler, has progressively exerted its influence ... In 1951 I spoke with A. J. Ayer about a "philosophy of reflection"; these words, which in France designated an incontestably venerable tradition, were meaningless for him. Much more recently, talking with students at Harvard, I found that many of their philosophy professors were discouraging them from looking for a relation between the almost exclusively analytic thought in which they were being trained and life – the problems that life poses to each one of us but which seemed in the professors' eyes to be merely matters for personal discretion. (1973: 17–18)

In this respect we might note that Derrida suggests that, contrary to a certain interpretation of his work, "a philosopher without the ethico-existential pathos does not interest me very much" (2001: 40). Analytic philosophers typically are not so interested in this existential pathos, as Marcel apparently also found, when, after he gave a talk on death, J. L. Austin (dying of cancer at the time) asked pointedly "we all know we have to die, but why do we have to sing songs about it?" (Scarre 2007: 65).

6. DERRIDA VERSUS SEARLE AND BEYOND

The debate between Derrida and Searle in the 1970s and 1980s, spurred by Derrida's engagement with Austin in "Signature Event Context", is perhaps the closest thing that the tradition has to an ongoing exchange of ideas between well-known analytic and continental philosophers, notwithstanding the sometimes aggressive and polemical stances taken by both Derrida and Searle. Both philosophers claimed that their interaction should not be understood as a clash between representatives of the sides of a "divide". In fact, Derrida accuses Searle of being Husserlian in relation to meaning and intentionality (indeed, there is a fairly close relationship between Searle and Husserl on the intentional, issues of naturalism aside), and Searle accuses Derrida of being Fregean in maintaining that unless a concept involves rigorous distinctions it is not an appropriate philosophical concept to use at all (a charge that Derrida accepts). Derrida even suggests that his own work is actually closer to Austin's than Searle's (Searle being the avowed inheritor and well-credentialled speech act theorist). Nonetheless, it has proved difficult for people to avoid this way of seeing it, if only out of a curiosity as to whether useful debate across the divide is possible. Analytic philosophers have widely proclaimed Searle the victor (Føllesdal 1996: 204; Glock 2008: 257), and have regarded Derrida's contributions as largely *ad hominem* attacks. It is not uncommonly alleged that, while Searle demanded clarity and calculable answers and solutions, Derrida compounded problem upon problem, such that the distinct became obscure and the obscure became distinct, and then proceeded to play with Searle's name (SARL). Of course, continental philosophers see Searle as having been convincingly refuted (in part because of his reliance on poor expositions of Derrida's work). The notoriety and significance of this interaction is partly retrospective. When Derrida was awarded an honorary doctorate at the University of Cambridge in 1993, a major controversy arose, with protests and expressions of derision from many analytic philosophers (especially Barry Smith and Ruth Barcan Marcus). Several analytic philosophers signed a letter stating that: "Academic status based on what seems to us to be little more than semi-intelligible attacks upon the values of reason, truth, and scholarship is not, we submit, sufficient grounds for the awarding of an honorary degree in a distinguished university" (Derrida 1995b: 420–21). The issue was put to a vote by the Cambridge faculty, and Derrida eventually received the award, but the animus on both sides was very deep.

In "Signature Event Context", Derrida is explicitly concerned with terrain that analytic philosophers often tend to think is their own: language and meaning, and the work of Austin in particular. Austin's speech act theory to some extent reconciles the Fregean and Wittgensteinian approaches to language. The broad idea is that a meaningful utterance performs three different acts at different levels. An utterance is a *locutionary* act, an act of saying, communicating the content of the sentence uttered (where this content is something like a Fregean sense). It is also an *illocutionary* act, an act *in* saying (making a promise, warning, judging, asserting, etc.). The illocutionary force of an utterance is the speech act it performs or attempts to perform; such force may be grammatically indicated, but usually is not. For each speech act, as before, there are conventional constitutive and regulative rules. Finally, and optionally, an utterance may be a *perlocutionary* act, an act *done* by saying. These are acts we usually describe in terms of their effect on the hearer, not in terms of speaker intention (e.g. frightening, persuading, amusing); like illocutionary acts, they go beyond locutionary content, but unlike illocutions they do not depend on the existence of conventions, and they are thereby not in the ambit of a theory of meaning in the way linguistic and social conventions are.

Such projects can be of interest to continental philosophy. Habermas, for instance, has sought to bridge the divide between Fregean (truth-conditional) and Wittgensteinian (use-based) accounts of meaning, albeit by attempting, transcendentally, to establish that the everyday practices of linguistic communication provide the basis for a context-transcendent understanding of the nature of truth and the argumentative justification of validity claims. Habermas accuses the semanticist tradition of committing three abstractive fallacies (confining linguistic meaning to sentences; tracing meaning back to propositional content of assertoric utterances; defining meaning in terms of objective, rather than socially mediated truth-conditions); the criticism here is reminiscent of Austin's own concerns (cf. Cooke 2002: 6).

On the other hand, the potential proximity between Derrida and Austin means that deconstruction might loom as more of an immediate threat than some other forms of continental philosophy. Indeed, Derrida alerts us to this counter-intuitive proximity when he states that he considers himself to be both a conceptual analyst and an analytic philosopher (cited in Glendinning 2001: 83). Few analytic philosophers would accept the latter claim, of course, and while Derrida says he is "very serious" and one can readily accept that his grammatology involves something like linguistic analysis, he admits that he found Kripke's *Naming and Necessity* bafflingly opaque (see S. Wheeler 2000: 2), and that he never found himself able to read and engage with even a "post-analytic" philosopher like Wittgenstein, despite some significant parallels with his work that are well attested to in the secondary literature. Frege and the formal-semantic tradition of analytic philosophy are also never given any serious attention throughout Derrida's long, and otherwise impressively diverse, oeuvre (although the work of Husserl mediates between Frege and Derrida, in that we have seen Husserl was engaged with Frege). While Derrida clearly wants to problematize one of the main meta-philosophical rationales for the divide in claiming identity with analytic philosophy, and while he is rightly wary of any too hasty postulation of an opposition with "fronts", the question remains as to just why Derrida might have been analytic philosophy's *bête noire* throughout the 1980s and 1990s.

After all, it is arguable that while Derrida, Davidson, Quine and Wittgenstein all use rather different methodologies and have inherited some very different philosophical cultures, they actually have some closely related targets in mind in their respective philosophies of language and meaning. Samuel Wheeler points out that all four critique the idea of a language, "in which we know what we mean, think our thoughts, and form intentions" (*ibid.*: 3). Derrida even maintains that "the idea that the meaning of a word or utterance should, ideally, be exact or definite in this way is not one prejudice or injustice among others in philosophy: rather it is *the* philosophical prejudice, *the* philosophical injustice" (in Glendinning 2001: 19). Without going into the details of Derrida's famous deconstructions of the speech–writing hierarchy, suffice to say that it is spoken language that gives rise to what, for him, is the illusion that language more generally simply allows us to express pre-formed thoughts, and the associated assumption of transparent meanings, which entail that "nothing about the expression of the concept adds anything to the concept" (Wheeler 2000: 218). If Derrida is right that there is no pure cognitive meaning without emotive feel and local particularity, then as Wheeler points out:

> the analysis of the difference between "John is illegitimate" and "John is a bastard" cannot be that a valuation is "loaded" on a neutral, purely cognitive meaning. More generally, if no principled distinction obtains between the pure meaning and the miscellaneous accidents of a sentence, then no principled distinction can be made between logical consequence and rhetorical connection among statements. (*Ibid.*: 219)[1]

39

Wheeler also succinctly captures one of the main consequences of Derrida's philosophy (and perhaps poststructuralism more generally) when he says that Quine's "web of belief must really be a web of desire and belief, both conscious and unconscious" (*ibid.*: 225). If that is so, aesthetic and psychoanalytic considerations become relevant to deconstruction, and one might even perform something like a deconstruction of the analytic imaginary as Michele Le Doeuff and others feminist theorists have done. Certainly metaphor is also central to other parts of continental philosophy, and we might consider Derrida's essay "White Mythology" (see Derrida 1982b), where an irreducible metaphoricity is argued to trouble univocal meaning, but also Ricoeur's *The Rule of Metaphor* (which criticizes Derrida's account of metaphor). Whatever the differences between these views, metaphor cannot be ignored as peripheral or inessential to philosophical discourse, and it is notable (from a deconstructive and feminist perspective) that the examples analytic philosophers commonly use often seem to run against the grain of their theoretical analyses, whether in regard to concepts or speech acts. "Sally is a block of ice" is, as Robyn Ferrell (1993) notes, a problematic example that concerns Searle in his *Expression and Meaning* (the successor to *Speech Acts*). For Derrida, valuation permeates our understanding of sentences, words or phrases, making any form of analysis that attempts to abstract from this to preserve an ideal content paradoxical. Moreover, any stipulated (definitional) cleaning up of language, whether through logic or other means, will need to be careful about its idealizing aspirations. After all, Derrida's basic point about language is that for something to be a language (or for communication to be possible at all), any phrase or sentence must be capable of being repeated in other contexts, in the absence of any particular speaker and addressee. If this is so, then stipulations and definitional analyses may be reasonable pragmatic decisions given certain aims, but they are not techniques that allow the philosopher to establish the essence of thought and language.

Without recounting the myriad claims and counter-claims in his polemical dispute with Searle (Derrida's contributions in this debate are collected in *Limited Inc.*, but Searle refused the publishers permission to include his), in the earlier essay "Signature Event Context", Derrida is interested in the way that Austin's speech act theory excludes from his investigation, at least provisionally, certain utterances that cannot qualify as successful or felicitous, and which are said to be somehow "hollow and void". This includes utterances that are made unintentionally (e.g. the performance of the act was not done at all or not done freely), and that involve parasitic use (e.g. where one plays with serious utterances say, on a stage, or in jest). Derrida's indebtedness to psychoanalysis commits him to problematizing the idea that the realm of the serious can be defined, as Austin and Searle would have it, as the presence at the time of speaking of a conscious mental state possessed by a unified subject who intends, believes and desires. Against such a view, Derrida contends that transformability of meaning (what he calls iterability) is a condition of possibility of language. To rule this out from start, or to consider it as unimportant and accidental, is to have an emaciated conception of both language and communication. Derrida calls his argument here a quasi-transcendental one: "quasi" because it is an enabling and disabling condition, since it also means that meaning can never be simple, never be clear and distinct, but is necessarily in a network that is liable to transformation. For related reasons, Derrida contends that the normal–parasitic distinction is also rendered problematic: "the promise I make to a friend is not more original than a promise in a play, because all language use is citational, iterable. E.g. I promise as I have seen others promise" (Kenaan 2002: 123). Every normal speech act has as its condition of possibility the prospect of: citationality; of not being understood; of the context of the statement (and hence its meaning on this view) being transformed; and so on. If iterability is constitutive of the possibility of language, then the distinction between normal and parasitic (and use and mention) becomes untenable, because putatively normal utterances must always be able to be read in contexts that make them parasitic. Derrida wants to show that the risk of communicative failure is a condition of the very possibility of language, not an accidental disruption to the original communicative relation of one presence to another.

Derrida would also contest the view that the essential explanandum of communication theory is successful communication (*ibid.*: 117). Partly because of a commitment to such a view, speech act theorists also tend to presuppose, if not explicitly declare, "that the opening gambit in the game of ordinary conversation is the use of an assertoric sentence by a speaker, the response to which is ultimately a 'yes' or 'no'" (Cobb-Stevens 1990: 102). Derrida's point in this regard would be that if the *telos* of speech is successful communication, then "the phenomena of speech are inevitably forced into a reductive dualistic structure; as instances of communication, they can either succeed or not succeed ... these two possibilities open to speech are not only antithetical, but are also hierarchically ordered" (Kenaan 2002: 124). For Derrida, this occludes the ambiguity of expression, including the ambiguity of the speaker's intent, along with the way in which we are solicited to respond in intelligent ways by situations that cannot adequately be reconstructed as involving a prior representation of intention. As Kenaan observes:

> the equation of non-success with failure covers up a wide intermediate spectrum – an intricate phenomenological landscape

> lying between success and failure – in which the actual life of
> language takes place … As long as the horizons of the philosoph-
> ical study of speech are set by such examples as "the cat is on the
> mat" … "the ball missed the hoop", then no room will be made for
> a consideration of the more tangled and complex – but no less
> common – ways in which misunderstanding dwells within under-
> standing. (*Ibid.*: 125–6)

To sum up, then, there seem to be two main worries about speech act theory that Derrida's work usefully illuminates: first, its predilection for understanding successful communication (within a fairly narrow scope, say the
translation of content from one mind to another) as the fundamental goal of
language; second, and following from this, the key distinction between normal (defined by the presence of success conditions) and parasitic (defined by
the absence of such success conditions).

In regard to the first point, Searle responds that common sense tells us
that communication is intrinsically purposeful or goal-directed; its *telos* is
the successful transport of meaning from one mind to another. If this is so,
Searle can then distinguish between normal speech acts and marginal/para-
sitic speech acts. Searle also thinks that Austin's methodological decision
to begin with cases of success is simple common sense: we need to start
with the simple cases, as Ockham's razor tells us, and this is just a matter of
research strategy with no deeper metaphysical significance. Indeed, Searle
and Austin argue that non-standard speech acts logically depend on standard cases, and hence the normal–parasitic distinction is claimed to be a logical rather than metaphysical one.

Derrida, however, reverses this position: so-called standard cases are
argued to depend on non-standard cases and to be inconceivable without
them. While Searle's advocacy of the principle of trying the simple things
first may seem to offer a pragmatic reason for starting with standard cases,
for Derrida the standard cases are, themselves, from the start, contaminated
by the non-standard; for any communication to be possible, language must
be able to function in contexts that are different from the one intended. If this
"quasi-transcendental" condition is not fulfilled, then there is no language.
Moreover, for Derrida the fact that there is an intrinsic self-referentiality
here – that we are talking about language in language, meaning from within
meaning, and so on – also means that Ockham's razor, a principle that
is characteristic of the sciences, is not readily applicable in this context.[2]
Instead, it is a sign of a metaphysical bias. For Derrida, Austin's philosophy
of ordinary language is marked by this exclusion, which is arguably far from
ordinary. Although he admires Austin's radically empirical method, Derrida
states:

> Austin's procedure is rather remarkable, and typical of the philo-
> sophical tradition that he prefers to have little to do with. It con-
> sists in recognising that the possibility of the negative (here, the
> infelicities) is certainly a structural possibility, that failure is an
> essential risk in the operations under consideration; and then, with
> an almost immediately simultaneous gesture made in the name of
> a kind of ideal regulation, an exclusion of this risk as an accidental,
> exterior one that teaches us nothing about the language phenom-
> enon under consideration.   (Derrida 1982a: 323)

Of course, this kind of purifying move in regard to meaning is not the special preserve of analytic philosophers. Husserl's *Logical Investigations* separates what he calls expression from indication in a related manner, and this is
subsequently contested by Merleau-Ponty and then by Derrida in *Speech and
Phenomena*. But it does suggest that Derrida would also have concerns about
the semantic-transformational side of analytic philosophy of language, which
involves a related purifying move, and they also show up some potential
problems with the more pragmatic analyses of speech act theorists such as
Austin and Searle, even though this neo-Wittgensteinian tradition has been
influential on philosophers as diverse as Lyotard, Habermas and Derrida
himself. It is for related reasons that J. J. Lecercle was moved to comment,
in a comparative essay on philosophy of language, that: "All I think I have
achieved is to remind you of the existence of the Channel: 'meaning' on one
coast, 'sens' on the other are rather different concepts" (1987: 38).[3]

It seems to us that in the late 1980s and early 1990s, the divide became
more vicious and fraught than ever before. Various other philosophical and
political incidents transpired. Charles Sherover and Joseph Kockelmans
were among the "pluralists" publicly protesting in 1987, on the front pages of
newspapers, the analytic control of the American Philosophical Association;
they even briefly orchestrated a coup. In *Fashionable Nonsense*, Alan Sokal
and Jean Bricmont attacked French theory and detailed their "hoax", which
involved submitting and having published an allegedly nonsensical essay
on science and poststructuralism in a humanities journal. In Australia, the
University of Sydney remained intransigently "split" in two by ructions that
at least partly pertained to the analytic–continental divide.

And yet, during this period there have also been other indications that perhaps the house is no longer quite so divided (or at least that its former inhabitants are prepared to sort through the rubble). First, essays devoted to the
topical, methodological and stylistic differences between analytic and continental philosophy have begun to proliferate.[4] Comparative books on specific representative authors from each tradition abound, and there are recent
books examining central continental philosophers and their relation to, and

differences from, analytic philosophy – for instance, Richard Cobb-Stevens's *Husserl and Analytic Philosophy* (1990), Robert Hanna's *Kant and the Foundations of Analytic Philosophy* (2001), Samuel Wheeler's *Deconstruction as Analytic Philosophy* (2000) and Paul Redding's *Analytic Philosophy and the Return of Hegelian Thought* (2007). Hubert Dreyfus's interpretative work on Heidegger and Merleau-Ponty has been significant, as has Ian Hacking's use of Foucault. In addition, a number of prominent philosophers trained in the analytic tradition have been perceived within that tradition to have jumped the fence. For instance, Robert Brandom, Charles Taylor, Donald Davidson and John McDowell are all associated with "post-analytic philosophy", a term that itself becomes part of the philosophical landscape during the 1980s and 1990s (see Rachjman & West 1985), possibly inspired by Rorty's *Philosophy and the Mirror of Nature*. John Mullarkey's *Postcontinental Philosophy* (2006) claims that the philosophies of immanence of Alain Badiou, Gilles Deleuze, François Laruelle and Michel Henry constitute a radical shift in continental philosophy (we might also include Quentin Meillassoux's "speculative realism" under this description), away from Heidegger, Jean-Paul Sartre, Merleau-Ponty, Derrida and phenomenology. Mullarkey argues that the shift occurred within France around 1988, and that continental philosophers working in Anglo-American countries have been slow to absorb it. In the past few years, serious meta-philosophical books on each tradition have been published, including Lee Braver's *A Thing of This World* (2007), Glock's *What is Analytic Philosophy?* (2008) and Glendinning's *The Idea of Continental Philosophy* (2007). (There have also been a number of "internal" works re-examining each tradition, such as Scott Soames's two-volume work *Philosophical Analysis in the Twentieth Century* [2003a,b].) Several journals have appeared in the past twenty years that include in their remit the goal of bridging the divide (*International Journal of Philosophical Studies, Philosophical Forum, European Journal of Philosophy, Phenomenology and the Cognitive Sciences*, etc.).[5]

Such meta-philosophy perhaps indicates that both traditions are in a period of transformation, no longer taking for granted the methods and conception of the value of philosophy that has been dominant throughout the twentieth century. Perhaps. Quite apart from the fact that many such encounters end in rancour rather than rapprochement, one might also think that this diversity only really occurs at the margins, and that most philosophers ignore or avoid it. For any genuinely post-analytic and meta-continental horizon to emerge, we feel that more attention to the typical practices and interests of each tradition is required. This will be our topic in Parts II and III.

PART II
METHOD

7. INTRODUCTION TO PHILOSOPHICAL METHOD

At the broadest level, philosophical methods differ because people do philosophy in different ways (Tugendhat 1976: 3–4). Given that they also inevitably influence one another, as a result groups or lineages of philosophers do philosophy in similar ways and such broad methods can be typed to at least some extent. Giving the notion of philosophical method more precision – for instance, considering argument forms, heuristics, mandated starting places (first philosophy; common sense) or the like as matters of method – is rather more committal, but at least some of the standard questions of philosophical methodology can be put at this level. Are the methods of philosophy distinctively philosophical? If they are, are they remotely suitable to the tasks they are put to? If they are not, in virtue of what does philosophical work differ from other intellectual productions? Again, it is clear that analytic and continental philosophers differ in their ways of doing philosophy, even where ways are picked out fairly broadly. Philosophers working in each tradition are influenced by different work, communicate with different groups, distribute authority and trust differently, and so on. Indeed, questions of philosophical methodology are closely bound up with the largely separate development of each tradition.

Analytic philosophy began in something of a methodological revolution, as we have briefly outlined in Part I, and the method was that of logical analysis. In his 1914 lecture at Oxford, Russell characterizes (analytic) philosophy as "the science of the possible", and in turn identifies this entirely with the deliverances of a particular *a priori* method, analysis directed at uncovering the logical forms of propositions:

> By concentrating attention upon the investigation of logical forms, it becomes possible at last for philosophy to deal with its problems piecemeal, and to obtain, as the sciences do, such partial and probably not wholly correct results as subsequent investiga-

tion can utilise even while it supplements and improves them ....
This possibility of successive approximations to the truth is, more
than anything else, the source of the triumphs of science, and to
transfer this possibility to philosophy is to ensure a progress in
method whose importance it would be almost impossible to exaggerate.   (1917b: 112–13)

The method of "logical analysis" was indeed behind much early analytic philosophy in general, whether accompanied by metaphysical or reductive goals
(as occasionally by Russell himself), or treated in less committal fashion as
a form of "same-level" analysis. Although it has retained an important and
perhaps privileged position, it would be entirely wrong to characterize the
whole analytic tradition methodologically in terms of logical analysis alone; at
the time of the early logical positivists the idea of analysis was already changing, and from the ordinary language movement on it is very clear that most
analytic work simply does not fit this description.

A second unifying thread one might pick out here involves language, and
the linguistic turn that analytic philosophy took: on this account, analytic
philosophy is primarily concerned with the nature of linguistic meaning,
and the analytic approach to traditional problems is by a kind of "semantic
ascent", in which we focus on the word "knowledge" rather than knowledge
itself, the word "truth" rather than truth itself, and so on. Logical analysis
then fits into place as one of several possible activities that one might engage
in, in the course of carrying out this project, which also neatly subsumes the
classical work of Frege and Russell on meaning and reference, many of the
positivists' concerns (Carnap's distinction, in *Logical Syntax of Language*,
between the formal and material modes, or his later distinction between
internal and external questions), the project of giving truth- or verification-
conditional accounts of terms or sentences, much ordinary-language philosophy, Wittgenstein's conception of philosophy, the philosophical impact
of Tarski's work on truth, the Davidsonian programme, the various liaisons
between philosophy and linguistics, and so on. The claim has certainly at
times been made by prominent analytic philosophers that the focus on
meaning is the job of the philosopher *tout court*; a representative early sample is that of Ryle in "Systematically Misleading Expressions":

I conclude then, that there is, after all, a sense in which we can
properly inquire and even say "what it really means to say so and
so". For we can ask what is the real form of the fact recorded when
this is concealed or disguised and not duly exhibited by the expression in question. And we can often succeed in stating this fact in
a new form of words which does exhibit what the other failed to

> exhibit. And I am for the present inclined to believe that this is
> what philosophical analysis is, and that this is the sole and whole
> function of philosophy. (1952: 36)

More recently, and in historical mode, Dummett has made much the same
claim about the analytic tradition itself:

> Only with Frege was the proper object of philosophy finally estab-
> lished: namely, first, that the goal of philosophy is the analysis of
> the structure of *thought*; secondly, that the study of *thought* is to be
> sharply distinguished from the study of the psychological process
> of *thinking*; and, finally, that the only proper method for analysing
> thought consists in the analysis of *language*.... The acceptance of
> these three tenets is common to the entire analytical school.
> (1978: 458)

Dummett himself acknowledges more recently that this conception is a
poor fit for some individuals (Gareth Evans is his stock example); these he
is forced to regard as analytic simply in virtue of their enculturation by analytic philosophers. But there are other, tougher, hurdles for his claim: for
instance, the fact that fields of philosophy that touch on normative issues
(ethics, political philosophy, aesthetics, epistemology, philosophy of science)
rely at least as much on strategies of "semantic descent" as on linguistic
methods (Cohen 1986: §2); or the fact that many naturalizing philosophers
who regard themselves as analytic discuss issues of substance and apparent philosophical relevance without making much use of semantic ascent
and without tackling the problem of meaning. A kind of "no true Scotsman"
strategy is possible here, in which the normative fields and the naturalizers
are regarded as being at the fringe and so peripheral to analytic philosophy,
but such a strategy seems to us extremely unconvincing, notwithstanding
the very great importance that questions about language and meaning have
had for the analytic tradition.

By now it is perhaps clear that alleged unifying features of analytic methodology are unlikely to be adequate to their task. Nonetheless, there are at
least two major methodological fragments within analytic philosophy that
are worth flagging as important, even if they are not endorsed by all analytics.

First, one can consider the use of formal logic in the pursuit of philosophical questions as a methodological commitment of its own. Unsurprisingly,
work on the logicist programme in the philosophy of mathematics by Frege
and Russell is in large part a direct application of the logical discoveries of
Frege's *Begriffsschrift* (*Conceptual Notation*), and Frege's *Foundations* and
Russell's "On Denoting" and *Our Knowledge of the External World* are exem-

plars of early work that could not be carried out without the resources of modern logic. This trend persists through Wittgenstein's *Tractatus Logico-Philosophicus* and the work of Russell's logical atomist period, both of which draw metaphysical conclusions from the features of classical logic, and many of the logical positivists – most notably the early Carnap in the *Aufbau* and the *Logical Syntax of Language* – carry out work that is very strongly inflected by formal logic.

Of course, all of this could also be rung up to the credit of logical analysis, but focusing on the logic in itself highlights a further pattern. Even in this early period, before the semantic revolution in logic of the 1930s, which accelerated the trend, it is clear that a give-and-take between logic and philosophy is under way. Logical systems generate explanatory agendas of their own within philosophical logic, and these can affect more generally philosophical discussions of such matters as truth, inference and the like; consider, for instance, the way in which the development of intuitionist logics has been used by Dummett in his arguments about the nature of truth and the prospects of anti-realism.[1] Metaphysical (or positivist) system-building or theory production can also be influenced by the extent to which fruitful isomorphisms with logical systems are possible; consider here David Armstrong's discussion of the Weiner–Kuratowski device (a formal way of defining ordered pairs out of unordered classes) as a reason for treating unordered classes as ontologically primitive, or the ways in which a variety of logics (temporal logic, deontic logic and epistemic logic, for instance) have been inspired by the standard alethic modal logics. On the other hand, philosophical concerns with the conditional, vagueness, reasoning about fictional objects and the like have prompted the development of new logical systems; most famously, C. I. Lewis's development of the normal alethic modal logics was prompted by dissatisfaction with the material conditional analysis of "if ... then" (the truth functional analysis on which "If *A* then *B*" is true unless *A* is true and *B* is false; see Lewis & Langford 1932). The pattern holds not merely for classical logic; other formal systems with inferential implications, such as probability theory, and other logical systems, such as modal logic, go through much the same process. Although it is not plausible to try to saddle all analytic philosophical work with this concern for logic, the symbiosis here – with philosophical theorizing following formal suggestiveness, and with philosophical needs prompting formal development – is a feature of much analytic work in practice that is quite distinct from logical analysis itself, or the linguistic turn.

Second, much recent analytic work is carried out in a strongly naturalizing attitude; consider the slogans that philosophy is continuous with the sciences, that there is no first philosophy, or such clarion calls as the following:

> In recognizing that philosophy is continuous with the sciences, we
> need not fear that philosophy will thereby be "eclipsed" by science.
> The constraints that science presents for philosophical theorizing
> should be welcomed, for philosophical theorizing unconstrained
> by empirical fact loses its connection with the very phenomena
> which we, as philosophers, seek to understand. Philosophy is an
> autonomous discipline, in the sense that it addresses a distinctive
> set of questions and concerns, and in this respect it is no more
> nor less autonomous than physics or chemistry or biology. This is
> surely all the autonomy we should want.   (Kornblith 2002: 27)

Although naturalizing philosophers have on occasion regarded their work as replacing or directly competing with traditional philosophy, the more usual tendency is for naturalizers to regard the project as one of *constraint*. For instance, the naturalized epistemology project launched by Quine in his "Epistemology Naturalized" (1977) broadly holds that traditional epistemology is to be responsive to the way that the relevant social, psychological and biological sciences are turning out. Such a naturalizer will, for instance, take seriously *empirical exploration of the initial data set* that epistemologists set out from (do people as a whole really have the same intuitions as the philosophers? [Goldman 1992]), or will *test the concepts or structures* posited by the epistemologist against descriptive work,[2] or will carry out philosophical work that is explicitly *conditional* on scientific or empirical claims,[3] or may even (in reductive mood) demand that philosophical analysis of epistemic concepts proceeds in entirely non-epistemic (or non-normative) terms. This by no means exhausts the range of naturalizing constraints that can be in play. In the philosophy of mind, for instance, on the analogy of water and H_2O, empirical functionalists believe that, while we can somehow *pick out* mental states in folk psychological terms, we have to look to the sciences to uncover what they really are. This is in effect a further naturalizing constraint, that in which our ordinary mentalistic conceptions are taken to serve a reference-fixing role only. And behind most such projects is a still further methodological commitment, that of *integration* with the relevant sciences. For instance, Paul Churchland's (1981) well-known attack on some aspects of folk psychology (most notably the propositional attitudes – desire, belief, etc.) is based on the charge that folk psychological categories simply *do not fit* into the emerging picture of the mind delivered by the natural sciences.

It seems to us that unifying accounts of analytic philosophical method have a fairly poor track record. But fragments of analytic philosophy can (and do) exhibit fairly large and well-developed methodological commitments. In addition, the conscious use, within the analytic tradition, of particular explicitly named and discussed philosophical methods is very much alive.

The upshot is that contemporary analytic philosophy displays a kind of conscious *methodological diversity*, in which it is not uncommon to come across conceptual analysis ("definition, question delegation, drawing distinctions, crafting adequacy conditions, teasing out entailments, advancing possibility proofs, mapping inference patterns" [Sorensen 1992: 15]), or linguistic analysis (semantic ascent, truth-conditional analyses), or formal methods (the translation of arguments into formal dress, the logical or probabilistic modelling of a situation), or the various forms of appeal to intuition or opinion (thought experiment, most obviously), or various naturalizing constraints (requirements of integration with particular sciences, deference to scientific results, treating philosophical work as "reference-fixing", etc.), or coherence-building methods (reflective equilibrium, inference to the best explanation), or simply work making use of stock argument patterns that have been thrashed out in the literature to at least some extent (ontological arguments, "missing explanation" arguments, etc.).

Of course, these methods are rather more narrowly specified than general "ways of doing philosophy". Yet the philosophical practices of different philosophers are generally built up from such atoms, and not randomly: philosophers who take naturalizing constraints seriously, for instance, also tend to make use of inference to the best explanation or some other coherence-building approach to argument. One could see the methodological commitments made in different forms of philosophical practice as reflecting differing conceptions of what it is to do good philosophy, and so as linking up with vigorous debates within analytic philosophy about the point of conceptual analysis, the correct relation to the sciences, and so on. But going straight to that debate is not compulsory, and in fact will merely bring us up against yet more not-very-adequate unifying accounts of the tradition. Timothy Williamson usefully distinguishes the more general practices of philosophy in terms of the *discipline* they exact, rather than the credos or philosophical theses they require commitment to, and as such he makes the point in *Philosophy of Philosophy* that more than one of them can (or should) be in play at one time:

> [W]hen philosophy is not disciplined by semantics, it must be disciplined by something else: syntax, logic, common sense, imaginary examples, the findings of other disciplines (mathematics, physics, biology, psychology, history, ...) or the aesthetic evaluation of theories (elegance, simplicity, ...). Indeed, philosophy subject to only one of those disciplines is liable to become severely distorted: several are needed simultaneously. ... Of course, each form of philosophical discipline is itself contested by some philosophers. But that is no reason to produce work that is

not properly disciplined by anything. It may be a reason to wel-
come methodological diversity in philosophy: if different groups
in philosophy give different relative weights to various sources of
discipline, we can compare the long-run results of the rival ways
of working. Tightly constrained work has the merit that even those
who reject the constraints can agree that it demonstrates their
consequences.   (2008: 285–6)

In similar fashion Beaney sees the strength of the analytic tradition as consisting in a kind of opening up of the notion of analysis well away from the logical
analysis of Frege and Russell; that is, it consists in the fact that "reductive and
connective, revisionary and descriptive, linguistic and psychological, formal
and empirical elements [of analysis] all coexist in creative tension" (2009).
Arguably this methodological diversity and *de facto* analytic pluralism are the
norm in contemporary analytic philosophy.

   Along with the positive methodological norms of the tradition that
Williamson and Beaney point to, we feel that analytic philosophy has also
historically come equipped with a set of *negative* methodological norms:
methods that are marked as in some sense dubious; disciplines that are simply too contested. This is not at all surprising, given the anti-idealist and
anti-psychologizing fervour of the early analytics. Some of the characteristic
tropes of continental philosophy fall into this to-be-rejected category, most
notably "immodest" transcendental reasoning, although it is arguable that
anti-psychologism cannot be identified with rejection of "conditions of possibility" arguments. We shall return to this throughout the book, but there has
been a constancy in the analytic attitude here, based on the commitments
that the early analytics assumed in accepting modern logic as a tool of analysis, and notwithstanding major changes on methodological issues within
analytic philosophy itself. The analytic attitude to transcendental reasoning
is in part a suspicion born of the anomalous status of that reasoning form in
comparison to formal logical and probabilistic forms of inference: the most
natural attempts to represent the logical structure of transcendental reasoning founder in triviality (it is just *modus ponens*) or invalidity (the conclusion simply does not follow). To represent transcendental reasoning more
adequately, we must fuse psychological and logical considerations together.
But one philosopher's fusion is another's confusion, and the analytic tradition is based in a thoroughly anti-psychologizing approach to both logic
and mathematics. While Dummett thinks that much analytic philosophy of
mind and epistemology is guilty of psychologism, we know that the first half
of Frege's *Foundations of Arithmetic* presents a strong attack on psychologism and defence of the analyticity of arithmetic, and Russell's *Principles of
Mathematics* more or less independently presents the same view:

> Philosophy asks of Mathematics: What does it mean? Mathematics
> in the past was unable to answer, and Philosophy answered
> by introducing the totally irrelevant notion of mind. But now
> Mathematics is able to answer, so far at least as to reduce the
> whole of its propositions to certain fundamental notions of logic.
> At this point, the discussion must be resumed by Philosophy.
>
> (2005: §3)

The overall picture, we suggest, is therefore one of a pluralistic tolerance for methods, constrained by something of a veto list. Of course this is not to say that analytic philosophers do not engage in such methods as immodest transcendental reasoning; it simply means that if they do, the resulting work tends not to influence the analytic dialogue, and it can serve as a marker of "non-analytic" status to some.

So there are at least some of the makings of a characterization of the analytic tradition in terms of method. But is this really the right way to approach the analytic tradition's understanding of itself? Recall the "content-neutral" characterization that we suggested in the Introduction. According to this, the analytic tradition can be seen as a particular kind of dialogue, characterized by ties of influence across generations and communication within them, in which inferential connectivity is especially valued. The present suggestion is that a more adequate understanding of analytic philosophy from the inside, as it were, would be arrived at if we supplemented the dialogic account with a set of broadly pluralist methodological precepts. Given the intransitivity of influence (and indeed of "inferential connectivity" across generations), the content-neutral account by itself leaves open the possibility that the analytic tradition might exhibit a kind of methodological drift, in which practices debarred or under serious question at one stage become central or normal at other stages. If so, and we were to seek an explanation for particular patterns of change or constancy in the analytic tradition, our data would simply be particular influences from philosopher to philosopher (not necessarily, although of course possibly, influence via reason); if people sought to engage in rapprochement exercises, yet maintained their dialogic connections to the analytic world, then on this account we would not particularly expect them to be "drummed out of the regiment".[4] By contrast, if the internal understanding of analytic philosophy involves there being some kind of methodological walls in place here, then patterns of constancy or change can now be explained much more simply by the existence and policing of such an understanding, and those engaged in rapprochement exercises are at least potentially liable to be considered as having departed from the tradition, even if they maintain their own dialogic connections with other analytic philosophers. The question is, then, whether this additional explanatory resource more adequately handles the actual practice of the analytic community.

This is a difficult matter to resolve. It is true that, on occasion, at least some contemporary analytically trained philosophers appear to have declined in analytic influence as a result of a non-analytic liaison or interest. The late Davidson and post *Mind and World* McDowell are straightforwardly part of the analytic dialogue in the sense that they continue to read analytic work, react to analytic discussions of their own work, attend conferences with (other) analytic colleagues, and so on. On the other hand, each has on occasion been regarded as having departed from the analytic tradition, precisely because of a flouting of analytic norms in some work (see Duke *et al.* 2010). There are cases in which analytic philosophers have engaged with continental work without in any way being drummed out of the regiment; examples are the pre-war Ryle with respect to Husserl and Heidegger, Dummett with respect to the early Husserl, and Brandom with respect to Hegel and Heidegger. But, of course, most such engagements are essentially critical or historical (or both); neither Ryle nor Dummett actually put into practice the methods of phenomenology in their own work.

At least in part, this issue is also complicated by the way in which the analytic tradition, as it changes, modifies its own understanding of past philosophers outside the tradition. In the early twentieth century, philosophical work done by British metaphysicians (such as McTaggart) or American pragmatists (such as John Dewey) was outside the analytic tradition on any count: the relevant dialogic connections of influence and communication (as part of a common project of maximising inferential connectivity) were absent, and neither McTaggart nor Dewey subscribed to early-twentieth-century analytic methodological canons. But of course, the analytic methodological canon has changed over time, and as a result influence networks have also altered. With the revival of metaphysics, much (at the time) non-analytic work in the early-twentieth-century British metaphysical tradition has become influential; under the influence of Quine and Sellars, much (at the time) non-analytic work in early-twentieth-century pragmatism has become influential. (There do not appear to be any converse cases, where work that was in its day considered straightforwardly analytic has since come to be regarded as falling outside the tradition: posthumous drumming out of the regiment does not seem to happen.) In the face of such examples, it seems to us that potential (inclusive) revisability is genuinely in play here, in the sense that the analytic tradition allows for the later re-evaluation and co-option of current philosophical work, regardless of present methodological canons. (The attitude is indeed much like that at play in analytic discussions of older historical figures: consider the common accusation that analytics read Hume, Aristotle and so on out of context and with an eye on ways of bringing them into relation with contemporary philosophy.) But partial revisability on some points is entirely consistent with inflexibility on others, and the co-option of traditional metaphysics, or pragmatic work, does not in itself provide much evidence that the analytic tradition is likely to become more tolerant to transcendental reasoning, genealogical projects and so on.

To the extent that the continental tradition is seen as beginning with Husserl's development of phenomenological analysis, clearly it also begins in methodological revolution. But of course earlier influences on twentieth-century continental philosophy, especially those in the tradition of critical philosophy, have also been in large part influences of method: Dilthey's hermeneutics, the Kantian commitment to transcendental methods, Hegel's dialectic and method of immanent critique and so on. Once again, the tendency over time has been to methodological diversity; phenomenology and transcendental reasoning have developed in myriad forms. Is there also a methodological unity here? Certainly, continental philosophy presents as less unified than the analytic tradition, containing as it does very different meta-reflections on philosophical method (some sceptical about the very idea) and with various diverse methods employed in practice: phenomenological, dialectical, hermeneutic, structuralist, psychoanalytic and transcendental. Nonetheless, there are some commonalities here. In different ways all of these methods are designed to shed light on what might be described as our time-embeddedness, and all are designed to exhibit something that is *not* simultaneously clear and distinct. Many are hence sympathetic to varying degrees to Leibniz's (and Bergson's, and Deleuze's) riposte to Descartes that clarity and distinctness are in fact mutually exclusive,[5] a philosophical objection that begins to explain some of the widely observed stylistic differences between analytic and continental philosophy. Again, the continental tradition generally exhibits a thoroughgoing wariness of any close link between philosophical method and either common sense (or proxies, such as folk psychology) or science; this is in contrast to the analytic tendency to retain at least one of these connections. Such a concern is perhaps partly presaged by Kant's critical philosophy (noting that there is a sense in which Kant's transcendental philosophy leaves everything as it is, and is certainly not incompatible with common sense), but it attains renewed vigour around the end of the nineteenth century. The "masters of suspicion" are an obvious source of this attitude, but consider also Bergson's critique of the intellect, or even Husserl's search for a method that would suspend the assumptions of the "natural attitude", including even the common-sense conviction that we have perceptual experience of an "external world". The relation between phenomenology and common sense is not simply oppositional, in that phenomenological descriptions typically remind us of pre-reflective dimensions of experience that have been both forgotten and presupposed, but the aim here is to describe levels of experience "beneath" the common-sense judgements of particular subjects, which are claimed to be the conditions of possibility for such opinions and judgements. Finally, in the poststructuralist thinkers, such as Deleuze and Derrida, this scepticism about any close methodological relation between philosophy and common sense is heightened.

Can we see contemporary analytic and continental philosophers as facing a common agenda of problems, with the division between the traditions simply marking the choice of different tools for tackling the job? Surely not. But it does not follow that the divide has *never* amounted primarily to a difference of opinion on philosophical method and not that of agenda. Indeed, Frege and Husserl begin with remarkably similar concerns, their differing attitudes to logic induce very different methodological commitments, and these in turn generate differing problem landscapes.[6] Different philosophical interests thereby build up around different methodological commitments, if only because the agenda that each tradition takes seriously is in part the outcome of a history of reflection on the possibilities and problems of the methods that it employs. Since methodological difference is today reinforced by differing literatures, evaluations of significance and assignments of trust and authority, it is not clear that a straightforward discussion about philosophical method can be held across the divide, even if it turns out that methodological difference has been behind the deepening of the divide. (The point here is fairly similar to the Kuhnian claim that Neil Levy [2003] picks up on in his conception of analytic philosophy as paradigmatic: methodological difference can be much more intractable than other kinds of difference, because giving way here can amount to giving up the whole project one is engaged in.) Nonetheless, for the reasons we have given above, there is at least some reason to regard this as a contingent matter; both analytic and continental traditions have exhibited methodological flexibility over time, in the sense that their methodological canons have changed, and as a result genuinely different networks of influence have arisen. The idea, then, that philosophers working in the one tradition might gain something from the critique or discussion of their methodological practices on the basis of criticism from the other tradition cannot initially be ruled out.

8. ANALYTIC PHILOSOPHY AND THE INTUITION PUMP

THE USES AND ABUSES OF THOUGHT EXPERIMENTS

Let us begin with an example, perhaps the most famous (or infamous) piece of science-fiction in recent analytic philosophy. Putnam asks us to suppose the existence somewhere in the galaxy of the planet Twin Earth, which is exactly like Earth except that the role of water – the clear colourless liquid that falls in rain, fills oceans and so on – is played by a different chemical (dubbed "XYZ") instead of H_2O. And here is the business end of what follows:

> [L]et us roll the time back to about 1750. At that time chemistry was not developed on either Earth or Twin Earth. The typical Earthian speaker of English did not know water consisted of hydrogen and oxygen, and the typical Twin Earthian speaker of English did not know "water" consisted of XYZ. Let Oscar$_1$ be such a typical Earthian English speaker, and let Oscar$_2$ be his counterpart on Twin Earth. You may suppose that there is no belief that Oscar$_1$ had about water that Oscar$_2$ did not have about "water". If you like, you may even suppose that Oscar$_1$ and Oscar$_2$ were exact duplicates in appearance, feelings, thoughts, interior monologue, etc. Yet the extension of the term "water" was just as much H_2O on Earth in 1750 as in 1950; and the extension of the term "water" was just as much XYZ on Twin Earth in 1750 as in 1950. Oscar$_1$ and Oscar$_2$ understood the term "water" differently in 1750 *although they were in the same psychological state*, and although, given the state of science at the time, it would have taken their scientific communities about fifty years to discover that they understood the term "water" differently. Thus the extension of the term "water" (and, in fact, its "meaning" in the intuitive preanalytical usage of that term) is *not* a function of the psychological state of the speaker by itself. (Putnam 1975: 224)

The last sentence indicates that Putnam's suppositions about the existence of Twin Earth and the features of the two speakers, and the intuitions subsequently elicited, are meant to establish a conclusion. This is a *thought experiment*; it is a piece of controlled speculation in which conclusions are drawn by specifying a situation (usually hypothetically or counterfactually) and then attending to our reactions to it. These reactions are conventionally dubbed "intuitions", and can be thought of as fallible intellectual seemings that are (apparently) effortless to produce, immediately given (on understanding of the relevant situation), reasonably stable from time to time, and very often able to be given a modal inflection (we can intuit that p is possible, or that it is necessary, or that it is impossible, etc.).[1] Like most, but not all, of its kin, the Twin Earth thought experiment *rejects a claimed necessity*, in that it provides evidence for a possible situation that serves as a counter-example to a necessary connection (here a functional claim) if our intuitions about the situation are correct. Moreover, it is a typical example of the use of the device in contemporary analytic philosophy (as opposed to most uses of the device in science), in that Putnam is not concerned to specify a situation that is *likely* to obtain in the real world, or that we *could bring about* were we to put our minds to it, or even to ensure that the specific situation is *physically possible*. Instead, Putnam is happy to sharpen his argumentative point by invoking unabashed science-fiction. And although many analytic thought experiments do limit themselves to the ordinary, the more famous of them tend to be bizarre in just this way.

Modern analytic philosophy is very heavily invested in thought experimentation. Some thought experiments (such as Twin Earth, or Searle's Chinese Room) have celebrity status and sub-literatures of their own, but analytic commitment to the practice is also demonstrated by sheer number. Thought experimentation is near ubiquitous in ethics (and normative theory in general), epistemology and philosophy of language, very common in philosophy of mind, metaphysics, the philosophy of religion and philosophy of science, and not at all uncommon in the philosophies of logic, mathematics and probability. Finally, analytic interest in the topic is also reflected by a growing contemporary literature on the nature and properties of thought experiments, in which the device is regularly treated as a stock philosophical method.[2]

Although their precise nature is controversial, there appears to be widespread agreement that Roy Sorensen is at least right in classifying philosophical thought experiments as either *necessity refuters* or (more rarely) *possibility refuters* (see Sorensen 1992: 153–7). Hidden necessities are legion in philosophical work, arising wherever a conceptual, logical, functional, inferential or constitutive connection is asserted (when knowledge is viewed as being equivalent to true justified belief, for instance), or wherever a possibility or state of affairs is ruled out (as when it is declared that there can be no truth without a truthmaker, for instance). Most thought experiments therefore serve straightforwardly as evidence in philosophical enquiry, allowing the agent to judge that a situation is possible. Some, less straightforwardly, are used in a kind of *reductio* mode to *undermine* the intuitive deliverances of other thought experiments: a classic example is Bernard Williams's (1973) *re-presentation* of a well-known personal identity thought experiment. In the original Lockean thought experiment, one is invited to imagine that a "mindswap" machine has been invented, such that if it is applied to A and B, the body of A will thereafter have apparent memories of B's life, psychological states identical to those of B, will claim to be B, and so forth, and the body of B will exhibit the same properties with respect to A. Imagine, further, that A was compelled beforehand to choose whether A's or B's body, after the operation, was to be tortured. If A chose A's body to receive the torture, B's body would afterwards express great relief at having made the right choice, and the conventional intuition from all this, argued for by proponents of the psychological theory of personal identity, is that A is now in B's body, and B is now in A's body. Williams begins with an apparently different case: that in which A is captured, and told that he is to be tortured tomorrow. Williams notes, correctly, that this would induce an entirely rational fear in A. The case is then varied: A is told that, before the torture, he is to have his memory wiped. Again, fear seems reasonable. Then A is told that, after the memory wipe, his memories will be replaced by those of a fictional person – and again fear seems rational. Further such modifications eventually lead to the Lockean scenario, but now with the strong intuition that A should fear that which will happen to A's body. In other words, the intuitive support the case originally gave the psychological theory now runs against that account. Again, some thought experiments simply *problematize*, drawing our attention to a theoretical difficulty that previously had not been attended to.[3]

Thought experiments tend to open philosophical debates rather than close them. In part this is because they are generally part of a process of clarification or exploration, but also because they can induce fairly familiar meta-debates that take off from the acknowledged limitations of the device. Common tropes here are for the opponent of the person proposing the thought experiment to dismiss it as too thin in detail, or alternatively too remote from actuality, or to suggest that the thought experiment rests on some kind of illegitimate "cuing" of our intuitions,[4] or to bring in historical information about the contested concept.[5] More simply, of course, the opponent might just propose variant thought experiments of their own; this is a game that two can play. Seen in this way, analytic thought experiments can be taken to play a useful but limited evidential role in a larger picture of analysis that includes direct argument, possibility modelling, formal analysis and other methods.

THE ANALYTIC TRADITION

Philosophical interest in thought experiment long predates the analytic movement. Examples of the *use* of thought experiment can of course be found throughout the history of philosophy since Presocratic times. The explicit philosophical *invocation* of thought experiment as a method has been a much more recent development. At first, recognition of thought experiment as a method for philosophy was fairly closely connected to the recognition of the method in science. The Danish chemist/physicist Hans Christian Ørsted appears to have coined the term "*gedankenexperiment*" in his 1811 work *Prolegomenon to the General Theory of Nature*[6] (itself strongly influenced by post-Kantian *Naturphilosophie*), and made deliberate use of the technique in his later work on electromagnetism. Through the nineteenth century, philosophical interest in the evidential use of hypothetical supposition occasionally emerges, although without making use of the term of art "*gedankenexperiment*". An example of a near coinage appears in Bradley's *Principles of Logic*, in a passage written in 1883:

> A supposition means thinking for a particular end, and in a special way. It is not a mere attending to a certain meaning or an analysis of its elements. It has a reference to the real world, and it involves a desire to see what happens. We may illustrate perhaps from other usages. "Say it is so for argument's sake", "Treat it as this and then you will see", are much the same as, "Suppose it to be so". A supposal is, in short, an *ideal experiment*. It is the application of a content to the real, with a view to see what the consequence is, and with a tacit reservation that no actual judgment has taken place. The supposed is treated as if it were real, in order to see how the real behaves when qualified thus in a certain manner.
> (Bradley 1922: 86–7, emphasis added)[7]

Neither Ørsted nor Bradley is very plausible as an influence on the analytic tradition of thought experiment. By contrast, Ernst Mach is an obvious candidate. Mach's 1897 essay on the subject (Mach 1976) provided the first detailed defence of the epistemic value of thought experiment in science, arguing that the device allowed sensory knowledge that might normally be cognitively inaccessible to come to consciousness through use in the imagined case. Mach is also responsible for some nice examples of the technique, and of course Mach was well known within philosophy – and particularly influential on some of the early analytics – for his vigorous brand of positivism. Since such early analytic philosophers as Russell and the logical positivists had scientistic leanings, a person aware of the current analytic commitment to the device, but ignorant of the details of analytic philosophy through the twentieth century, might think that thought experiment entered the analytic tradition in this way – consciously, through the influence of Mach – and early on.

Yet this does not seem to have happened. In early twentieth-century anglophone philosophy, explicit reference to thought experiment – about the clearest evidence of Mach's influence on this point that one might have – crops up in passing in *other* traditions, rather than the early analytics. A representative sample is the pragmatist Ferdinand Schiller's suggestion, in opposition to the new post-Fregean logic, that "it is perfectly possible to conceive [the] syllogism, *as it occurs in real thought*, and as alone it *can* occur therein, as a thought-experiment with reality which forecasts the course of events we are entitled to *expect* on the strength of past experience" (1921: 16). Moreover, even the *use* of thought experiment is rare in the science-leaning end of the early analytic tradition. In most cases, early analytic thought experiments appear to have been treated as straightforward *illustrations* or passing *demonstrations* of a point secured in another way (as in the case of Russell's evocation of the five-minute-old Earth[8]). True, Russell is sympathetic to the application of imagination to philosophical problems,[9] but the imagination is to wander through the world of forms, and not through hypothetical empirical situations. The models provided by the Fregean analysis of number and the Russellian analysis of definite descriptions are meant to liberate the analyst from the tyranny of surface form in analysis, and Russell's principle of abstraction and his account of classes provide powerful tools for avoiding commitment to metaphysically suspicious entities – but it is still analysis that does the work of philosophy, and analysis is not to be performed by thought experimentation.[10] Notice how very different this view is from the more recent – and also older – approach to analysis as involving the identification of necessary and sufficient conditions for the application of a term or concept, a practice that lends itself to thought experimentation.

Of the early figures in the analytic tradition, only Moore – who is not in any sense a Machian – made sustained use of thought experiment, and then only in a special case. Moore believes that propositions as to which things have intrinsic value cannot be argued for; they can only be recognized. In *Principia Ethica*, therefore, he recommends that questions about intrinsic value be settled by the "method of absolute isolation", in which one imagines a situation in which the relevant thing exists alone, and then notes whether or not such existence would nonetheless be good (1989: §§55, 57, 112–13). There are some signs that Moore would be prepared to take the method

61

of thought experimentation further, at least within the field of ethics. For instance, he remarks:

> Wild and extravagant as are the assertions which metaphysicians have made about reality, it is not to be supposed but that they have been partially deterred from making them wilder still, by the idea that it was their business to tell nothing but the truth. But the wilder they are, and the less useful for Metaphysics, the more useful will they be for Ethics; since, in order to be sure that we have neglected nothing in the description of our ideal, we should have had before us as wide a field as possible of suggested goods.
>
> (*Ibid.*: §71)

Moore's preparedness to make such use of thought experiment, has, however, little to do with his involvement in the nascent analytic movement. Rather, it has to do with the subject matter of ethics itself, and the way that discussion of it had developed. Appeals to intuition as elicited by described cases appear regularly in earlier ethical argument (Kant or Henry Sidgwick, for instance), and Moore's discussions perhaps influenced the later ethical intuitionism of H. A. Prichard and W. D. Ross.[11] Here again there are passages that clearly contemplate thought experiment; for instance, in Prichard's judgement as to how moral agents should reason when afflicted by doubts about their obligations: "The only remedy lies in actually getting into a situation which occasions the obligation, or if our imagination be strong enough in imagining ourselves in that situation, and then letting our moral capacities of thinking do their work" (Prichard 1968: 16–17).

But for Prichard and Ross, as for Moore, the thought experiment was accepted as a technique in part because the epistemology of the situation was thought to be *highly unusual* – ethical knowledge was to be delivered by intuitions that were in some sense incapable of error, being a kind of direct knowledge of the moral properties of states of affairs.[12] There is no general licence here for thought experiment; indeed, the notion of intuition in play here is, in its (limited) infallibilism and curious direct acquaintance epistemology, in some ways more similar to the notion of intuition employed by Bergson (the means by which we gain non-relative knowledge) than to later analytic understandings of intuitions as either beliefs or dispositions to believe. For this reason, the tolerance to thought experiment on display here arguably had little influence on later analytic tolerance of the device; indeed, we share Scott Soames's suspicion that one can see Ross's work as "inadvertently feeding the rather widespread suspicion about the place of normative ethics, and other evaluative matters, in philosophy that typified the attitudes of many important analytic philosophers in the '30s and '40s" (2003a: 342).

The method of absolute isolation is, in effect, one in a group of "reci-pes for speculation" that can be adapted to different circumstances, and thus prompt thought experimentation throughout philosophical history. For obvious reason it has special relevance to questions about the intrin-sic or extrinsic nature of properties. A further device of this kind is what Simon Blackburn calls "spinning the possible worlds" (1984: 312); holding the intrinsic properties of an agent fixed and altering (in supposition) the envi-ronment. Putnam's Twin Earth is an example of a thought experiment that puts this into action, and similar argumentative machinery lies behind much recent work on indexicals, demonstratives and so on. Although such a device does not appear directly in the early analytic literature in thought experiment form, it is arguably present as a kind of *standard* when modalized concepts such as verifiability are to be elucidated. Schlick's examples of when someone is, in principle, capable of verifying a proposition are a very modest form of world-spinning along these lines; in effect, the agent is to be placed in just the right spatiotemporal location to obtain the relevant kind of evidence in a world otherwise identical to the actual world. Such a standard licenses a kind of thought experiment in those who are to put the verifiability criterion into practice: to assess a putatively verifiable sentence, I have to engage in an act of imaginative speculation and then note whether the agent in my scenario would be justified in counting the event as one of verification.

Now, other familiar philosophical recipes for speculation do also make occasional appearances in the early-twentieth-century literature; for instance, Laplace's demon (in various disguises) was pressed into occasional philosophical service, largely by non-analytic philosophers.[13] And on such occasions there was not always a protective wall limiting the use of the tech-nique, as there was for Moore and the intuitionists. But the general contrast here between past and present analytic practice remains clear: given the cur-rent ubiquity of analytic thought experiment, these are very thin beginnings indeed. The difference between early and late tolerance of thought experi-ments is one marker of a major methodological change within the analytic tradition, tied to changing conceptions of analysis, a revision in attitudes to intuition, and perhaps to a wider move toward coherence accounts of justification.

The specifically analytic climate seems to us to have changed from the 1930s, with the turn to ordinary-language philosophy and the associated resistance to systematic accounts of meaning.[14] If we must pay attention to "what we would say" in philosophy, we have to license the outlining of an imaginary situation and the treating as evidence our (classificatory, lin-guistic) reactions to it. This is very close to thought experiment in the lin-guistic mode, and it lends itself to an obvious adaptation if attention turns from linguistic to conceptual analysis. It is true that many of the classics of the ordinary-language movement do not make much use of this possibility, instead appealing to ordinary language in the critique of traditional or other analytic arguments or terminology (consider Ryle's discussion of systematically misleading expressions, Austin's attack on the sense-data tradition in *Sense and Sensibilia*, Austin's worrying at Moore's use of "could" and "should", Peter Strawson's criticism of the translational practices of formal logic in his *Introduction to Logical Theory*, and so on). But on more free-ranging occasions, the ordinary-language movement was clearly permissive of thought experimentation. Consider, for instance, Austin's well-known donkey-shooting demonstration:

> You have a donkey, so have I, and they graze in the same field. The day comes when I conceive a dislike for mine. I go to shoot it, draw a bead on it, fire: the brute falls in its tracks. I inspect the victim, and find to my horror that it is your donkey. I appear on your doorstep with the remains and say – what? "I say, old sport, I'm awfully sorry, &c, I've shot your donkey by *accident*"? Or "by mistake"? Then again, I go to shoot my donkey as before, draw a bead on it, fire – but as I do so, the beasts move, and to my horror yours falls. Again the scene on the doorstep – what do I say? "By mistake"? Or "by accident"?   (Austin 1961: 185 n.1)

This is a thought experiment in a linguistic framework; it concerns directly our judgements about the terms "by accident" and "by mistake", but these in turn provide potential evidence as to what our concepts of accident and mistake are (or, in even more realist mode, as to what the relevant universals might be). Similarly, Ryle's torrent of passing examples and counter-examples in *The Concept of Mind* rises to the level of thought experiment whenever he extracts a conclusion about what we would call clever, intelligent, voluntary, imaginative and so on, from a quickly sketched imaginary context of judgement. Of course the thought experiments of Ryle and Austin are determinedly ordinary, but the ordinary-language movement can also show examples at the more science-fictional end of thought experimentation; most notably, and despite his official suspicion of abnormal supposition, Wittgenstein is a very fertile producer of *outré* thought experiments.[15]

Such methods outdistanced ordinary-language philosophy itself. The boom in thought experimentation can be dated to the late 1950s, when individual thought experiments began to develop lengthy literatures of their own.[16] Some of these thought experiments still retain philosophical bite – consider Sidney Shoemaker's discussions of personal identity (involving Locke-inspired "puzzle-cases" of mind-, brain- or personality-swap) or Edmund Gettier's famous counter-examples to the tripartite analysis of knowledge as justified true belief. The methodological change here is marked not merely by an increase in the rate of thought experimentation, or by an increased tendency to discuss particular examples; instead, something of a broader shift in attitude has occurred within analytic philosophy. Since the 1960s, the analytic literature has to some extent *organized itself* around particularly evocative examples of thought experiment, in part because the thought experiments involved, unlike mere illustrations, admit of more than one response. In addition to Putnam's Twin Earth, consider Searle's Chinese Room, Quine's gavagai, Jackson's Black-and-White Mary, the trolley-car cases in ethics and Newcomb's problem in decision theory. Each of these is a battleground, a permanently contested territory, with variants on each thought experiment acting as a spur to new theory.[17]

It is tempting to see this shift in attitude as being connected with the general revival of analytic metaphysics, and there is certainly a connection between the device and the preparedness of contemporary analytic philosophers to rest their conclusions on appeals to intuition, considered as a fallible but useful guide to underlying beliefs, conceptual structure, the meaning of public terms or even the nature of universals. Equally, it is worth noting that the eliciting of intuitions (whether by thought experiment or in other ways) itself received something of a theoretical fillip at around the same time, with the post-Quinean growth in the use of coherence-building devices in analytic philosophy that we discuss in Chapter 9 (reflective equilibrium, inference to the best explanation, etc.). However, there may also be external factors coming into play here; the burgeoning of analytic journals post-war, for instance, may well have furthered discussion of cases, and the development of literatures around them. Certainly it is difficult to see how ongoing discussion of and tinkering with thought experiments could be done naturally in a community for whom the monograph is the more natural unit of publication, like the continental community. Additionally, the structuring of philosophical work around standard thought experiments – the star system, as applied to thought experiments – might also to some extent have come about because of further background norms of the analytic dialogue of the kind that we have suggested lie behind the theoretical conservatism of the tradition. Analytic literatures involve standard cases or patterns of argument, classical ways of putting an objection, and a range of other devices for keeping the background assumptions of dialogic participants in step (as we suggest, to improve the inferential connectivity of analytic work). A tendency to retain the details of especially successful thought experiments (or to hold most parameters fixed while varying others for a particular argumentative point) furthers this goal, but it also means that the organization of analytic sub-literatures around thought experiments will not be especially surprising.

CONTINENTAL PHILOSOPHY AND THOUGHT EXPERIMENTS

It is notable that thought experiments are not regularly deployed in continental philosophy. Of course, there are persistent uses of certain stories or fictions that at first glance look like thought experiments, like Hegel's influential "master–slave" dialectic in *Phenomenology of Spirit*, Nietzsche's invocation of the eternal return of the same, Sartre's novelistic examples illuminating bad faith and absence, or Deleuze's engagement with the Robinson Crusoe tale,[18] but they do not seem to function equivalently. In a certain sense, Hegel's account of the development of self-consciousness via a battle for recognition is a fiction, but it also has another status, being inferred as a transcendental condition to explain social life and the necessary "co-imbrication" of the "I–we" relation. Is it short and pithy, and does it allow for a deductive conclusion to falsify a claimed necessity or possibility? Is it a test for consistency or best understood as a claim about what is conceivable or possible? No. It is meant to be both grounded in experiential data of a phenomenological and historical kind, and, at the same time, world-disclosing, allowing us to look at the world and our place in it anew.

Although few of the most famous continental figures explicitly explain their reluctance to use thought experiments, their more general reflections on methodological matters suggest they harbour the conviction that something often goes awry in philosophies that uncritically mimic the use of thought experiments in science. To put it another way, there is thought to be an intrinsic problem (or at least risk) with thought experiments that strip a problem back to its basics. Such cases appear decisive only because of their abbreviated and schematic form; more generally, this abstraction belies the complexity of social life and functions on the basis of certain tacit philosophical presuppositions that are either controversial (such as the assumption of a rational, self-interested agent who is extricable from their past), or are not really practically conceivable.

In distinguishing the phenomenological technique of eidetic analysis (imaginative variation) from the typical analytic use of thought experiments, J. N. Mohanty (1991) claims that the latter is based on mere logical possibility, not on what he calls eidetic possibility. Mohanty's claim is that while we may be able to logically conceive of the possibility of, say, body-splitting in Derek Parfit's teletransporter device (which promises to create a replica of us on Mars), we cannot *concretely imagine* this. In other words, it cannot be "lived", or a "concrete intuition", as Husserl might say. If this is right, the intuitive responses that a bizarre or science-fictional thought experiment evokes from us are unlikely to be very helpful in soliciting our views about personal identity. To put the problem another way, it seems clear that thought experiments need to meet some kind of sufficient resemblance condition to be effective as an argument for or against a given view, and Mohanty's view is that this condition is frequently lacking. What might such a sufficient resemblance condition be? Scientific thought experiments rely on one seeing the resemblance between the imagined scenario and an actual experiment that might be conducted, and ideally will be. In philosophy, of course, things are not so simple, but it seems that an appropriate requirement will be some connection to actual experience or to a large body of existing analytic work on the thought experiments in question. Indeed, these scenarios presuppose a shared community of experts for their meaning, familiar with the array of conceptual analyses and the pitfalls that a given thought experiment entails for particular perspectives. As such, they serve as heuristic devices against which views in their neighbourhood are sharpened, as part of a testing process. But of course this is rather uncompelling for any philosophers not already enculturated in this way. For those unfamiliar with this background, thought experiments can seem stale and deprived of depth. For those in the know, on the other hand, the experiments have depth because of the communal work on given problems.

Some of these problems are exacerbated when thought experiments are given an explicitly normative or action-guiding flavour. Many thought experiments cut out an imagined time-slice wherein one is asked to imagine a situation without our past or even projected futural possibilities, and to make decisions on the basis of this determination. This highly abstract and "thin" scenario is assumed to nonetheless shed light on our "thicker" practical situation. In Rawls's famous "veil of ignorance" thought experiment in *A Theory of Justice*, for example, we are limited in both of the above temporal ways, having neither knowledge of, nor an affective relation to, our past abilities or interests, and having virtually no knowledge of how any future redistributive arrangements might affect us. The same is evidently true of the various thought experiments and rationality paradoxes that one encounters in game and decision theory. Bernard Williams (1976: 97) generalizes this point to claim that thought experiments put us in a situation but without our history, including all of the associated information and background that we require in order to make choices. As such, he suggests that they are *exclusively forward thinking*; the past is only relevant in order to predict the future. As such, one of the key continental rejoinders to any uncritical reliance on the efficacy of thought experiments would be that that they give insufficient attention to the background, the memorial traces (including the unconscious) that are at play when our categorical judgement is appealed to in such a manner. Given the growing acknowledgment within analytic philosophy of many of these meta-philosophical limitations, however, the key question is whether analytic philosophers are sufficiently cautious in their actual use of such experiments in their work.

These kinds of themes have analytic analogues, and within the analytic literature there are materials one could use in reply. For instance, Williamson has on occasion induced real-world Gettier thought experiments in his audiences, to make it clear that complaints about possibility or non-actuality can simply miss the point; in *Philosophy of Philosophy* he comments:

> What is striking about real-life Gettier cases is how little difference they make. They are not markedly more or less effective as counterexamples to the target analysis than imaginary Gettier cases are. Those who found the imaginary counterexamples convincing find the real life ones more or less equally convincing ... Conversely, those who were suspicious of the imaginary counterexamples are more or less equally suspicious of the real life ones. (2008: 193)

Again, and with an eye on some of the same concerns as have been expressed above, there is an analytic literature that examines the nature of imaginative conceiving, the connection between conceivability and possibility, and the reliability of the transition from the one to a claim about the other. The upshot can be a precisification that removes the concern, or locates it in a way that allows the issues at stake to emerge more clearly: for instance, in the wake of divided opinions about the conceivability of his zombie thought experiment for epiphenomenalism, David Chalmers (2002) has claimed that the possibility claim that his argument requires is a minimal species of epistemic possibility: this obtains when we cannot know *a priori* that the situation cannot obtain.

We can, however, pose a more radical challenge to the use of thought experiments via the work of Deleuze. In *The Logic of Sense, Difference and Repetition* and elsewhere, Deleuze repeatedly discusses two interrelated assumptions that conspire together to produce what he considers to be a false or dogmatic image of thought. These two foundational assumptions are termed "good sense" and "common sense". Common sense, like Bergsonian analysis, is said to be that which allows us to decide on the categories that will be used to determine a solution, as well as to settle the value of those categories. Common sense thus bears directly on methodological issues, including how a problem should be divided up such that a solution might be ascertained. It functions predominantly by recognition (we recognize that this fits into that category), and is described by Deleuze as "a faculty of identification that brings diversity in general under the form of the same" (1990a: 77–8). In other words, it identifies, recognizes and subsumes various diverse singularities (or particularities) and gives them a unity. Good sense then allocates things into the categories. It functions by prediction, and by choosing and preferring (1994: 33, 226), and it is frequently assumed to be naturally oriented to truth. It starts from massive differentiation and then resolves, or synthesizes it. When taken together, Deleuze argues that this model of recognition (including labelling) and prediction is profoundly conservative. It precludes the advent of the new; good sense and common sense are concerned with the recognition of truths rather than the production of them.

On this view, it is "common sense" that we draw on to ascertain whether or not a particular thought experiment gets a grip on a fundamental moral or political issue, or is an appropriate way of dealing with the dilemma at hand. We recognize that a particular hypothetical scenario – say Plato's ring of Gyges, which makes us invisible – stands for a broader problem, in this case the role of fear of consequences in preventing human selfishness (this fear is, of course, removed if we are invisible since crimes could be committed without worries about being caught and punished). A large part of this process depends on our intuitive response to whether the proposed analogy holds; for instance, whether Judith Jarvis Thomson (1971) is right in claiming that the pro-life position that women do not have a right to abortion is analogous (in the relevant ways) to waking up and finding oneself tied to a famous violinist and becoming their effective life support without any possibility of freeing oneself from this arrangement. Usually, the abbreviated form of the experiment or analogy means that the information that is needed in order to make any such adjudication is not given, but we are nonetheless solicited to trust our response. If this is inconsistent with something else we have stated about, say, abortion, we are then exhorted to modify our understanding of the relevant moral and epistemological distinctions in order to incorporate that which was revealed by the thought experiment. This is what Deleuze calls "good sense", where we attempt to resolve a problem by selecting one set of alternatives over another, or at least providing criteria for such adjudication. The function of good sense is hence to resolve the question at hand by reference to our intuitions on the thought experiment at hand (and its suitability to stand as a marker for the more general problem) and to our rational principles. In attempting to decide in this manner, however, we run the risk of reducing complex problems to questions that admit of clear and distinct answers. Likewise, Rawls's famous "veil of ignorance" scenario at times appears to reduce the problem of justice to a judgement between the distributive principles of utilitarianism, liberalism and strict egalitarianism. In both of these cases problems are understood in a manner that restricts them to a determinate range of possible outcomes; we move from the past as complex and unpredictable to the future as simple, predictable and amenable to calculation.

Such a case against thought experiment will almost certainly leave most analytics cold. Deleuze is in effect making a claim about a causal mechanism of judgement, just as (say) the psychologists Amos Tversky and Daniel Kahneman do, in positing the use of heuristics in judgement. For instance, they posit a "representativeness" heuristic, in which, in considering whether object A belongs to class B, or event A arises from process B, "probabilities are evaluated by the degree to which A is representative of B, that is, by the degree to which A resembles B" (1982: 4). Such accounts can indeed have implications for our views on the reliability, fallibility, limitations or corruption of thought experiments. But there is no *special* problem for thought experiment, here; Deleuze is in effect concerned with classificatory judgement, whether of an actual situation or not. Second, theoretical concerns about bias need not lead us to stop thought experimentation any more than concerns about road conditions need prevent driving. To the extent we accept Deleuze's concerns, or otherwise believe the device of thought experimentation is on a topic less reliable or skewed, we can carry out the thought experimental equivalent of driving slowly: we can vary the details of experiments, note the reactions of people from different backgrounds, alter frame stories, look for real-world examples, consider how well our reactions cohere with our other judgements and so on.

There is another aspect to the Deleuzian case, however: the claim that such common-sense/good-sense practices cannot result in genuine concept creation. The complicated genesis of our intuitions has been ignored, and the method cannot possibly involve a problematization or critique of the sociopolitical circumstances that have contributed to those intuitions in the first place; as such, it will be bound to the preservation of the status quo. For Deleuze, such an appeal to intuition remains pre-critical (and not befitting the philosopher), within the dogmatic image of thought and reliant on common sense, despite the immediate appearance of both strangeness and objectivity many thought experiments evince. In effect, this is the charge of analytic conservatism, which we take up in Chapter 9.

ANALYTIC CONCERN WITH THOUGHT EXPERIMENTS

From about 1960 to the 1980s, although analytic philosophy became progressively more invested in thought experiment, analytic philosophers themselves did not have much to say about the nature of the device or its growing importance in their work. It hardly played a starring role in analytic discussions of the nature and methods of analytic philosophy; Jonathan Cohen's *The Dialogue of Reason*, for instance, makes only passing mention of particular thought experiments, focusing instead on the issue of the role of appeal to intuition (however it might come about) in analytic philosophy. The reliability of thought experiment did, however, in this period come up for debate on occasion, with some philosophers expressing a kind of scepticism about the technique in general. Well-known examples are those of Hare, who, in his "What is Wrong with Slavery?" (1979), effectively denies that remote possibilities (such as those in which the institution of slavery would maximize utility) are at all relevant to moral concepts cut to fit the actual world, and Daniel Dennett, whose characterization of thought experiments as "intuition pumps" contains both endorsement and caution:

> Each setting of the dials on our intuition pump yields a slightly different narrative, with different problems receding into the background and different morals drawn. Which version or versions should be trusted is a matter to settle by examining them carefully, to see which features of the narrative are doing the work. If the oversimplifications are the *source* of the intuitions, rather than just devices for suppressing irrelevant complications, we should mistrust the conclusions we are invited to draw. These are matters of delicate judgment, so it is no wonder that a generalized and quite justified suspicion surrounds such exercises of imagination and speculation. (1981: 459–60)

The attitude here is that thought experiments are fallible tools like most methods in philosophy; their fallibility does not preclude their use, but it does ensure we should carefully check the results.

A straightforwardly positive account of thought experiment does not seem to have been strongly accepted through this period. In part, this may have been due to a lack of consensus about semantic ascent and the legitimate ambitions of philosophy: if it was unclear whether the Gettier industry, say, was working out the meaning of "knowledge" or the structure of the concept of knowledge or the nature of Knowledge, then it would be equally unclear exactly what the evidential role of the host of Gettier thought experiments really was. From the 1960s on, the analytic tradition *did* become much more inclined to conduct analyses in "possible worlds" terms, and one might even be able to point to a reasonably standard set of assumptions about the philosophical machinery involved in counterfactuals, say, but that would not necessarily produce unanimity on the nature of thought experiment. For instance: Saul Kripke famously maintains that "[p]ossible worlds are *stipulated*, not *discovered* by powerful telescopes" (1981: 44). Such a conception of counterfactual supposition certainly has implications for our preferred account of what a thought experiment might be up to, but it does not by itself settle the question of the reliability of intuitions elicited *by* the counterfactual supposition, let alone questions about whether all of this amounts to conceptual analysis or something else.

We suspect that many analytic philosophers of the period who made use of thought experiments, if challenged in their practice (for instance, by a Deleuzian), would have echoed Ted Sider's comments on the methodology of analytic metaphysics:

> I have no good epistemology of metaphysics to offer. It should not be thought, though, that this uncertainty makes metaphysics a worthless enterprise. It would be foolish to require generally that epistemological foundations be established before substantive inquiry can begin. Mathematics did not proceed foundation-first. Nor did physics. Nor has ethics, traditionally.   (2001: xiv)[19]

Such a view might not, in the case of thought experiment, be given straight. For thought experiments are broadly devices for eliciting intuitions, and so both challenge and defence might primarily focus on the evidential role of intuition itself. These are distinct issues (since one can make direct appeals to intuition, as philosophers often do, without bringing in the machinery of thought experiment), but whether focusing on thought experiment itself or intuition there is obviously something attractive about such analogies for those who rely on the method. Equally attractive is the assimilation of philosophical thought experiment to the scientific thought experiment tradition; if Galileo's falling weights, Einstein's elevator and the like can yield genuine knowledge, and indeed major conceptual revolution (challenging the Aristotelean account of gravity in Galileo's case; challenging Newtonian mechanics in Einstein's case), then why not Putnam's Twin Earth or Jackson's Mary?

However, there are reasons why such considerations might not seem especially compelling in the case of thought experiment. First, as we have suggested, heavy reliance on thought experimentation (especially bizarre or science-fictional thought experimentation) has been a relatively *recent* development for the analytic tradition. It does not amount to going on in the same way as the earlier analytic tradition; indeed, it marks something of a departure from that tradition. Appeals to track record therefore peter out fairly quickly, or at least run into a history in which the great and the good resolutely shun the device. Second, it is at least controversial whether philosophical and scientific thought experiments really are to be grouped together as the one device. At least one strand in the current literature on thought experimentation considers precisely this issue. Third, and perhaps most importantly, the onus of proof here has arguably moved with the development of the experimental philosophy movement within analytic philosophy. Experimental philosophy, among other things, uses the methods of psychology to broadly test the prevalence and robustness of the intuitions that philosophers report. The purpose is in part negative (to uncover potential sources of bias in intuition elicitation), and in part constructive (in natur-alizing spirit, to integrate philosophical practice with contemporary psycho-logical work on the nature of judgement, inference and concept formation). For present purposes, what is relevant is that the negative side of the project very often targets the method of thought experiment. Two examples:

(i) The analytic epistemological literature has been strongly influenced by Gettier's famous thought experiments exhibiting cases where agents appear to have true justified beliefs without having knowledge about the matter in question – or at least, so the prevailing intuition of the philosophical com-munity goes. Jonathan Weinberg, Stephen Stich and Shaun Nichols (2001) have claimed that the reported intuitions may be an artefact of the typical background of the anglophone philosopher. For instance, they claim on the basis of a study they have conducted with students at Rutgers that while most people with a Western European ethnic background intuit that the agent in a Gettier example lacks knowledge, when people with an East Asian back-ground are presented with these thought experiments, they divide on the issue roughly 50–50.

The implications of this are difficult to assess, even if we do not take issue with the conduct of the study, as has been done. Perhaps the result is no more surprising than evidence that people from different communities have (to some extent) different ethical standards, or than the obvious facts that different communities have very different systems of etiquette or languages (after all, epistemology, ethics, etiquette and language are all normative sys-tems, and differences in norms are a fact of anthropological life). Perhaps the word "know" has acquired different meanings in different sub-communities; perhaps convergence would result again if it were reflective (rather than ini-tial) opinion that was measured. But obviously even if such responses are acceptable, the prospect of such findings does prompt serious reflection on the point of philosophical enquiry via thought experiment.

(ii) The analytic ethical literature leans especially heavily on the device of thought experiment, although not with the confidence of Moore, Prichard or Ross. Rather, thought experiment is seen as an intuition-eliciting device that plays a role within a wider process of reflective equilibrium, in which our intuitions about particular cases and our moral principles or rules are to be brought into coherence with one another (this is taken to be the epis-temological underpinning of much ethical work, as is often acknowledged, simply because of an alleged lack of serious alternatives; see e.g. DePaul 2006: 616). And, of course, many of the resulting thought experiments are science-fictional or bizarre in form (consider Judith Jarvis Thomson's violin-ist example, or the endless variants on the trolley-car problem). Drawing on both work in the experimental philosophy movement and the "heuristics and biases" tradition within cognitive psychology, Cass Sunstein (2005) argues that moral reasoning is very often carried out through heuristic "short cuts", which induce typical biases in our moral judgements, and as a result, treating unusual situations as guides to our moral beliefs – as analytic philosophers often do – is folly. We can simply learn nothing through such thought experiments. The echo of Hare's caution about ethical thought experiments here is very strong.

Once again, much may be said in reply. In establishing that certain intuitive reactions are incorrect, Sunstein appears to simply beg the question against the non-consequentialist. But however good such replies are, the empirical work behind such challenges again demands some reply, and most such replies induce costs for the philosopher. At the least, the simple evidence of systematic disparity in judgement can be uncomfortable for the moral philosopher. An explanatory agenda has arisen for the moral philosopher that to some extent unpicks the broad consensus in the field that its methodology is adequately secured. As for the epistemologist in the case of the Gettier thought experiments, the choice appears to be between an unpalatable restriction of some kind (our job is to analyse people like us/surprisingly many people are simply wrong) and some kind of naturalizing takeover.

The experimental philosophy challenge is very much current and unfinished business for analytic philosophy. However, although the possibility has not, as far as we know, been discussed, the challenge here also has some implications for the practice of some continental philosophers. Broadly speaking, evidence about the extreme context-dependence of intuitive judgements on apparently irrelevant features of narrative frame, choice of wording and so forth is also evidence that can feed into scepticism about any philosophical project, however ostensibly non-psychological, that makes claims about the possibility of gaining knowledge by attending to our presentations, by mental acts of judgement, and so on.

The past twenty years or so have also seen a more traditionally philosophical discussion of the nature, reliability, ineliminability and defeasibility of thought experiment within analytic philosophy. Views here range from the claim, in the spirit of Moore, Ross and Prichard, that thought experiment puts one into direct perceptual contact with a Platonic world of laws (Brown 1991), to the straightforwardly empirical claim that thought experiment is disguised argument and always in principle eliminable in favour of the direct argumentative mode (Norton 1996). For present purposes, what is notable about this literature is that some analytic philosophers value thought experiment precisely on grounds of the conceptual innovation or change the device allows. This is a theme first developed (in the case of scientific thought experiments) by Thomas Kuhn, extending Mach's idea of thought experimentation as making use of a kind of tacit knowledge derived from experience. Kuhn remarks:

> [T]hought experiment is one of the essential analytic tools which are deployed during crisis and which then help to promote basic conceptual reform. The outcome of thought experiments can be the same as that of scientific revolutions: they can enable the scientist to use as an integral part of his knowledge what that knowledge had previously made inaccessible to him. That is the sense in which they change his knowledge of the world. And it is because they can have that effect that they cluster so notably in the works of men like Aristotle, Galileo, Descartes, Einstein, and Bohr, the great weavers of new conceptual fabrics.   (1977: 263–4)

Tamar Szabo Gendler, who along with Sorensen is perhaps the figure most central to recent analytic discussion of the device, argues that although thought experiment is indeed eliminable, in the sense that it may be replaced by direct argument and direct appeal to intuition whenever it serves the function of illustrating a contradiction (as necessity refuters generally do), direct argument offers far fewer resources for identifying ways of *altering* our theoretical commitments or conceptual framework in order to avoid the problem uncovered by the thought experiment (see Gendler 1998). In this sense, according to Gendler, Kuhn is entirely right to link thought experimentation to conceptual change. The tacit knowledge employed in making sense of a hypothetically described situation can play a role in any conceptual reorganization the situation provokes, and as a result conceptual reorganization is much more likely to attend to the deliverances of our experience. In this way, thought experiment can offer a kind of reflective, reorganizational knowledge that might not be available through other means.

Gendler's primary goal here is the rehabilitation of the scientific thought experiment, and one might wonder whether such conceptual change is really very often on the agenda with respect to the thought experiments of philosophy. Twin Earth is an interesting example here. Putnam's thought experiment is concerned to establish the thesis of content externalism (as he puts it, the claim that meanings ain't in the head), and to argue for a particular model of conceptual structure, on which natural kind concepts such as water have a "stereotype" (water is what fills the lakes, what we drink, etc.) as well as an underlying essence (water is whatever *this* stuff is, and this is a matter of its microphysical constitution). These are theses that are commonly accepted at present within analytic philosophy (content externalism much more than the stereotype/essence account), but were not commonly accepted before

Putnam's work. Moreover, the change in perspective here was not simply a change in what one was prepared mentally to sign up for; philosophers appear to have a genuinely different perspective now on the nature of mental content. That this is a *conceptual* change is, of course, difficult to argue, but there is at least one piece of evidence that Putnam's achievement is on a par with major theory change in science. Independently of Putnam's work, and as a result of empirical work rather than thought experimentation, cognitive psychologists hit on much the same theory transition: from an account of concepts as structured by necessary and sufficient conditions to an account on which concepts are structured by some kind of similarity measure involving exemplars of the relevant category, and perhaps with an underlying core (see e.g. Rosch 1973, 1999). The change has been significant within that field, and although it has not led to unanimity it has opened up a range of highly interesting accounts of conceptual structure. If one is prepared to credit this as a cognitive achievement involving conceptual change, it is difficult not to credit the Twin Earth thought experiment with having done similar work within philosophy.

It seems to us that the issue with Gendler's account, as with the critique from experimental philosophy, has to do with the *outré* nature of many analytic philosophical thought experiments, and that this is also the chief concern that can be distilled from Deleuze's concerns about common sense and good sense. Certainly, if a thought experiment's chief value over direct argument is in allowing one's tacit, experientially based knowledge to play a role in any conceptual reorganization that is to follow, then it is indeed a problem if the situation involved has been described in too thin a fashion to allow such tacit knowledge to come into play, or if the situation is so bizarre that one's tacit knowledge is no guide at all to what is going on.[20] Concerns of this kind can highlight the tension between the methodological autonomy claimed by the analytic philosopher and the broad project of integration with the sciences, but the example of Putnam's Twin Earth shows that the criticism here can be overstated. Twin Earth is bizarre science-fiction, but not to be dismissed entirely for that reason. The same extremely cautious but non-dismissive attitude holds good, we think, for much analytic thought experimentation.

9. REFLECTIVE EQUILIBRIUM

COMMON SENSE OR CONSERVATISM?

The analytic method of reflective equilibrium is at once a method of doing philosophical work and a defence of the resulting work against various possible sceptical attacks. Its first employment was in Nelson Goodman's *Fact, Fiction and Forecast*, certainly one of the most influential analytic works of the mid-twentieth century. After setting out a version of Hume's problem of induction (the problem of justifying as rational our confidence in inductively formed beliefs, such as the belief that the sun will rise tomorrow or that gravity will continue to work on cars), Goodman suggests that the problem can be avoided if we take seriously the idea that our particular judgements about induction and our general inductive principles justify each other through a continuous accommodation that seeks a point of stability:

> The point is that rules and particular inferences alike are justified by being brought into agreement with each other. *A rule is amended if it yields an inference we are unwilling to accept; an inference is rejected if it violates a rule we are unwilling to amend.* The process of justification is the delicate one of making mutual adjustments between rules and accepted inferences; and in the agreement achieved lies the only justification needed for either.
>
> (1983: 64)

Although reflective equilibrium remains influential as a potential defence against the sceptic within the philosophy of science and general epistemology, in contemporary analytic work it is more commonly employed in analytic ethics and political philosophy, a situation almost entirely due to John Rawls's seminal book *A Theory of Justice*. Rawls himself uses the method of reflective equilibrium in order to negotiate the difference between our moral/political intuitions about what is fair and just and the moral/political theory that is endorsed by our rational judgements under the test of the "veil of ignorance", but he also makes it clear that this is not, in his opinion, an isolated case; in his words, reflective equilibrium is "a notion characteristic of the study of principles which govern actions shaped by self-examination" (2005: 48). Under Rawls's influence, the practice very rapidly spread through normative ethics and political philosophy in general. It has been contended that the method of reflective equilibrium is *the* generally accepted methodology in normative ethics, endorsed by many different kinds of philosopher, including both Kantians and utilitarians (see Gaut 2003: 147; Hooker 2003b), and regardless of the philosopher's particular views about metaphysics, epistemology and philosophy of language (Hooker 2003a: 10, 15).[1]

The reflective equilibrium process involves a stepwise working backwards and forwards between our provisional judgements about particular cases (intuitions) and applicable rules govering them (principles), with the goal of increasing their coherence; the goal is to arrive at a more reflectively justifiable – if not necessarily final – position. Goodman himself was concerned with what Rawls calls "narrow" reflective equilibrium: a process of coherence adjustment that concentrates on the judgements, rules and background epistemic desiderata that one *actually* begins with. Needless to say, such a process may simply prove unsuccessful if equilibrium is not to be locally found; indeed, it runs the risk of simply uncritically affirming one's initial errors.

The intent behind Rawls's own "wide" approach in *A Theory of Justice* is to avoid the conservatism inherent in the Goodmanian version of the method. To leave open the possibility of a radical shift in our conception of justice, Rawls suggests that we must bring into play *all* imaginable sets of roughly coherent judgements, rules and desiderata in a choice situation that is itself governed by such factors, until some sort of stable equilibrium is achieved. Obviously this is something of a counsel of perfection,[2] but analytic ethicists do on occasion consciously steer away from the narrower forms of equilibrium in the attempt to avoid the dangers of conservatism. Consider Peter Unger's use of the device in *Living High and Letting Die* (a work that certainly does not seek to affirm current charitable practice), which includes among its fallible revisable starting points the following:

> By contrast with Preservationists, we in the minority hold that insight into our Values, and into morality itself, won't be achieved on an approach to cases that's anywhere near as direct, or as accommodating, as what's just been described. On our contrasting Liberationist view, folks' intuitive moral responses to many specific cases derive from sources far removed from our Values and, so, they fail to reflect the Values, often even pointing in the opposite direction. (1996: 11)

To put the wide/narrow point another way, there is a difference between an understanding of reflective equilibrium that prioritizes certain starting intuitions or sentiments (which we have reason to believe, or at least no reason to doubt, have *independent* value or credibility), and a reflective equilibrium that prioritizes overall coherence with our other beliefs (and hence adds to this equation *dependent* credibility), which might include our theories of personal identity, human flourishing, rationality, the findings of science and so on.

Goodman's innovation is not without pre-analytic roots. These might include dialectical thinking in general, and as Christine Korsgaard (1996: 61ff.) points out, a similar (if simpler and more one-sided) test of *reflective endorsement* may perhaps be found in both Hume and Sidgwick, according to which a faculty cannot be normative unless it returns a positive verdict when it takes itself and its own operations as its object. However, the motivation for the very widespread acceptance of reflective equilibrium within analytic normative theory is more specifically analytic. If the evaluative categories of (individualist) epistemology are at all apt for philosophical work, then how one finds it acceptable to carry out such work will obviously depend on the epistemological picture one is committed to, and the possibilities indicated by it. Even those who shun first philosophy agree, minimally, that there has to be some kind of consistency between the account one gives of justification or knowledge, and the ways in which one thinks philosophical knowledge or justification can be obtained. Within the early analytic movement, such concerns about consistency typically revolved around both empiricist limitations on the sources of knowledge, and the limitations of a foundationalist account of the structure of knowledge. Reflective equilibrium and related devices in use in contemporary analytic philosophy are by-products of a wider trend within the movement: the move away from the empiricist foundationalism of the logical positivists. In effect, for many within the analytic movement, the method of reflective equilibrium is a way of getting out of an awkward epistemic predicament. Hence, although it is certainly possible for use of reflective equilibrium to proceed for other reasons, assessment of the role it plays within analytic philosophy demands at least something of a look at the wider analytic engagement with empiricism, and the resulting sceptical concerns.

Those within early analytic philosophy who were strongly influenced by the sciences either endorsed, or sought to stay close to,[3] a moderate form of classical empiricism, in which the Kantian category of the synthetic *a priori* was rejected, but the category of analytic truths was regarded as non-empty (logical and mathematical truths, as well as conventional truths, being located here). Such an empiricism was very rapidly seen by the logical positivists in particular as having heuristic value as a razor in the philosophy of science, culling methods of enquiry that seem, at first sight, to be worth exploring, and so allowing many dead ends to be identified and avoided at the outset. For example, empiricism of this kind sharply constrains the kinds of probabilities that we can make sense of, in effect undermining the classical account of probability; it generates serious difficulties with the idea that we can come to know the causes of an event; it plays an essential role as a premise in positivist arguments for a verificationist approach to meaning; it is the background against which "first-person" introspectionist approaches to psychology were assailed within that field; it generates difficulties for theories positing unobservable objects or properties (and so pushes some scientists and philosophers to a kind of instrumentalism or fictionalism); and it was thought to either do away with or seriously constrain acceptable accounts of scientific explanation.

Of course, the empiricist razor became something of a chainsaw outside the philosophy of science, in large part because verificationist criteria for meaningfulness debarred much traditional metaphysics, religious theorizing and ethics. However, even without the verificationist trappings, moderate empiricism was itself a tough environment in which to explain ethical or metaphysical knowledge, or indeed any philosophical activity that appeared to proceed on the basis of intuition or which claimed *a priori* knowledge of matters that did not appear to be logical, mathematical or conventional. For instance: if (as analytics generally did) we accept Hume's observation that there is no valid argument from descriptive premises to a normative conclusion, if empiricists are right to demand that all knowledge of the world be based in experience, and if our experience is directly of descriptive matters, then the foundations of ethical knowledge simply do not seem to be there. Of course, these kinds of challenges are not insuperable problems – one can, for instance, adopt a non-cognitivist ethics, or attempt to reduce metaphysical issues to those of logic or language – but the natural result of such manoeuvres is that the substantive problems of traditional ethics and metaphysics tended to be ignored in favour of meta-ethical issues, semantic reductions and so forth. Moreover, the sceptical tendencies of empiricism had special bite within epistemology itself: through the early twentieth century, empiricist difficulties with the problem of induction (and later, the Pyrrhonic problem of the criterion and Goodman's "new riddle" of induction) became notorious. A response to sceptical arguments about such matters was therefore very much on the empiricist agenda.

Allied to moderate empiricism was a further early analytic commitment: that of foundationalism. Western philosophical conceptions of knowledge have traditionally exhibited a strong tilt towards the idea that one's beliefs are justified only if they are either themselves foundational (basic, self-justifying or beyond justification) or are grounded in the right kind of way on beliefs that have this property. In medieval and early modern times, a particular "classical" form of foundationalism about knowledge (or *scientia*) became standard, broadly based on Aristotle's account of demonstration in the

Posterior Analytics. According to this tradition, the requisite foundational beliefs are to be *infallible* (immune from error), *incorrigible* (immune from refutation) and *indubitable* (immune from doubt), and the grounding relation is to be essentially deductive. This picture was gradually dismantled over early modern times, in favour of various forms of fallibilist foundationalism, but foundationalism of any kind turned out to have difficulties in answering sceptical attacks (the more so if empiricist scruples about intuition and the synthetic *a priori* are respected). Foundationalism can also lead to specifically *philosophical* embarrassment, quite apart from sceptical concerns. The problem is seen wherever, for instance, our alleged knowledge of a philosophical account of knowledge fails to meet its own standards (as is arguably the case for Hume's epistemology in the *Treatise*, as noted above), or where an allegedly foundational standard is taken as such only because of a covertly circular procedure (as is arguably the case for Descartes's account of clear and distinct perception in the *Meditations*), or indeed where any particular choice of foundation appears simply dogmatic (a situation the positivists themselves generally tried to resolve through various conventionalist devices, albeit unsuccessfully[4]).

The epistemic pressures here can be brought out by a further sceptical concern: the Pyrrhonian *diallelus*, or wheel, dilemma. In Chisholm's (1982) formulation, the dilemma arises because of our commitment to both the following claims:

(1) I can identify instances of justified belief *only if* I already know the criterion or principles for justification.
(2) I can know the criterion or principles for justification *only if* I can already identify instances of justified belief.

Together these claims entail that we can't be justified in believing anything. Chisholm notes that philosophers have generally resolved the problem through a kind of "Methodism", in which (1) is accepted and (2) is rejected. The challenge for any such view is to plausibly explain how one *could* be justified in believing in a criterion of justification before being justified in particular beliefs. The alternative "particularist" rejection of (1) and acceptance of (2) appears to beg the question, but Chisholm claims that there are resources in the medieval account of *opinio* that allow us to avoid that conclusion. On this view, our basic beliefs act as *signs* of other states of affairs according to epistemic principles. We can work these principles out by considering instances of justified belief that we identify (so this "critical cognitivism", as Chisholm calls it, is a particularist account), but to identify such instances is *not* necessarily to be initially justified in doing so; it requires us merely to satisfy, rather than knowingly apply, the relevant principles. By a bootstrap procedure,[5] then, we reach the anti-sceptical goal of having justification in both our particular judgements and our epistemic principles.

The similarities between this approach and Goodman's form of reflective equilibrium are apparent, but it is equally apparent that particularism faces some potentially damaging objections. Despite some intriguing applications, Chisholm's idea has not standardized into a general analytic technique.[6] Conversely, what makes Goodman's technique so attractive for many analytic philosophers is that it lines up with a more general epistemological sea change within the analytic tradition. Despite some dissenters in the nineteenth century – most famously John Stuart Mill (1843) and William Whewell (1840) – foundationalism had remained the dominant picture of the structure of justification within anglophone philosophy until the middle of the twentieth century. This consensus more or less collapsed with the publication of Quine's extremely influential article "Two Dogmas of Empiricism" (1953b), in which he argued that there was no stable sense in which a statement could be true in virtue of meaning alone (that is, no stable sense in which a statement could be purely analytic). Given the close connections empiricists thought obtained between *aprioricity* and analyticity, this in turn suggested that all knowledge is *a posteriori*, and so in some sense provisional or revisable. Quine's criticism of the analytic–synthetic distinction therefore led analytic philosophers to take more seriously the idea that justification has a *coherentist* structure. On this view, justification is primarily a property of belief *systems*, rather than of individual beliefs. A belief system, in turn, is justified to the extent that it forms a coherent web, where this is some kind of measure of the logical consistency of the system and the degree to which its members are inferentially and explanatorily well knitted together.[7] Beliefs that fail to cohere with such a network as a whole are unjustified for the agent; since justification is a matter of doxastic context, no belief is guaranteed to be justified come what may.

Coherentism provides new resources in combating scepticism. For instance, the coherentist can point out that, along with basic truths of mathematics and logic, our belief in the inductive regularities of the world sits at the inferential centre of our belief networks, tightly knitted to many of our ampliatively formed beliefs. In similar fashion, it suggests that ethical or other philosophical knowledge might well be unproblematic; certainly, that it is not to be rejected because an appropriately secure foundation cannot be identified. Goodman's reflective equilibrium is in effect a local version of this idea. Following Quine's article, a number of other local coherence-building inferential processes were identified, explored and put to work within the analytic literature. For example, analytic philosophy now makes regular use of *inference to the best explanation*, an argument form in which we accept that claim that serves as the best explanation of the relevant evidence among those explanations we can generate (Harman 1965, 1968). A well-known example is Jerry Fodor's (1975) original case for the language of thought hypothesis. Again, coherence-building lies behind Quinean appeals to *theoretical virtue*; preferring, *ceteris paribus*, those theories that are (for instance) close to current belief, modest, simple, general and/or refutable (Quine & Ullian 1978: ch. 6). Such appeals are less commonly employed within analytic philosophy, but they do occur.[8]

The Quinean revolution in analytic epistemology has certainly been contested; many contemporary philosophers reject either his naturalism or his aposteriorism, and analyticity has made something of a revival. But coherence is arguably a virtue in more or less any piece of philosophical work; certainly the goal of increasing local coherence is sensible on many particular occasions of judgement. Hence, inference to the best explanation, appeals to theoretical virtue and reflective equilibrium will retain at least some defeasible evidential force on most epistemological accounts, even in the absence of a more general commitment to coherentism. In the particular case of ethics, however, the issue is whether such defeasible evidential force is actually defeated. Certainly, some philosophers have been prepared to argue that the relativity of moral views from society to society might be enough to put any such local coherence-building project into question. Hare, for instance, makes this point in the following way:

> The appeal to moral intuitions will never do as a basis for a moral system. It is certainly possible, as some thinkers of our own time have done, to collect the moral opinions of which they and their contemporaries feel most sure, find some relatively simple method or apparatus which can be represented, with a bit of give and take, and making plausible assumptions about the circumstances of life, as generating these opinions; and then pronounce that this is the moral system which having reflected, we must acknowledge to be the correct one. But they have absolutely no authority for this claim beyond the original convictions, for which no ground or argument was given. The "equilibrium" that was reached is one between forces which might have been generated by prejudice, and no amount of reflection can make that into a solid basis for morality. It would be possible for two mutually inconsistent systems to be defended in this way: all that this would show is that their advocates had grown up in different moral environments.
>
> (1981: 12)

Note that such an objection (one that many continental philosophers would endorse) simply begs the question if we are convinced that coherence standards of justification are in general required; moreover, an analogous objection is completely unpersuasive in some other cases where equilibrium methods are appealed to, such as the coherence between our general beliefs about the legitimacy of induction and our particular beliefs about the persistence of particular inductive regularities in the world. In other words, the objection in effect is pointing out that, if we are not pure coherentists about such matters, narrow reflective equilibrium plays no real anti-sceptical role in the ethical case. And since wide reflective equilibrium is a much more committal process, involving genuine changes in one's practice, the upshot of Hare's criticism is that reflective equilibrium is not a universal cure-all, which allows analytic ethicists to continue to theorize on the basis of elicited intuitions in the way they would otherwise have been inclined to do, but now secure in the knowledge that the epistemology of ethics has been put on a firm footing. And of course the uncomfortable point is that many analytic ethicists may have invoked the method in just such a spirit.

Obviously the strength of any such charge will vary with the evidence of bias or variation in belief in a particular case. But there is a broader issue here, which we feel is one of the points of difference between the two traditions; that of the legitimacy of conservative techniques within analytic philosophy (or particular fields, such as ethics). In the epistemic sense at issue here, conservatism is the view that "a proposition acquires a favorable epistemic status for a person simply by being believed" (Foley 1983: 165). The method of narrow reflective equilibrium is evidently conservative in this sense, and so to a sceptical continental philosopher might well be taken to be overly invested in the preservation of common sense and what is already thought to be known. Wide reflective equilibrium, by contrast, is less easily attacked on conservatism grounds, in part because it brings with it the kind of commitment to revisability that Quinean aposteriorism involves: it requires a process of perennial updating; back and forth adjustments between overarching philosophical views, intuitions and empirical data provided by science; and as such any equilibria reached will be entirely provisional. But of course much actual philosophizing will depart from this sort of idealized standard; often when reflective equilibrium is invoked and claimed to support a given view, no such rigorous process has actually taken place. Our time, after all, is finite. While our intuitions may theoretically be subject to revision in wide reflective equilibrium, when it is recognized that we do not have an eternity for decisions and that all of our various beliefs form a part of an intricate system of interconnected cultural convictions, it seems eminently unlikely that the process will involve anything like a *radical* challenge to our basic convictions and intuitions. Moreover, at any particular point in the reflective equilibrium process – whether wide or narrow – the equilibrium reached will be, in part, a function of the particular judgements we hold at that time. The methods of both wide and narrow reflective equilibrium therefore accord significant value to our everyday intuitions and immediate judgements, from moment to moment, and hence, to common sense.

Finally, the way in which wide reflective equilibrium seeks to *avoid* undue conservatism might also be brought into question. There is certainly something bizarre in the idea that an agent can, through such deliberation alone, arrive at the appropriate equilibrium, no matter how remotely the equilibrium point is from the agent's starting place. To continental eyes, the method seems to tacitly presuppose a variant on the rational and disinterested subject, in that it quite radically abstracts from the choices we make and the way most of us live. Carl Knight inadvertently expresses this risk when he notes that the subject of any wide reflective equilibrium process "must undergo any experiences that may offset biases in his or her formative influences" (2006: 222). This sounds like a noble ambition, but is it tenable, either in the conception of a subject that it presupposes, or in the conception of the philosopher that it advocates? The philosopher here is modelled on the conceptual persona of the judge: as rational, probing, impartial and devoid of affect. By contrast, consider analogous methods in the continental tradition that also seek to bring theory and prior belief into relation. The continental tradition generally does not take the method of dialectic to be inherently conservative in this way, or to exhibit the same deference to common sense; in Merleau-Ponty, for instance, what is dubbed "hyperdialectic" is meant to be a dialectic between the perceptual faith (prereflective experience, prior to opinions or beliefs) and philosophical elaborations or articulations of it. Moreover, continental usages of dialectic tend to stress the historicity or embeddedness of the subject; the abstracting tendencies of reflective equilibrium are not present here, nor the explicit grounding of a set of initial beliefs or opinions. In this sense, continental usages of dialectic are quite different from the analytic understanding of that process; as Merleau-Ponty remarks in *The Visible and the Invisible*:

> The bad dialectic is that which thinks it recomposes being by a thetic thought, by an assemblage of statements, by thesis, antithesis, and synthesis; the good dialectic is that which is conscious of the fact that every thesis is an idealisation, that being is not made up of idealisations or of things said ... but of bound wholes where signification never is except in tendency.　　　　(1969b: 94)

Many analytic philosophers would reject such ambitions (and the associated critique of reflective equilibrium) on the grounds that they betray an unsustainable philosophical ambition, and a misguided meta-philosophical dismissal of common sense. Consider, for instance, Moore's "two hands" argument against scepticism about the external world, on Bill Lycan's (2001) interpretation. Moore's idea is that at least some pre-reflective opinions have the power to defeat philosophical argument, because our responses to an argument can only be guided by a method of *differential certainty*. Any argument at all from a set of premises to a conclusion, if valid, leaves us with the choice between accepting the premises and therefore the conclusion, or rejecting the conclusion and therefore rejecting the conjunction of all of the premises. We can only make this choice, in turn, by comparing the relative plausibility of the conjunction of all of the premises and the negation of the conclusion. If it turns out that the conjoined premises are relatively more plausible than the negated conclusion, we treat the argument as giving us evidence for the conclusion; if the negated conclusion is more relatively plausible than the conjoined premises, we treat the implausibility of the conclusion as evidence for a defect in the premise set. But such judgements of plausibility inevitably bring in common-sense belief (a category that, for Lycan, includes not just common-sense claims about the existence of hands, but also knowledge claims about such matters; *ibid.*: 48–9). The standard philosophical arguments for scepticism about the external world begin with plausible (even compelling) philosophical claims about knowledge or justification, and draw conclusions that fly in the face of common sense, but the method of differential certainty then simply tells us that we must have gone wrong somewhere in the premise set. On this view common sense is not irrefutable, but its status in possession is not at all trivial. It can be overturned by evidence ("careful empirical investigation and scientific theorizing"), but, as Lycan remarks: "No purely philosophical premise can ever (legitimately) have as strong a claim to our allegiance as can a humble common-sense proposition such as Moore's autobiographical ones. Science can correct common sense; metaphysics and philosophical 'intuition' can only throw spitballs" (*ibid.*: 41).

There is a pragmatism behind this view that regularly receives expression in the analytic literature. It is not that common sense is always especially valuable; however, it is where one is at the pre-philosophical moment. As Williamson (2008: 242) notes, one must start off from somewhere, and one cannot help but start from where one is, and to judge things accordingly. Other pragmatic themes also make regular appearances in the analytic literature; for instance, on the "Canberra Plan" approach to philosophy, associated with that city in Australia, common sense is implicated in the background beliefs that yield the meanings of our concepts, and so is an inescapable starting point for the methods of conceptual regimentation. Again, for the coherentist, the familiar image of Neurath's raft is used to point out that we simply cannot throw all of common sense into doubt at once. Indeed, analytic philosophers who defend conclusions running in the *face* of common sense nonetheless will often acknowledge points of this kind. In defending modal realism against all comers, David Lewis unsurprisingly faces a challenge from common sense, and his response is a textbook example of the attitude:

> Common sense has no absolute authority in philosophy. It's not that the folk know in their blood what the highfalutin' philosophers may forget. And it's not that common sense speaks with the voice of some infallible faculty of "intuition". It's just that theoretical conservatism is the only sensible policy for theorists of limited powers, who are duly modest about what they could accomplish after a fresh start. Part of this conservatism is reluctance to accept theories that fly in the face of common sense, but it's a matter of balance and judgement .... The proper test, I suggest, is a simple maxim of honesty: never put forward a philosophical theory that you yourself cannot believe in your least philosophical and most commonsensical moments. (1986: 134–5)

For continental philosophers this is a rather strange and unimaginative test of a philosophical theory; indeed, it is one that threatens, at least if Lewis himself took it seriously, to end philosophy. It also seems to assume that our intuitions and everyday common sense are free of metaphysical commitments. But the analytic approach to common sense is not only backed by pragmatic considerations and/or to coherentist epistemologies. Some analytic philosophers have explicitly articulated, as part of their understanding of the point of philosophizing, a commitment to common sense. Consider Russell's well-known comments about the relation between philosophy and pre-theoretic belief or common sense:

> Philosophy should show us the hierarchy of our instinctive [i.e pre-theoretic] beliefs, beginning with those we hold most strongly, and presenting each as much isolated and as free from irrelevant additions as possible. It should take care to show that, in the form in which they are finally set forth, our instinctive beliefs do not clash, but form a harmonious system. There can never be any reason for rejecting one instinctive belief except that it clashes with others; thus, if they are found to harmonize, the whole system becomes worthy of acceptance. (1912b: 25)

The idea here is not that pre-theoretic belief is to trump all philosophical conclusions, but rather that philosophical work represents a kind of rational reconstruction of pre-theoretic belief, which allows us to put it on to a firmer footing and in some sense voluntarily assent to it. Although pre-theoretic beliefs are certainly defeasible, they are *not* to be brought into play as already suspect, so to speak, or ripe for revision; the job of the philosopher is not to begin with the aim of getting somewhere else (see e.g. Cohen 1986: 91–7; Lewis 1973: 88). Of course, this does not preclude our getting to very remote locations; Russell (1953) also, appalled by the apparent triviality of ordinary-language philosophy, urges that philosophy is not simply to recapitulate unreflective common sense. From this point of view, the widespread reliance on reflective equilibrium methods in analytic ethics is best judged case by case, rather than defended in the whole, or dismissed as entirely problematic.

10. THE FATE OF TRANSCENDENTAL REASONING

A significant methodological difference between analytic and continental philosophers comes out in their differing attitudes to transcendental reasoning. It has been an object of concern to analytic philosophy since the dawn of the movement around the start of the twentieth century, and although there was briefly a mini industry on the validity of transcendental arguments following Peter Strawson's prominent use of them, discussion of their acceptability – usually with a negative verdict – is far more common than their positive use within a philosophical system or to justify a specific claim.[1] By contrast, in the continental traditions starting with Kant but enduring throughout the twentieth century and beyond, some form of transcendental reasoning is close to ubiquitous (some of the structuralists might be exceptions), notwithstanding that what one means by the transcendental is significantly reconfigured by phenomenology, and then the genealogical turn, as well as by a more constructivist understanding of philosophy in which its value is seen as partly bound up with the transformative potential of concept creation. Concerns about the status of transcendental reasoning certainly exist for continental philosophers, but continued creative use persists, and there is no general agreement that transcendental argumentation is especially problematic. In fact, it is more commonly claimed, and it is certainly frequently implied, that a transcendental dimension is of the essence of philosophy. Any philosophical activity that does not reflect on its own conditions of possibility is naive, or pre-critical, and the sometimes pilloried continental enquiries into the "problem of modernity" are but one way of attempting to reflect on the conditions of contemporary philosophical discourse, subjectivity and cultural life more generally. Of course, any suggestion that a transcendental dimension is necessary to philosophy need not automatically entail a critique of analytic philosophy. Instead, it might be maintained that to the extent that analytic philosophers do meta-philosophy of some kind, especially in dwelling on the relation between experience and reflection on that experience (not so much from nowhere but rather from "within"), they are also perhaps minimally transcendental philosophers, noting that a certain common-sense pragmatism or naturalism might short-circuit or limit the significance given to such reflections. Much of this chapter will hence be concerned to offer both an explicit and implicit rationale for the divergent attitudes of analytic and continental philosophers *vis-à-vis* transcendental reasoning. We give an incomplete account of what transcendental arguments are, review the major analytic criticisms of them, gesture towards some of the recent continental appropriations of such arguments (focusing on the themes of embodiment and time), consider the extent to which analytic criticisms apply to such usages, and attempt to bring to the fore the differing explanatory norms that justify these divergent practices.

ANALYTIC ATTITUDES TO THE TRANSCENDENTAL

Robert Stern notes in the introduction to his *Transcendental Arguments and Scepticism* that there is a "widespread conviction that there is something vaguely disreputable or even dishonest" about transcendental arguments (2004: 1). This seems a fair report of the peripheral and doubtful status of transcendental argument in contemporary analytic philosophy; that is, in the period after both Strawson's influential defence of the argument form and the subsequent publication of well-known objections by Stephan Körner and Barry Stroud. For the past thirty years or so, transcendental arguments have neither been used nor analysed extensively in the analytic journal literature, and when such prominent analytically trained philosophers as Putnam, Davidson[2] and McDowell[3] do make use of them, it appears to be taken to be a sign of non-analyticity in a way that it was not for Strawson.[4] Sometimes this is explicit, but more often it is implied by the comparative lack of attention that they receive in the standard-bearing analytic journals. Beyond the situation of these well-known "post-analytic" philosophers, there are other indications that the transcendental has become problematic for analytic philosophy – for instance, Pascal Engel (1989) denies that many of those who are generally taken to be French analytic philosophers should be considered thus, precisely because of their residual allegiance to the transcendental. Arguably, analytic and continental philosophy of religion are also largely separated on this point, and a related methodological division is apparent within pragmatism (see Pihlstrom 2003).

The analytic and continental understandings of transcendental argument share common ground in Kant's *Critique of Pure Reason.* Although he never uses the term himself, what we call a "transcendental argument" is something of an abstraction from Kant's practices of transcendental deduction and transcendental exposition;[5] it is whatever Kant is up to in such canonical passages as the "Transcendental Deduction of the Pure Concepts of Understanding", the "Second Analogy" and the "Refutation of Idealism". It might seem, then, that differing views about the transcendental across philosophy could be understood as differences about how to handle the Kantian heritage: differences about the dependence of transcendental argument on the transcendental philosophy in general, or about the most fruitful way to generalize on, or depart from, the model established by Kant's usage. And, given the well-known differences in the interpretation of Kant in the two traditions, this is not an unreasonable view,[6] but the move back to Kant brings into prominence a basic problem in discussing the differing analytic and continental receptions of transcendental reasoning; there is arguably no common referent here. Kant is indeed read across both traditions, but it does not follow that there is anything like a neutral characterization of the transcendental argument form available to both analytic and continental philosophers. Consider, for instance, the following characterization of the transcendental argument form:

> A transcendental argument is an inference from a state of affairs that indisputably obtains, to the existence of a further, contested, state of affairs that is recognised to be a necessary condition for this obtaining (a "condition for its possibility"). The uncontested state of affairs is almost always subject-involving – it might involve such first-personal matters as having knowledge, or certain experiences, or beliefs, or conceptual capacities, or it might involve inter-subjective relations or practices of some kind. The contested state of affairs may or may not be subject-involving. The structure of such an argument is then as follows:
> (1) Subject-involving state of affairs p obtains.
> (2) A necessary condition for p obtaining is that q obtain.
> (C) Hence, q obtains.

This is fairly standard, but it is equally standard at this point to reject the characterization as inadequate. If this is all a transcendental argument comes to, then it is a special case of reasoning by *modus ponens* and so of no great theoretical interest. One might seek a different inferential frame for the argument (interpreting it as a species of inference to the best explanation, say) but again the result is nothing distinctive. Much of Kant's own practice is missing in this skeletal characterization – most obviously the intended role of such demonstrations as in some sense securing synthetic *a priori* principles or concepts – and one can select from the two post-Kantian traditions many different ways of adding flesh to these bones, in the form of further conditions or constraints that attempt to capture the distinctive feature (and so the distinctive possibilities) of such reasoning. For instance, one might highlight the nature of the claim made by the second premise – it might be that the notion of necessity in play here is not simply conceptual or logical; or that the condition it expresses is to be thought of as a type of non-logical, non-psychological dependence relation; or that the goal of the transcending manoeuvre is to reconceive the two states of affairs so as to understand them as distinct though connected. Others bring in the contextual surrounds of a transcendental argument: it might be that it has an essentially anti-sceptical function; or that it starts from the explanatory question "how is p possible?"; or that the kinds of conclusion that it can establish are themselves premises for a further (transcendentally idealist) project. There is no general agreement across the traditions (or indeed within each) on each of these matters; different ways of understanding transcendental argument have developed in parallel. Indeed, it is not unusual for this state of affairs itself to be celebrated as a mark of the vitality of the method; for instance, Karl Ameriks remarks:

> Even if Kant's system is a multilayered complex that has only one root in common sense ... it is no crime if the other root of his work (the "transcendental" arguments), like all good philosophy, is inextricably involved with some abstract and endlessly disputable concepts. The fertile ambiguity of these concepts ... has by now surely demonstrated their worth.   (2006: 38)

Although one might dispute Ameriks's contention that there is an inextricable connection between good philosophy and endlessly disputable concepts, the short outline above should make it clear that, historically speaking (and in continental philosophy), the "fertile ambiguity'" he celebrates is certainly present. But, of course, much of the fertile ambiguity of the transcendental argument form is *not* on display in analytic treatments of it. It seems to us that the point to be explained, in looking at the analytic attitude to transcendental reasoning, is not so much the interpretative difference here as the fact that the interpretative difference is so largely absent from the analytic literature. This is not necessarily a mark of analytic ahistoricity; indeed, analytic examination of historically important argument forms can often vector in on such "fertile ambiguity" precisely in an attempt to work out whether it is indeed so fertile. Contemporary analytic discussions of the ontological argument form generally distinguish Anselmian, Cartesian, Kantian and Gödelian forms, with numerous variations depending on whether conceptual, experiential, modal or other circumstances are used to launch them. Why is there not the same sustained analytic persistence with transcendental modes of reasoning?

In the early analytic context, at least, the answer seems to in part involve the way that empiricism functioned as a *methodological* constraint, rather than merely as a truth claim. Even non-empiricists among the early analytics (such as Russell, for much of his career) nonetheless took empiricist scruples very seriously as a mark of epistemic respectability. To take transcendental reasoning seriously is to disregard this "negative heuristic". Methodological worries of this kind are never with just the particular issue at hand; rather, the potential cost is in the confounding of the whole research programme (of analytic philosophy, in the one case, and of its relation with modern science, on the other). Hostility to transcendental reasoning was therefore part and parcel of Russell and Moore's formative attempts to distance themselves from British idealism. While Russell in his early period generally maintained that mathematics involved synthetic *a priori* knowledge, he was careful to avoid transcendental justifications for such claims.

The move within the early analytic period to a more thoroughgoing empiricism made transcendental reasoning even more difficult to take seriously. The logical positivists influentially rejected the synthetic *a priori*, suggesting that such knowledge claims amounted to poetry, mysticism or nonsense. Of course, in different ways, Wittgenstein's Tractarian picture, the verification principle and the multiple languages view that Carnap puts forward in his mid-career "Empiricism, Semantics, and Ontology" seem to have a synthetic *a priori* status by their own lights, as has often been noted (BonJour 1998: ch. 2; Sacks 2006), but this was not taken as any kind of spur to transcendental reasoning. Instead, epistemological self-application difficulties were seen as theoretical problems arising within the overall empiricist project, hardly to be solved by jettisoning that most basic commitment. Rather, within the empiricist analytic tradition such problems were most obviously to be resolved by adopting a more thoroughgoing coherentism and the radical empiricism of Quine. Transcendental reasoning ran squarely up against the research programme of the emerging analytic movement; to take it seriously was to be a philosopher of some other kind.

Given this attitude, it is hardly surprising that analytic discussion of transcendental reasoning could come about only with the rise of obviously non-positivistic and even non-empiricist schools within that tradition, constrained not in the least by methodological empiricism. Most obviously these conditions obtained for the mid-century ordinary-language movement in England. The key change in the analytic literature was the conception of transcendental argument as a separate argument form with a logical or semi-logical structure, capable of being recognized in the work of other philosophers, past and present, and perhaps available for use in analytic projects. The first clear attempt at an analytic treatment of a transcendental argument *form* is Austin's isolation of transcendental argument as a distinctive (if limited) method of reasoning in his 1939 paper "Are there A Priori Concepts?" When the argument form makes its appearance in the analytic tradition, it does so in the teeth of a characteristically pointed piece of Austinian rhetoric:

> People (philosophers) speak of "universals" as though these were entities which they often stumbled across, in some familiar way which needs no explanation. But they are not so. On the contrary, it is not so very long since these alleged entities were calculated into existence by a transcendental argument: and in those days, anyone bold enough to say there were "universals" kept the argument always ready, to produce if challenged.   (1961: 33)

Next Austin sets out a particular argument for the existence of universals, and clarifies what he means here by "transcendental argument": "This is a *transcendental* argument: if there were not in existence something other than sensa, we should not be able to do what we *are* able to do (viz. name things)" (*ibid.*: 34). After a little discussion of the very limited knowledge of universals such an argument can yield, Austin presents a further argument for the existence of universals, notes that it is also transcendental in this sense, and then raises what one could take to be a difficulty with any general strategy of using such arguments repeatedly (rather than as one-offs, as it were):

> Now it must be asked: what conceivable ground have we for identifying the "universals" of our original argument with the "universals" of this second argument? Except that both are non-sensible, nothing more is known in which they are alike. Is it not odd to suppose that *any two* distinct transcendental arguments could possibly be known each to prove the existence of the *same* kind of thing?   (*Ibid.*: 35–6)

It is perhaps not surprising that the first analytic discussion of the transcendental argument form turns out to be an obituary, but there are other points worth noting here.

First, in treating transcendental argument as a form *entirely* detachable from its Kantian heritage, Austin is making a characteristically analytic move. The implication is that this is something we can lift out of the general milieu of transcendental idealism or critical philosophy and treat on its own or recognize at work in other contexts, something that is in some sense available for analysis as a logical or semi-logical structure. This abstracting move remains entirely usual in analytic discussions of transcendental argument.

Second, considered as such a form, in Austin's hands the transcendental argument becomes much the same sort of device as the standard argument forms of the ordinary-language school, say the paradigm case argument, or the argument from excluded opposites. In each of these cases, the argument form involves reasoning to a state of affairs from a capacity we have that pre-supposes it. One can see Austin, then, as offering a very "thin" understanding of transcendental argument, on which the argument form comes down to a kind of logical or conceptual relation between capacity and ground. Austin's version is unusually austere, purged of most of its Kantian heritage. This is surely in part due to the context of ordinary-language philosophy itself, inclined to be suspicious of traditional metaphysical (or critical) terminol-ogy. In such a context, one can see Austin's version of the transcendental argument, like Hume's account of causation, as something of a revisionary clean-up job: the intention is not to engage in Kantian exegesis, let alone to enjoy the "fertile ambiguity" that Ameriks celebrates; rather, it is to identify an argument form that can in theory be put to general service as a philo-sophical technique (because sufficiently purged of links to the transcendental philosophy), but that is perhaps not as useful a technique as its proponents suppose. Austin's transcendental argument form is (by his lights) a bad argu-ment form, but a clear one.

The ordinary-language movement also offers the first explicit analytic rejection of this view, and the first sign of a more optimistic role for tran-scendental argument. Peter Strawson's 1959 monograph *Individuals* is subti-tled "An Essay in Descriptive Metaphysics", and in his introduction Strawson is concerned to outline descriptive metaphysics as a middle way between revisionary metaphysical activities and the ordinary activities of philosoph-ical analysis (such as the appeal to paradigm cases). In setting out the case for going beyond analysis, Strawson highlights the limits of analysis as a path to *understanding*:

> Up to a certain point, the reliance upon a close examination of the actual use of words is the best, and indeed the only sure, way in philosophy. But the discriminations we can make, and the con-nexions we can establish, in this way, are not general enough and not far-reaching enough to meet the full metaphysical demand for understanding. For when we ask how we use this or that expres-sion, our answers, however revealing at a certain level, are apt to assume, and not to expose, those general elements of structure which the metaphysician wants revealed. (1959: 9–10)

Descriptive metaphysics is the project of tracing such structures, and it requires arguments that are at the same time explanations and even, per-haps, dramas (Strawson 1966). For Strawson this is the natural home of tran-scendental argument; he regards Kant as a descriptive metaphysician, and the "reidentification" argument he puts forward in §2 of the first chapter of the book is the exemplar of the analytic transcendental argument. Our conceptual scheme of a single unified system of spatiotemporal relations is the framework within which we organize our individuating thoughts about particulars, but a condition of our having such a scheme is our acceptance of the persistence of at least some individual particulars through periods of non-continuous observation; hence we are justified in believing in the persistence of (some) individual particulars (1959: 25–40). This is recognizably transcendental, and Strawson concludes a discussion of it by pointing to the way the argument is intended to serve an explanatory role.

Being descriptive, Strawson's transcendental argument is explicitly modest (as Austin's was not): it concerns only the tracing of our conceptual commitments and the structure of our conception of the world. Nonetheless, Strawson holds that it has value in defeating the sceptic, since the argument shows the sceptic "pretends to accept a conceptual scheme, but at the same time quietly rejects one of the conditions of its employment" (*ibid*.: 35). To say the least, this conclusion has been strongly contested in the analytic literature (and Strawson himself came to drop it, and to adopt a more cautious attitude to transcendental argumentation; 1985: 20–23). Two objections have had especially great influence in the analytic literature.

First, as Stroud (1968) points out, the sceptic has hardly been defeated. For the conclusion of a modest transcendental argument simply tells us a fact about how we take things to be, how we need to think about the world. It is a further step from this claim to the claim that this *is* how things are. The proponent of the argument can only (immodestly) take this step if the premises of the argument are bolstered with a commitment to a thesis strong enough to bridge the gap (idealism, or verificationism, for instance). Yet this is a premise the sceptic will not accept. Stroud goes further, pointing out that the utility of the transcendental argument is in question even if such a background is assumed, since direct (non-transcendental) argument from idealism or verificationism is now sufficient to establish the conclusion.

Second, as Körner (1966, 1967) and Stroud (1968) both point out, the necessary connection identified in Strawson's arguments (between experiential fact and transcendental ground) is itself difficult to defend against the sceptic. For the only necessity in play here is a necessity apparently arising out of our conceptual framework. Hence a suppressed premise of the argument is that no other conceptual framework is available. Yet it is difficult to see how this unique applicability is to be established. The objection here is in fact a version of a concern Russell set out in classical form in *The Problems of Philosophy*: the necessities established by transcendental reasoning must be relative necessities, in that they depend on features of our conceptual framework that themselves might well be contingent.

Both of these objections are widely known within the analytic community, having been discussed in the literature particularly in the decade after Stroud's first paper on the topic. This suggests a straightforward *internal* explanation of the current analytic attitude to transcendental reasoning: the contemporary analytic attitude to the transcendental is a function of the literature surrounding and examining the Körnerian and Stroudian objections to the argument form – and the upshot of this episode is that analytic philosophers now simply have reason to regard transcendental arguments as bad arguments, and as a result there has been a decline in interest in the argument form. There is indeed something to this explanation, but it is nonetheless a little too straightforward as it currently stands, for two reasons.

First, it does not explain the differences in the analytic treatment of what one might call dubious argument forms. There are several other historically influential argument forms that receive ongoing study and elaboration in the analytic literature, even though they are generally regarded as entirely unsuccessful. The ontological argument, for instance, remains a lively subject of discussion in the analytic journals, and is the subject of several recent monographs (e.g. Dombrowski 2006; Everitt 2004; Oppy 1995; Sobel 2004). True, there exist proponents of the argument who believe it to be sound, but they are very much a minority. One might in the same way regard Putnam and Davidson as part of a minority on the subject of transcendental reasoning, but it is only in the case of the transcendental that being in the minority is taken as a sign of non-analyticity. One might point in the same way to ongoing analytic discussions of Cartesian arguments for dualism, ancient Greek arguments for fatalism or McTaggart's argument for the unreality of time. Why does this pattern of continuing analytic attention to doubtful argument forms not hold good for transcendental argument?

Second, the internal explanation does not explain the differences in the analytic treatment of these particular objections and close relatives. Objections much like those of Stroud and Körner can be raised against other argument forms that remain central to the analytic literature. Many argument forms that *ostensibly* see off the sceptic – argument patterns based on reliabilism, say, or those based on some form of contextualism – fall foul of sceptical replies of a Stroudian flavour. Many argument patterns are valid only within the scope of particular assumptions, or can lend only coherence-building support to a position; they might therefore seem open to Stroud's follow-up objections about the utility in argument of the transcendental argument form. Körnerian worries about strong claims of necessity arise wherever an argument depends on a claimed necessity or impossibility, for instance, in arguments based on thought experiments of the kind Sorensen calls "possibility refuters" (1992: 153–7). These are certainly not the most common use of thought experiment in the analytic tradition, but they are a respectable minority, and they involve claimed necessities (thinly disguised as claims about impossibility). Each of these situations is one in which a Stroudian or Körnerian move might be made or has been made, pointing to a sceptical counter-move or an overly confident claim of necessity. Yet in none of these cases is the fact of objection of this kind taken as debate-closing in the way that it apparently has been for transcendental reasoning. The internal explanation is simply incomplete; the best explanation is that the analytic attitude to transcendental reasoning genuinely depends *also* on particular norms and habits peculiar to the analytic tradition.

Stroud's sceptical objection can seem puzzling or nit-picking to continental philosophers who are generally unconcerned with the anti-sceptical role of transcendental arguments. Yet focusing on the *sceptic* as the opponent can be a little misleading. Arguably Stroud's objection causes far more general trouble for the argument *form*, and this is where the analytic assimilation of transcendental reasoning to semi-logical argument forms makes something of a difference. Any argument form at all that can be taken without (too much) distortion out of its dialogic context can be recharacterized as having an anti-sceptical function, in that it could in principle be wielded in a different context against someone sceptical about its conclusion. Similarly, any putatively anti-sceptical argument that has the same kind of potential transferability can simply be seen as an argument for its conclusion, no matter what the dialogic context it arises in. Issues to do with justification are inescapable, and logical and epistemological questions regarding the validity of their deployment in a given system still need to be raised, even if the overall aim is more to furnish ontological accounts of our situation in the world than to provide secure foundations for knowledge. Of course, if the continental philosopher maintains that philosophy is an exercise in concept creation, and nothing more than that, perhaps they might be entitled to ignore Stroudian worries, but on our view such a position would be untenable on other grounds, and it is not in fact a position that any continental philosopher unambiguously subscribes to. Stroud's point can also simply be taken as a reminder that the transcendental argument form is limited, when considered as a form of argument, demonstration or proof. This still leaves open other roles for transcendental reasoning, since there is an obvious explanatory value in exhibiting the connections between distinct parts of one's conceptual scheme, even if the premises one starts from are unlikely to be accepted by those who question one's conclusion, but it does make the argument form considered *as* an argument form (in the analytic way) somewhat problematic.

The internal force of the Körnerian objection is also apt to be misjudged by those outside the analytic tradition. Analytic caution about claimed necessities is marked, and arguably is the result of two quite distinct developments.

On the one hand, from the middle of the twentieth century the analytic tradition has become increasingly committed to a form of naturalized epistemology and radical empiricism. Quine's influential arguments against the analytic–synthetic distinction carried over into a suspicion of necessity itself and the project of *a priorist* reasoning in philosophy. Such exercises as Strawson's could, at most, show the structure of a conceptual framework that we happen to hold, and no part of which is beyond potential revision. Certainly, in many dialogues within analytic philosophy this change in attitude means that necessitarian reasoning is contested even by those who admit the existence of necessities; the attitude here is captured by Dennett's oft-repeated remark that philosophers too often mistake a failure of imagination for an insight into necessity, and by the neo-Humean dictum that necessities are theoretical costs, to be minimized wherever possible. In the particular case of Kantian transcendental argument, such warnings are, of course, accompanied by several awful historical examples: most egregiously, for the analytic tradition, Kant's own confidence in the finality of the logic of his day and his sandbagging by the rise of non-Euclidean geometries (and the later non-Euclidean interpretation of relativity theory).

On the other hand, the analytic tradition contains an internal puzzle over necessity that also sounds warnings about transcendental reasoning. The early-twentieth-century development of modal logics led, surprisingly to those involved, to a problem of massive overabundance. The pioneer of formal modal studies, C. I. Lewis, found five distinct logical systems that he felt could serve as candidates for our ordinary understanding of necessity, but it rapidly became clear that there are many more, and that there are complex interrelations between them. Each of these distinct modal logical systems is consistent and non-trivial, and each yields a distinct sense of necessity; moreover, this growth in the modelling of alethic necessity itself has been followed by a wave of treatments of temporal, deontic and other necessities, and by rather more involved post-Kripkean diagnoses of recurrent equivocation between types of necessity. As a result, contested philosophical argument forms that turn on necessities have to be treated with very great care even by those who are fully supportive of apriorist reasoning; clarity, rather than fertile ambiguity, is especially at a premium in this territory.

What, then, of our previous observation that transcendental reasoning appears to meet something of a double standard within analytic philosophy? While analytic caution about the invocation of necessity is suspended in some cases, there are general norms within analytic philosophy marking such cases out as genuinely less problematic than the transcendental case.

First, and most obviously, some claimed necessities are more readily defensible because they have an immediate connection to the concept of logical contradiction. For instance, consider a fairly hackneyed argument against one form of polytheism that Sorensen gives as an example of possibility-refutation at work: if it were possible for there to exist two completely omnipotent beings, then it would be possible for one to desire to bring about a state of affairs that the other desires not to bring about and so (by the given definition of omnipotence) for the state of affairs to both be brought about and not brought about; but this is impossible, and so the polytheist hypothesis is as well. Transcendental arguments do not make similarly secure claims about the necessity of the connection between an agential and a non-agential state of affairs obtaining.

Second, the analytic conception of the relation between philosophy and common sense also serves as a marker of the anomalous status of transcendental premises. Much analytic work is carried out in the spirit of David Lewis's conception of the role of the philosopher:

> One comes to philosophy already endowed with a stock of opinions. It is not the business of philosophy either to undermine or to justify these pre-existing opinions, to any great extent, but only to try to discover ways of expanding them into an orderly system.
>
> (1973: 88)

Such an attitude can allow for the philosopher to arrive at highly unusual places (such as Lewis's own modal realism). But it does place certain limits on the kinds of *premises* that will be readily accepted, and on the whole they are conservative limits. Premises that do not receive the immediate backing of intuition (or in some other way fail to be credentialled by common sense) are open to doubt. If such premises are claims about the necessity or impossibility of a certain state of affairs obtaining, and it is not clear (as it is in the polytheist argument case) that the necessity or impossibility is logical, definitional or conceptual in nature, then we suggest that the doubt becomes a form of permanent contestation. No matter how detailed the philosophical work that takes one to the claimed necessity, it remains an entirely provisional claim in the sense that its rejection is conceivable. As such, our claim is that transcendental reasoning runs up against a fairly standard *positive* heuristic of analytic philosophy, in that a transcendental argument will never or rarely be able to play a constructive role in the fruitful development of an analytic position.

CONTINENTAL ATTITUDES TO THE TRANSCENDENTAL

In continental circles, transcendental reasoning is controversial and perhaps even permanently contested terrain. Certainly it is contested by all of the great philosophers of the tradition and the risks associated with such forms of reasoning are acknowledged. But it is not controversial enough to induce general abstinence. Instead, the implicit rationale seems to be something like Pascal's wager. Believing in the efficacy of transcendental arguments, if they work, may result in tremendous results (a Copernican revolution); if they do not, some important concepts will have nonetheless been created. Better that, on this view, than disbelieving and being the underlabourer of science. While various continental philosophers have subjected Kant's conception of the transcendental to problematization and critique, few have thought that this signalled the end of the transcendental project. Rather, the aim, scope and structure of transcendental reasoning is instead consistently reinvented by all of the major philosophers associated with this tradition. Indeed, the assumption is more that whatever his failings, Kant's transcendental project (and the project of philosophical critique more generally) achieved something of the utmost importance. The German idealists all described themselves as transcendental philosophers, and the revival of interest in Kant in the late nineteenth and early twentieth century in neo-Kantianism (Cassirer in Germany, Léon Brunschvicg in France, etc.) produced significant revisions in the understanding of transcendental methods and arguments.

In the twentieth century, transcendental reasoning has continued to be frequently deployed in continental philosophy in very different ways. To cite some extremely familiar proper names that encompass most of the major areas usually associated with continental philosophy, we might think here of: Husserl, and the phenomenological intention to use such arguments to reveal *the* transcendental, a whole "region of being" that was previously unexplored (it is thus both a method and an object of enquiry, as with Kant); Heidegger, and the association of the transcendental project with both phenomenology and hermeneutics; Sartre, who synthesizes the work of Husserl and Heidegger and gives transcendental philosophy an existential turn, as well as a famous phenomenological "proof" of the existence of the other; Merleau-Ponty, whose account of an omnipresent bodily intentionality seeking equilibria with the world through the refinement of our "body-schema" and the acquisition of flexible habits and skills is argued to be the condition that ensures that sensory experience has the form of a meaningful field rather than being a fragmented relation to raw sense data; Deleuze, who espouses "transcendental empiricism" and rejects the possible as a category, instead looking to show how particular specific things are actualized, and who deduces the necessity for the "virtual"; Derrida, who consistently talks about "quasi-transcendentals" in association with themes such as *différance* despite also deconstructing the transcendental philosophy of Husserl, Heidegger and others; and Gianni Vattimo, whose project has been characterized as temporalizing the *a priori*. Luce Irigaray discusses the "sensible transcendendental", Bernard Stiegler and Jean-Luc Nancy are both invested in transcendental philosophy,[7] as are Jean-Luc Marion, Michel Henry and the thinkers of the theological turn in phenomenology, as well as various contemporary German philosophers of discourse ethics and recognition, including Habermas, and Karl-Otto Apel, whose concern is primarily with performative contradiction and the way they provide transcendental conditions for communicative rationality (see Apel 1987). For each of these philosophers, transcendental arguments operate differently, with more or less scope, and more or less claimed universality, and are more or less able to be formalized in deductive terms.[8]

While we cannot, for each of these distinct continental conceptions of transcendental reasoning, establish whether the analytic criticisms apply, it is useful to abstract a little from the important differences between these varied projects and proffer a generalization. All these philosophers exhibit, to varying degrees, what Alan Murray (2002) calls an *anteriority complex*. We shall explore two particular kinds of claims of anteriority that are major factors in contemporary continental philosophy today: those revolving around body/perception and time (some would claim that place subtends this opposition). These particular foci allow us to directly consider transcendental reasoning by some influential phenomenological and poststructuralist thinkers; moreover, family resemblance versions of one or another of these positions are in evidence in most of the usual suspects. Indeed, without wanting to unify these two trajectories, they do seem to each be complicit in what Mark Sacks calls *situated thought*, which:

> is construed as being the thought that one would have from a particular point within a framework, the content of which is informed by it being grasped as if from that perspective. It is not bare propositional content as if from nowhere, but is rather informed by being phenomenologically embedded and directed. (2005a: 444)

According to Sacks, much of the difficulty associated with transcendental arguments arises from the tendency to understand them as articulating relations between concepts or propositional contents. Construing transcendental arguments as formally valid inferences cannot be adequate, and while they can be "modestly" understood as conceptual claims easily enough, for any transcendentally reached conclusion to be *a priori* true requires some kind of shifting to the level of experience. As a result, the thinker needs to be co-implicated with what is thought. This phenomenological (or performative) element thus links all transcendental arguments that are not merely analytic to a kind of minimal phenomenology, at least in the relation between the propositional content and the speaker/experiencer of such content. While there is certainly a circularity here, it is one that is part of reflection and not something that can be overcome. What is interesting and significant for us here is that Sacks's account helps to explain why time, place, space and the body (elements of any situation) are central to continental philosophy's pre-occupation with transcendental reasoning. A transcendental argument must bear some relation to experiences that are possible (or actual) in this world, or to concepts that structure our world, as is the case with the "historical *a priori*" of Foucault's early work, especially *Archaeology of Knowledge* and *The Order of Things*, which are avowedly transcendental.

EMBODIMENT, PERCEPTION AND BEING-IN-THE-WORLD

Let us start with transcendental arguments about the body, perception, motor-intentionality or being-in-the-world, most of which come from phenomenology. While Heidegger has a complicated relation to transcendental philosophy, there are myriad chains of priority claims in *Being and Time*, often posed in the telltale language of "primordiality" and the "always-already". Famously, the ready-to-hand is claimed to be a condition of possibility of apprehending objects as present-at-hand, or as unready-to-hand. While philosophy has traditionally prioritized the theoretical encounter with things, on Heidegger's view Dasein associates with things first and foremost on a practical and immediate basis that he calls the ready-to-hand, which refers to the availability of things for our use and deployment in relation to the completion of tasks. For Heidegger, useful things are necessarily in a situation and are always related to other useful things by a rich network of contextual associations (1962: §§14–24). In the derivative mode of knowing that he terms the present-at-hand, entities become material objects that are available for inspection (or mental constructs, although Heidegger would not put it thus), rather than as tools for our use. Against the Cartesian view (which arguably includes materialism in this respect), the world is not primarily the scientific world, but the practical one of everyday life, and the transcendental claim is that any present-at-hand analysis never leaves behind the practical but presupposes it, in the sense that it is made possible by it.

Some closely related claims are put forward by Merleau-Ponty in *Phenomenology of Perception*. Often associated with the thesis of the "primacy of perception", rather than rejecting scientific and analytic ways of knowing the world Merleau-Ponty argues that such knowledge is always derivative in relation to the more practical aspects of the body's exposure to the world, notably our bodily intentionality that seeks equilibria or "maximum grip" with the world through the refinement of our "body-schema" and the acquisition of flexible habits and skills. For him, these aspects of bodily motility and perception are the transcendental conditions that ensure that sensory experience has the form of a meaningful field rather than being a fragmented relation to raw sense data, and this kind of know-how (the "I can") is also said to be the condition of possibility of knowledge-that (the "I think"). Of course, philosophical reflection is required to illuminate this priority of know-how. Whether or not this is an insuperable problem is debatable, but for most phenomenologists it is, rather, a fertile occasion for thought precisely of the transcendental variety. Without dwelling on this here, a good concrete example of Merleau-Ponty's claim is the argument that, to put it bluntly, grasping is a condition of possibility of pointing; the ability to point to one's nose (an abstract, reflective activity) depends on one's ability to grasp one's nose (a practical response to solicitation from the world, say a mosquito bite, or a need to scratch). This claim is made by Merleau-Ponty based on studies of the injuries that afflict a pathological patient (Schneider), phenomenological descriptions of what is involved in these two ways of inhabiting space, the alleged inabilities of empiricism and intellectualism to adequately describe or explain either the phenomenology or the empirical facts of the case (hence it involves inference to a better explanation), and also transcendental reflection about enabling conditions for our experience of the world (motor intentionality). His basic claim is that the understanding evinced in grasping can be independent of the understanding involved in pointing, but that the reverse does not apply.[9]

This kind of practical non-cognitive grasping is, for Merleau-Ponty (and Dreyfus, Sean Kelly and others working in this tradition), largely what takes place in learning, and bound up with this privilege given to motor intentionality and skilful coping is a suggestion that such basic activities involve non-inferential perceptual norms. As Dreyfus and Kelly put it:

> The agent feels immediately drawn to act a certain way. This is different from deciding to perform the activity, since in feeling immediately drawn to do something the subject experiences no act of the will. Rather, he experiences the environment calling for a certain way of acting, and finds himself responding to the solicitation ... If this account of the phenomenology is correct, then there is an irreducibly normative component to the experience of perceptual objects ... it is "right" or "appropriate" to stand a certain distance from a picture. (2007: 52–3)

While few phenomenological descriptions are uncontested, all phenomenologists will maintain that our perceptual field is normatively structured. Perception has an orientational structure (up/down, figure/ground,[10] etc.) that solicits us to optimally come to grips with it, and we see things in terms of actions and in relation to potential uses of them by others. If we grant for the moment that there are non-inferential perceptual norms of this kind, then it is at least open to make a case of the kind Sacks puts forward: one on which beliefs can be justified without appeal to inductive or other non-deductive evidence, and yet not in virtue of anything like straightforward conceptual analysis. Of course, an analytic philosopher suspicious of transcendental reasoning might maintain that to show that something is non-inferential is not to show that it is infallible,[11] nor that it is prior to inference. Indeed, the more controversial part of any such argument would be to establish in what sense these non-inferential aspects (say Heidegger's ready-to-hand, or Merleau-Ponty's bodily intentionality) are the ground for inference. Brandom (2002: 302–22), for example, refuses to concur with Heidegger on this. It need not follow from this that transcendental arguments are intrinsically misleading, however, but rather that they are deployed as part of a package deal.

Indeed, these kinds of phenomenological arguments are not straight *a priori* arguments. While they depend on experience, and claim that certain enabling conditions make possible this experience, phenomenological reflection also allows us to attend through reflection (to some extent) to these so-called enabling conditions, which were previously in the background; they also become perspicuous in cases of break-down (when things are unready-to-hand). This need not lead to a problem of infinite regress. Bodily intentionality is (claimed to be) primordial, and not everyone must see the claimed necessity, nor indeed need the process of coming to see this putative necessity itself be immediate. On the contrary, it depends on detailed descriptions of phenomena and the structures of experience, and the concepts involved in such descriptions are capable of alternative understandings (see Taylor 1995b). Empirical data will hence rarely establish that a transcendental argument is wrong *tout court*, since the difficult task is always to describe each of the premises/concepts in detail, and there is often sufficient ambiguity in the situation to allow for the reconstruction of a transcendental argument that fits with empirical findings. However – and this is the key point – not any reconstruction will be possible; the empirical remains an important constraint. The important question for the continental philosopher here is just when such reconstructions become a pathological attempt to immunize one's theory against any possibility of error. This is always a judgement call, depending on an array of background norms regarding justification and explanatory comprehensiveness. It does suggest, however, that cognitive and empirical science cannot be ignored by any phenomenologist working in this particular embodied transcendental tradition, and that empirical discoveries can and should (potentially) be able to cast doubts on the claims of transcendental philosophy.

There is, however, a strong and a weak (immodest and modest) way to interpret Heidegger and Merleau-Ponty's claims to a primacy of the ready-to-hand and embodied perception. They might just be a timely reminder to any cognitivist philosophy that something is left out when structures of cognition are posited everywhere (a reminder of persistent and lurking fallacy). The stakes are raised, however, when it is declared that the non-inferential ground *necessarily* could not be explained or understood within the mechanistic and inferential terms of science: that, say, the dynamics of the lived-body (and not just what it feels like from the inside) will necessarily remain a mystery to the body as an object that is known by science, psychology, biology and so on (see Bermudez 2006). This is where the anteriority complex becomes, perhaps, a more apt term. But if we do not take this more immodest step, how does what we have described thus far fare in relation to the standard analytic objections to transcendental reasoning?

The problem is that *nothing* seems to bridge the Stroudian–Kantian gap between appearance and reality, although from the phenomenologist's perspective that very gap itself presupposes the ready-to-hand, and bodily coping, as its condition of enunciation. From the analytic point of view, therefore, at best these kinds of thoughts are an appeal to some kind of coherence condition; for instance, a kind of reflective equilibrium concerning our judgements and pre-judgements (see Malpas 1997: 16). The "transcendental" move is no doubt thought of by its proponents as involving more than just the transformative potential of concept creation or an inference to the best explanation, but (on this view) it then becomes rather unclear why the continental philosopher does not make out that part of the case that *can* be made in such theoretically uncontentious terms. In other words, what is wrong with charitably interpreting Heidegger or Merleau-Ponty as giving an inference to the best explanation, and so protecting them from Stroudian critique? While some of their arguments can be plausibly reconstructed in such terms, it is exegetically inaccurate to do so. They deploy various stronger claims of necessity than would be endorsed by a standard fallibilist inference to the best explanation, and the preference of many continental philosophers for anti-mechanistic and non-reductive explanations seems to be doing some work in their justifications for these stronger claims of necessity.

TIME

We have suggested that one of the other key trajectories *vis-à-vis* transcendental reasoning concerns time, a link that was first noted in Kant. In his reflections on the phenomenology of internal time-consciousness, Husserl famously suggests that our integrated experience of a melody – even on first listening – implies that any so-called "now" must have a retentive element that retains the past notes, and a protentive moment that anticipates future elaborations. No doubt there are other possible explanations one might give here, but these, Husserl would claim, presuppose these same aspects of time-consciousness; as Merleau-Ponty says of the Humean principle of association, an impression by itself can never cause another impression.[12] Whether these arguments are satisfying or not would need to be considered in depth, but we have here a transcendental claim, and one that is developed by the existential phenomenologists, perhaps especially by Heidegger. In *Being and Time*, temporality is claimed to be a necessary condition for Dasein; it is the ground, without which there is no Dasein at all. Heidegger claims that what he calls "understanding" depends on the futural ecstasis of time; that "attunement" (or mood) is structured by the past ecstasis of time (throwness, having-been); and that "fallenness" is fundamentally an attachment to present things that denies these other escstases. To put it bluntly, understanding, attunement and fallenness can hence only be understood through time.

If philosophy of time is important to phenomenology, it is also a central feature of poststructuralism, where the conception of the transcendental is rendered somewhat more modest, localized to times and places, historicized (to greater and lesser extents) in an effort to avoid some of the problems associated with the Kantian and Husserlian conceptions, and so often without the strong claims to synthetic *a priori* knowledge. Transcendental arguments have increasingly been buttressed by phenomenology, hermeneutics and genealogy; it seems that extra forces are marshalled, just as Stroud says they must be, to avoid begging the question. But for both genealogy and phenomenology the transcendental dimension remains crucial rather than an unnecessary add-on. Of course, there is also an important sense in which poststructuralism's genealogical or deconstructive analyses take the critical dimension of Kant's Copernican revolution so seriously that they quite frequently put the lie to the necessitarian ambitions of transcendental philosophy. In archaeological, genealogical and deconstructive analyses, any claims to transcendental neutrality or to having established a uniquely applicable condition (or set of conditions) for experience that holds for all times and places is radically relativized. While this is often done immanently, by analysis of textual inconsistencies, or by contextualizing these claims historically (rather than by deductively formalizing the argument), the ultimate result is that many philosophers in this tradition can concur with the force of Stroud and Körner's objections, although the pressing question then concerns the way their work is still proffered in the name of transcendental philosophy itself. Deleuze, for example, criticizes Kant for tracing the transcendental from the empirical and reinvents transcendental philosophy so as to avoid this mistake. The minimal transcendental significance of this "temporal turn" consists in the idea that "beings are disclosed within changeable cultural horizons of interpretations, and these cultural horizons are the transcendental conditions (the temporalised *a priori*) for the meaning and intelligibility of things in general" (Woodward 2008). It might be argued that this historicizing does not really avert analytic concerns, in that it continues to involve a question-begging kind of anti-realism. Or, if it does avert them, it might be that it brings with it other commitments that are equally anathema to many analytic philosophers (relativism, say). Transcendental reasoning in this guise is both modest (in the sense of not universalist) and, *prima facie*, immodest, in arguing for the existence of discernible epochs in a manner that most historians would be wary of.

It seems to us that the key transcendental arguments in poststructuralism revolve around questions concerning the condition of possibility for change, novelty and difference. Where there is difference, the question then concerns the genetic conditions of specific changes, and what might be deduced to hold more generally that explains these specific changes. Deleuze's project in *Difference and Repetition* is a straightforward example. He attempts to establish that repetition is not, and never could be, the simple repetition of the same, and a key part of this project is his demarcation of three different approaches to time – habitual time, memorial time and futural time – all of which, he contends, involve repetition, as well as difference in repetition.

The first synthesis of time, for Deleuze, is that of habit, which founds the phenomenological experience of the "living-present". On this view, time is constituted by an originary synthesis that operates on the repetition of instants; it contracts the independent instants into one another to constitute the living present. The past and the future then become but aspects or dimensions of this living present (which is not itself an instant): the future is that which is anticipated to occur, whereas the past is the preceding instants and background conditions that are retained in the contraction that makes up the present. This living-present also sets up a directionality or arrow of time in that it goes from the past to the future, and from the particular to the general. On Deleuze's partly Humean view, then, habit is the condition of the self or ego that accompanies the contractions of the living present; the "I" is produced by myriad habitual syntheses of time. It is clear enough that habit involves some kind of repetition, but for Deleuze, habit also involves difference primarily because "habit draws something new from repetition – namely difference (in the first instance understood as generality)" (1994: 73). Habit is hence not simply a *mechanical* repetition; rather, it also involves a pre-reflective recognition (based on the passive synthesis) that the activity that is being engaged in is something that has been done before. For example, in the famous Humean series AB AB AB AB, it is habit that introduces a difference between one set of the series and the next, leading us to expect a B whenever we encounter an A. As Deleuze suggests, "when A appears, we expect B with a force corresponding to the qualitative impressions of all the contracted ABs. This is by no means a memory, nor ... a matter of reflection" (*ibid.*: 70). His point is that it is not that we reflect on the past, or even consciously remember the past, but that we simply know how to go on in a non-reflective way. While this process partially depends on the past experiences that are involved in the synthesis, at least according to Deleuze, there is no memory (except what is sometimes called procedural memory) involved in the living present of habit (*ibid.*: 70). This passive synthesis of time occurs *in* the mind; it is not carried out *by* the mind.

While this habitual explanation of time, in which the chain of events or passing present moments constitute time, seems to offer an adequate explanation of the constitution of the "living-present", the present also passes in the time that is thus constituted (it can be exhausted and is hence not co-extensive with time *per se*), and his basic question is hence something like, "why is it that a habitual present, or temporal 'now' moment, can pass?", or "why is it that the present is not totally co-extensive with time?" Deleuze suggests that this necessarily refers us to a virtual or transcendental condition for the living present, as Bergson also maintained, as we shall see in Chapter 17. To put this another way, there needs to be a *second* synthesis of time that causes the present to pass, and this, he argues, is the time of the past, or memorial time (*ibid.*: 79). The fundamental idea is that we cannot represent a former present (i.e. the past) without also making the present itself represented in that very representation. So, if we think about our past, we also in some sense bracket away the present, or cause the present to cease to be. This means that whenever we remember, there will be two main aspects to this: first, the "actual" memory of that past; but also a representation of the present (or the self) as itself being engaged in remembering. Deleuze describes these two aspects as memory and understanding (*ibid.*: 80). We can, perhaps, schematize his argument as follows: (1) the present passes; (2) "no present would ever pass were it not past 'at the same time' as it is present" (*ibid.*: 81); (3) hence to explain this we need to posit a "pure past" (a virtual past) that has never yet been present. And, as Körner suggests, the perhaps suppressed premise here is that no other explanation will suffice. According to Deleuze, then, this second synthesis of time, the past, is the *ground* that means that any "present" always necessarily passes (as it is bracketed away in the attempt to remember), and it hence allows for the arrival of another "present" (*ibid.*: 81–2).

Deleuze ultimately contends, however, that neither of these modes of time are sufficient, since they do not properly institute time in thought. Although we no doubt *can* think habitually, and although there is "understanding" involved in memory (as the present is also bracketed away with the past, and this enables the necessary distance for something tantamount to reflection), this is not genuinely critical thought. Deleuze argues that truly philosophical thought involves a futural form that breaks open time (*ibid.*: 88), and interrupts time, even if it always also pertains to time. Deleuze associates this affirmation of pure difference, of the future, perhaps surprisingly, with Nietzsche's famous thought of the eternal return of the same. He transforms it by putting a peculiar inflection on Nietzsche's notion of the eternal *return of the same*, instead exalting the eternal *return of difference*. Again, we can schematize this argument: (1) there is actual change/difference (the new sometimes happens; creativity occurs); (2) neither of the first two syntheses of time adequately explain this, although they both presuppose change/difference; (3) there must, therefore, be a third temporal synthesis oriented to chance and difference. The synthesis that is involved in futural time is not conjunctive, but instead must be conceived of as disjunctive, in that the only unity of the eternal return is the negative unity that difference does, in fact, return (*ibid.*: 126).

There are intuitive problems with the notion of difference returning, but in this brief account of *Difference and Repetition* we can see the manner in which the unknown future serves as a condition for explaining genetic change/difference, something that is also the case, albeit in different ways, with the other poststructuralist thinkers. Of course, these arguments will not convince everybody, either in summary form or in Deleuze's own (far more nuanced) account. To those sceptical, this might all seem a bit murky, and murkiness is indeed one of the potential risks associated with transcendental arguments, in Deleuze and also in other philosophers. While Derrida, for example, is one of the great (internal) critics of transcendental philosophy, there are nonetheless arguably also some important slides in his work – from questions of transcendental priority to ethical priority, for example – that are made possible by the ambiguities and imprecisions that are part and parcel of transcendental philosophy. For example, it is not always clear how to understand statements such as: "There where the possible is all that happens, nothing happens, nothing that is not the impoverished unfurling of the predictable predicate of what finds itself already there, potentially, and thus produces nothing new" (Derrida 2005: 57). Derrida's language here is strong, but is he simply making a conceptual point about the limitations of our concept of possibility, something that could be by definition true (or at least true-given-our-genealogical-history), or is it a claim that bears on reality, however loaded that term may be? There is an important difference between what Stern (2004: 10–11) refers to as concept-directed and truth-directed transcendental arguments, but Derrida's quasi-transcendental claims can almost always be read in both of these ways, and so the problem (within which deconstruction avowedly situates itself) revolves around whether we understand Derrida primarily as a genealogist of concepts, as a transcendental philosopher,[13] or as an ethicist, albeit in a highly restricted sense. Derrida might contest this contrast, suggesting that concepts and metaphysics are inextricably intertwined, but is this opposition between the event and the predictable predicate a *necessary* one? Derrida claims it to be a condition of thinking the event, but is this really the only manner in which one can account for, or think, the event? Is every philosophy of mediation, of continuums, necessarily condemned to be unable to explain the event? It is not clear that this is so. Presumably "tipping points" of various kinds can still be theorized, and the risk is that transcendental reasoning of this sort depends on a contrast that excludes other possibilities; the claim to any given unique necessity is thus not itself made good, as Körner has noted.

CONCLUSION

The key explicit objections that analytic philosophers raise – the general objection from empiricism, Stroud's "idealist/verificationist" objection and Körner's worries about the impossibility of establishing the uniqueness of any alleged condition – are sufficient to make one wary of transcendental arguments, although they are not sufficient (at least for one of us) to discredit them. From two different sides we have developed the point that bound up with each of these concerns is an array of associated explanatory and justificatory norms that genuinely differ across the divide. They suggest that we are in a situation akin to what Jean-François Lyotard calls a *differend*: a dispute in which two parties cannot agree on a common rule or criterion of judgement that would allow for a tribunal of arbitration. In conclusion, let us consider again how this might be so.

The empiricist objection has been in the background during much of the above discussion, but it is fundamentally a worry about the ampliative ambitions of the transcendental move, and the methodological disaster that unconstrained transcendental theorizing threatens to visit on philosophy. Moreover, the worry these days often concerns the naturalistic ambitions of much analytic philosophy quite as much as empiricism itself. How could such reasoning be sensibly incorporated within a framework that often regards the finding of the sciences as epistemically privileged and that seeks coherence (and even perhaps eventual integration) between its disparate knowledge claims? *Prima facie*, not easily, although there are a couple of important points to note here. First, one would need to fill out just what the commitment here to methodological empiricism or naturalism means, since there are many different ways of understanding this, and perhaps the particular version of naturalism being endorsed or presupposed is itself dogmatic or problematic (*partes extra partes*). That is certainly what Merleau-Ponty would maintain. Second, a wide range of non-positivist variants on empiricism and naturalism have now been developed within analytic philosophy, and so the question of the compatibility of transcendental arguments with such views has to be rethought in this context. McDowell engages in this kind of project in *Mind and World* and elsewhere, and it is not a coincidence that most of the major continental philosophers associated with transcendental arguments (including Husserl, Bergson, Heidegger, Deleuze) are either anti-naturalists, or take a critical and transformative attitude to both nature and the natural sciences. Certainly elements of vitalism can be discerned in the work of Bergson, Heidegger and Deleuze. At the same time, various contemporary philosophers working with transcendental arguments in phenomenology and philosophy of mind are engaged in projects of naturalizing phenomenology, or perhaps more aptly "phenomenologising nature" as David Morris (2007: 535) puts it, intimating that the former project remains impossible given certain well-entrenched accounts of nature (e.g. nature is the scientific, *tout court*), and that perhaps what needs to happen is something rather more radical: "nature is not space-time-matter unfolding according to laws, nature is moving being organising" (*ibid.*: 541). We cannot address this here, except to say there is some support for this kind of view within cognitive science and continental-inspired philosophy of mind. On such views, empirical analyses must be relevant, and in a relation of mutual constraint with any purported transcendental claim, and transcendental claims must be potentially refutable by empirical analysis, noting that empirical analysis is never completed once and for all, and that the negative heuristics associated with empiricism and naturalism are somewhat looser than those deployed by most analytic philosophers. Transcendental reasoning, on this view, earns its keep much like any other theoretical approach with predictive implications.

The Stroudian objection lends itself less to such middle-way approaches. There does indeed appear to be a question-begging assumption of something like anti-realism in virtually all non-externalist uses of transcendental arguments (we say "something like" because while to an analytic philosopher the dictum "being is phenomenon" has to be idealistic, to many phenomenologists it is a middle way between idealism and realism). However, two rejoinders might be offered. One might concede the point, as Taylor (1995b: 25) does, but nonetheless maintain that transcendental analyses still establish necessary conditions for our own self-relation – *for ourselves* we are, for instance, necessarily embodied subjects – and insist that this has significance for the humanities and social sciences writ large, even if we should be metaphysically modest regarding what it means about reality *per se*. Second, one might point out that Stroud's influential criticisms of transcendental argumentation are not premise-free, presupposing a logical and metaphysical gap between me and everything else, as well as that knowledge has primacy over action (Avramides 2001: 253).

This charge of partiality could be extended to the analytic project of classifying and formalizing different argument types. While undoubtedly useful in many contexts, this can also create problems of its own. The risk is that a characteristically analytic or decompositional approach obscures the manner in which thought itself is (at least sometimes) synthetic. Effective reasoning is arguably more complicated than this, and for the continental philosopher to think otherwise would be to mistake the means of reasoning for the end; that is, to confuse particular useful tools of thinking with the task itself. In that respect, as we have seen, most continental philosophers will maintain that there is inductive support (or support by inference to the best explanation) for the ostensibly non-inductive method of transcendental argumentation. Even for those not interested in the sciences, the history of Western philosophy would be another such ground, including both its problems and its successes.

We have seen that almost all transcendental arguments depend on a certain active involvement. In that sense, they do beg the question against the sceptic, and they do call for a certain abeyance of incredulity (a certain trust) in reading and reflection, or at least in moments of them. Philosophers have to be critical, but none are critical all of the time, and for a transcendental argument to work one has to be taken along by a story of sorts (a description, a genealogy, etc.), one has to imagine and reconstruct experiences (from an embodied situation), and one has to critically and sceptically reflect in another moment, using various other devices of argumentation. One can, of course, err in navigating these dual demands. We can be bewitched by sophistry. But this also means that, without some trust, transcendental reasoning will never work, in the sense of being useful or helping to induce a perspectival shift. The analytic community has, by and large, decided not to trust such arguments; the continental community, by and large, has put a significant degree of faith in them. As James (1956) made clear in a more general epistemic context, the precise trade-off between the goal of avoiding false beliefs and the goal of seeking true beliefs can properly differ from agent to agent, and that is the situation we have here between the traditions. The analytic decision is arguably reasonable given the difficulties there are in finding a constructive role that transcendental reasoning can play within the norms of the analytic community. The reasonableness of the continental decision requires consideration of the value of the activity of engaging in this wager while also critically reflecting, and the value of the perspective that that dual combination affords. In that sense, transcendental arguments are circular, but so, it might be argued, are philosophical methodologies oriented around seeking reflective equilibrium, the use of thought experiments, and an explicit or implicit commitment to common sense. The circularity need not be vicious in any of these cases, but it sometimes is in all of them. Jeff

Malpas (2003: 5–6) has observed that the comparison of analytic and continental approaches to transcendental arguments might help to bridge the divide or to deepen it. Our feeling is that the latter is rather more likely in this case. Perhaps, however, these rather stark differences need to be made perspicuous in order for a genuine conversation to be possible.

11. PHENOMENOLOGY
RETURNING TO THE THINGS THEMSELVES

The tradition of phenomenology has proved remarkably resilient, enduring throughout the entirety of the twentieth century and beyond. In fact, it continues to be one of the primary research fronts of contemporary continental philosophy (both on the European continent and beyond), as well as a tradition that many of the great continental philosophers have aligned themselves with – Husserl, Edith Stein, Heidegger, Sartre, Merleau-Ponty, Levinas, Ricoeur, Gadamer, Arendt, Derrida, Henry, Marion and so on – while also reinventing in more or less radical ways. In recent times, the term phenomenology also crops up repeatedly in analytic philosophy of mind where it roughly designates the qualitative character of experience, or what are sometimes called qualia. Of course, in Husserl and the tradition stemming from him, phenomenology has come to mean something rather more specific than merely a term that is interchangeable with "what it is like". By the same token, if we describe phenomenology as a descriptive method for studying and reflecting on experience and its variegated structures, it is not radically divorced from some important analytic concerns either, and it is perhaps for this reason that philosophers such as Ryle and Austin (and the early pragmatist, C. S. Peirce) have sometimes wondered whether their own projects might best be called phenomenological.

It seems to be phenomenology's more grandiose methodological aspirations that analytic philosophers have been troubled by, rather than any kind of wholesale rejection of the worth of all phenomenological description (although there have been wholesale rejections too). There are also concerns about the imperial ambitions of phenomenology; most major phenomenologists did not think of their work and their method (of "waking to wonder" as Eugene Fink once described it) as one philosophical technique among many, that might be of use for some purposes and not for others. While it is true that phenomenological analyses (especially Husserl's) sometimes proceed very slowly and avoid generalization beyond established findings, phenomenologists have tended to see what they do as essential to philosophy *per se*; this raises the hackles of analytic readers. While the idea of doing away with phenomenology *tout court* seems unlikely, the real division pertains to just what is done with these descriptions of experience and just what their significance is claimed to be. Are they viewed as platforms from which necessary and essential conditions might be established (and if so, what is their relation to empirical conditions?), or as defeasible psychological descriptions of experience that are of little philosophical significance? While the latter answer alone does not make one an analytic philosopher, since some continental philosophers would endorse such a dismissal of phenomenology albeit for different reasons, it is certainly a view that is widely shared within the analytic community.

That said, analytic criticisms of phenomenology have been many and varied, orienting themselves around the following interrelated claims: that phenomenology amounts to a form of foundationalist subjectivism (and thus a variant on the Cartesian project); or that is it a form of psychologism (as with Frege's initial charge against Husserl's *Philosophy of Arithmetic*); that it uses an introspective methodology that privileges a first-person perspective that has been invalidated by the social sciences (as Dennett suggests); that it assumes some kind of incorrigibility of our access to phenomena (and some kind of "correlation", to use Meillassoux's term from *After Finitude*, between "phenomena" and "reality") and is thus vulnerable to "arguments from illusion" of various kinds, not only those that are sceptical in inspiration but especially those coming from science that suggest that phenomenology is naive (this is also Dennett's position); that it partakes in the myth of the given (a strange charge given that precisely what all phenomenology denies is the passive sense-data-type model as ground for knowledge); and finally that its reliance on transcendental reasoning means that it falls prey to all the problems that we detailed in Chapter 10. In effect, much of contemporary analytic philosophy sees phenomenology as one more in a series of thoroughly doomed empiricist endeavours to complete the Cartesian programme, alongside such programmes as phenomenalism and Berkleyan idealism. This chapter will consider these various charges, as well as the prospects for Dennett's "hetero-phenomenology": that is, an objectivist phenomenology.

THE CONTINENTAL PHENOMENOLOGICAL TRADITION(S)

Fundamentally, phenomenology is committed to the importance of starting with experience, adequately describing that experience on its own terms, and then seeking to build a theory on those descriptions. The motto "return to the things themselves" is arguably primarily negative in orientation: it stems from worries about philosophical abstractions and metaphysical positions losing touch with what Husserl called the life-world (*Lebenswelt*) or what Heidegger in *Being and Time* called "average everydayness". As such, a phenomenologist should not start with a theory (or metaphysics), and then turn to experience to try to confirm (or falsify, as in Popper's alternative idealization of scientific practice) that theory or hypothesis. Phenomenology is often characterized as depending on the first-person perspective rather than the third, but this opposition is more complicated than it seems since any first-person perspective is oriented to something beyond the person, and, for the phenomenologist at least, any third-person perspective must be understood from somewhere and somewhen. If the sciences offer an account of perception, thought and so on in terms of causal relations between already determinate entities, phenomenology seeks to disclose the original experience of the world that such explanations take for granted. Such an ambition means that one's philosophical method will need to be suitably tailored so as to recover this experience without betraying it through the activity of philosophical reflection and, of course, through the use of language. The difficulty of this task is sometimes thought to constitute an objection to phenomenology, although most phenomenologists offer detailed and plausible accounts of the relation between the reflective and pre-reflective domains. It does mean, however, that phenomenologists must use a method that differs substantially from two of the dominant philosophical methods. As Merleau-Ponty puts it in *Phenomenology of Perception*, "the demand for a pure description excludes equally the procedure of analytical reflection on the one hand, and that of scientific explanation on the other" (2002: ix). Only by avoiding these tendencies, according to him, can we "rediscover, as anterior to the ideas of subject and object, the fact of my subjectivity and the nascent object, that primordial layer at which both things and ideas come into being" (*ibid.*: 219). The point here is that to start from the subject–object polarity is to neglect something more fundamental: what we might call being-in-the-world in Heidegger's terminology.

While we have referred to phenomenology in the singular, it must be acknowledged that *what phenomenology is* remains fundamentally contested in contemporary continental philosophy. None of the major philosophers associated with the phenomenological movement have precisely the same understanding of its method and aims. Indeed, the ambiguity of the Husserlian motto "return to the things themselves" partly prescribes that this be so. Although one can find phenomenologically inclined descriptions, arguments and the German equivalent of the term itself in Kant, Hegel and others, Husserl is widely acknowledged to be its methodological founder. But even Husserl did not consistently deploy one given phenomenological method; instead he frequently revisited his account of it, and argued for distinctions between different kinds of phenomenology in his own work. What, then, allows these various concerns to hang together?

Pivotal to all versions of phenomenology is a concern to start with experience and build any theory from that. Likewise, an indebtedness to Brentano's conception of intentionality – the directedness of mental states – is also ubiquitous. Brentano has arguably been equally influential for the analytic traditions, but for continental philosophy the significance is largely in Brentano's influence on Husserl's seminal *Logical Investigations* of 1900–1901. Here Husserl characterizes the two main components of the phenomenological method:

1. The negative move consists in suspending judgement on anything that might prevent us attending to the "things themselves", to experience (the famous *epochē*, or suspension of the "natural attitude" that assumes, for example, that there is an outside world).
2. The positive move involves a "return" to the specific mode of appearing of the phenomenon and requiring some kind of search for essences (technically called an *eidetic reduction*, or *eidetic analysis*).

Phenomenology of this kind is not simply a form of introspective subjectivism. It involves a search for essences, or exemplifications, and hence retains a generalizing tendency. In fact, Husserl famously goes so far as to proclaim that phenomenology is a rigorous science, although he insisted that it is a science of consciousness rather than of empirical things, and as such it is methodologically distinct. Phenomenology aims to look at particular examples without theoretical presuppositions (such as the phenomena of love-relations in Sartre, of two hands touching each other in Merleau-Ponty, etc.), before then discerning what is essential to these experiences, as well as reflecting on enabling conditions for those experiences.

This broad technique of argumentation is employed, admittedly in very different ways, by all of the subsequent phenomenologists, although for Heidegger, Sartre and Merleau-Ponty, "pure" phenomenology is impossible. In order to understand "concrete" human life, they maintain that we need to pay more attention to our essential historicity without abstracting from this by privileging rational reflection. In other words, there is a certain inextricability from our social world (*Lebenswelt*) that makes pure phenomenology and the postulation of the transcendental subject impossible, and necessitates a turn to history (and to hermeneutics, genealogy and deconstruction as we shall see later). In *Phenomenology of Perception*, Merleau-Ponty therefore argues that phenomenology is essentially, and necessarily, existential philosophy (2002: xiv), which is to say that any attempted reduction to the "things themselves", or experience, will actually end up by revealing the ways in which experience is permeated by the social situation we are in. In other words, the attempted phenomenological reduction is necessarily incomplete, but for Merleau-Ponty this inability to complete it does not herald the end of phenomenology – it actually reveals much about the human situation, notably our ties to the world. Being-in-the-world hence emerges in its full richness only against the background of the reduction (*ibid.*: xiv). Merleau-Ponty's commitment to "existential phenomenology" means that the unity of the world is first lived as ready-made or already there, not produced as a conscious judgement, as some (perhaps unfair) readings of Husserl suggest. Any phenomenological reduction is not to be understood as the purification of consciousness of all empirical involvement and the "natural attitude", but rather as the reflective effort to disclose our pre-reflective engagement in the world, and an elaboration of bodily intentionality is central to Merleau-Ponty's account of this (Toadvine 2008).

Since these developments, Derridean deconstruction (particularly his *Introduction to Husserl's Origin of Geometry* and *Speech and Phenomena*) and Deleuze's *Difference and Repetition* and *The Logic of Sense* have subjected phenomenology to two rather more vehement forms of critique. In particular, reservations are proffered by both Derrida and Deleuze in regard to Husserl's implicit and explicit philosophy of time, as well as his conception of the transcendental ego and the manner in which it serves as a condition for meaning (Sartre had also already rejected this in *Transcendence of the Ego*). The analytic charge of subjectivism against phenomenology is hence also partially reflected within continental philosophy (although most do not accuse Heidegger's phenomenology of this). Marxists and psychoanalysts have also been concerned that phenomenology falls victim to something closely related to the "user illusion", arguing that it does not offer resources for understanding the manner in which the material forces of production interpellate individuals to think, feel and act in certain ways. Poststructuralist philosophers have also raised something like this charge against phenomenology. Phenomenological analysis suggests our experience is unified, has a certain kind of mineness about it (Heidegger), even if there is no ego or "I" that is revealed in our phenomenology. Likewise, there seems to be a commitment to experience being meaningful, which is something that Deleuze, Foucault and other poststructuralists contest for roughly social-constructivist reasons (sense is produced, not basic). These neo-Nietzscheans maintain that at a fundamental level there are but conflicting drives/desires, and conscious experience will (at best) fail to see the significance of this, and (at worst) systematically misunderstand what is really happening at the level of unconscious desire and hence at the level of society. But even with the rise of poststructuralism (and more recently speculative realism, Badiouian metaphysics, etc.), phenomenology remains an important part of contemporary continental philosophy, and it is a formative – albeit contested – influence on all of the new philosophies. Indeed, it is notable that in *Difference and Repetition* Deleuze calls for a new and more radical phenomenology (i.e. one that is not encumbered by common sense and thus tacitly still a form of *doxa*), and Derrida was a Husserlian for a long time before he subjected aspects of this project to both a (quasi-) transcendental and phenomenological critique. One therefore needs to be careful about too quickly instituting an outside (or beyond) of phenomenology in contemporary European thought. Phenomenology remains alive, in the sense that it is the subject of both ongoing research and ongoing critique, and we have also seen recently a "theological turn" in French phenomenology, through the work of philosophers such as Marion, Henry and others.

ANALYTIC PHENOMENOLOGY TODAY

As we have noted, Brentano's conception of intentionality – the directedness of mental states – has been influential in the analytic traditions, although there is considerable disagreement as to whether this is a feature to be resolved in analysis (reductive or non-reductive), or rather a given to be built on (as in the so-called Austrian School of Chisholm and his followers). Moreover, many analytic philosophers have taken earlier Husserlian phenomenology quite seriously, and have even been interested in related philosophical problems. Husserl's concerns in the *Logical Investigations* arose out of a literature (Bolzano, Brentano, Frege) important to early analytic philosophy, and in many ways they are continuous with the concerns of modern philosophers of language and of mind. Precursors of ideas given analytic expression in the work of David Kaplan, Searle, Jack Smart and others have been found in Husserl, although obviously situated in a very different methodological context. Of the two main components of the Husserlian phenomenological method, analytic philosophers (along with most later phenomenologists) question the possibility of a universal *epochē*, and the point of a particular *epochē*, and the subsequent stage of eidetic reduction is seen as simply carrying out conceptual analysis in an unnecessarily convoluted form. For Husserl, the reduction or *epochē* is meant to allow a grasp of the relation between subjectivity and objectivity by isolating the *noema* – the object as it is perceived, thought, remembered – rather than the object itself. Analytic philosophy would not accept this distinction by and large, or would assimilate it to the distinction between representation and object.

The transcendental dimension of Husserl's work receives new emphasis in *Ideas I*, where Husserl holds that the result of the reduction is the discovery of transcendental consciousness, a new region of being; the claim is that our experience of objectivity has as its condition this transcendental region of being. This is something of a sticking point for many analytic philosophers. Instead, there is a fair degree of respect for the earlier *Logical Investigations*, evinced by the fact that well-known analytic philosophers such as Kevin Mulligan and Barry Smith can consider themselves Husserlians. There is also an interesting overlap between the work of the "Munich phenomenologists", primarily inspired by the *Logical Investigations*, and later analytic work. Most notably, Adolf Reinach's analysis of the foundations of civil law has been held to be a forerunner of Austinian speech act theory.[1]

There is also, undoubtedly, limited and particular use of phenomenological methods in analytic philosophy of mind. Partly because of such occurrences, Glendinning claims that phenomenology cuts across the "divide", rather than follows its contours. For him, various philosophers normally thought to be "analytic" can also be said to be phenomenologists; he cites as examples Austin, Ryle, Stanley Cavell, McDowell, Putnam, Cora Diamond and Wittgenstein (Glendinning 2007: 23). Austin, Ryle and Wittgenstein have indeed on occasion allowed that their work could be considered to be a phenomenology of sorts,[2] but the term only seems to apply if broadened considerably. If we do this, it is indeed possible to characterize some analytic philosophical work (especially work at the behaviourist end of philosophy of mind) as phenomenological. However, it seems equally well described as a strand of analysis paying special attention to the embedding of linguistic expressions or conceptual classifications in contexts of human activity; the divide now recurs as the division between this kind of "phenomenology" and that kind with a more Husserlian inheritance.

In fact, it is equally plausible to maintain that early analytic philosophy was just as concerned with rejecting phenomenology as it was with idealism, even if with ordinary-language philosophy the situation becomes rather more complicated. The critique of idealism that guided Russell and others early on was, as we saw in Part I, preceded by the Fregean critique of Husserl's "psychologism", and although phenomenology was inaugurated after this with *Logical Investigations*, it has been received by many in the same way. This was followed by Carnap's critique of Heidegger for transgressing the limits of what can be meaningfully spoken of, and since that time few analytic philosophers have seriously entertained phenomenology as a worthwhile method. While that is arguably still the dominant view today, the past fifteen years have seen greater engagement with phenomenologists, as analytic philosophers have become more concerned with their own history, and as cognitive science has developed models of the mind less antagonistic to phenomenology than, say, computationalism. The growth may also be due to greater analytic preparedness to countenance a pluralized conception of the philosophical project. From the other direction, there has been a concern within continental philosophy with naturalizing phenomenology, as well as with thematizations of its importance for cognitive science, and the anti-naturalist flavour of phenomenology has been somewhat diminished. This suggests a new and improved opportunity for meaningful dialogue between players from both "camps". However, we suggest that residual meta-philosophical concerns, which we shall now outline, continue to preclude anything like a genuine rapprochement here.

ANALYTIC CRITICISMS OF PHENOMENOLOGY

In an early review of Heidegger's magnum opus, *Being and Time*, Ryle remarks: "it is my personal opinion that ... phenomenology is at present headed for disaster and will end up either in a self-ruinous subjectivism or a windy mysticism" (quoted in Passmore 1978: 497). For most analytic philosophers, Ryle was entirely right; the phenomenologist's preference for a (largely) first-person methodology, the deployment of transcendental arguments, an apparent anti-realism (or at least a tendency to give comfort to constructivist views) and either an anti-naturalism or unwillingness to engage with science present a package deal that is deeply suspicious. Perhaps the failure of phenomenology to integrate with the sciences is the major issue here (as we shall see below), but there are other related concerns. Searle suggests that phenomenology is not only very limited, but is on the verge of "bankruptcy" (1999: 1), "and it does not have much to contribute to the topics of the logical structure of intentionality or the logical structure of social and institutional reality" (*ibid.*: 10). Searle goes on to suggest that one of the main problems with phenomenological methods is that, using them, most of the important questions in philosophy and science cannot even be stated. This idea (that phenomenology has little to offer the analytic philosophy of mind) elides the fact that the phenomenological focus is more on the mind–world relation rather than the mind–brain relation. It is hence fairer to say, as Shaun Gallagher and Dan Zahavi do in *The Phenomenological Mind*, that "phenomenology is concerned with attaining an understanding and a proper description of the experiential structure of our mental/embodied life; it does not attempt to develop a naturalistic explanation of consciousness" (2008a: 9). Presumably, however, the only reason one would advocate any such conception of the philosophical task is that such a starting point is not felt to be intrinsically distorting, or at least is considered to be less distorting than starting with any of the major alternatives (which might include folk psychology, an idealized rational subject, linguistic analysis, the conception of philosopher as servant to science, or the philosopher as the "orderer" of various disparate knowledge claims).

And in this respect, many analytic philosophers will simply disagree; Dennett, referring to phenomenology, famously says that the "first person science of consciousness is a discipline with no methods, no data, no results, no future, no promise. It will remain a fantasy" (2001). We shall explore Dennett's claims in some detail, since his own conception of heterophenomenology has been the subject of sustained dispute by various phenomenologists, but let us first turn to the argument from the "fact" of illusion, and whether this presents an insurmountable obstacle to phenomenology, as is sometimes alleged.

ARGUMENTS FROM ILLUSION: SCIENCE AND THE USER-ILLUSION

Any compelling case of perceptual illusion is *prima facie* a theoretical problem for phenomenology, which in its various differing guises contains a commitment to the primacy of perception, the primacy of the pre-reflective (or the ready-to-hand), and a commitment to the fruitfulness of the very notion of returning to the phenomena themselves. As such, "if the phenomenal world is equated with the perceptual world and asserted to be the real world, and if illusion and hallucination are acknowledged to occur within the perceptual world, then it would seem that one is forced to grant reality to illusions and hallucinations" (Dillon 1988: 93). There are broadly two concerns here that are worth elaborating on.

The first concern is the broad objection that perceptual illusion puts paid to the use of phenomenology in completing the Cartesian project. Having been mistaken once (as we all have been), how can we know that we are not systematically mistaken? Without an answer to this, what can attending to the percept really tell us that is veridically reliable, informative and useful? Clearly this kind of objection to the epistemic and ontological primacy of the phenomena was not compelling to phenomenologists who were not (unlike, say, the sense-data theorists, phenomenalists, etc.) looking for an entirely secure foundation for knowledge. In addition, this kind of argument from illusion seemed to many to presuppose a dualist ontology between the thing-in-itself and our experience (representation) of it, and in the continental tradition there has been a long-standing view that such an ontology must be avoided. For Merleau-Ponty, this is exactly the problem for both empiricist and intellectualist accounts of perception. The former gives way to a radical scepticism; the latter banishes error and ambiguity in favour of apodictic judgements of consciousness. Phenomenology (even with Husserl) purports to escape the subject–object, self–world, phenomena–noumena (thing-in-itself) dualist-type worries, by making a methodological manoeuvre that has ontological commitments if not metaphysical ones. There is an epistemic primacy of phenomena; certainly in the existential phenomenologists this becomes a primacy of the ready-to-hand, or bodily coping, and so on. But in a more or less sustained way, there is also an *onto-logical* primacy of phenomena: hence the title of Renaud Barbaras's book, *The Being of the Phenomenon* (2003), and Heidegger declares in *Being and Time* that phenomenology *is* fundamental ontology. While the meaning of Being is simultaneously disclosed/covered over by the "phenomena", it is clear that for Heidegger we do have an important pre-ontological access to Being through such phenomena.

As Martin Dillon points out, phenomenologists usually have at least two strategies to undermine arguments from illusion. They will need to show: (i) that the phenomena of illusion do not undermine phenomenological ontol-ogy, and, to make the point in an even stronger (transcendental) fashion, that illusion cannot be understood without reference to phenomenology; and (ii) that there is a viable distinction between the phenomenal world and the subjective world, which allows for mistakes, corrections and so on occurring in the subjective world, without leading us to give up on the philosophical and ontological primacy of the phenomenal world. The first point the phe-nomenologist will make in relation to (i) is that our experience is intrinsic-ally temporal. As such, we should not take our ambiguous perception (at one instant) as a knock-down reason to impugn the testimony of phenomena *per se*. After all, the very apprehension that we have made a mistake and been taken in by an "illusion" is itself perceptual; the erroneous perception is cor-rected by another perceptual experience. As Dillon puts this point, "for the illusion to be an illusion, there must be a unitary phenomenon that reveals itself first in one mode and then in another" (1988: 95). Furthermore, per-ceptual experience is rarely clear and distinct, and phenomenologists hence typically distinguish between systematic illusion and the ambiguity that is a necessary consequence of being a situated and involved perspective, and hence not having a view from nowhere. A stronger claim might also be that the experience of hallucination is phenomenologically differently from regular experiences of the world, thus allowing for the needed distinctions. Merleau-Ponty, at least, claims that this is attested to by patients experi-encing hallucinations (2002: 334). If this kind of reasoning is compelling, the need for insisting on a disjunction between phenomenality and reality, between consciousness and its causal object (and hence the "hard problem" of consciousness, as Chalmers labelled it), is arguably partly attenuated.[3] Finally, of course, the phenomenologist would attempt to undermine any strong scepticism by pointing out, in transcendental manner, the extent to which the sceptic presupposes what they are purportedly doubting.

But the issue of justification need not be posed as a sceptical concern. A second concern with phenomenology comes from the sciences. There is a reasonable body of evidence to the effect that we are frequently misguided in our own reports about what we have experienced, and the claim is then that phenomenology cannot stand in the face of *systematic* error. To put it more plainly, our phenomenological descriptions of the structures of experience, even if we are very careful and well trained, might simply be wrong, an example of the "user illusion", to borrow Benjamin Libet's phrase regarding time-consciousness.[4] Jean-Michel Roy puts the problem for phenomenology in the following terms:

> If … consciousness is intrinsically deceiving, it somehow makes a cognitive system victim of a fundamental phenomenological illusion under which it either takes its phenomenological properties for what they are not, or it imagines having phenomenological properties that it is in fact deprived of. The objection is an old one, and it is at the heart of Comte's arguments against the possibility of an introspective investigation of an observational kind, to which both Brentano and Wundt strove to find adequate answers. As a result, a cognitive system is made incapable of simply gaining real access to what has been assigned to the phenomenological investigation as its domain, and such an investigation cannot therefore contribute to the elaboration of a cognitive science.
>
> (2007: 9; see also Petitot *et al.* 2000)

The question, then, is: are we indeed systematically deceived in our phenomenological experience? We think Roy and others are right to suggest that phenomenologists are committed to a "no" answer to this question. This does not entail that phenomenologists are committed to incorrigibility, however, since for very few of them does consciousness exhaust the mental. On the contrary, phenomenologists are often concerned to examine background enabling conditions for our experience of intentionality, including our habitual ways of comporting ourselves that we are usually not conscious of. Nor does it prevent phenomenologists from accepting many of the findings of psychoanalysis, even including the positing of an unconscious.[5] Yet phenomenology would lose much of its claimed philosophical significance if it turns out that we are systematically duped about the structures of our experience, perhaps even if at the same time it turned out that the semantics of the way we make sense of our inner life is given by phenomenology.

Although inauthenticity or bad faith may predominate, phenomenology assumes that there must be resources within experience itself that, when properly attended to, disclose our situation and reveal the manner in which we can tend to misconstrue our own experiences, usually by constructing an overarching theory out of a particular restricted aspect of experience (indeed, in this sense there is something in experience that both empiricism and intellectualism get right). The phenomenologist must hence offer an account of why philosophers and people more generally think that there are such things as sense data or an essential self, or that social cognition necessarily involves inference, to take one of the points on which many analytic philosophers and many phenomenologists will part company, as we suggest in Chapter 20. There may be a certain naivety in the phenomenological optimism about experience here, but it does not mean that a phenomenologist must take phenomenology to be the whole story. Such theorists can, and (we think) should, consider other resources: psychoanalysis, neurology, cognitive science, analytic philosophy of mind and so on. There are plenty of things that phenomenology cannot accomplish on its own and contemporary phenomenological practice arguably largely reflects this fact (even if this was not always historically thought by phenomenologists to be the case).

Allegations of the user-illusion also return us to the ongoing worry that phenomenology is a form of psychologism or subjectivism. Another way of putting this might be to say that the concern is that phenomenology reduces objective possibility to subjective imaginability. Arguably, however, phenomenology seeks meaning clarification, and possibility is not reduced to imaginability, but only explored thereby (Mohanty 1991: 270). We might also reaffirm the point that to call phenomenology a form of subjectivism, psychologism, or introspection is somewhat misleading. Human consciousness is understood as intrinsically directed at, and open to, the world, hence as Morris succinctly puts it: "the stress of phenomenology falls not on an acting of introspecting, but on forging concepts adequate to experience" (2007: 534). When phenomenology is criticized for being subjective, often the critics evince a misunderstanding of phenomenology, construing it as nothing other than subject reports of "what it is like", rather than *analyses* of the variegated structures of experience, including the structural conditions for particular subjective reports. Consider, for example, Thomas Metzinger's claim that the phenomenological method cannot provide a method for generating any growth of knowledge since there is no way one can reach intersubjective consensus on claims such as "this is the purest blue anyone can perceive" versus "no it isn't, it has a slight green hue". As Zahavi points out in response, "these claims are simply not the type of claims that are to be found in works by phenomenological philosophers and to suggest so is to reveal one's lack of familiarity with the tradition in question" (2007: 28).

DENNETT AND HETEROPHENOMENOLOGY

One well-known analytic philosopher who has had much to say about phenomenology in recent times is Dennett. Throughout his career, Dennett has held to the slogan "content before consciousness": that is, to the idea that philosophical problems of consciousness have to wait on the working out of the theory of content. In *Consciousness Explained*, among other works, Dennett claims that we have no coherent concept of consciousness that is not, at bottom, content-based. Our self-conception is regularly astray here; indeed, Dennett thinks, it is constructed on the fly, and involves numerous acts of fudging and recasting that give us a spurious narrative unity. Nonetheless, Dennett is interested in phenomenological work, albeit from an unusual angle. He distinguishes *heterophenomenology*, an outside or objective phenomenology that is third-personal, from the Husserlian tradition of *autophenomenology*, which is focused on turning inwards and introspecting, and is hence subjective or first-personal. The point of heterophenomenology is to bring first-personal phenomenological claims made by subjects into play as data for cognitive science; these are data that are genuinely needed, providing, as they do, what Dennett calls a "manifest ontology" of the agent, which is genuinely defeasible within cognitive science. Indeed, this defeasibility is much of the point; unless some way is found to bring scientific work and phenomenological description together, there is simply no way that the sciences can take phenomenology seriously, and taking it seriously means running the risk of finding that we are phenomenologically deluded. The project cannot be performed more directly, Dennett thinks, because in autophenomenology one is essentially analysing one's own experiences, reflecting on one's own first-person perspectives, and this is not capable of scientific integration.

Dennett retains the name "phenomenology" for this activity because a putative methodological agnosticism is in play here, that is, the technique of bracketing:

> Heterophenomenology, I argue, is a cautious, controlled way of taking subjects seriously, as seriously as they could possibly be taken without granting them something akin to papal infallibility, while maintaining (contrary to everyday interpersonal communicative practice) a deliberate bracketing of the issue of whether what they are saying is literally true, metaphorically true, true under-an-imposed-interpretation, or systematically-false-in-a-way-we-must-explain. (2007: 252)

The existence claims made in first-person reports, studied from the outside, are to be suspended by the heterophenomenologist; the benefit of such an approach is that "the world as it appears to the subject is an inter-subjectively confirmable theoretical posit, and can consequently be studied in a scientifically respectable manner" (Zahavi 2007: 23). The clear implication is that this is not the case with autophenomenology because of its alleged reliance

on the method of introspection, and because phenomenologists have confused observation with theorizing. They cannot neutrally describe experience,
qualia, the "what it is like", without theorizing about it. As Dennett puts it
in *Consciousness Explained*, our "personal power of self-observation of our
conscious mind" is subject to error, an intrinsic weakness that the phenomenological tradition ignored, instead adopting a "doctrine of infallibility", or
at least of "incorrigibility" (1992: 67). Suffice to say that both claims are highly
contentious. We have already seen the sense in which it is not true of the philosophy of Merleau-Ponty, for one. But Dennett continues, "What we are fool-
ing ourselves about is the idea that the activity of introspection is ever a matter
of just 'looking and seeing'. I suspect that when we claim to be just using our
powers of inner observation, we are actually engaging in a sort of impromptu
theorizing" (*ibid*.). There is no such thing as a pure conscious observation,
in the sense of passively apprehending something entirely given, and consequently free of any sort of interpretation or construction on the part of the
cognitive system. When we try to neutrally describe, we inevitably end up
introducing a theoretical explanation. He adds, "We are remarkably gullible
theorizers ... because there is so little to 'observe' and so much to pontificate
about without fear of contradiction" (*ibid*.: 68).

Except for the clause that there is "so little to observe", many post-
Husserlian phenomenologists will acknowledge the theory-embeddedness of
observation, and hence the difficulties of phenomenological description. But
it is not clear that the attempt (without its subsequent take-up by the heterophenomenologist) cannot provide philosophically useful insights. The analytic philosopher will presumably agree that a method is not to be shunned
merely because of its fallibility; the issue here is essentially the pragmatic
question whether (auto)phenomenology in actual practice furthers philosophical work of value. Here judgements differ between the traditions, and
again something of an impasse is reached.

It is interesting to recognize that phenomenologists have reversed the
complaints that Dennett makes against them. If Dennett maintains that
phenomenologists inevitably practise (bad) theory while they purport to
describe, they respond that in his philosophy of mind as a whole he inevitably offers and relies on a (bad) phenomenology while purporting to offer an
objective theoretical explanation. As Zahavi puts it:

> Dennett's heterophenomenology must be criticized not only
> for simply presupposing the availability of the third-person per-
> spective without reflecting on and articulating its conditions of
> possibility, but also for failing to realize to what extent its own
> endeavor tacitly presupposes an intact first-person perspective.
>
> (2007: 39)

Gallagher and Zahavi follow this theme up:

> Hetero-phenomenology itself, however, involves something of a
> fantasy. The fantasy here is the idea that in the study of conscious-
> ness or the mind, science can leave the first-person perspective
> behind, or neutralise it without remainder. In attempting to say
> something about consciousness, hetero-phenomenology fails to
> acknowledge that its interpretations of first-person reports must
> be based either on the scientist's own first-person experience
> (what he understands from his own experience to be the experi-
> ence of x), or upon pre-established categories that derive from folk
> psychology or from obscure, anonymous, and non-rigorous forms
> of phenomenology. (2008a: 18)

Once more we seem to have reached an impasse, this time one that
is based on the extent to which it is problematic for a philosophical field
to fail to integrate with the sciences in the manner Dennett calls for. But
this impasse is not simply the divide in disguise; as our earlier discussion
of thought experiment and the experimental philosophy movement shows,
many analytic philosophers who value methods based on the elicitation of
intuitions exhibit the same discomfort that the phenomenologist feels here.

We hope we have done enough here to show that phenomenology *en
masse* cannot be easily rejected on the grounds that it involves introspection, is committed to incorrigibility about the mental and must naively ignore
empirical data and experimentally derived scientific insights. There are many
reasons, no doubt, for preferring alternative approaches to philosophy (and
philosophy of mind), but these caricatures do not manage to adequately capture them. That said, we have seen that the package deal presented by phenomenology is suspicious to most analytic philosophers given various norms
of that tradition, and in Chapters 18 and 20 we look at some of the topical
consequences of these methodological differences.

12. GENEALOGY, HERMENEUTICS AND DECONSTRUCTION

Without wanting to unify genealogy, hermeneutics and deconstruction, this chapter will highlight the manner in which these three differing trajectories together ensure that sustained textual engagement, and a concern with culture and history (including the history of philosophy), constitute a method of sorts that undergirds large parts of contemporary continental philosophy. While the treatment of the history of philosophy by certain philosophers can seem negative, with apparently sweeping terms of critique such as "logocentrism", "metaphysics of presence", "incredulity towards grand narratives" and so on, there is a positive aspect to this attempt to "unearth" and extract from the archive some of the historical conditions of differing formations of subjectivity and objects of knowledge. Certainly all three trajectories insist on the conceptual and historical presuppositions of theoretical frameworks, and they hence all partake in what we will come to call the "temporal turn" characteristic of twentieth-century continental philosophy, a manner of proceeding that is distinct from some of the norms and methods of analytic philosophy, most notably those associated with the linguistic turn, but also perhaps the more general analytic concern with argument and rationality. This is not to say that there are not analytic philosophers engaged in hermeneutic activities, for instance in conducting historical enquiries; Ian Hacking's explorations of the historical origins of concepts of probability and statistics are of clear relevance to analytic philosophy of science but also clearly involve something like hermeneutic and genealogical techniques.

While there are important differences between hermeneutic and genealogical thinkers, and thus between hermeneuticists and poststructuralists (who tend to be aligned with genealogy), they do share a related lineage. In *Being and Time*, Heidegger argues that hermeneutics is essential to both Dasein's self-understanding and the meaning of Being. He also undertakes a task of destructive retrieval in relation to the history of philosophy, and while his claims regarding the former are central to the work of Hans-Georg

Gadamer and hermeneutics, it is his claims regarding the latter that are more central to Derrida and deconstruction. If it is fair to say that genealogists and deconstructionists are more explicitly aligned with critique than hermeneuticists, then it is also perhaps not surprising that they have been subject to a greater frequency of critical rejoinder by analytic philosophers. In contrast to the philosophers associated with genealogy, hermeneutics is less a "school" with overlapping views about a given subject matter, and as such it is ostensibly more neutral, being applicable to any philosopher substantially concerned with understanding and interpretation (as Føllesdal [1996: 205–6] suggests). Analytic caution about hermeneutics tends to reflect well-known arguments about the extent to which the methods of the social sciences and humanities are distinct from those of the natural sciences, but this is an internal divide within that tradition. Even genealogical theorizing is not necessarily felt to be intrinsically misleading for analytic philosophers, although at least three overlapping concerns arise here: that it commits the genetic fallacy; that the historicism involved entails a problematic relativism (or even idealism as we explore in Chapter 16); and that it leaves us no place for normative judgement.

CONTINENTAL PHILOSOPHY: A HERMENEUTICS AND GENEALOGY OF OURSELVES

Let us begin by attempting to situate hermeneutics and genealogy within some broader tendencies within continental philosophy. Only Nietzsche and Foucault explicitly use the name "genealogy" for their methods, yet something related to it is far more pervasive, and arguably even characteristic of continental philosophy writ large. The emphasis on interpretation coheres with the dominance of transcendental reasoning in the post-Kantian tradition, as well as with Hegel's dialectical method of immanent critique (i.e. the teasing out of oppositions and contradictions with a concept that gives rise to their sublation and the transformation of the concept). It shares connections with what Ricoeur and Gadamer call a "hermeneutics of suspicion" (see Ricoeur 2004: 64, 144; see also Gadamer 1984), which refers to the deployment by Nietzsche, Freud and Marx of methods that are not only suspicious of one's access to their own minds and much existing philosophy and theory, but also psychologically and physiologically oriented. The matter of (self-)interpretation also lies in part behind continental concerns with the problem of modernity (see Pippin 1991); for the analytic tradition this is either not seen to be a problem or, if it is conceded to be a problem deserving of philosophical reflection, it is exceedingly far from the *raison d'être* of philosophy. And the idea of a critical philosophy has been around at least since Kant: critical theory, genealogy and deconstruction can all be differently situated within this tradition. In his well-known essay "Nietzsche, Genealogy, History" (1971), for instance, Foucault claims that two traditions in modern philosophy come out of Kant's work: "an analytic of truth" and "an ontology of present reality", which he also calls "a genealogy of ourselves". As Foucault writes in "The Art of Telling the Truth":

> In his great critical work Kant laid the foundations for that tradition of philosophy that poses the question of the conditions in which true knowledge is possible and, on that basis, it may be said, that a whole stretch of modern philosophy from the nineteenth century has been presented, and developed as the analytics of truth. But there is also in modern and contemporary philosophy another type of question, another kind of critical interrogation ... The other critical tradition poses the question: what is our historical present? What is the present field of possible experiences? ... It seems to me that the philosophical choice confronting us today is this: one may opt for a critical philosophy that will present itself as an analytic philosophy of truth in general, or one may opt for a critical thought that will take the form of an ontology of ourselves, an ontology of the present. (1994: 147–8)

Now, questions remain to be posed about just what is being intimated by the idea of an "analytics of truth", and just why the idea of doing an "ontology of the present" is bound up with genealogical analyses of the past. In addition, an analytic metaphysician or ontologist is unlikely to be looking to offer an ontology of the *present* in the first place (indeed, that temporal inflection might be considered an oxymoron) and is instead typically concerned, as Glock (2008: 121) notes, with such apparently timeless questions as: what kind of things exist? And what is the nature or essence of those things? Perhaps Putnam (2005: 15–16) is right to comment that ontology means something different for analytic and continental philosophers. Precisely because of this, Foucault's diagnosis is helpful, since almost all the usual suspects associated with continental philosophy are indeed interested both in what Foucault calls an ontology of the present and the consequent need to reflect on the background conditions for any given form of reflection. Moreover, it also seems clear that an ontology/genealogy of the present/ modernity will have to be more interpretive than analytic (see Ophir 2001), although one can, and perhaps should, attempt to do both.

This general conception also comes out in Habermas's essay "Taking Aim at the Heart of the Present" (1986), which was an obituary for Foucault. Although his position is clearly distinguished from Foucault's, Habermas retains an allegiance to the sociocritical conception of the task of the philosopher. Indeed, the philosophical concern with the problem(s) of modernity, and the various explicit critiques of the alleged reification of instrumental reason or calculative thinking in the work of many continental philosophers, also fit Foucault's descriptions, as do the manner in which so many continental philosophers associate reflections on time with normative considerations and political philosophy, and critique the present in the name of the future (more or less defined, more or less utopian). So too does the transcendental dimension associated with most continental philosophers. As Sacks puts it, successful transcendental reasoning involves *situated thought*, which necessarily involves forms of self-reflection regarding the relation between given propositional content and the thinking of such contents (as such, psychological matters are not radically disassociated from truth, although one obviously needs to be careful articulating this relation). Another way of putting Sacks's point about transcendental philosophy and situation might be to consider the notion of the background that is a focus of much of continental philosophy in its various forms: we might think here of talk of horizons, life-world (*Lebenswelt*), motor-intentionality, transcendental fields, absorbed coping, context and the interest in the social, historical and psychological conditions for certain kinds of philosophical utterance and ways of living. For Husserl, Heidegger, Merleau-Ponty and others, central to their phenomenological reflections is an attempt to make more perspicuous previously inarticulated background conditions. For genealogists such as Nietzsche and Foucault, the point is generally to see the historical contingency of these background conditions, and thus to open up a space for the new and different in the relation between the thinker and the delineated historical *a priori* that structures their thoughts. While the terminology of transcendental philosophy may not be there in the work of Nietzsche (and Foucault in his genealogical period), it is arguable that this kind of structure – having a perspective on a perspective from "within" – is still characteristic of their philosophy, even though it is also true that in a certain sense Foucault inverts Kant by showing that what appears to be necessary is in fact contingent.[1]

A final piece of evidence for the Foucaultian claim about two traditions stemming from Kant involves the dialectical thinking that plays such a major role in continental philosophy. While analytic philosophy has sometimes made claims to being a dialogue of reason (see Cohen's book of that name), and Socrates' dialogical conception of the task of philosophy has some echoes in analytic practice, what goes by the name of the dialectic in nineteenth- and twentieth-century continental philosophy is something rather different: it has tended to be a critical methodology with a historical purview that has been allied with change and transformation. Hegel and Marx are, of course, the major figures associated with dialectical thinking, and Hegel himself claimed that the task of philosophy is to grasp its own time in thought. Marxian dialectic claimed to have reversed Hegel's idealism and its complacent emphasis on thinking: what matters is changing the world more than understanding it, although arguably, of course, we cannot do one without the other. Horkheimer and Adorno's critical theory also offers us a negative dialectics in the book of that name, and in *The Visible and the Invisible* Merleau-Ponty labels his own philosophy "hyper-dialectic", or "hyper-reflection". This emphasis on the necessity and inevitability of interpretation of ourselves, and of contemporary life more generally, is also illuminated in different ways in the methods – hermeneutics, genealogy and deconstruction – that we shall now consider.

HERMENEUTICS

Hermeneutics began with the interpretation of religious and classical texts, but in a chain of influence from Schleiermacher to Dilthey to Heidegger, it becomes concerned not only with interpretation of texts more generally, but also with broader questions about the possibility of communication and ontology. Heidegger suggests that Dasein – roughly coextensive with the the term human being even if deliberately not reduced to that – is the only being that can raise the question of its own being, is concerned with its own being, and for whom its existence is in question. Heidegger's point is that Dasein stands out from mere immersion in the world, and is self-interpreting (1962: §9). Another way of putting the point might be to say that understanding is not something we do, but something that we are (Ramberg & Gjesdal 2005). On the simplest level, for Heidegger "understanding" is bound up with the recognition and projection of possibilities. Dasein is always already aware of possibilities and in the mode of the ready-to-hand, for example, the world presents itself in a particular light in relation to something that we are about to do, or some project that we are about to engage in (1962: §31). Moreover, for Heidegger, analytical enquiry and "interpretation" are nothing more than the working out of the possibilities that are already projected by the "understanding" (*ibid.*: §32). This means that all interpretation is at least partially grounded in something that we see in advance, in what he terms the forestructure of our understanding. For Heidegger, this is because in interpretation there is "never a pre-suppositionless apprehension of something presented to us". To offer a few examples of this structure of our understanding that he also terms the "existential-hermeneutical as" (*ibid.*), we inevitably hear a certain particular spluttering sound *as* a lawnmower starting up, we perceive the door *as* an escape route if we are being chased, we see the ruins *as* they were in their former glory, perhaps *as* evidence of the decline of the Roman Empire if they are in the relevant location, and Heidegger's fundamental claim is that we cannot get outside this mode of "seeing as" (which is related to what Wittgenstein calls seeing an aspect in *Philosophical Investigations*). Moreover, although it is sometimes useful, the attempt to see something free of this "as" structure is also deficient and derivative: the object or experience is "deworlded", and thus, at least in one sense, no longer understood at all. This means that there is no such thing as a pure perception that is without theoretical and practical background and contextualization. Rather, all perception is inevitably also an interpretation. Heidegger's account of the forestructure of our understanding involves some subtle distinctions that we cannot consider here – for example between fore-having, fore-sight and fore-conception (*ibid.*) – but he rejects the suggestion that this position commits him to a vicious relativism. While he admits that the structure of understanding and interpretation that he describes is circular, he argues that, far from this being a problem, the mistake is actually to yearn for a stable form of knowledge that is independently justifiable and therefore not circular. On his view, this would inevitably fall foul of something akin to the learning paradox that Meno famously described (and which is closely related to the paradox of analysis). What is decisive, Heidegger consequently argues, is not to get out of the hermeneutic circle, but to come into it in the right way. We must have a vague understanding of what it is that we are looking for, as contained in the ready-to-hand and its pre-ontological conception of the meaning of Being. This conception of interpretation heralds the renewal of a hermeneutical method that has since been productively explored by several of Heidegger's students, most notably Gadamer, who extended Heidegger's remarks in his magnum opus *Truth and Method*. While hermeneutics remains influential within continental philosophy, it has been contended that in its Gadamerian form it places too much emphasis on the authority of tradition, thus either leaving no room for critical judgement and reflection (Habermas) or presupposing a fused shared horizon of meaning that ignores some of the complexities of communication (Derrida).

ANALYTIC HERMENEUTICS

While some of these same issues have come up in the analytic reception of hermeneutics, we note that there is also a tradition of analytic hermeneutics that includes many of those philosophers usually among those deemed to be post-analytic. The *Stanford Encyclopedia of Philosophy* entry on this topic proclaims: "Hermeneutics has provided the critical horizon for many of the most intriguing discussions of contemporary philosophy, both within an Anglo-American context (Rorty, McDowell, Davidson) and within a more continental discourse (Habermas, Apel, Ricoeur, and Derrida)" (Ramberg & Gjesdal 2005). With the exception of the still (sadly) divisive figure of Derrida, and with the addition of Gadamer who is clearly fundamental both to hermeneutics and to many rapprochement projects, we have an account here of some of the main figures of potential convergence in relation to the "divide" between analytic and continental philosophy. We should not too quickly conclude that this is an example of genuine crossover, however, since it is arguable that some of the post-analytic philosophers are arguably no longer part of the analytic mainstream, as evidenced by where they are now publishing and citation patterns (see Duke *et al.* 2010). More philosophically, there is an important contrast between the practical hermeneutic holism of Heidegger and Dreyfus (in which the understanding of know-how is context-bound and not formalizable outside that context) and Davidson's more theoretical holism (Braver 2007: 243). In *Inquiries into Truth and Interpretation* (2001e: 125–39), Davidson offers a hypothetico-deductive account of what is going on when we are confronted by an interlocutor whom we are attempting to understand. As Pascal Engel puts it: "On Davidson's view, the interpretation of action is not a scientific explanation but, like it, consists in testing hypotheses against data. The data and the hypotheses differ … but it is a form of hypothetico-deductive explanation nevertheless" (1991: 143).

While Davidson might agree with continental hermeneuticists that the causal explanations of the physical sciences cannot be unproblematically employed in relation to the social sciences – and indeed is famous within analytic philosophy for maintaining a similar claim about the relation between the biological sciences and psychology – the spirit of his account of radical interpretation does not seem to be readily amenable to the perspective of most phenomenological hermeneutics.

Two other candidates for the label of "post-analytic" actually seem closer in spirit to the hermeneutic philosophy of the continental tradition: Charles Taylor and Bernard Williams. In Glock's (2008: 90) view, both are "instrumental" historicists (studying the past is necessary to achieving some other ends) rather than "intrinsic" historicists (studying the past offers the only genuine philosophical insight). Continental philosophers, from Heidegger to Derrida, are also generally instrumental historicists, primarily wanting to study the past to illuminate the present. For some continental philosophers, however, study of the past is an indispensable instrument. For Gadamer in *Truth and Method* for example, it is *only* the appreciation of the way in which we are shaped by tradition that makes genuine philosophical insight possible – "History does not belong to us, we belong to it" (2005: xvii). Analytic philosophers will not generally endorse an indispensability claim of this kind.

NIETZSCHE'S GENEALOGY OF MORALS

While the explicit endorsement of a genealogical method is restricted to *On the Genealogy of Morals*, a related methodological practice does seem to be in play elsewhere in Nietzsche's work. David Cooper brings out well the sense in which something like genealogy might be characteristic of Nietzsche's more general project, and not merely of limited and restricted relevance in one book (as Brian Leiter [2002: 165–92] maintains). On Cooper's view, Nietzsche's work, and the method of genealogy more generally, bring together two accomplishments that philosophers do not typically have: a historical sense and a knowledge of physiology. Together they might be thought to constitute the conditions of life (or the background) that we usually do not attend to when we focus on present morality, our conscious experience of free will, and other philosophical issues. As Cooper puts it:

> What the "physio-psychologist" uncovers – the drives, needs, instincts, affects, lurking behind our "foreground estimates" – the historian confirms on a diachronic scale, exposing, for example, how shifting modes of evaluation have been shaped by and expressed "conditions of life" opaque to the evaluators themselves. (2003: 2)

On the Genealogy of Morals famously begins: "We are unknown to ourselves, we men of knowledge – and with good reason. We have never sought ourselves – how could it happen that we should ever find ourselves?" (1989: Preface, §1). If these promises regarding genealogy are fulfilled, then the Nietzschean project threatens to expose conceptual analysis (and perhaps analysis more generally) as merely skirting the surface of things, never getting to the background or the subterranean conditions (psycho-physiological) that are always at work within philosophy.

In both Nietzsche and Foucault's hands, genealogy is to be distinguished from traditional historical practices. Genealogy does not think of the permutations and combinations of history as governed by reason, or progressing in any teleological manner. Likewise, there is not claimed to be one pure origin that is sought: diversity and conflict are endemic however far back we go. That said, genealogy nonetheless purports to give a hidden history, a hidden psycho-physiology, which highlights the constitution of certain types, both particular subjects as well as modes of thinking and evaluating (affirmative, negative, etc.). Ideas are thus often treated as something like symptoms, either of a given culture, or of the healthy or the diseased, active or reactive types. To evaluate truth claims or concepts via psychology can look bizarre (or, in a dialogic context, *ad hominem*); depraved people, for instance, may still have some remarkably good ideas. But Nietzsche (and to a lesser extent Foucault) is concerned primarily with value, and in this terrain there is arguably greater justification for such a move.

What, then, is the genealogy that Nietzsche offers us? Nietzsche's basic point is that three naturally occurring psychological mechanisms – *ressentiment* (essay 1), internalized cruelty (essay 2) and will to power (essay 3) – explain the ascetic morality that Nietzsche says we continue to live by despite the "death of God". The reason why Nietzsche calls himself an immoralist, and calls for a revaluation of all values, is because of the conviction that contemporary European morality has encouraged mediocrity and conformity, and made greatness highly unlikely. What *On the Genealogy of Morals* adds to this general Nietzschean revaluation is that it traces the development of modern-day moral beliefs from immoral beginnings in violence, suffering and resentment. According to Nietzsche's quasi-historical genealogy, Judaeo-Christian slaves turned inwards, and posited a soul – an interior mental reserve – as a last resort in order to allow them to escape from, and eventually turn the tables on, their more powerful Graeco-Roman oppressors, who were clearly in control in the physical realm. It is at this time, Nietzsche suggests, that the doer becomes separated from the deed: "The slave revolt in morality begins when *ressentiment* itself becomes creative and gives birth to values: the *ressentiment* of natures that are denied the true reaction, that of deeds, and compensate themselves with an imaginary revenge" (1989: 1, §10). Whereas "noble" morality basked in its own greatness and only denigrated those lesser as an afterthought (what Nietzsche calls the good–bad morality of masters that he associated predominantly with Graeco-Roman times while also acknowledging the Mongols and the Japanese), the Judaeo-Christian slaves first of all denigrated their oppressors as evil and only secondarily affirmed themselves as good by contrast (what Nietzsche calls the good–evil morality of slaves). The former is affirmative: the latter is negative and tends towards bitterness, because so much time and energy is invested in denigrating those who have control. Nietzsche thinks this revaluation was initially a move of some genius, but since that time the advent of a priestly caste – acting as an intermediary between masters and slaves – has contributed to the masters having a bad conscience (they could act otherwise; they are hence responsible), and Western history has since seen the triumph of the weak (and the negative) over the strong (and the affirmative). What we count as good is partly the result of the resentment of those who were weak, and this morality that valorizes humility, poverty, chastity and so on still persists without the context in which it made sense.

Now, what is the status of these kinds of claims? This is clearly not traditional history. Although Nietzsche and Foucault both adduce substantial historical evidence for their claims, it is hard to imagine that a debate about historical sources might lead either of them to change their mind. From an unsympathetic perspective, the conclusion might be that they are merely perpetuating myths, as Habermas alleges in *The Philosophical Discourse of Modernity* (1990: 120–30), or that the theories behind the stories are, through the device of quasi-history, rendered unfalsifiable, as Popper might have contended. These genealogies also seem to verge on committing the "genetic fallacy" of holding that an analysis of the origins of a given value or belief system can call into question its present functioning. That said, Nietzsche consistently insists that one cannot assume that the original function of something coming into being is congruent with its contemporary function and meaning. So the question is: just what is the relation between a genealogical description of how a given morality allegedly came about, and Nietzsche's intended critique of such morality and revaluation of all values? Just how does an investigation of the origins of our morality shed light on its current value? It is an open question whether Nietzsche satisfactorily resolves this problem. One available view, which is characteristic of analytic readings of Nietzsche, is that while Nietzsche gives us great insight into the causal powers of morality and the manner in which it prevents the flourishing of great people, doing a genealogy is not necessary – and is in fact superfluous – to establishing these points (Leiter 2002: 171).

FOUCAULT: GENEALOGY AND POWER

In "Nietzsche, Genealogy, History", Foucault explicitly aligns his genealogical period (which is associated with *Discipline and Punish* and the first volume of *History of Sexuality*) with Nietzsche's work. According to Foucault, genealogy fundamentally opposes:

> an attempt to capture the exact, and pure essence of things ... because this search assumes the existence of immobile forms that precede the external world of accident and succession ... If the genealogist refuses to extend his faith in metaphysics, if he listens to history, he finds that there is "something altogether different" behind things: not a timeless and essential secret, but the secret that they have no essence or that their essence was fabricated in a piecemeal fashion from alien forms. (1984: 78)

Rather than confuse itself with a quest for their "origins", genealogy is said to cultivate the details and accidents that accompany every beginning: it is hence concerned with multiplicity rather more than identity. Unlike, say, a Hegelian or Marxian conception of history, or in a different way the idea of history presupposed by the traditional historian, Foucault is opposed to *all* conceptions of history as progression, or that posit an outside of time from which a given totality can be measured. Genealogy thus affirms the marginal and the discontinuous and traces their impact on the present, and this knowledge is itself explicitly affirmed as a perspective. The goal is to say something about what really happened, by explaining trajectories that surface histories might ignore by assuming the discrete existence of their object. It is also, and perhaps most importantly, to produce a mutation in our understanding of our relation to the past, that opens up new possibilities for conceiving of our future.

Foucault himself was arguably also attentive to the charge of the genetic fallacy in his work; it seems to have partly motivated his move from a methodology of archaeology to one of genealogy. For instance: while, in *The History of Madness* (better known in English in the abridged form *Madness and Civilisation*), Foucault is highly critical of the treatment of madness in modern culture, according to his own method it is difficult to justify this judgement, since we cannot get outside history to act as critic in this way. If Foucault's early analyses of the constitution of domains of knowledge tacitly breached its own methodology by presupposing a view from nowhere (or by presupposing that one could actually be on the side of the mad, which is the subject of Derrida's [1978a] deconstruction of Foucault), with the method of genealogy this kind of critical intent and the interpretive rather than structuralist (and quasi-scientific) dimensions of his project are foregrounded. While Foucault's genealogies of prisons and the history of sexuality end up being very critical about the narratives of emancipation associated with both these structures of contemporary life, and while some would protest that he cannot say that power is everywhere and then make moral judgements about particular arrangements of power as Charles Taylor, Nancy Fraser, Habermas and others have suggested (see Patton 1989; Taylor 1984a), arguably such criticisms are misplaced, because they assume that a given culture is hegemonic and that it has a single, univocal tradition. And, of course, this is not so; societies are complex, made up of many different virtues and many different practices. Some of these practices can be used to counterpose and critique other practices and in this case his aim is specifically to offer an ontology of ourselves; as such, the inconsistency of the earlier archeological period is thus overcome.

Other questions remain, however, including the charge of the genetic fallacy. Despite the fact that Taylor is one of Foucault's main critics, Taylor actually offers a justification of the need for doing history of philosophy in terms quite close to Foucault's (noting that Foucault's archives extend far beyond the canonical texts of the history of philosophy). Taylor maintains that the key philosophical task is to articulate our current philosophical framework, but the question then becomes one regarding precisely *how* analyses of the past achieve this. First, Taylor asks us to consider whether it is merely fortuitous that the greatest challengers of the Cartesian conception of the mind – his heroes, Hegel, Heidegger and Merleau-Ponty – all had a deeply historicized conception of the task of philosophy. An understanding of the past is necessary, in his opinion, to furnish contemporary philosophy with perspectives distinct from the current status quo (Taylor 1984b: 20–22). But is this the *only* way? What about attending to synchronic rather than diachronic diversity, as Glock (2009: 90) asks, or indeed employing the imagination through thought experiment? While genealogical analyses would obviously be relevant if a given belief or practice deployed historical references that *could* be undermined (such as descriptions regarding the naturalness, or ubiquity of a state of affairs), are they relevant if there is no such explicit story that a genealogy could help to undermine? Or is there always a (deconstructive) story to tell about that which resists authorial intention, that which haunts us on account of the complicated inheritance of the words and concepts that we have been bequeathed and that are transformed with use (iterability) as Derrida might maintain? While one can attempt to give conditions for the use of a concept (without which you simply are not part of the language-game) as many analytic philosophers do, it might be alleged that the specification of such rules "would typically play only a minor role in characterizing what the word means, what concept(s) it expresses" (Cooper 2003: 8). The application of these terms might be reasonably stable, but their meaning might be fluid; certainly this is part of what Nietzsche's genealogies of punishment seek to show and something that Derrida's work further explores.

DECONSTRUCTION AND GENEALOGY

Although we address deconstruction in more detail elsewhere, it is worth noting here that the relation between deconstruction and genealogy is a close one.[2] Deconstruction inherits from Heidegger the idea of performing a destructive retrieval in relation to the history of philosophy, and binary oppositions in texts and culture more generally are seen to be pervasive. Moreover, because of the conviction that philosophy has certain constitutive blind spots, the whole point of deconstruction is to occupy the margins of philosophy: not wholly outside philosophy, but not quite within it either. Without leaving philosophy behind, and without announcing some new science (such as grammatology) or turning to literature instead, Derrida wants to practise a double reading, one that is literal and faithful to a text (or concept), and another that is more violent and transgressive, and disrupts stable or received certitudes. The latter cannot be merely capricious, however, or the deconstruction in question will have no force; it will be wilful and random. While this is precisely the charge that Searle (unfairly, for one of us) makes with respect to Derrida's reading of Austin, if we concede that this is not always the case in Derrida's deconstructions, then it might be maintained that a condition of possibility of deconstruction (which is said to be "always already" at work in texts) is that meaning is never simple, but always multiple (albeit not indeterminate) and this gives genealogy an ongoing role in problematizing texts. If words and concepts have a multifarious and complicated history that subsists in them, then the possibility of deconstructive readings is readily apparent. Indeed, it is no accident that etymology plays a fairly important role in deconstruction and continental philosophy generally. Such etymologies are often not strictly faithful, and yet it is not that they are simply made up *ex nihilo*. They attest to something conceptual, and thus something with which an etymologist could concur, but they also relate it to broader tendencies with cultures, epochs and traditions.

CONCLUSION: THE GENETIC AND ANTI-GENEALOGICAL FALLACIES

We have seen a number of worries expressed about genealogical analyses, notably that they risk being *ad hominem*, and confuse an analysis of origins with the evaluation or justification of the present (both charges are indebted to analytic philosophy's general worries about psychologism). Of course, there are features of a situation that can make an inference from genetic circumstances reasonable, as most analytics would concede. For instance, numerous philosophers have offered a "natural history" of God, in which the origins of religion are traced in societal power structures, individual psychology and so forth. If religious beliefs have their origins in wish-fulfilment, for instance, then although they may nonetheless be true, at the very least a non-theist explanation can now be given as to why religious belief is so prevalent. Genetic considerations play exactly this role – blocking certain arguments, perhaps shifting the onus of proof, adding coherence to a worldview – in analytic discussions of religion (Mackie 1983: ch. 10). Genetic questions are thus almost always a reasonable factor in any evaluation, and the minimal premise upon which genealogy would seem to rely – the claim that the past subsists, albeit in altered forms, in the present – does not seem particularly controversial, having conceptual and linguistic registers as well as more committal metaphysical ones.

A key motivation for genealogy is that it is linked with change, in that an important condition for transformation of a culture and society is to understand that the particular developments that have occurred are not inevitable. As such, one pragmatic reason for offering a genealogical account might be that recognition of something *as* an error (say that we generally act slavishly, or conservatively) is not itself a strong force for change, but the additional recognition of problematic psychological motivations through which the error has arisen may be more likely to induce change. As such, Nietzsche, Foucault and others might be seen to employ a double tactic, a double methodology: genealogies can provide relevant rational evidence, but they can also be rhetorically compelling as a force for change in a way that an argument on its own might not be.

Still, despite these ecumenically acceptable remarks, analytic philosophy is not strongly invested in genealogical enquiry. Is this because it falls victim to an anti-genealogical fallacy (J. Williams 2005: 114), the presupposition of an atemporal view from nowhere in which concepts are thought to be like manna from heaven (to redeploy Robert Nozick's phrase)? We here return to the common charge regarding the alleged atemporality and ahistoricality of analytic philosophy. Quine certainly advocated paying no attention to the history of philosophy and Gilbert Harman reputedly had a note on his door at Harvard that proclaimed "JUST SAY NO TO THE HISTORY OF PHILOSOPHY". Nonetheless, this is perhaps not an affliction that characterizes most analytic philosophers today. Glock, for example, contends that analytic philosophers are usually neither historiophobic nor anachronistic (distorted) in relation to the past, and in *Tales of the Mighty Dead*, Brandom says:

> There is a familiar perspective from which neither the historical story nor its metaphysical rationale would appear as of the first importance. Analytic philosophy in its youth was viscerally hostile both to historical philosophical enterprises and to systematic ones ... This self-understanding was never unanimous ... With time it has become clearer, I think, that commitment to the fundamental analytic credo – faith in reasoned argument, hope for reasoned argument and clarity of reasoned expression ... – is not incompatible with ... perhaps even requiring, both historical and systematic forms.   (2002: 1)

Atemporal tendencies in analytic philosophy there certainly are, however, and in this respect we find the divide running through the middle of the movement, rather than between it and the continental tradition. What Strawson calls the "Homeric struggle" within analytic philosophy of language, between "use theories" (emphasizing a context of application) and "truth-conditional theories" (using logical resources), is extremely widely known and keenly appreciated within the tradition: each side has trump cards, and cost assessments here are very difficult. For this very reason, however, many analytic philosophers will regard the charge of ahistoricism as hardly decisive; if the most intractable problems of meaning can be resolved merely by accepting the mathematician's heaven, then so be it.

In the main, continental philosophers, with their interest in the conceptual and historical presuppositions of thought, do not tend to (err in) this direction. Nietzsche famously says "only that which has no history can be defined" (1989: 2, §13), and in *The Will To Power* suggests that "what is needed above all is an absolute skepticism towards all inherited concepts" (1968: §409). Sometimes, continental philosophers do invite the charge of the genetic fallacy and it is no doubt an attendant risk of such forms of philosophizing. But such risks are not, in our view, discussion enders; rather, they are better understood as a call for more information. To invalidate a person's perspective because their view is understood to be symptomatic of their position in the class structure, or on the basis that it is merely an expression of unconscious wish-fulfilment, is clearly problematic. Forms of continental philosophy that proceed in this manner are just as coercive in their theories of meaning as the logical positivists were. Reasoning about a position on its own merits is indeed worthwhile. So is it the case that both of these extremes – ahistorical conceptual analysis, or historicized genealogy – are insufficient on their own? Perhaps, and that possibility is enough to motivate and take seriously intermediate positions. Although we can hence argue for the desirability of a rapprochement in regard to these extremes at this highly theoretical level, the devil is in the detail.

13. STYLE AND CLARITY

Stylistic differences between the traditions have been noticed (and parodied) from the very start. And while style is an intrinsically personal thing (Kripke has a different writing style from David Lewis, as do Derrida and Badiou, etc.), it is also difficult to dispute that there are some overlapping stylistic norms at play across these traditions. Of course, matters of style are obviously affected by the influences within each tradition; graduate programmes will inevitably end up socializing their students (usually via modelling rather than explicit directives) into particular ways of comporting themselves, both in written and oral communication. Analytic philosophers also generally self-identify as such (as do continental philosophers in Anglo-American countries), and certain overlapping tropes are also likely to flow from this self-identification, as well as an interest in demarcating such a philosophical style from other styles. It is hence perhaps not surprising that the history of "othering" of allegedly non-philosophical styles that was inaugurated by Russell continues to this day. The important question for us, however, is just what role these stylistic differences play in the divide. Are they symptomatic of underlying methodological or doctrinal commitments, or differences in their conception of the role of philosophy (perhaps creating perspectives versus limning reality), or are these stylistic differences the only real marker of the divide?

Those who argue that style is the main difference between the traditions tend to also have a deflationary view about the divide; indeed, they can point to stylistic variation in the common philosophical heritage (that between Aristotle and Plato, or between Spinoza and Berkeley, say) as evidence that stylistic difference need not indicate that philosophers fall within different traditions. We think, however, that style is not a sufficient explanation of the analytic–continental divide on its own, and that matters of style here are not easily separable from issues of both methodological practice and topical substance. We will hence draw together some of the different pragmatic and philosophical justifications given for these kinds of strategies and styles. They pertain, in the main, to the issue of the relation between the respective goals of clarity and creativity, and the omnipresence (on one view) of metaphysical assumptions in the language that we have inherited, as well as to aesthetic and sociopolitical issues.

STYLE VERSUS PHILOSOPHY, OR STYLE AND PHILOSOPHY

Whether or not it is descriptively accurate of current analytic practice, the tradition's self-image has repeatedly placed a premium on clarity and simplicity of expression. Arguments are to be isolated and put in the clearest possible form; confusion is to be avoided by particular attention to matters of language; claims are to be considered as such, and not to be left lurking behind hypostatized entities. The stylistic norms here are therefore linked closely both to the conception of philosophy as analysis (interpreted broadly, including such practices as reflective equilibrium, thought experiment and so on), and to the central role, for the analytic tradition, of explicit argument and reason-giving. Analytic philosophy prides itself on being clear, transparent and literal rather than figurative; the regulative ideal, at least, is a minimalist style that is plain-speaking (even if sometimes technical), in the effort to secure against ambiguity. As Moore put it in *Principia Ethica*:

> It appears to me that in Ethics, as in all other philosophical studies, the difficulties and disagreements, of which its history is full, are mainly due to a very simple cause: namely to the attempt to answer questions, without first discovering precisely *what* question it is which you desire to answer. I do not know how far this source of error would be done away, if philosophers would *try* to discover what question they were asking, before they set about to answer it; for the work of analysis and distinction is often very difficult: we may often fail to make the necessary discovery, even though we make a definite attempt to do so ... At all events, philosophers seem, in general, not to make the attempt, and, whether in consequence of this omission or not, they are constantly endeavouring to prove that "Yes" or "No" will answer questions, to which *neither* answer is correct, owing to the fact that what they have before their minds is not one question, but several, to some of which the true answer is "No", to others "Yes".   (1989: vii)

Somewhat more succinctly, in the *Tractatus*, Wittgenstein says: "Everything that can be put into words can be put clearly" (2003: 4.116). Of course, the Latin titles of both of these influential books sit somewhat uncomfortably with the plain-speaking and rhetoric-free (self-)interpretation of some analytic philosophers, what one might call the Carnap style. There are, of course, bravura stylists in analytic philosophy: Fodor and David Lewis, for one kind of example, or Wittgenstein for another – Wittgenstein remarks in *Culture and Value* that "philosophy really only ought to be written as poetic composition" (1984: 24). And there are, of course, stylistic fashions and tropes in analytic philosophy as with any other mode of writing: certain kinds of playfulness, certain kinds of dry remarks or in-jokes, deliberately *outré* ways of framing thought experiments and so on. The normative ideal is nonetheless generally to indulge such stylistic adornments only when clarity is not endangered. As we have seen, this is partly because much analytic work is seen as part of a communal project of problem identification and resolution, which aims at making the philosophical work of one integrate reasonably smoothly with that of another; this has immediate effects on style and the need for stylistic indicators of common reference or content.

For related reasons, Pascal Engel (1999) counter-poses the style of the straight line (AP) with the style of the circle (CP), and there is, we think, an important contrast to be drawn here with continental philosophy in this respect. While no continental philosopher thinks that they work alone, without a community, and while almost all thematize intersubjectivity in detail, the normative image of the philosopher is far more iconoclast and individualist than this. Moreover, it is preoccupied more with monographic books and diachronic issues in relation to the history of the entire tradition than with journal entries that reply to one another, and hope to build knowledge or understanding in a progressivist and quasi-scientific manner. Of course, some of the exegetical scholarship in journals such as *Kant-Studien* or *Heidegger Studies* does aim to develop knowledge on a particular thinker in a progressivist manner, and so there is perhaps a distinction to be drawn between interpreters and original philosophers. In respect of those with ambitions and claims to being original and systematic philosophers in their own right, Deleuze and Guattari interestingly remark at one point in *What is Philosophy?* that philosophy is syntagmatic whereas science is paradigmatic (1994: 124). Although such a diagnosis does not seem to be accurate when applied to analytic philosophy – or at least the self-conception of most analytic philosophers – on Deleuze and Guattari's view it is culture (and sometimes the artist, sometimes the scientist) that provokes and inspires the philosopher, but there is little hope for a communicative ethics among groups of philosophers working on similar problems that will gradually allow for progress in the discipline. Similar if less strident positions are held by many of the other major continental philosophers and this partly accounts for the different styles and techniques of the two traditions. Of course, Wittgenstein also remarked in

Zettel that "the philosopher is not a citizen of any community of ideas. That is what makes him a philosopher" (2007: §455), but if analytic philosophy in more recent times can be understood as paradigmatic, and as having a consequential dialogic conservatism as we have suggested, then tropes of clarity of expression and common sense are inevitable.

On the other hand, we might note that Nietzsche frequently attacks language as secondary, weak and falsifying of experience, and Bergson is also deeply distrustful of language. In *The Creative Mind*, he notes:

> Language is, I grant you, pervaded with science; but the scientific spirit demands that anything may be questioned at any moment, and language needs stability. Language is open to philosophy; but the philosophical spirit inclines towards endless renewal and reinvention, for that is how things work, whereas words have definite meaning, a relatively fixed conventional value: they only express the new as a recomposition of the old. This is usually and perhaps imprudently called "reason", the conservative logic that rules communal thinking: conversation sounds very much like conservation. (Quoted in Lecercle 2002: 21–2)

As Lecercle glosses this position in *Deleuze and Language*, words freeze concepts, and make any philosophy concerned with such concepts dependent on common sense. These kinds of Bergsonian worries have been carried on in Deleuze's work, and whatever we might want to say about a linguistic turn in continental philosophy, significant parts of this tradition are wary of language, especially in its representational functions. Moreover, there is rarely an advocation of communicative norms of rationality that are part of both ordinary conversation and philosophical discourse. Of course, Habermas and Apel are obvious exceptions in this regard, since they attempt to show that the everyday practices of linguistic communication provide the basis for a context-transcendent understanding of truth and the argumentative justification of validity claims. Nonetheless, according to Badiou's synoptic account of French philosophy post-1940, the sixth unifying factor of what he claims to be a period of philosophical richness on a par with only two other moments in history – ancient Greece, and early German idealism – is that all of the major figures aimed to create new forms of philosophical expression appropriate to the new forms of existence in modern life, particularly in regard to art, love, politics and science. They wanted "to create a new style of philosophical exposition, and so to compete with literature; essentially, to reinvent in contemporary terms the 18th-century figure of the philosopher-writer". The close relation between existentialism and literature is well known, but Badiou adds:

> In France, by the 1950s and 60s it was philosophy that was invent-
> ing its own literary forms in an attempt to find a direct expres-
> sive link between philosophical style and presentation, and the
> new positioning for the concept that it proposed ... It is at this
> stage that we witness a spectacular change in philosophical writ-
> ing. Forty years on we have, perhaps, grown accustomed to the
> writing of Deleuze, Foucault, Lacan; we have lost the sense of
> what an extraordinary rupture with earlier philosophical styles it
> represented. All these thinkers were bent upon finding a style of
> their own, inventing a new way of creating prose; they wanted to
> be writers.   (2005: 72–3)

We might add to the French philosophers Badiou mentions. For Irigaray and other of the "French feminists", neutral language is an illusion and to avoid the biases (including gendered) that are enshrined in language we need to use language in new ways. Indeed, for all these philosophers one might offer a political defence of complicated writing in relation to creativity and the new. Certainly it is clear that any interest in the conditions of possibility of the new (different) will incline one to look to performatively enact what is being philosophized about.

While Badiou's account of French philosophy is not meant to apply to all continental philosophy writ large, we can, to some extent, generalize his ana-lysis. Some German philosophers – for example Habermas, Axel Honneth and Apel – loom as possible exceptions, and this stylistic difference between French and German philosophy might help to explain Éric Alliez's (1997: 82) observation that there is an American–German alliance that centres around a renewed Kantianism and communicative ethics, and has figures such as Habermas, Gadamer, Brandom and other pragmatists involved. But even if this assessment is plausible, it seems to us that Badiou is nonetheless clearly being overtly patriotic when he restricts his ascription of stylistic innova-tions in philosophy to France. We might think of Adorno, for whom analytic philosophy's plain-speaking style is felt to be politically pernicious, feeding into a certain instrumental rationality characteristic of our technological age. Heidegger held related positions and his later work hence turned to poetic language, which is neither designative nor habitually sedimented, and can remind us of what has been taken for granted and foreclosed on by our technical uses of language. Antonio Negri, Georgio Agamben, Nietzsche, Kierkegaard, Walter Benjamin and Martin Buber are among many other non-French continental philosophers for whom style is vital to their phil-osophy, and where there is also a strong suspicion of communicative norms of everyday discourse and rationality providing any kind of telos for philoso-phy. If we extend Badiou's characterizations of post-1940s France to include many other continental philosophers (but not all: we are proposing family resemblance criteria, not necessary and sufficient conditions), we can see that the clichés about the styles of the differing traditions are not entirely false. While one side gives a negative valence to a given style, the other side gives a positive valence to that same style.

Writing of the style that analytic philosophers valorize, William Barrett complains, for example, that "an 'analytic' philosopher ... earns this title by grinding away at the consequences of this or that particular proposition as if filing a legal brief ... But philosophy is a way of seeing rather than the tedious business of a lawyer's brief" (1979: 66). Certainly the charges of logic-chopping and scholasticism are not uncommon, and this gripe that analytic philosophers are lawyer-like in their stipulations and problem-solving activities might be thought to include both ordinary-language philosophy and more formally oriented philosophers. Of course, it is not just continental philosophers who make such allegations. Dennett, for instance, is as impatient with much analytic work as he is with the continental style: "we philosophers tend to wander back and forth between cramped, blinkered, nibbling exercises on the one hand, and advertisements for grandiose but half-baked visions on the other" (2008: 22). Again, philosophers such as Cora Diamond (1996) and Raimond Gaita (1999), who are arguably neither analytic nor continental, reject much analytic moral philosophy on the basis that the vocabularies employed in these domains of thought does not allow these philosophers to get a grip on the lived experience that they are seeking to shed light on.

On the other hand, we have seen that Hare (1960: 115) alleges that continental philosophers produce "verbiage disguised as serious metaphysical inquiry", "build monstrous philosophical edifices" and so on. Hare's comments are uncharacteristic only for their candour and aggressiveness, rather than for the sentiments that they express. When analytic philosophers "other" continental philosophy, the key feature pointed to is almost inevitably the absence of the clarity required for one to be part of the game of giving and asking for reasons. For many analytic philosophers, reading the work of many continental philosophers involves an experience of the contravention of these norms; perhaps it even induces a feeling of a loss of integrity, as Williamson has noted (see Baggini & Stangroom 2002: 151). And this is not a one-way street, of course. It can be an uncanny experience reading any work that one is not familiar with (but perhaps especially philosophical work), and, as Glendinning emphasizes in *The Idea of Continental Philosophy*, this feeling of unease ensures that when justifications are given for a refusal to engage with any given "other", considerations to do with style are almost inevitably invoked.

Derrida's work, for example, is often claimed not to meet accepted standards of clarity and rigour. In their letter to *The Times* newspaper denouncing the award of Derrida's honorary doctorate by the University of Cambridge, Barry Smith and the other signatories contend that this is so "in the eyes of philosophers, and certainly among those working in leading departments of philosophy throughout the world" (Smith *et al.* 1992). Indeed, many post-modern or poststructuralist philosophers are criticized for threatening to reduce philosophy to style (Davey 1995). Such clichés, although frequently unfair, are not entirely false either. We have seen that continental philosophy often involves a move to a hermeneutics of textual interpretation and pays great attention to matters concerning expressive style. This is perhaps especially evident in Nietzsche, and in poststructuralist thinkers inspired by Nietzsche, including the strategy of textual reading with which Derrida and deconstruction have long been associated. Deconstruction begins with the assumption of something like the principle of charity and of respecting authorial intention, but then seeks to show at the level of consequences in the text (i.e. an *undecidable* word or concept that does not quite fit the logic of the argument) how such a principle proceeds to undermine and contaminate itself, and thereby opens the text to alternative reading(s) that problematize the author's avowed intentions. One attends with greater and greater specificity to the aporias and tensions of a text, sometimes playing creatively with the text. This preoccupation with style and textuality can be laboured. Reading Derrida's *Glas*, or Deleuze and Guattari's *Anti-Oedipus*, is tough going for many continental philosophers too. Who is not impatient with Derrida, Deleuze, Heidegger or Irigaray, at least from time to time, wishing that they would just tell us what they mean? Of course, this is not such a simple matter when one is attentive, as those working in the continental tradition almost invariably are, to the historical genealogy of concepts and ideas that persist in our manner of expression and contain various metaphysical assumptions: as Derrida says in *Limited Inc*, "one shouldn't complicate things for the pleasure of complicating, but one should also never simplify or pretend to be sure of such simplicity where there is none. If things were simple word would have gotten around" (1988: 119). Moreover, Derrida (and others) often offers arguments as to the necessary co-imbrication of stylistic concerns with those pertaining to content, as we see perhaps most famously in Derrida's *Dissemination* and the essay "Plato's Pharmacy", which contests the Platonic divide between the philosophers and the sophists. But are Derrida's arguments presented in the clear and distinct manner that analytic philosophers prefer and are accustomed to? They are not, and it is perhaps for this reason that Glendinning (2010) calls non-analytic ways of doing philosophy (including Derrida's) non-argumentocentric. While some would claim that any such mode of reasoning and persuading is not philosophy, this need not be the case, and the normative question is whether philosophy should embrace style (and even rhetoric) or seek to minimize it as much as possible because there are cognitive norms that serve to legislate in some manner what counts as a good philosophical style. As Engel puts the latter claim:

> any kind of inquiry must conform itself to certain cognitive norms, that the norms are, in an important sense, objective, and that a kind of philosophical inquiry which respects these norms will bear most of the characteristics of what is generally called "analytic philosophy", whereas other forms of philosophical practice, currently called "continental", do not bear these characteristics.
>
> (1999: 219)

Engel explicitly aligns such cognitive norms with the norms of common-sense communication, however, and here we reach another impasse. Should this common sense ground and anchor our philosophical styles and methods, or does that commit one's philosophy to theoretical conservatism, to being nothing more than the shuffling of the deck of cards, redistributing things from time to time? But what else might philosophy be? Critique, or "first philosophy"? These are both live possibilities, of course, and a central part of the self-understanding of many continental philosophers, but the critical disavowal (explicit or otherwise) of the importance of common sense frequently leads to accusations of mysticism and obscurantism, charges that are quite commonly levelled at many of the major continental philosophers. The stylistic differences between analytic and continental philosophers are hence not superficial as some have alleged. On the contrary, they are intrinsically bound up with an array of methodological differences that we have already enumerated in Part II, as well as the topical differences that we shall treat in Part III.

14. PHILOSOPHY, SCIENCE AND ART

This chapter concludes Part II's focus on method, by briefly analysing the respective conceptions of the role and value of philosophy in each tradition, as well as how it relates to scientific (and hence the relation of philosophy to naturalism) and artistic endeavours (and hence the relation of philosophy to concept creation).

PHILOSOPHY AND ART

Let us begin with art, which has historically been associated more with continental philosophy than analytic philosophy. It is uncontroversial to claim that almost all of the major continental philosophers have been heavily concerned with art (Husserl seems to be an exception), and with the relation of art to the creation of the new. In no particular order consider: Walter Benjamin, Adorno, Merleau-Ponty, Sartre, Derrida, Deleuze, Foucault, Heidegger, Bergson and so on. This is so, even if they propound inaesthetics, like Badiou, since this is just the name for the philosophical reflection on art that nonetheless gives art primacy with respect to philosophy, and even if some Marxist traditions have been highly wary of certain forms of art. On the other hand, Richard Campbell (2001) suggests, with some plausibility, that there is a tacit Platonism that persists in the analytic tradition. Even if few analytic philosophers will explicitly proffer a Platonic rejection of art and excise the poets from Athens, and even if there are plenty of analytic philosophers working in aesthetics and the philosophy of art (such as Nelson Goodman and Arthur Danto), an engagement with art is not mandatory for the major systematic philosophers in the tradition and as a group they are not preoccupied with art in the way that most continental philosophers are. How many analytic philosophers, for example, write multiple essays on an artist such as Paul Cézanne (as with Merleau-Ponty), or a book on Francis

Bacon (as with Deleuze's *Francis Bacon: The Logic of Sensation*)? We might think, equally, of Frankfurt School critical theorists, such as Benjamin and Adorno (whose writings on music, like Nietzsche's and Schopenhauer's, have been influential), as well as Heidegger's discussion of Van Gogh in "The Origin of the Work of Art" (collected in *Basic Writings*). Derrida has written *The Truth in Painting*, co-curated and written exhibitions at the Louvre (published as *Memoirs for the Blind: The Self-Portrait and Other Ruins*), and designed gardens with highly reputed architects (Peter Eisenmann). This trajectory has been extended in more recent times by Jacques Rancière, Bernard Stiegler, Jean-Luc Nancy, Elizabeth Grosz, Rosi Braidotti and others. Moreover, many continental philosophers have written for major art catalogues and journals. And it is not just the work of the usual suspects stemming from the continent that evinces this tendency. Most contemporary continental philosophers working in Anglo-American countries also have a reasonably thorough understanding of the history of art. Is this true of most analytic philosophers? Probably not. But, even if it were, it seems fair to maintain that it does not inflect their philosophical work. Do Anglo-American philosophers cite Jackson Pollock and Picasso? Not frequently. Few analytic philosophers write novels, as have Sartre, Simone de Beauvoir, Julia Kristeva and Badiou, and the existentialists saw their literary outputs as not radically different in kind from their philosophical treatises, just as analyses of poetry have been philosophically central to Heidegger (Rainer Maria Rilke, etc.) and Derrida (Stephan Mallarmé, Paul Celan, etc.), who have both used poetic techniques in their philosophical writings. Badiou even claims that much of twentieth-century French philosophy is explicitly an attempt to come to terms with not only changes that had swept society, but also changes that swept the world of art. Of the period between 1940 and the 1990s he writes:

> French philosophers evinced a profound attraction to modernity. They followed contemporary artistic, cultural and social developments very closely. There was a strong philosophical interest in non-figurative painting, new music and theatre, detective novels, jazz and cinema, and a desire to bring philosophy to bear upon the most intense expressions of the modern world. Keen attention was also paid to sexuality and new modes of living. In all this, philosophy was seeking a new relation between the concept and the production of forms – artistic, social, or forms of life.   (2005: 71)

When it comes to political philosophy, to give another example, few analytic philosophers devote any kind of sustained attention to the political value of art, but in *What is Philosophy?*, Deleuze and Guattari famously suggest that it

154

is vital to the summoning forth of a new people and a new earth, thus breaching the boundaries between art and politics, as does Rancière in his *Politics of Aesthetics* and various related works.

Continental philosophy has dominated literary theory in the United States, where Derrida, Paul De Man and others made a big impact. It also dominated cinema studies and film theory until perhaps the early 1990s. Certainly while psychoanalysis, structuralist, Marxist, critical theory and poststructuralist perspectives dominated film theory in the 1970s and 1980s, Noël Carroll and others instituted an analytic-cognitivist turn against this "grand theory". Today, analytic philosophy of film has begun to dominate the field, a development that Robert Sinnerbrink (2010) argues threatens to amount to a philosophical disenfranchisement of film (see Bordwell & Carroll 1996). While it is also the case that post-analytic philosophers such as Cavell and Stephen Mulhall have done important work in film, and the artistic terrain more generally, it is only recently that the research paradigm of analytic philosophy has played a significant role in discourse about film, both within and outside of philosophy.

PHILOSOPHY AND SCIENCE

It is equally uncontroversial to claim that many of the major analytic philosophers have been heavily concerned with science and the interplay between philosophy and science (in no particular order consider Russell, Hempel, Carnap, Popper, Reichenbach, Salmon, Dretske, Dennett, Fodor). But this is much less univocal a tradition; an equally distinguished list of major analytic philosophers are clearly resistant of this trend (consider Dummett, Wittgenstein, Alvin Plantinga, Davidson, Putnam, Chisholm, Sellars, Lewis), and have quite distinct views of the value of philosophy (some more and some less friendly to the sciences). Terry Pinkard (1999) is correct to note that "respect for science and a naturalistic outlook tends to run high in American analytic philosophy, much less so in British analytic philosophy". Indeed, in his latest book, Michael Dummett suggests that the transatlantic divergence with respect to naturalism is perhaps the beginning of a further divide within analytic philosophy:

> If the scientism so prevalent within present-day American philosophy is intensified, a breach may open up between present analytic philosophy as practiced in the UK and as practiced in Britain and continental Europe. This in itself may help to bring about rapprochement between European philosophers of different traditions. (2010: 150)

While debates about the relation between philosophy and science are hence hotly contested within analytic philosophy itself, there is nothing like the quasi-utopian understanding of their profession maintained by some continental philosophers. This difference can partly be explained by the adoption, within much of the analytic tradition, of Hume as the first contemporary philosopher, and of a corresponding disregard for the fusion of normative and non-normative claims, and we have seen that most continental philosophers – from the Frankfurt School, to phenomenological arguments for the normativity of their descriptions of being-in-the-world, to Levinas, Derrida and others – maintain that there is a necessary co-imbrication of the "is" and the "ought".

While some analytic philosophers maintain that the job of the philosopher is simply to clarify the discourses of the sciences (a view that is arguably not shared by any continental philosophers), perhaps by also eliminating folk psychological ideas that do not reflect these findings, many more analytic philosophers conceive of the philosophical task as an attempt to integrate the disparate knowledge claims of the sciences with everyday folk psychology and common sense. This requires something like a process of perennial updating, back and forth adjustments between philosophical (cum scientific) views and folk psychology, in attempt to maintain reflective equilibrium. Given that science is certainly changing all the time, analytic philosophy, which endeavours to be responsive to this, must consequently also change all of the time. On both of these understandings, however, it is clear that there is something of a deferential relation to the ideal findings of the sciences (certain of which are more privileged than others). The deference at play here involves an interesting phenomenon that is worth bringing out explicitly. Naturalizing philosophers in the Quinean tradition regard philosophy as continuous with, but constrained by, the deliverances of the relevant natural sciences and mathematics. Such continuity and constraint imply inferential connections between the two, and in fact this is a common naturalistic move. Quine's ruling scepticism out of court in naturalized epistemology, for instance, amounts to making his philosophical conclusions conditional on the sciences he trusts being right. Yet if a conditional connection is made out between a scientific matter and a piece of philosophy in this way, one might think *both* sides are hostage to it. If the scientific claim turns out to be true, the philosophical claim follows by *modus ponens*. But if the debate in philosophy goes against that philosophical claim, *modus tollens* tells us that the scientific claim is false as well. Of course, naturalizing philosophers are not at all inclined to draw that conclusion; rather, they will diagnose philosophical pathology. The conditional here is a *one-way* conditional, so to speak. Hence analytic deference to science – wherever it exists – is generally rather stronger than a mere continuity claim. The deference here is genuinely to the sciences, too; by contrast, *within* the analytic literature no such one-way conditionals can be readily discerned. Where inferential connections between different philosophical positions are accepted, analytic philosophers are apt to employ both *ponens* and *tollens*.

Continental philosophy's engagement with the sciences is generally both critical and transformative. It is rarely about establishing reflective equilibrium between the knowledge claims of various domains. It may be foundationalist in regard to science, as is the case with Husserl's projected rigorous science of consciousness that would establish a foundation for particular knowledge claims (especially those concerning logic and mathematics), and Heidegger's ontico-ontological project, in which, for example, biogenetic and sociological treatments of death are both said to presuppose his own existential analysis of death (1962: §52). On the other hand, continental philosophers might also see the sciences as privileged points of provocation, as akin to a stimulus for reflection. There are more than two possibilities, of course, but the point we want to establish here is that the overarching aim is usually not the coherentist conception of philosophy as showing how each of the differing knowledge claims can be reconciled within an overall worldview (e.g. physicalism). Although we have seen that many contemporary phenomenologists are engaged with the cognitive sciences in a manner that makes them coherentists of a sort, it remains the case that the majority of continental philosophers typically critically/creatively engage with science (non-deferentially), or are uninterested in the so-called hard sciences, or are comparatively ignorant of it. This is not to reinstate the account offered by Sokal and Bricmont in their infamous *Fashionable Nonsense*, and nor is it to deny that Badiou and Deleuze, for example, are well apprised with Zermelo–Frankel set theory and differential calculus, respectively. The deferential relation is not apparent in Deleuze's work, however, and in Badiou's work love, art and politics are equally as privileged as science. This is also the case with other important continental philosophers of science such as Gaston Bachelard and Georges Canguilhem (1988; see also Norris 2000). Similarly Husserl was thoroughly invested in the sciences and mathematics (non-deferentially), and his and Heidegger's anthropology and use of the term *Lebenswelt* (life-world) was influenced by Jacob Von Uexküll's discussions of animals and humans, just as Merleau-Ponty was profoundly influenced by Gestalt psychology and Bergson was by Darwinian evolution. Badiou sums up post-1940s French philosophy as wanting to "abandon the opposition between philosophy of knowledge and philosophy of action, the Kantian division between theoretical and practical reason, and to demonstrate that knowledge itself, even scientific knowledge, is actually a practice". As he elaborates on this point:

> French philosophers sought to wrest science from the exclusive domain of the philosophy of knowledge by demonstrating that, as

a mode of productive or creative activity, and not merely an object of reflection or cognition, it went far beyond the realm of knowledge. They interrogated science for models of invention and transformation that would inscribe it as a practice of creative thought, comparable to artistic activity, rather than as the organization of revealed phenomena. This operation, of displacing science from the field of knowledge to that of creativity, and ultimately of bringing it ever closer to art finds its supreme expression in Deleuze.

(2005: 70–71)

If Badiou's account is at all plausible – and we think it is both in relation to France and also, to some extent, more widely – nothing like this takes place in analytic philosophy of science. Instead, there is typically an acceptance that science is correct *tout court* (or at least that privileged sciences such as physics and mathematics are correct), and then philosophers have the job of accommodating other dimensions of experience with these fundamental truth claims. Another way to highlight this contrast might be to observe that the alliance of philosophy, science and common sense amounts to something like a Holy Trinity for Russell. Indeed, Russell cannot forgive Plato, Spinoza, Hegel and Bergson because "they remained 'malicious' in regard to the world of science and common sense" (1914: 48–9). We do not want to exaggerate the sense in which continental philosophy, indebted to the masters of suspicion, rejects common sense and science, but the attitude to both is generally one of critical wariness. It is not that science is wrong, or that it has not enabled us all to live well, in certain respects. The notion that science is solely disclosive of truth is, however, typically felt to be of a piece with scientism, and with the work of the Frankfurt School and Heidegger any such privilege given to science is associated with a calculative way of thinking that is considered to be cause for concern, since philosophical questions are themselves thus abjured and it is felt to have consequences for society writ large. Instrumental reasoning is thus privileged, along with a co-imbrication of science and technology, which is discussed at length in Lyotard's *The Postmodern Condition*. Without considering this social dimension further, there are myriad theoretical concerns about scientific reductivism expressed by Bachelard, Merleau-Ponty, Husserl, Deleuze and Habermas, to mention but a few.

CONCLUSION

Obviously a concern with art and a concern with science are not sufficient to make one a continental philosopher or an analytic philosopher, respectively, and hopefully no one would propound such a crude account. Is there nothing to be said regarding the divide in this respect? Glendinning (2007: 8) argues that our relation to science, and its contested status as Western culture's epistemological ideal, is the major split within academic philosophy, but, for him, it is a schism that cannot be understood in terms of continental philosophy as predominantly anti-science versus analytic philosophy as predominantly pro-science. A concern with avoiding generality and clichés is a great virtue of Glendinning's book, but in this case we think he blinds himself to the obvious. There are exceedingly few, if any, thoroughgoing scientific naturalists in continental philosophy (perhaps Meillassoux is close), contrary to the analytic tradition where they feature reasonably heavily. Despite a certain philosophy of science reading of his work that has been promulgated in recent times, the following quote from Deleuze's *Difference and Repetition* captures what is arguably the prevailing "continental" mood: "every time science, philosophy and good sense come together it is inevitable that good sense should take itself for science and a philosophy (that is why such encounters must be avoided at all costs)" (1994: 224). Certainly there is a suspicion of strong scientific naturalism evinced in the work of the vast majority of continental philosophers ever since Husserl, and there are also a great many phenomenological and ontological accounts of nature (e.g. Merleau-Ponty), something that most analytic philosophers would find untenable (even McDowell is not prepared to go this far in *Mind and World*). As such, there are enough overlapping ideas about the power of philosophy and its relation to science to say that this is an important difference between the two traditions, even though there is nothing like unanimity in the relation between analytic philosophy and science.

Of course, to say that continental philosophy of science is generally quite distinct from analytic naturalism does not provide much by way of a description of what is distinctive about continental philosophy since there are, again, many ways in which one might not be an analytic naturalist. Even our slightly weaker contention that there is a significant difference between continental philosophy's critical and transformative engagements with science and the deferential relation to the best (or ideal) findings of the sciences in much analytic philosophy (which helps with various other family resemblance features to give it a minimal unity) is still to define continental philosophy by exclusion. But we are not seeking here to establish the philosophical unity of analytic and continental philosophy, respectively, simply by pointing to some of the differences it exhibits when contrasted with the other tradition's engagements with science and art. Rather, we hope to have begun to exhibit a kind of package deal in their respective methodological preferences and commitments throughout Part II and we now turn to some of the topical differences that follow from this.

PART III
INTERPRETATION OF KEY TOPICS

In Part III of this book, we examine some topical consequences of the traditions' respective methodological preferences. Of course, any comparative project of this kind will be partial, since analytic and continental philosophers do not so much give divergent answers to the same questions as divergent answers to different questions. The standard differentiations between the subdisciplines of philosophy – that is, epistemology, metaphysics, ethics and so on – are usually not treated in strict separation by continental philosophers; on the other side, connections between them that are taken seriously in analytic philosophy have no continental equivalent. Nonetheless, we think a topic-based approach to difference (and potential interaction and rapprochement) has its merits. For instance, the differing analytic and continental attitudes to representationalism about the mind and the significance of the body come out fairly clearly by considering the way the philosophy of mind and action have developed in the two traditions (as we do in Chapter 18); again, differing attitudes to the epistemological tradition, expressivist manoeuvres, representationalism and folk psychology can be brought out by considering the problem of other minds (as we do in Chapter 20). Again, the differing attitudes of the two traditions to a series of metaphysical and/or semantic issues can be brought out at least in part by considering the subjects of ontology (Chapter 15), truth and objectivity (Chapter 16) and time (Chapter 17). We are thus able to pinpoint some of the key points of methodological and topical difference that have (in the main) hindered dialogue and rapprochement, while also revealing their overarching different conceptions of the importance and value of philosophy itself.

Of course, in any such exercise, fairly short shrift has to be given to the variety on offer within each tradition, but a discussion that focuses on central tendencies has other merits. For instance, it can bring out the kinds of similarity relations that back a (minimal) family resemblance account of each tradition. This is a fairly uncontroversial suggestion with respect to analytic philosophy, although there has been some rethinking within that tradition of the importance of the usual indicators (as in Williamson's identification of a representationalist, rather more than linguistic, turn). However, we think it is also possible to justify a family resemblance characterization of continental philosophy in part on topical grounds; there is a characteristically continental attitude to time (notwithstanding some obvious disputes), an anti-representationalism about the mind, an anti-theoretical approach to ethics and politics, and an enduring concern with intersubjectivity. Together with the undeniable ties of influence within the tradition of such figures as Kant, Nietzsche, Husserl and Heidegger, these commonalities suggest that the tradition is rather more than an opposition that is defined into existence by analytic border guards trying to establish what analytic philosophy is not.

15. ONTOLOGY AND METAPHYSICS

"First philosophy", in the sense of mere metaphysics, is common to both traditions: analytic and continental philosophers reflect on the nature, structure and inhabitants of the world. But "first philosophy" has also been taken to be the view that such metaphysical/ontological enquiry is to precede empirical enquiry, common sense or the deliverances of the sciences, and this has always been contested within the analytic tradition. Important worries about such first philosophies were expressed at the outset and subsequently, and partly because of the premium placed on avoiding nonsense or tautology through careful linguistic or conceptual analysis, analytic philosophy has tended to more piecemeal projects in this field. Even if contemporary analytic philosophy has considerably broadened its metaphysical horizons, many analytic philosophers would nonetheless contend that this kind of caution remains a necessary safeguard against speculative metaphysics and/or nonsense. On the other hand, the positivist thread within analytic philosophy can be overstated; abstract metaphysics has obviously been revived since the "modal revolution" in philosophical logic and philosophy of language, and much contemporary analytic work is influenced by "analytically co-opted" metaphysicians such as McTaggart.

By contrast, it seems evident that continental philosophers by and large (even with the declarations of the death of philosophy as any kind of ultimate arbiter of knowledge) retain a strong commitment to first philosophy and to ontology, at least in the minimal sense that a preoccupation with Being is part and parcel of the scene (even where it is contested). We should not conclude, however, that continental philosophy is entirely blind to analytic philosophy's worries about first philosophy. While Husserl and Heidegger offer first philosophical projects, turning the page on what has gone before and calling for a new philosophical beginning, the continental tradition also encompasses a historicist concern with such pronouncements and their associated transcendental claims, and philosophers such as Derrida and Deleuze hence shy away from according philosophy any privileged role *vis-à-vis* other disciplines (although the latter still sees philosophy as privileged in regard to concept creation). Even Badiou begins his magnum opus, *Being and Event*, by noting that, "there is a general agreement that speculative systems are inconceivable" (2007: 2). It is no longer a question of asking "'How is pure mathematics possible?' and responding: thanks to a transcendental subject. Rather: pure mathematics being the science of being, how is the subject possible?" (*ibid.*: 6). Philosophy is not ontology on this account (rather, set-theoretical mathematics literally *is* ontology). As becomes clear in Badiou's *Manifesto for Philosophy*, the role of philosophy is to mediate between (or demonstrate as compossible) set theory and what he calls the "truth procedures" of art, love, politics and science. Given this, we must complicate any suggestion that continental philosophy is preoccupied with first philosophy and analytic philosophy is not. It is perhaps fair to say, however, that in the analytic, rather more than the continental, tradition, first philosophical projects are perpetually questioned on epistemological grounds. Before exploring this disparity, let us start with a brief recitation of Heidegger and Sartre on two of the more disquieting philosophemes for most analytic philosophers: Being and Nothingness.

BEING AND NOTHINGNESS: HEIDEGGER, SARTRE AND BEYOND

Suggesting that the whole corpus of Western philosophy has posited the *presence* of things as the ultimate reality and therefore the proper object of philosophical investigation, Heidegger famously asserts in *Being and Time* (1927) that the entire tradition has thereby ignored the most fundamental philosophical problem in the process; the problem of that which allows things to be present at all, or what he calls the problem of Being. The term "Being" has a long history in philosophy as the most universal but indefinable concept; it is frequently invoked but, on Heidegger's view, rarely understood. This is partly an issue of ineffability; Being exceeds all of our resources for attempting to describe it and Heidegger hence deliberately resists any such project. While the question of Being is necessarily shrouded in darkness, Heidegger argues that we do have some lived understanding of the meaning of Being, albeit a vague one, and it is for this reason that our *own existence* is at issue in pursuing this apparently opaque question. Being is presupposed in all our everyday practices, and the tension between our lived understanding of Being and the philosophical tradition's inability to offer any cogent theoretical account of it underlies the need to ask about the meaning of Being. For Heidegger, ontology just is the study of Being, or the conceptually developed account of that which allows things to be, and Heidegger opposes his procedure of "fundamental ontology" (concerned with Being) both to traditional metaphysics (concerned with what *is*, and focusing on particular beings of the world, rather than Being *per se*) and to scientific enquiries into facts. Ontic enquiry examines entities, beings, that which is present; ontological enquiry examines that which allows entities to be, "presencing", or Being. Heidegger argues that this difference has been covered over and ignored, and he suggests that this is because philosophers have been ill at ease with time (hence the title of his book), invariably construing Being as timeless, eternal and unchanging. Philosophers have sought to make Being present, *either* in empirical things (beings) *or* in the realm of that which is transcendent and "otherworldly" (such as the changeless and eternal world of Plato's Forms). Rather than consider the question of Being – the fundamental ontological question of what allows empirical things to show up for us, and for there to be a meaningful "world" – Western philosophy has frequently posited one special thing that makes all of the other empirical things possible. Most obvious among these explanations is God, but Heidegger holds that other ontologies ("onto-theologies") equally rely on a transcendent thing that makes possible all the other things (this is also roughly what Derrida deconstructs as being committed to a "metaphysics of presence").

In *Being and Nothingness* (1943), Sartre foregrounds the importance of nothingness and negation. This project has important predecessors, most obviously in Hegel, but also in Heidegger. In the early chapter "The Origin of Negation", Sartre looks at some preontological experiences of negation that we have, and argues that they suggest an ontology. He brings forward and analyses three main phenomena in considering negation: our ability to pose a question, our pre-reflective apprehension of destruction and our apprehension of absence. In regard to destruction, Sartre suggests on one level there is not *less* after the storm, just something else (1993: 8). What we (humans) apprehend on a pre-reflective, or a pre-judicative level – that is, before judgement – is this destruction. Generally, we do not have to reflectively judge that a building has been destroyed, even if this sometimes undoubtedly is the case. We disengage from the "given" (the mass of rubble) to see it in terms of that which it is *not* – the building, say, in its former glory before being wrecked by the storm (*ibid.*). Humans introduce the possibility of destruction into the world (and they simultaneously apprehend and introduce fragility into the world), since objectively there is just a change. But Sartre claims that this introduction of a *negatite*, as he calls it (a coinage indicating something like negativity), is not through an act of judgement. Rather, we apprehend the nothingness, and we disengage from the given, prior to reflection. Sartre's basic question is: how could we accomplish this unless we are a being by whom nothingness comes into the world, that is, free? Of course, there are various obvious replies that Sartre argues against, including that such *negatites* are just imposed by our mind, and are thus subjective or psycho-logical and not warranting any ontology of Being and Nothingness. We can-not consider this in any detail here, except to say that Sartre has to establish that non-being does come to reality only through humans, and also deny that non-being is thereby an abstraction, merely subjective or psychological (see Catalano 1985: 55).

In regard to absence, Sartre famously describes walking into a cafe expect-ing his friend Pierre, and immediately having an intuition of Pierre's absence (rather than making a rational judgement that Pierre is not present). When he looks at the next person to come in, he nihilates them; that is, he imme-diately sees them in terms of what they are not – Pierre. Nor is it that Sartre can find Pierre's absence in some precise spot in the cafe. His point is that this absence pervades the entire room and everything in it. Now Sartre's expectation for Pierre to be there obviously in some sense brings about the absence of Pierre. But Sartre argues that he discovers the absence, again pre-judicatively. He finds it in the cafe, and it is, he says, an "objective fact for that moment" (1993: 10). If we try to play some kind of mental game, and flippantly judge, for example, that the pope or the president is also not in the cafe, while the content of the judgement is true, it does not engage us in the same way (*ibid.*). Hence judging that someone is not there through reflec-tive thought is phenomenologically entirely different from the pre-reflective case. The point, again, is that we could not apprehend absence, and perceive that which is not in the cafe, were consciousness not radically separate from the realm of things (*ibid.*: 27). Such analyses (presented here very schemati-cally) are the foundation for Sartre's insistence on our radical freedom. All of his various examples of negation involve a rupture, or a break, from what is given, or from that which *is*, to posit that which is not given. Sartre con-cludes that particular instances of negation are made possible by non-being (or nothingness) and not the other way around. Nothingness is part of the ontology of the human–world relation.

Of course, some continental philosophers (e.g. Levinas and Marcel) think that philosophies of Being are a mistake, and some (Nietzsche and perhaps Deleuze) oppose philosophies of becoming to those of Being, but familiarity with philosophies of Being is certainly a major branch, if not the trunk, of the continental tree. While Derrida might quibble about aspects of Heidegger's ontico-ontological difference, and might foreground the distinct non-neutrality of Heidegger's allegedly neutral fundamental ontology (see *Aporias*), the questions that Heidegger is interested in are not to be dismissed as a non-starter, or an obvious linguistic error, as they have been by many analytic philosophers. In Levinas's case, although his book *Otherwise than Being or Beyond Essence* continues his critical relation with Heidegger (and to philosophies of Being more generally), structurally there are similarities between Heidegger's critique of the metaphysics of presence and Levinas's rejection of what he calls the "imperialism of the same", in which the philosopher's predilection for knowledge attempts to domesticate and absorb all that is unknown within a totalizing system of categories. Levinas, however, holds the first question of philosophy to be not ontological (in either Heidegger or Quine's sense) but rather the proto-ethical question: how does my being justify itself?

ANALYTIC METAPHYSICS

Contemporary analytic metaphysics is, to some extent, the return to a project that the older analytic tradition had put into question. Many contemporary metaphysicians see continuities between their own practice and the Aristotelian project of accounting for being *qua* being, or Leibnizian metaphysical system-building. In this sense, there can be a "pre-critical" flavour to analytic metaphysical work, which can weigh up arguments and appeal to metaphysical principles (the identity of indiscernibles, the truthmaker principle, the principle of unrestricted composition), and do so with the intention of getting at the structure of the world, rather than merely the structure of our concepts. However, although an often rationalist past is drawn on, the empiricist tendency in analytic philosophy remains very influential, and much work in this mode retains the flavour of the linguistic turn.

The upshot can appear to be something of a conscious disconnection between epistemology and practice; as Sider puts it:

> I follow the descriptive metaphysician in taking ordinary belief about metaphysical matters seriously, but follow the prescriptive metaphysician in aspiring to more than autobiography. This conception of the nature of metaphysics is, I suspect, common to many of the practitioners of contemporary analytic metaphysics. Unfortunately, I also share with my fellow practitioners the lack of a good answer to a very hard follow-up question: why think that *a priori* reasoning about synthetic matters of fact is justified?
>
> (2001: xiv–xv)

Sider's reply, in effect, is to appeal to the conception of metaphysics as attempting to make coherent or model our (defeasible) common-sense beliefs; a kind of reflective equilibrium and appeal to theoretical virtue at once. The process licenses appeal to intuition (the small considerations out of which David Armstrong [1978] builds his case for universals, say, or the extent to which Chisholm's [1989] notion of an event captures all our common beliefs about them), but imposes theoretical constraints as well. In effect, it allows for the positing of metaphysical entities (particular accounts of propositions, facts, states of affairs, events, properties and so forth) to meet explanatory needs arising from common opinion; it also allows for the adjustment of common opinion to preserve theoretical virtues that particular metaphysical accounts enjoy.

This is the kind of activity best displayed, rather than described, and Davidson's (2001c) seminal work on events provides a straightforward example.[1] Consider (1a) and (2a) below:

(1a) Brutus murdered Caesar.
(2a) Brutus murdered Caesar quickly.

If we were to translate these sentences into an appropriate logic, the natural approach would involve picking a two-place relation to hold between the terms in each case, yielding a pair of sentences with the forms of (1b) and (2b):

(1b) F(Brutus, Caesar)
(2b) G(Brutus, Caesar)

But, Davidson points out, this will not do. Whereas (2a) logically entails (1a), (2b) does not logically entail (1b); a structural component respecting this relation has been effaced. Yet what could the structural component be? Davidson argues that our only plausible alternative is to think of the underlying logical structure of sentences such as (1a) and (2a) as something like:

(1c) There is an x such that (x is an event and F(x, Brutus, Caesar))
(2c) There is an x such that (x is an event and F(x, Brutus, Caesar) and x is quick)

Now the required inferential connections are respected. But the consequence is that the adverbial constructions involved in our ordinary beliefs commit us to the existence of events. Hence, Davidson thinks, we have reason to posit such entities. Notice that here a theoretical constraint is defeasibly imposed (we do not want to lightly ignore the semantics of language suggested by the logical discoveries of analytic philosophy), but so too is a defeasible commitment to common sense (we are disposed to accept the ontological commitments uncovered in our ordinary way of speaking).

Consider such work in the light of Russell's views on the relation between metaphysics and logic during his logical atomist period. In the last of his 1918 "Lectures on Logical Atomism" ("Excursus into Metaphysics: What There Is"), Russell remarks:

I think the importance of philosophical grammar is very much greater than it is generally thought to be. I think that practically all traditional metaphysics is filled with mistakes due to bad grammar … [by analysis] you can get down in theory, if not in practice, to ultimate simples, out of which the world is built, and … those simples have a kind of reality not belonging to anything else.

(1956: 269–70)

Russell makes it clear that analysis is meant to primarily cut away apparent metaphysical commitments, and the simples are more or less posited simply as the thinnest set of metaphysical commitments that will correspond to the logical form uncovered by these analyses. This picture is updated for the post-positivist analytic tradition in Quine's very influential 1948 essay "On What There Is" (1953a). Quine believes that our basic standard of ontological commitment is provided by the existential quantifier: I am committed to there being whatever I am existentially quantifying over in my statements about the world; "to be is to be the value of a bound variable". But, like Russell, Quine also holds that such commitments can alter as we learn ways of paraphrasing our statements that avoid such quantification. This is, broadly, the tradition that Davidson is working in.

The Quinean approach to metaphysical questions is arguably dominant in analytic philosophy today. Quine's own tilt towards privileging the ontological commitments of science is much less popular, however; moreover, Quinean scruples within logic have been largely set aside with the rise of possible world semantics. As Michael Loux and Dean Zimmerman point out, the difficulties that result when we try to be Quinean in such an environment, in turn, explain the metaphysical methodology sketched above:

> Quine's criterion of ontological commitment was very import-
> ant to philosophers like Chisholm and Lewis. Both are rightly
> regarded as champions of a chastened approach to metaphysics:
> one that neither shies away from the traditional problems of ontol-
> ogy, nor falls back into the arcane, untethered system-building that
> had given metaphysics a bad name; and both regarded Quine's
> criterion as an antidote to the besetting sins of traditional meta-
> physicians … The metaphysics of Chisholm, and, later, Lewis look
> nothing like Quine's, however. For Quine, it is the deliverances of
> science alone that should determine our ontological commitments
> … Once all our ordinary convictions are taken into account, the
> traditional problems of metaphysics return with a vengeance, as
> they do not for Quine. As a result, ontology must be responsive to
> other areas of philosophy; a particular ontological scheme shows

its adequacy by its usefulness in the resolution of problems else-where. Desiderata for an ontological scheme include both sim-plicity (a point about which Quine would agree) and scope. One metaphysical system is superior to another in scope in so far as it allows for the statement of satisfactory philosophical theories on more subjects – theories that preserve, in the face of puzzle and apparent contradiction, most of what we take ourselves to know.

(2003: 4–5)

This metaphysically optimistic tradition is arguably dominant today, but it has many analytic sceptics. The deflation of metaphysical questions to seman-tic issues is still extant, occasionally under the influence of the positivists (Carnap's "Empiricism, Semantics and Ontology" is key here), and occasion-ally because metaphysical work is "read down" as conceptual enquiry, or implicitly stipulative definition. Finally, there is a long-standing tradition of more overtly "prescriptive" metaphysics within analytic philosophy, occasion-ally inspired by innovations in logic (such as plural quantification). And at this point, the analytic tradition and the revisionary projects of continental metaphysics have recently come into some contact.

BEING: A LINGUISTIC ERROR

One way of coming at the "divide" is in terms of whether or not there is a real question that Heidegger (and the post-Heideggerians indebted to him) is concerned with in the opening sections of *Being and Time* (1962: §1–8), or whether this question rests on a linguistic confusion and is essentially meaningless. Carnap, of course, intimated the latter in his engagement with Heidegger in "The Elimination of Metaphysics Through Logical Analysis of Language"; the use of "being" as a noun can be analysed in terms that deny the need for a theme of Being. There are similar worries about philosophies of Being expressed by Ayer, Quine, Peter van Inwagen, and Paul Edwards in *Heidegger's Confusions* (2004). Continental philosophy is considered by Ayer, for example, to be "very largely an exercise in the art of misusing the verb 'to be'" (quoted in Heinemann 1953: 4). For him, talk about being and nothingness in Heidegger and Sartre is just logical incompetence, akin to the pre-Kantian mistake of taking existence to be a property (Ayer 1952: 43–4). Van Inwagen holds that the Heideggerian reawakening of the question of the meaning of Being is untenable: "it is my position that the questions Heidegger wishes to make once more available to us were never really there" (2009: 474). He goes on to suggest that: "what Austin said of 'exist' … he might equally well have said of 'be': 'The word is a verb, but it does not describe something that things do all the time, like breathing, only quieter – ticking over, as it were, in a metaphysical sort of way'". Van Inwagen adds that:

> the vast difference between me and a table does not consist in
> our having different sorts of being (*Dasein, dass sein,* "that it is");
> it consists rather in our having vastly different sorts of nature
> (*Wesen, was sein,* "what it is") … Sartre and Heidegger and all
> other members of the existential-phenomenological tradition are,
> if I am right, guilty of ascribing to the "being" of things features
> of those things that should properly be ascribed to their natures.
> That is why they deny that being is the most barren and abstract
> of all categories. (*Ibid.*: 477–8)

On this view, Quine's criterion of ontological commitment – that we are committed to the existence of those things that are quantified over (posited in locutions of the form "There is an *x* such that …") in our best scientific theories – captures the univocal sense of being or existence. Van Inwagen concedes that Heidegger and others like him would have a ready response to this: "what Quine calls 'the ontological question' (What is there?) Heidegger would dismiss as merely the most general ontic question" (*ibid.*: 474). As Max Deutscher (2009: 36) puts a version of this reply, while a Quinean might argue that the comment "horses have being" can be understood as the same as "there is at least one thing that is a horse", Heidegger might *always* reply by asking for the meaning of "is" when we make this latter claim. Admittedly, one can make the question of Being something without possible rejoinder or objection in this manner, by saying that any formal grounds for putting the question out of bounds already presuppose an uncritical answer to it, but the existential phenomenological tradition would certainly maintain, along with speculative metaphysicians such as Bergson and Whitehead, that "existence is more than the silent, featureless pendant of the 'existential' quantifier ('for some x'). The 'is' of existence is not to be reduced to the 'is' of instantiation" (Bradley 2003: 438).

Of course, van Inwagen's position is not without critics within analytic philosophy. Quite apart from the tradition of free logic, the more anti-realist end of the analytic tradition can take issue with univocal notions of existence. Putnam, for instance, complains:

> what we see in this brief account of the revival of ontology within
> the supposedly chaste precincts of analytic philosophy is … that
> once we assume that there is, somehow fixed in advance, a single
> "real", a single "literal" sense of "exist" … we are already wandering
> into cloud cuckooland. (2005: 84)

This pragmatist challenge to analytic metaphysics is one that many continental philosophers would concur with although, as Putnam pointedly notes in his later work, Heidegger was not the only major twentieth-century philosopher to value the *Lebenswelt*, the life-world, and to condemn the tendency of metaphysicians to take it less than seriously.

16. TRUTH, OBJECTIVITY AND REALISM

The differing commitments and interests of the analytic and continental traditions emerge especially clearly with respect to truth and realism, in part because of explicit critique across the traditions on this point. Notwithstanding the influence of pragmatist and coherence understandings of truth, the analytic tradition has a broadly objectivist understanding of truth, which backs analytic concerns with the (alleged) anti-realist tendencies in continental philosophy. In this chapter, we compare the two traditions' respective understandings of truth and its association with metaphysical realism. We shall argue that the distinction between these two traditions follows largely from the primacy of the proposition in analysis. The modern account of truth is seen within analytic philosophy as hardly won from a pre-existing fog of confusion, in which use is confounded with mention, sense with reference and the semantic with the epistemic. Truth is to be sharply (categorically) distinguished from satisfaction, obtaining or existing, and is standardly conceived of either as a semantic property of some kind (on much the same level as provability, or significance), or as a predicate that picks out no property in the world. We shall outline the development of this view of truth within analytic philosophy, and then consider contemporary concerns with the relation between accounts of truth and metaphysical realism. The analytic perspective will be contrasted with the more ontological (historical) and sometimes constructivist account of truth typical in continental philosophy. We conclude by considering the frequent accusations of relativism levelled at continental understandings of truth, and the charge that continental philosophy, from phenomenology to poststructuralism and beyond, remains committed to forms of idealism.

TRUTH IN THE ANALYTIC TRADITION

In *A Thing of This World*, Lee Braver proposes a diagnostic test for the classification of philosophers:

> To discover a particular philosopher's place, we would ask how he conceives of his work and the goal of philosophy. Is he after timeless truth that escapes the contingent empirical factors that happen to have made him what he is, even if only as an inaccessible ideal, or does he view truth as itself the product of such factors?
> (2007: 513)

This notion of "timeless" truth is certainly key to the analytic tradition, as is made clear by early analytic criticism of pragmatist accounts of truth, or accounts in the idealist tradition (such as Brand Blanshard's [2002: 260–69]). Truth and falsity are directly considered in the philosophy of logic, but the analytic motivation to carry out such investigations is primarily driven by considerations of meaning and metaphysics. Obviously, a truth-conditional theory of meaning makes the connection between truth and meaning concerns immediately apparent, but even a use or an intention theorist can feel the need for clarity on the nature of truth, especially in the borderlands in which concerns of language shade into concerns of metaphysics. The standard options that an analytic philosopher will consider, in making sense of linguistic practices, show this very clearly. If we are confronted with a way of talking, the sentences of which appear to be metaphysically loaded, the analytic tradition furnishes us with a number of models for understanding what is going on:

  (i) We may simply, in direct (or naive) realist mode, take such talk as being truth-apt and indeed often true, some kind of direct report of the facts.
 (ii) We may prefer a reductive realism, taking such talk to be truth-apt and often true in virtue of reducing to a more respectable kind of talk.
(iii) We may regard such talk as essentially instrumental – although truth-apt – concerned more with furthering some other goal than meeting the assertoric norm of truth.
 (iv) We may decide on a kind of eliminativism or error theory, allowing the practitioners to settle semantic matters as they wish (and so ensuring the truth-aptness of their utterances), but pointing to reason to hold their assertions to be typically false.
  (v) We may adopt some form of non-cognitivism, deciding that such talk is non-truth-apt because not really declarative, serving instead another purpose somehow related to our attitudes (and we might then, in the face of well-known difficulties, let this ramify into a "quasi-realist" view).

174

(vi) We may, more simply, hold it to be non-truth-apt because it is non-literal, serving a metaphorical or artistic purpose of some kind.

(vii) We may, for local or global anti-realist reasons, decide that an understanding of the talk involves consideration of justification conditions, because the subject matter is not one that the concept of truth properly applies to.

Fragments of this range of alternatives can be found, for instance, in analytic discussions of the language of ethics, religion, mathematics and folk psychology, and unsurprisingly there has been a great deal of "technology transfer" between these debates, in which models newly worked out in one domain are put to the test elsewhere. Yet obviously such debates wait on a clear idea of what is involved in regarding talk as *truth*-apt. Hence what it is for something to be true is a general concern in all of these cases.

Analytic theorizing about the nature of truth, in turn, is connected to a debate about the bearer of truth. Is it a linguistic entity (such as a sentence), an abstract object (such as a proposition), or a speech act of assertion (a "statement", in the jargon)? The fact that many putative truthbearers (such as the sentence, or the Moorean proposition) have internal structure – for instance, grammatical structure – suggested a natural account of truth for sentences, which was developed in different ways by Russell and Wittgenstein. On this view, a sentence is true just when it *corresponds* to some state of affairs that obtains, where this correspondence is a matter of *congruence*: the structural components of a true sentence (or perhaps its underlying logical form) are articulated together in the same way as the parts of the relevant obtaining state of affairs.[1] The logical atomist project is motivated in part by this conception of truth. Yet correspondence theories need not be so metaphysically committal. J. L. Austin (1979), more cautiously, abandoned the structural idea and opted for a correspondence theory of statements (in the above sense) built not on congruences between the structure of the entity and the world, but on correlations established purely by convention. On his account, a statement is true if the specific situation it is linked to by demonstrative convention (conventions governing what, in the circumstances of utterance, the statement is taken to be about) is of the type it is more generally linked to by the descriptive conventions of the language group. For example, the descriptive conventions of English hold that statements of the form "That is a brown dog" apply to certain kinds of situations; hence, if I were to point and say "That is a brown dog", my statement is true just if the situation indicated by my demonstrative pointing (given our conventions of pointing, usage of "That" and so on) is of the type of situation that we apply this statement to (i.e. I am pointing at a brown dog).

Austin's concern to expunge the metaphysical commitments of the correspondence theory, rather more than his particular account of truth, has

175

been widespread in analytic philosophy. A range of deflationist accounts of truth have been advanced, which seek to explain the function of the word "true" without finding a property for it to attach to. Although the first clearly deflationist account dates from the 1920s (Ramsey's redundancy theory of truth), that such accounts of truth are prominent is due to the semantic revolution in logic in the 1930s and after, which to some extent had the effect of demystifying the notion of truth as it was used in that field. Tarski's (1956) seminal "semantic theory of truth" is the model here, an account of truth-in-a-language that defines that notion recursively,[2] by exploiting the logical form of the sentences of first-order logic. In addition to such "formal correctness", Tarski points out that his definition is "materially adequate", in that it entails all instances of the following equivalence (expressed in the relevant language, and where p is any sentence of the object language and S is some name of p):

(T) S is true if and only if p. (E.g. "Snow is white" if and only if snow is white.)

Tarski's definition does not directly apply to natural languages (on pain of contradiction); even if it did, the concept of truth, if analysed along his lines, would decompose into truth-in-English, truth-in-Polish and so on. But the Tarskian model has proved suggestive; given an account of meaning, we can fix the truths of a language – and that is all that can be said about truth. Tarski's work has also been exploited in the opposite direction by Davidson, who in effect uses convention (T), together with the assumption that we do understand truth, to develop a theory of meaning. This "inversion of the primitive" is not at all unusual in analytic philosophy; perhaps the best example in contemporary philosophy is given by the rival traditions explaining possible worlds in terms of propositions, and propositions in terms of possible worlds. The notions of assertion, truth, meaning and understanding form an interconnected complex, allowing similar explanatory reconnections to be developed by philosophers with different programmes.

More recently, and largely under the influence of Dummett, such analytic discussions of truth and meaning have been directly connected to apparently metaphysical debates about realism.[3] The philosophical tension between empiricism and realism, of course, long pre-dates the analytic movement, but it has remained a perennial topic of interest or concern to that tradition, emerging in such well-known episodes as Russell's struggles with empirical respectability, the logical positivist movement, the long career of phenomenalism and the flourishing of instrumentalist or interpretationist views on everything from the unobservables of science to the entities of folk psychology. In one sense Dummett simply falls into place in this history, as another for whom empiricist scruples have put into question some form of realism, but he also marks something of a change in the sequence; the traditional epistemic–metaphysical showdown is reworked in semantic form.

Dummett's starting point is the conviction that metaphysical issues in philosophy depend on the prior settling of issues about meaning; indeed, that paradigmatically metaphysical debates (such as that between the realist and the idealist) amount to little more than semantic claims together with a "picture", or "metaphor". In turn, Dummett suggests, an enquiry into meaning (appropriately sensitive to the constraint imposed by our understanding of our language; that is, by our knowledge of meaning) puts into question the idea that our statements or thoughts could have truth-conditions that outrun all possible evidence we might have for them. Building on Wittgenstein, Dummett develops the theme that our ability to acquire concepts, and to manifest them in use, entails, instead, a justification-conditional account of meaning (or, in a variant, a truth-conditional account of meaning employing a concept of truth implicating evidentiary considerations in some way). For example, Dummett suggests that the evidence-transcendent (uncheckable) aspect of the realist concept of the past is something that might well vary from person to person, precisely because there is no way to ensure that new English speakers have acquired the same concept (with respect to this aspect of it) as each other. A consequence of this position is that the concept of evidence-transcendent truth itself comes under serious question; a second (arguable) consequence is that at least one basic tenet of realism has been undermined: the claim that statements of the relevant domain have objective truth-conditions. Dummett's advocacy of this position is nuanced; although he regularly considers the prospects of an entirely global anti-realism along these lines, it is perhaps more accurate (and in the spirit of the intuitionist logic that accompanies the view) to say that he holds that we cannot rule a global anti-realism out, and have local reasons, within particular discourses, for adopting the view. Of course, the exact characterization of realism and the commitments that a realist signs up for in adopting that view are themselves in dispute; Dummett's attempt to translate metaphysical questions into the semantic realm is generally resisted by realists themselves, who conceive of the view in much the following way:

> An object has independent existence, in some sense, if it exists and has its nature whatever we believe, think, or can discover: it is independent of the cognitive activities of the mind ... It is not constituted by our knowledge, by our epistemic values, by our capacity to refer to it, by our imposition of concepts, theories, or languages ... For the realist, the world exists independently of the mental. (Devitt 1997: 15–16)

Arguments similar to Dummett's have been developed by Putnam, and there is indeed something of a connection between Dummett's verificationist roots and the American pragmatist tradition. Consider, for instance, Putnam's characterization of realism, clearly a cousin of Dummett's own view:

> The world consists of some fixed totality of mind-independent objects. There is exactly one true and complete description of "the way the world is". Truth involves some sort of correspondence relation between words or thought-signs and external things and sets of things. I shall call this perspective the externalist perspective, because its favourite point of view is a God's eye point of view. (1981: 49)

The analytic debate here between the realist and the anti-realist has produced a great variety of intermediate positions. Perhaps most notable, as an extension of Dummett's ideas, is that of Crispin Wright (1992), who draws from the deflationist tradition in order to argue for the utility of a notion of "minimal" truth, agreed on by realist and anti-realist alike. A predicate is a minimal truth predicate for a particular domain of discourse, roughly, if it ensures that statements possess some assertoric content, that is, if it respects (a slight variant on) Tarski's condition (T). Not every domain of discourse will possess a predicate meeting this test (those for which expressivism of some kind holds will not, for instance). Once such minimal conditions of truth-aptness are met for a particular domain, Wright suggests that the question of realism devolves into the question of the presence or absence of further, essentially independent, features. Wright's list here includes Dummett's original concern (the extent to which sentences in the domain can be evidence-transcendent); whether it is *a priori* that divergence of opinion in the domain indicates cognitive error on the part of at least one agent; whether the truth-conditions of sentences in the domain feature in explanations of other sorts of facts; and whether, under ideal epistemic conditions, a congruence between the agent's beliefs and the facts of the domain is to be explained by the beliefs tracking the facts or the facts reflecting the beliefs (the "Euthyphro contrast"). Since these criteria can diverge, the ways in which a discourse can be realist or anti-realist can vary, and a kind of particularism about the whole issue emerges.

As a result of these developments, and continuing realist opposition to the whole anti-realist tradition, the analytic tradition at present contains a range of anti-realist models of varying degrees of ambition. At the least, the resources are present for an analytic reworking and recharacterizing of traditional concerns about the irrealist overtones of much continental work.

CONTINENTAL ANTI-REALISM

Analytic philosophers have regularly pointed to idealist tendencies in continental philosophy through the history of the twentieth century. In recent times, two continental philosophers have advanced roughly the same interpretation: one (Meillassoux) regarding it a major problem, and the other (Braver) apparently regarding it a virtue. We start with Braver's recent book, *A Thing of this World*.

On Braver's view, Kant and Hegel opened up a faultline in the realism that has dominated Western philosophy since Plato, an anti-realist faultline that has resonated with continental philosophy ever since. While, in one sense, Kant is a realist, in that he posits the noumenon or thing-in-itself, he also maintains that there is no possibility of determining correspondence or fit between our representations and the thing-in-itself. Braver sees the subsequent history of continental philosophy as an attempt to free itself from Kant's remaining realism. Here, realism is to be understood in common (as far as that is possible, given disagreements there about it) with the analytic tradition; Braver's "realist matrix" is developed with an eye on the characterizations of realism provided by Putnam, Dummett and Devitt.

Braver suggests that four interwoven and partially overlapping theses can be found in analytic characterizations of realism, each strictly speaking orthogonal from the others. Realism can be taken to involve: (i) the mind-independent existence of objects or states of affairs; (ii) truth as correspondence between thoughts, beliefs, propositions and what really obtains; (iii) some kind of uniqueness claim (there is only one way to capture the determinate structure of reality); (iv) an assertion of bivalence – well-formed declarative statements are (leaving vagueness issues to one side) either true or false. The list is, to analytic eyes, reminiscent in part of Wright's local indicia of realism, although the differences are also striking; Dummett's attempt to characterize realism in terms of bivalence has, for instance, won much less support than the related suggestion that the realist claims that we are in a position to understand evidence-transcendent truth-conditions. However, Braver (2007: 14–22) also suggests that (analytic) realism involves a further thesis: that of the passive knower. This contrasts directly with the active knower of many Kantian and post-Kantian trajectories.

The matrix established, Braver contends that Kant, Hegel, Nietzsche, Heidegger (early and late), Foucault and Derrida dispute various of these realist theses in an increasingly radical fashion. If this is right, the divergence on realism simply *is*, more or less, the analytic–continental divide. Of course, any such progressivist and linear understanding of the history of continental philosophy faces obvious problems. Meillassoux himself is an obvious exception to the trend Braver highlights (wanting to reinvigorate both realism and the thing-in-itself), but also, and more critically, the continental tradition itself encompasses differing, albeit usually partly overlapping, inheritances. And while it is also probably true that through analytic eyes most of these philosophers are best considered as anti-realists, most continental philosophers would resist this, instead claiming that they are methodologically agnostic on this issue (Husserl), or that they have found a middle way between idealism and realism (Heidegger, Merleau-Ponty and Sartre), or that the problem is itself misleadingly posed (Hegel and others). For the moment, though, let us admit with Braver that few continental philosophers appear enthused by standard proxies for realism, such as the principle of bivalence, or truth as correspondence, or related ideas such as truth as correctness and adequation (or coherence for that matter, albeit perhaps to a lesser extent). If these general assessments are more or less correct this *might* be taken to legitimate Braver's claim that continental philosophers are anti-realists. However, it might also be taken to indicate that their concerns with reality and truth do not easily map onto the problems with which analytic philosophers are concerned under these headings.

The issue here is precisely one of topic. While Braver claims that analytic and continental philosophers can be shown to engage with the same problem, albeit in different ways and ignorant of each other's work, very few continental philosophers actually talk about truth in any sustained way; a whole constellation of analytic concerns is absent. As Foucault says of his own intellectual tradition: "There have not been that many people ... in the twentieth century who have posed the question of truth ... I see only Heidegger and Lacan" (2005: 189). In recent times, Badiou, well known for calling for a return to "truth" as the pre-eminent concern of philosophy against what he takes to be its devaluation in poststructuralism, derides the idea of truth as correspondence and implies that no serious philosopher has ever accepted such a view. Clearly he has not read much analytic philosophy (and his interpretation of the history of philosophy is also rather wilful). But comments like this lend further weight to the idea that it is not the same issues that are being addressed by the two traditions: that there is no easy way to compare analytic and continental concerns in this broad area. This is so even without noting that Badiou (2001: 70) characterizes truth (following Lacan, but otherwise iconoclastically) as that which punches a hole in knowledge, including accepted justification processes, and so on. Indeed, Braver also pays almost no attention to the work of Lacan. When we consider that Deleuze and Derrida in different ways endorse Lacan's psychoanalytic suggestion that a "logic of symptoms" is more important than an "ethics of truthfulness", and when we consider that Badiou is also heavily indebted to Lacan, the omission seems telling. Of course, none of these points invalidate Braver's effort to instigate a conversation between analytic and continental philosophers regarding realism and truth; rather, they put into question the view that there is a potential conversation here waiting to be discovered, if we were only ecumenical enough to see it. Indeed, such a view seems curiously like a realist endorsement of the thing-in-itself, and this supposition does not fit easily with Braver's own descriptions and advocation of a historicist and relativist ontology; again, it seems to elide the differing analytic and continental reactions to the Kantian heritage that emerged in our consideration of transcendental reasoning. In pursuing these questions, we focus on Heidegger and Foucault in this chapter as representatives of the continental tradition, since both of their accounts of truth (and realism) have been highly influential and they make perspicuous some of the interpretive difficulties involved in construing continental work as anti-realist. We shall then return to the issue of realism and anti-realism in relation to phenomenology, and Meillassoux's critique of "correlationism". This does seem in some ways closely related to an analytic realist position, but the fact that Meillassoux's worries are both presented and received within the continental tradition as radically new is also, arguably, another indicator of the pervasiveness of the "divide".

HEIDEGGER AND MERLEAU-PONTY: REALISM AS THE FORGETTING OF BEING

According to Heidegger, there is a tendency to construe that which is present-at-hand (that which presents itself as independent of us, and which we neutrally observe) as more real than the ready-to-hand (that which is used in relation to our own purposes, and is meaningful by dint of its existence in a culturally saturated milieu, or what Heidegger calls an "equipmental totality"). While he unambiguously denies the assumption that what is present-at-hand is alone real, or most real, there are some difficult interpretive issues in understanding *Being and Time* as simply saying this. In particular, it is not entirely clear whether Heidegger is committed to the characteristically anti-realist view that present-at-hand reality is in fact dependent on Dasein, or whether he is an ontic (empirical) realist about such entities. While Braver does not think Heidegger is a genuine realist about present-at-hand-objects, since things are only present-at-hand (or show themselves as independent) *for* Dasein, some others philosophers do take this view. Taylor Carman, for example, maintains that:

> Being is ... inextricably bound up with Dasein's understanding of the intelligibility of entities as entities, but it is emphatically not an entity brought into existence by Dasein. Without Dasein there would "be" no being, which is to say there would be no under-

standing of being, so that *that* and *what* entities are would add up to nothing intelligible. But occurrent entities would still be, nonetheless … To say that entities exist independently of us is not to assert the being or existence of anything like being or existence, as if it too were a kind of entity, that is, something that is alongside or in addition to the entities themselves. It is consistent, then, to say that although being consists solely in our understanding of being, occurrent entities are independent of us and our understanding.

(2002: 202–3)

Carman's position is not uncommon: quite a lot of scholarship asserts the realism of Heidegger. What does seem to be undeniable, however, is that Heidegger is concerned with and opposes what might be called reductive metaphysical realism, a realism about the existence of the object that allows the question of Being (roughly the condition of possibility of the presencing of objects) to be reduced to issues to do with correspondence between our claims about particular entities.

Some similar concerns are also present in the work of Merleau-Ponty. While it might be argued that he is actually committed to a form of realism about both body and world, his own claims to the contrary highlight the extent to which metaphysical realism is philosophically dangerous territory. Any naive realist commitment to things in the world independent of us inclines us to commit what he calls, in *Phenomenology of Perception*, the "experience error", which makes perceptions out of the things perceived. This is an error in which the object as known by sciences and "objective thought" is retroactively read back on to the initial perception of the object. Merleau-Ponty is, for instance, prepared to say that our perceptual experience of the Müller–Lyer illusion is more ambiguous than we tend to think; our initial phenomenological experience of the two lines, he alleges, gives them to us as neither equal nor non-equal (2002: 6).

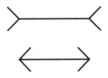

Our objective knowledge that this is an illusion, revealed by someone telling us or by our using a ruler, is then retroactively reinterpreted back into the initial perception. We hence tend to think that we did perceive the diagram as involving unequal lines, but this recollection about our "seeing as" is not phenomenologically accurate. For Merleau-Ponty, bivalence thus is not characteristic of the perceptual order.

Some related issues crop up in regard to Heidegger's views on truth. Like Badiou, Heidegger sometimes derides the idea of truth as correspondence, suggesting that it has made no headway in thousands of years. In his later work, the Greek notion of *alētheia* comes to play the key role. As John Sallis puts it:

> The phenomenological analyses of *Being and Time* issue in a rede-termination of truth, one which does not metaphysically oppose truth to appearances, true world to apparent world, but rather displaces the opposition: truth as the opening/openness of the very site of self-showing. It is precisely for the sake of enforcing this displacement that Heidegger insists on distinguishing between truth as aletheia and truth as correctness.
>
> (Quoted in Braver 2007: 199)

In Heidegger's own words:

> Truth as "correctness" is not of the same essence as truth in the sense of "unconcealedness". The opposition of correctness and incorrectness, validity and invalidity, may very well exhaust the oppositional essence of truth ... above all for modern thinking. But that decides nothing at all concerning the possible oppositions to "unconcealedness" as thought by the Greeks ... We stand too uncritically under the prejudice of the opposition between truth and falsity taken for granted a long time ago.   (1998a: 26–7)

In the Greek understanding of *alētheia*, there is a revealing/concealing process and they are not simply in opposition. All revealing also involves a concealing, and vice versa. Correctness and incorrectness are in a more stark opposition, however, but Heidegger suggests that they are ontologically derivative of *alētheia*.

FOUCAULT ON TRUTH AND KNOWLEDGE

Foucault succinctly sums up his enduring fascination with truth in the following way: "My general theme isn't society but the discourse of true and false, by which I mean the correlative formation of domains and objects and the verifiable, falsifiable discourse that bear on them" (1996: 295). On Braver's interpretation, Foucaultian genealogy and archaeology attempt to dispel the realist illusion: "*The Order of Things* claims that the way things are changes along with the way they are known at these times of epistemic transition"

(Braver 2007: 358). If this is so, then there can be no essence of truth, and no reality to which true claims correspond, outside of what is accepted as true within a given *epistēmē*, or power–knowledge relation. In somewhat Kuhnian fashion, while Foucault (1972: 224) might say that Mendel spoke the truth from our perspective (not eternally), he was not "within the true" of biological discourse at his time. Not only can there be no identification of a real enduring thing that is simply differently interpreted, but the metaphysical implication seems to be that there is no real enduring thing *tout court*. Few analytic philosophers will accept such a view, since it seems to constitute a strong (that is, overly committal) form of relativism or constructivism.

But does Foucault consider the realist question simply one that should not be posed, epistemically, or does he consider it in some sense wrong? There is significant debate on this in the literature. It is sometimes maintained that, while the justification of truth can only occur discursively for Foucault, there is a brute reality that impacts on our experience that has an epistemic role that Foucault simply – wilfully – denies. Truth itself also seems to be epistemic for Foucault, however, which is a position that few analytic philosophers will accept. Now some of this ambiguity is due to Foucault's shifting between different senses of truth; perhaps as many as five according to C. G. Prado's (2005) analyses, including a constructivist understanding (truth is a product of power relations), a criterial understanding (truth is relative to particular discourses), an experiential or parrhesic conception (those experiences of truth that subvert any given power arrangement), and a meta-perspectivist conception (in which it is insisted there is no way of reconciling these conceptions of truth). Although they interpret this dimension of his work differently, it is also worth noting that both Todd May and Prado maintain that there is indeed a realist dimension to Foucault's work, contrary to Braver's anti-realist interpretation. As was the case with Heidegger, it is simply difficult to locate Foucault with respect to the "realist matrix".

STAR-MAKING AND SEX-MAKING IN CONTINENTAL PHILOSOPHY

In *After Finitude*, Meillassoux contends that many continental philosophers are "correlationists" to either a weak or a strong degree (depending, roughly, on the extent to which their inheritance is Kantian and Hegelian), and so cannot adequately account for the reality of ancestral claims regarding "arche-fossils" (including in physics, biology, etc.) that pre-dated human subjects. This consequence obtains because of the continental commitment to the claim that the past is only available to us *as* knowledge in the present, or knowledge of the past for us now; they are presentists of a sort (for whom only that which is present is real), perhaps even tacit verificationists, and are thereby committed to saying both yes and no to the question whether events before human experience are real. Meillassoux thinks this characterization holds good of phenomenologists, but it might also be applied to the Foucaultian position, which, as we have just seen, "is interested in the *correlative* formation of domains and objects and the verifiable, falsifiable discourse that bear on them" (Foucault 1996: 295, emphasis added). And Meillassoux is certainly right in seeing an epistemic problem for Foucault, for whom we cannot claim that Mendel's theory corresponds to any eternal fact, apart from saying that it is true *for us* now. Indeed, Foucault himself briefly considers a possible rejoinder to his book *History of Sexuality*: that he is offering a history of sexuality without any given "sex", and thus is offering a form of idealism (1990a: 151). For him, however, any claim that there must be a biology, a brute sex, underlying experience, seems like a metaphysical investment in a Kantian noumenal and hence rather speculative.

Issues like this played a significant role in the mid-century analytic reception of continental philosophy. While Royaumont was something of a failure according to all concerned, an interesting philosophical meeting transpired between some of the key protagonists in 1951 that presaged the lack of genuine intellectual engagement of the later affair. In Georges Bataille's recounting:

> It so happened that I met A. J. Ayer last night, and our reciprocal interest kept us talking until about three in the morning. Merleau-Ponty and Ambrosino also took part … We finally fell to discussing the following very strange question. Ayer had uttered the very simple proposition: there was a sun before men existed. And he saw no reason to doubt it. Merleau-Ponty, Ambrosino, and I disagreed with this proposition, and Ambrosino said that the sun had certainly not existed before the world. I, for my part, do not see how one can say so. This proposition is such as to indicate the total meaninglessness that can be taken on by a rational statement … I should say that yesterday's conversation produced an effect of shock. There exists between French and English philosophers a sort of abyss which we do not find between French and German philosophers. (2004: 112)

Without wishing to dispute Bataille's assessment of an abyss between philosophy on the continent and philosophy in Anglo-American countries, we might note that there are some similar discussions in analytic philosophy, perhaps most saliently the work of Goodman and his essays on "star-making",[4] and Dummett's consideration in "The Reality of the Past" of a form of anti-realism about the past based on a kind of correlationism very similar to that which Meillassoux identifies. From the analytic point of view, indeed, such tendencies are generated by empiricist limits; the logical positivists themselves had difficulty with the realist attempt to establish the existence of the external world, since verificationist theories of meaning make knowability a condition of meaningfulness and any given statement of metaphysical realism is rather difficult to verify. *Prima facie*, however, one might be tempted to dismiss continental philosophy as idealist on the basis of Bataille's bemusement faced by Ayer's proposition, Merleau-Ponty's apparent unwillingness to assent to the proposition in question and Meillassoux's critical characterization of the post-Kantian tradition of continental philosophy. But is it the case that Goodman, Foucault, Bataille, Merleau-Ponty (and Derrida, where this issue also crops up in the context of his infamous idea that "there is nothing outside of the text") simply do not understand science? More likely is Meillassoux's charge that although they understand the relevant science (which in this case is also enshrined in common sense), their philosophies commit them to positions (idealist ones) that make them unable to adequately account for stars and suns being around before humans.

Of course, there are many possible rejoinders. In Heideggerian language, we might say, as Braver does, that "obviously we didn't make the stars in the sense of physically constructing those bright, faraway things. But ontologically we are responsible for their having the mode of Being that they do as things which we experience" (2007: 195). On Braver's interpretation, the notion of the independence of things (the being-in-itself of things) is nonsensical without humans, so while there is no ontic (empirical) dependence between us and the stars, there is an ontological dependence. While this returns us to the question of whether or not it is correct to interpret Heidegger as an antirealist, Heidegger does seem to say (as Meillassoux alleges that he does) both yes and no to the question of the reality or otherwise of fossil ancestry and the existence of stars before humans were around. The question is whether it is a mistake (or a confusion, or a misuse of language) to maintain such a position, or whether there are different temporal orders between the geological time of the earth and the physicist's time, say, on the one hand, and lived-time in its manifold varieties on the other hand, that demand a complicated answer of this kind. It seems clear that Meillassoux and various analytic philosophers are correct to maintain that we have the resources (notably, but not only, through the sciences) needed to think a time before any givenness to consciousness (indeed, arguably the empirical condition of givenness itself). We shall explore the compatibility or otherwise of this insight with phenomenological treatments of time in Chapter 17.

For now, we reaffirm that phenomenologists generally aim to bracket such metaphysical questions, and instead attend to the phenomena. As Merleau-Ponty says: "we must not, therefore, wonder whether we really perceive a world, we must instead say: the world is what we perceive" (2002: xvi). Of course, analytic philosophers typically resist the conflation; world (or being) and perception of that world (or being) are simply distinct, on pain of the impossibility of error. Although we noted in Chapter 11 that Merleau-Ponty and other phenomenologists seem to be able to avoid the charge of incorrigibility, it is clear that this sort of concern is less present in the continental tradition; indeed, it is denied as an epistemic possibility by some. For Braver, such obduracy indicates anti-realism, but the matter is arguably not that simple; this is one of the points at which the differing attitudes of each tradition to the notion of representation matter. Phenomenologists can be readily interpreted (in the metaphysical register) as advocating a form of direct realism that simply does without intermediaries like representations between organism and environment. Both of these options – the anti-realist and the direct realist interpretations – have some plausibility. We might maintain that the existence of these dual possibilities is reflective of an inconsistency or lack of clarity at the heart of the phenomenological project, or we might conclude that it shows that the analytic matrix of realist options cannot be superimposed over the work of continental philosophers without presenting an uncanny picture of the philosophers in question (albeit often enlightening) and without categorization problems like this cropping up. Similar issues do arise within analytic philosophy, but the categorization prospect is not as fraught and complicated as it is in regard to the continental tradition, whose shared inheritance of these terms from Kant has also involved a substantial reconfiguring of them. As such, we think that philosophers ought to be careful about ascribing anti-realism to continental philosophy writ large.

17. TIME

A CONTRETEMPS

In the late 1980s, the American economist Jeremy Rifkin claimed that "a battle is brewing over the politics of time" (1987: 10)[1] because he felt that the pivotal issue of the twenty-first century would be the question of time and who controlled it. We think that a battle over the politics of time (and the metaphysics of time) is also a major part of what is at stake in the differences between analytic and continental philosophy. Very different philosophies of time, and associated methodological techniques, serve to define representatives of each of these groups and also to guard against their potential interlocutors. To begin to illustrate this, let us offer a patchy history of philosophy of time in the early twentieth century, the period in which the idea of a "divide" between two ways of doing philosophy began to be entrenched.

In the early twentieth century, the philosophical agenda on time was set in particular by the work of McTaggart, Russell, Husserl and Bergson. At the same time, of course, physics was undergoing a revolution in its understanding of space and time, and philosophical accounts of time were forced to engage with this, as well as with the traditional philosophical literature on the subject (the influential work of Carnap and Reichenbach, among the logical positivists, and Heidegger, is in this period). Einstein's 1905 paper on relativity itself begins, implicitly, with a philosophical point. As a follower of Hume and Mach, Einstein is sceptical of the empirical propriety of the concept of absolute simultaneity, and he proposes in its place an essentially conventional – but empirically respectable – account of synchronization. This, together with further postulates (about the constancy of form of laws of physics across all inertial frames of reference, and the constancy of the speed of light for all inertial observers), immediately yields apparently counter-intuitive results about the interrelation of time, space and velocity. For instance, if A travels at close to the speed of light away from and then back to a stationary twin B, the subjective ages of the two twins will be found to now differ. The theory of relativity might thereby be thought to call into question the notion of

188

objective time, but a further development (the four-dimensional understanding of Einstein's theory, in terms of "Minkowski space–time") complicates the picture. Rather than time and space being separable, we need to think of a single space–time manifold with four dimensions, of which time is a one-dimensional sub-space, and in which transitions are neither purely spatial nor temporal, but rather "space-like" or "time-like" to varying degrees. Such a position entails a radical change in our understanding of space and time, as Hermann Minkowski made clear in proposing the model: "Henceforth space by itself, and time by itself, are doomed to fade away into mere shadows, and only a kind of union of the two will preserve an independent reality" (1952: 75). Evidently, such a view gives no special place to the "now". Unsurprisingly, philosophers influenced by these developments therefore generally reject presentism, the claim that only the present (and not the past or the future) is ontologically real.[2] In fact, it is usually accepted that four-dimensionalism in physics means that our experience of the "now" (the "immediate present") and the notion of temporal becoming are but subjectively compelling illusions. This constitutes quite a challenge both to common-sense conceptions of time and our everyday experience of time.

The analytic discussion of these matters was also, however, strongly influenced by J. M. E. McTaggart's work, although more in framework than in detail (see McTaggart 1993). McTaggart was part of the British idealist tradition rejected by the early analytic movement, although he himself maintained friendly relations with his former students Russell and Moore. Moreover, the actual argument of his 1908 paper "The Unreality of Time" (or at least the part concerned with the incoherence of the A-series) has had at best patchy support within analytic philosophy. Briefly, McTaggart distinguishes two ways in which events in time can be ordered. The A-series corresponds to a psychological experience of succession that roughly corresponds to what the phenomenologist might call the natural attitude in regard to time, with certain events being futural, coming to be present and then moving into the past and the even further past. All of these temporal designations are relative to a given "present", from which certain events are seen to be in the future and others in the past. To put this another way, for the A-series, events in time can be ordered according to their possession of properties such as being two days future, being present, being one day past and so on. Yet events in time can also be ordered relationally, in terms of the one being two days earlier than the other, one day earlier than the other, simultaneous with the other, one day later than the other and so on. This B-series of time – of before, simultaneous with and after – involves a structure that maintains permanent relations between events.[3] Analytic work on time largely accepted this distinction, in so far as it polarized around two perspectives – presentism and eternalism – that respectively take the A-series and the

B-series properties or relations as primitive. The claim here can be put in different registers; for instance, a "B theorist" who holds that the real temporal features are the relations between times need not hold that all tensed statements can be translated into the B-series language without loss of meaning. Many analytic philosophers go on to hold that the results of modern physics support the eternalist position. Advocates of the A-series are hence forced either to dispute this claim about modern physics, or to argue that if it is true then modern physics leaves out something fundamental about the nature of time and temporal succession. This latter approach, although less common in analytic philosophy, seems to be the position that most continental philosophers are explicitly or implicitly committed to, as we shall see.

The continental "temporal turn" reached its "tipping point" at the same time as the Einsteinian revolution in physics, but proceeded quite independently; arguments against any ontological privilege accorded to the "now" and any conception of time based on a succession of instants were also raised by these philosophers, but their reflections went in another direction. Bergson emphasizes the importance of a non-measurable lived time (*durée*) that is also said to be the proper medium of thinking (via "intuition" rather than the intelligence), and as a result proposes radical alterations to the way we think about memory. For him, the past remains real and part of all of our experience, existing as what he calls a virtual temporality (a time that is real, but not present); it is not reducible to the linear order that clock-time, or the succession of instants model gives us, in which we proceed from past to present to future. In fact, in *Matter and Memory* he refers to a notion of the "pure past" that coexists with the present, and constitutes it; the present, on this view, is a dimension of the past rather than vice versa. Around the same time, Husserl's rich analyses of internal time-consciousness demonstrated that rather than conscious life comprising a series of punctal "now" moments, there is a necessary intertwining of anticipative "protention" in relation to the future and "retention" of the past. His concern was to describe our experience of time, as well as to delimit some of the non-empirical conditions of possibility for any experience of time. For most phenomenologists, it is this relation between protention, primal impression and retention that makes possible the experience of, say, temporal flow. We need not have an actual experience of protention, but we must deduce such features in order to explain coherently our experience of, say, listening to a melody. In other words, these features are claimed to be the transcendental conditions of temporal experience in its myriad forms, and these time-constituting phenomena are not themselves determinable as occurring in the present, past or future in the same way as the events that historically happen. In a different way, Heidegger also argues in *Being and Time* that time has a transcendental significance; both for Dasein and ontologically, a philosophical priority must be accorded to the "not yet", the "to come", the possible and the future. This has been influential on much of the ensuing continental "tradition", especially French phenomenology and poststructuralism.

Consider the dialogues that did and did not occur during this formative period of the "divide". It is telling that there was very little substantive engagement between the phenomenological/Bergsonian accounts of time and the anglophone (analytic and idealist) discussion of McTaggart's position. There was, of course, the series of polemical encounters between Russell and Bergson we briefly outline in Part I, and one of the major points of contention between them concerned time, in part because of its central role in justifying Bergson's method of intuition. As James Bradley puts it, Bergson argues that "the real nature of time resides not in its segmented parts but in its given, experiential character as duration: the irreducible, purely qualitative, cumulative flow of a multiplicity of states which forms an indivisible, heterogenous continuum" (Bradley 2003: 441). All attempts to understand time (or, for that matter, life) by partitioning it into quantifiable items are bound to fail. They are spatializing abstractions that use the "intelligence" to break things down into their sub-components, but for Bergson time is irreducible and cannot be analysed by reference to anything that is non-temporal. The real nature of time was thought to pertain to this experiential (and, simultaneously, transcendental) characteristic, not to the four-dimensional manifold advocated by physicists and analytic philosophers; the former is the condition for the latter, rather than the other way around. Russell was, unsurprisingly, antagonistic towards such a view, and, on the basis of work in physics and mathematics, not prepared to accept the qualitative (and ontological) difference between time and space that Bergson insisted on. On a similar basis, J. J. C. Smart, Quine and many other analytic philosophers have argued that there can be no objective ontological difference in kind between the past, the present and the future, just as there is no ontological difference between here and there. It is merely subjective mental perspectives that divide the spatiotemporal block into a past part, a present part and a future part. Partly because of some similar considerations (which emerge also in Russell's well-known analysis of Zeno's paradoxes in *Our Knowledge of the External World*), Russell even felt entitled to proclaim that time was an "unimportant and superficial characteristic of reality" (1917a: 21). To Bergson, on the other hand, time is closer to ultimate reality, a transcendental condition of the spatial, of change and of life.

Competing philosophies of time were also part of the background to the polemic between Heidegger and Carnap in the early 1930s. After all, we have seen that Heidegger's *Being and Time* argues that Being is not an entity, and that the question of Being has a vital relation to time. Carnap, Reichenbach and other logical positivists[4] were substantially concerned with the philosophical implications of the theory of relativity, especially in regard to space and time. Carnap wrote a thesis setting out an axiomatic theory of space and time, and Reichenbach became a well-known philosopher of science who wrote many books on the philosophical implications of Einsteinian physics. Both became major figures in the United States in the 1930s (Reichenbach after some years in Turkey), and were instrumental in the rise of analytic philosophy there. On the other hand, Heidegger's *Being and Time* gave almost no consideration at all to Einsteinian physics. His later work, where he talks of "time-space" rather than Einsteinian space–time, indicates his feeling that Einsteinian physics (like Newtonian physics, which is more directly addressed in *Being and Time*) continued to treat time as a spatial entity (a thing).

While logical positivism as a programme has been largely abandoned in analytic philosophy, some of the crucial differences that were apparent at this stage (and earlier in the Bergson–Russell debate) have recurred throughout the twentieth century. Most notably, the analytic tradition harbours reservations about transcendental philosophizing about time, and contains a strong sub-culture of deference to the best findings of the relevant sciences, while the vast majority of continental philosophers, by contrast, typically use transcendental arguments and are either critically/creatively engaged with science (non-deferentially) or entirely uninterested in it. What this means for the philosophy of time is well captured by Keith Ansell-Pearson's summary of the Bergson–Russell debate:

> the physicist gives us space–time in which time has no independent meaning; but the philosopher holds that space–time is really spatialised time and not time at all. The physicist then retorts that the time of the philosopher is merely phenomenological or psychological. (2002: 44)

Ansell-Pearson's "physicist" is a proxy for many analytic philosophers, including Russell, Carnap, Reichenbach and myriad recent four-dimensionalists. If this characterization is valid, it seems plausible to maintain that even when discussions on the philosophy of time apparently proceed in the same direction, they do so in parallel, as it were, on locally incommensurable rails. Since Heidegger, for instance, continental philosophy has been wary of references to immediacy, intuitions or any postulation of an undivided "now", but this is done in a manner that is radically distinct from the analytic four-dimensionalist criticism of presentism. Yet even this "distorted parallelism" claim is too weak; each tradition's approach to the question of time additionally incorporates some kind of rejection of the other. Something like what Lyotard (1989) calls a *differend* bedevils analytic and continental philosophy at this point: that is, a case of conflict between two parties that does not allow for the possibility of a rule or criterion (or even a linguistic vocabulary) by which the dispute may be fairly decided.[5] This would appear to rest, in part, on differing methodological and meta-philosophical allegiances. For most continental philosophers, the very possibility of philosophizing, questioning and thinking requires that one consider the relation between time and "subjectivity",[6] whereas the analytic enterprise simply elides this as part of the general rejection of transcendental reasoning. The divide here only gets reinforced when metaphysical or transcendental reflections on time become associated with sociopolitical critique, as happens with Hegelo-Marxist philosophers and, in a different way, in the poststructuralist guise of continental philosophy that we shall now consider.

TIME AND POLITICS

Many of the most famous continental philosophers have seen an intimate relation between philosophies of time and normativity, including sociopolitical issues – think of Hegel, Marx and Heidegger, all of whom have challenged the conception of time as involving a series of moments, a linear trajectory that clock-time regulates and subjects to our control. In fact, it is this understanding of time, as about measurement, and thus as amenable to calculation, prediction, arithmetical division and ultimately time-keeping, that all of the different poststructuralist thinkers also challenge, sometimes on ethico-political grounds but also on philosophical ones. Most frequently, the philosophical reasons given here rely on various forms of transcendental argument, which are taken to explain why linear clock-time (or theoretical ideas of time that are dependent on a clock-like series of moments) is an abstraction from lived time, or is dependent on the existence of a past that cannot be recalled and a future that cannot be anticipated, and incoherent without them. Methodologically speaking, the prolific use of transcendental arguments within continental philosophy constitutes a major point of difference with analytic philosophy as we have seen, but to view this as the fundamental meta-philosophical cause of the analytic–continental divide would be to ignore the fact that many of the other major continental methods (including genealogy, hermeneutics, "intuition" for Bergson, and phenomenology) are also bound up with philosophies of time and an interest in the historical presuppositions of concepts. They are all methods that develop and affirm our essential historicity, as does the conception of reason that is invoked.

In more recent times, an emphasis on the future (and the event) that defies anticipation and hence cannot be understood as "soon to be present" is arguably shared by Levinas,[7] and all the major thinkers said to be poststructuralist.

Derrida and Deleuze certainly emphasize a conception of the future whose significance lies in the way in which it simultaneously interrupts any "now" or present moment and is a condition of possibility for any event worthy of the name. Indeed, they both also invoke Hamlet and maintain that an event can only occur when time is "out of joint" in the way that they associate with futurity; otherwise there is no possibility of the event but merely a pre-programmed or deterministic outcome. They assert that it is this aspect of the radical singularity of any event that needs to be emphasized, as a counterbalance to conceptions of time in which the future is treated as known and apprehended according to either the habitual expectations of the present, or the predictions and calculations that are based on what we presently know. On this view of the future, it is fundamentally not amenable to prediction and calculation. By contrast, analytic epistemology arguably endorses or makes room for a calculative model in relation to the future, in the articulation and defence of inductive processes that are formal or semi-formal (most obviously, in the use of probability theory in straight prediction, Bayesianism in decision theory, and so on). Perhaps there is a similar approach inherent in the standard analytic thought experiment, which usually specifies a situation with no past.

While holding that we cannot avoid anticipating the future, and that we must try to predict and calculate future consequences for any decision that hopes to be responsible (that is to say that we must prepare), Derrida's work intimates that exclusive adherence to these kind of relations to the future can be dangerous. If such a calculative relation to the future becomes dominant in a given milieu, it *can* lead to the absolutist violence of fascism and communism. Less dramatically, and more frequently, it can lead to the minor fascisms of everyday life in which no one dies but conceptual and interpersonal violence nevertheless takes place. This means that Derrida will not name the future. Democracy and justice must instead be understood as "to come" and unable to ever be actualized in a present situation. This futural dimension of time that he refers to is said to intervene in the time of the present and break it open, without ever fully coming to presence. A similar predicament afflicts our relation to the past. One cannot attain a self-contained present that is immured of the past, and yet this past cannot be presented before us and recognized in its totality. To put this another way, the influence of the past on our present is largely unspecifiable, despite what some psychoanalysts suggest, yet they are right in seeing such influence as being pervasive. Borrowing from Levinas, Derrida maintains that there is something akin to an "ethical past", an immersion in the weight of history that is immemorial but nonetheless subsists in the form of traces. This ethical past cannot be represented or recalled, one cannot assume responsibility for it as a totality, and the trick is hence not to see the past as an origin to which one might return.

194

In his analyses of the times of Chronos and Aion in *The Logic of Sense*, Deleuze makes some closely related points. He describes two different aspects of time that he also calls the *time of the present*, where the past and future are only dimensions of the present contracted into it, and the *time of the past and future*, where the present is only a dimension of the past and of the future. Chronos is described as the time of actual events where all past and future events are synthesized into an indivisible present akin to Bergson's *durée*. On this view, which is similar to that of Augustine and contemporary analytic metaphysical presentists, no reality can be ascribed to that which *is* not actual, but unlike such presentists the present is still extended and has past and future dimensions. For Deleuze, however, the time of Aion is equally real and is described as the disruptive moment in which any given present is always dividing into both the past and the future, such that there is, in fact, no present. Only the past and future truly subsist in time on this view, and Deleuze hence calls Aion the time of the eternal and the time of the pure event. In *The Logic of Sense*, the reversals in Lewis Carroll's Alice books give us some kind of indication of this second order of time, Aion, and they also help explain the association of this order of time with nonsense. In Carroll's world, which Deleuze thinks is also ours, characters are punished before having done anything wrong, or they cry before pricking themselves. Now, there may be empirical explanations for such behaviour, of course, but, for Deleuze, these follow from a reality that is both Chronos and Aion. Empirical explanations fail to see that what has occurred is never wounding or traumatizing because of any particular actuality, whatever it may be, but that we are wounded because of the prospect of worse "to come" in the future, or because of the relation that any given actuality bears to the complex of temporal syntheses that is our past (or, to phrase this more positively, we are likewise inspired and touched by events because of their relation to the time of Aion). As such, it is the future and the past that affect us; an openness to the future that necessarily resists our calculative entreaties and that immemorial past which cannot be represented as a totality. If rationality purports to be atemporal, albeit with its claims being expressed in the present tense (inference and verification are of the present tense),[8] then there is something that will always elide such forms of reason. For Levinas in *Time and the Other*, rationality (and he would also say scientific time) involves a synchronization of the diverse that cannot comprehend diachrony: in this case, the past that subsists and the future that cannot be anticipated but instead disrupts (1987: 103–4).

This account of a continental "temporal turn" could easily be extended. Sartre's paradoxical conception of consciousness in *Being and Nothingness* (it is what it is not and is not what it is) revolves around his account of time, just as Merleau-Ponty's philosophy of ambiguity in *Phenomenology of*

Perception clearly revolves around temporal matters: "I know myself only in my inherence in time and in the world, that is, I know myself only in my ambiguity" (2002: 345). The tradition of critical theory owes a great deal to Benjamin and his philosophy of what we might call messianic time (which also heavily influenced the work of Agamben), as well as to Marx and others. In many of its guises (e.g. Herbert Marcuse) critical theory also relies heavily on psychoanalytic techniques that trace the impact of the past within the present. Gadamer and other hermeneutic philosophers arguably also take this "temporal turn", albeit without the poststructuralist valorization of the future as difference, novelty and so on. For Gadamer, *Verstehen* and phronesis are given greater import, as are our common-sense prejudices, which are seen as the ground of any possible understanding. It is also worth noting the existence of some recent important books on time by Alliez (1995), Lyotard (1991) and Stiegler (1998), and the fact that Badiou's philosophy of the event is also arguably pre-eminently concerned with a rupture within time. Furthermore, in *The Life of the Mind*, Hannah Arendt (1978) develops Augustine's characterization of humans as "homo temporalis". In the nineteenth century, it is not only Hegel and Marx who might be considered, but also Søren Kierkegaard, whose *Concluding Unscientific Postscript* is primarily concerned with the manner in which the genuinely religious life involves a contradiction between temporal existence and eternity, as well as the manner in which the choice, or leap of faith, occurs at an instant in which time (lived time) and eternity are envisaged to intersect.

While we have obviously run together some widely divergent and competing accounts of time in this characterization of continental philosophy, it remains the case that there is an overarching preoccupation with time in the work of all these philosophers and movements. Moreover, time is understood in a manner that pertains more to social life than to Einstein and other developments in physics (the time of our lives rather than the time of the universe, as David Hoy [2009] puts the contrast), along with a certain anti-presentism about time that carries with it an ethico-political inflexion. For all these philosophers, there is an intricate and complicated structure of time that, if simplified (e.g. treated linearly, spatially, etc.), can degenerate into problematic political positions and to violence. Institutions and societies are worthy of critique to the extent that any of the above chronopathologies takes on a dominant form. Now, this account of time and its relation to ethico-political matters is unlikely to be taken seriously by many analytic philosophers, possibly on account of the charge that such claims remain psychological points buttressed with transcendental claims that are never adequately made out. But even assuming that it were, it remains to be seen just what kind of relation these accounts bear to existing philosophy of time in analytic philosophy, and it is to this question that we now turn.

TIME IN CONTEMPORARY ANALYTIC PHILOSOPHY

While time has been a major area of philosophical enquiry in analytic meta-physics, philosophy of science and personal identity, no wholesale turn like that which we have associated with continental philosophy ever takes place. An explicit engagement with time is not a mandatory aspect of any gen-uinely original philosophy, although the less piecemeal and more system-atic projects must give philosophy of time serious attention. Moreover, such philosophers often envisage themselves as clarifying or making philosophical sense of the physics, which is ultimately the truth about time, or as "situat-ing" it within a framework of other epistemological and metaphysical claims. Many contemporary analytic philosophers are hence four-dimensionalists about time, developing an account of time that supplements or is explicitly constrained by post-Einsteinian physics. It would, however, be a simplifica-tion to argue that the difference between analytic and continental philoso-phies of time is reducible without remainder to the issue of the status of the philosopher's role in relation to the findings of physics. There are, after all, plenty of analytic metaphysicians of time who do armchair philosophy about time involving conceptual analysis, and who are not particularly concerned with the latest developments in physics. In fact, there is a split between the four-dimensionalists who bite the physicist's bullet and say that the passage of time (and the experience of the "now") is an illusion, and others (such as John Bigelow and Arthur Prior) who would claim it is a Moorean fact and not an experiential illusion, a split that can be traced all the way back to the work of McTaggart. Perhaps it is possible to argue for the compatibility of presentism and relativity/four-dimensionalism, but such views are yet to be widely accepted.

Both of these dominant trajectories will be considered here, but if time and method are bound up with one another, according to many continental philosophers, then it must be asked: is there an implicit philosophy of time underwriting some of the major methodological practices of analytic phil-osophy? To put it another way, what do the main philosophical methods presuppose about the analytic philosopher's time-embeddedness, for want of a better term? Perhaps some of the methodologies that are used are tempor-ally restricted, reliant on the present even while the content of their avowed philosophical positions is generally stridently anti-presentist as McCumber's work argues (see *Reshaping Reason*). We have seen that the main methods associated with continental philosophy – genealogy, hermeneutics, decon-struction, transcendental reasoning and so on – are not deployed in the analytic tradition. As Robin Le Poidevin and Murray MacBeath (1993: 16) note, it seems that Kant's first antinomy (time has a beginning; time has no beginning – cf. Kant 1929: A427/B455, A434/B462) or Aristotle's aporias (we maintain both that time is an entity and that it is not an entity) are the source of the analytic feeling that *a priori* arguments for time having a certain structure or topology are doomed to end in failure. Bill Newton-Smith's *The Structure of Time* (1980) argues that the structure of time is a matter that can only be settled empirically; physicists alone can determine, for example, whether or not time is bounded. In a related vein, in *Time's Arrow and Archimedes' Point* (1996), Huw Price seeks to re-establish an Archimedean point for knowledge outside of the relativism that seems to be a consequence of the special theory of relativity and our various anthropocentric biases, most particularly the fact that our philosophizing and thinking about time is greatly affected by our own finite status as creatures in time. Price adopts the reverse procedure to Heidegger and attempts to dispel rather than dwell on this paradoxical temporal structure by reinstating an objective atemporality, a view from "nowhen".

When analytic philosophers do metaphysics of time, a kind of formal or structural fertility is often on display. The nature of time might be explored in part through an investigation of the properties of various temporal logics, which might exhibit forward or backward branches, temporal loops, continuous, discrete or integral times, or various fusions of temporal and alethic possibilities. Again, the choice of differing logical models for time (Prior-style modalized systems, or standard first-order systems quantifying over instants) can be taken to have wider metaphysical implications. Metaphysical conclusions are often plumbed here through semantic analysis, much as in the tradition outlined in Chapter 15: the eliminability or ineliminability of A-series terms might be taken to have consequences for at least the implicit commitments of our everyday language. Again, many thought experiments concerning time are distinctly science-fictional: consider the way Richard Swinburne (1990) and Ernest Sosa (1983) argue for the existence of temporal subjective facts by asking us to imagine that someone knows all that there is to know about time, history and dates, but does not know which date is the present one, or Sidney Shoemaker's (1969) case for the conceivability of "frozen time", or the numerous ongoing analyses of time-travel, as philosophers attempt to decide whether the asymmetry of causation is related to the asymmetry of before and after.[9] Radical revisions to our common-sense understandings of time are countenanced by many of these philosophers. Nowhere does it seems that a chronological, linear understanding of time as a succession of instants is dominant, and yet nowhere is there any kind of reflection like that for which continental philosophers go in for, whether they be phenomenologists, poststructuralists and so on. Can we even situate the "continental" perspectives that we have considered in terms of the debate between two views on the nature of temporal reality – presentism and eternalism – that have dominated analytic philosophy? Both seem to fail to capture what is at stake in continental reflections on time, whether at the beginning of the twentieth century or the end. Continental philosophers since Heidegger want to dispute the philosophical priority of the present, as most of the analytic eternalist camp does, but also to insist (unlike eternalists) on temporal becoming, on ontological distinctions between past, present and future, as well as between time and space. This conjunction of claims has no obvious equivalent in analytic philosophy, perhaps because it is not readily compatible with physics. Of course, there are some analytic philosophers who feel that the eternalism and presentism alternatives are unduly restrictive, including those who maintain that the debate is merely verbal because each side is using the word "real" in a different sense: one untensed and the other tensed.[10] Nonetheless, perhaps owing to the analytic tilt on developing inferential connections so dialogue and communal progress can be made, much of the debate revolves around evaluating the pros and cons of two (or at most three) main accounts of time: presentism, eternalism and, to a lesser extent, the "growing universe" theory. None of these frameworks resemble in either methods or conclusions the kind of positions and arguments proffered by Deleuze and Derrida, or for that matter by Husserl and Bergson. Consider, for example, the commonly espoused (old) B-series claim that (i) the semantics of "past", "present" and "future" can be explicated entirely, without loss of meaning, in terms of relations to the time of utterance (for instance, to say "The 1950s are past" is to say no more than "The 1950s are earlier than the time of utterance"), and (ii) the idea that there is such a thing as the passage of time arises entirely from an incorrect understanding of such semantic matters. This idea that the past might become part of an omni-temporal space–time block, rather than retain its own significance, is, we think, precisely what the notion of an immemorial past (Derrida), or a virtual past (Bergson and Deleuze), would deny.

There is, likewise, a genuine clash between the phenomenological accounts of time and what analytic philosophers are interested in. In one sense, this is perfectly understandable. Phenomenology focuses on describing our experience of time, which might include the interplay between the three different temporal dimensions as they are differently experienced in, say, boredom, anxiety or listening to a melody. In addition, phenomenologists delimit some of the non-empirical conditions of possibility for the experience of time. They hence examine subjective experience, and the conditions of possibility for that experience, whereas physicists are concerned with objective or physical time. What are we to make of these very different accounts? Can they both be true? It seems we are faced with a choice between some form of pluralism or reductionism. We can be pluralists, and say that both are right in their own domain (roughly the subjective versus the objective, the phenomenological versus the naturalistic), but this risks a resulting vacuity or lack of philosophical depth; worse, unless we are pre-pared to countenance a radical dualism, it ignores the clear signs that neither framework is particularly commensurable with the other. Indeed, if physical time and psychological time are two different kinds of time, then extensive commentary is required regarding their relation to one another, something that is generally not forthcoming in the work of either analytic or continental philosophers.

Alternatively, we can be reductive and say that one of these two philoso-phies of time derives from (or is a mistaken reflection of) the other, which is the more fundamental. It seems to us that both analytic and continental phil-osophers adopt this option more than ecumenical pluralism, although the methods and rationale provided for these orders of priority and reductions are very different. How else might we explain the suggestion made by many analytic philosophers that subjective/psychological time is an illusion, even though psychological time is discovered first by each of us as we grow out of our childhood, and even though psychological time was discovered first as we evolved from our animal ancestors (Dowden 2010)? Consider, on the other hand, Gallagher and Zahavi's following claim in *The Phenomenological Mind*:

> There is no pure third-person perspective, just as there is no view from nowhere. To believe in the existence of such a pure third-person perspective is to succumb to an objectivist illusion. This is, of course, not to say that there is no third-person perspective ... but it is a perspective founded upon a first-person perspective, or, to be more precise, it emerges out of the encounter between at least two first-person perspectives; that is, it involves inter-subjectivity. (2008a: 40)

On their view, the conditions of subjective time are also the conditions of possibility of intersubjectivity, which are, in turn, the condition of possibil-ity of the objective time of the physicists. Moreover, for them any account of time that ignores its experiential development in humans, that gives no attention to questions of conditions of possibility of temporal experience, will be one-sided.

Indeed, issues pertaining to the genesis of knowledge and its development are important to all continental philosophers, thus inviting the charge of perpetuating the genetic fallacy as we have seen. Sometimes this is perhaps a fair charge, but the reverse position is also a risk – what James Williams (2005) has termed the anti-genealogical fallacy, an accusation that might be bestowed on any view that thinks that concepts come from nowhere, or that we might translate our overdetermined and messy language, with its history of associated concepts, into a pure language that overcomes such difficulties. Yet, *prima facie*, our experiences of time and the way we learn about the world are through and through temporally tensed, since we navigate in the world through our bodies and their temporal anticipative capacities. For example, the perception of an object is informed by procedural memory (habits) and it also gives us hitherto undisclosed sides, sides that our attention might be directed towards in the future. For most continental philosophers, at least from Husserl, Sartre and Merleau-Ponty on, such experiences are the transcendental condition of our experience of a world at all, from which scientific analyses are based. Analytic philosophers might accept that a condition of the development of the hard sciences is this embodied dimension, but insist that issues to do with the truth (or metaphysical reality) of what is discovered leave such genetic questions behind. Does this commit many analytic philosophers to positing a view from nowhere, as Nagel criticized, or, more to the point, does it commit them to positing an atemporal view from "nowhen", as Price has happily accepted in *Time's Arrow and Archimedes' Point*? We cannot adequately resolve this dispute here, but it seems that we have encountered a contretemps that helps to explain the rather pervasive non-engagement between representatives of analytic and continental philosophy in the twentieth century. There will, no doubt, be counter-examples to any thesis like this, but this chapter has nonetheless begun to show what distinguishes the philosophies of time of large parts of continental philosophy from much of what takes places in analytic philosophy.

18. MIND, BODY AND REPRESENTATIONALISM

While philosophy of mind, loosely construed, is present in any philosophy, it is fair to say that philosophy of mind in analytic philosophy has taken a particular direction in the twentieth century, partly owing to developments in the cognitive sciences such as psychology, neurology, biology and linguistics, and other scientific disciplines. If the mid-century "identity theory" of the mind was largely a philosophical response to problems with behaviourism, more recent developments in analytic philosophy of mind have generally sought to integrate themselves with the cognitive sciences. A certain approach to cognitive psychology became dominant in the 1960s, bringing with it a philosophy (empirical functionalism) and an artificial intelligence (AI) research programme ("Good Old-Fashioned AI") based on the characterization of the mind as a computational system operating on language-like representations. The concern to integrate with these sciences (in the hope of propagating solutions) has not been so clearly evident in continental philosophy of mind, notwithstanding the enduring influence of Gestalt psychology, psychoanalysis, Saussurean linguistics and social sciences such as anthropology.[1] Partly because of this, but also because of some deep philosophical differences, if you pick up any textbook from the last two generations on the philosophy of mind, the major figures associated with continental philosophy will generally be absent, except perhaps for a passing mention of Husserl's thesis that all consciousness is consciousness *of*, or directed towards, something. This absence in textbooks, as well as the absence of genuine trends of cross-citation, alerts us immediately to the pervasiveness of the divide, especially given that philosophy of mind is the primary concern of analytic philosophy in recent times and that phenomenology is a discipline and method that is heavily concerned with consciousness and mind.

To some extent, however, this is unsurprising. Phenomenology, as we saw in Chapter 11, does not generally concern itself with some of the main questions that have preoccupied analytic philosophy of mind, concerning the nature of mind (material or otherwise), mental states and mental processes. On the other hand, phenomenology is clearly not entirely irrelevant to any science of perception or consciousness, and there is an overlap (and consequent contestation) with analytic philosophy of mind on some other issues here, especially in regard to reflections on self-consciousness, intentionality and time-consciousness. In addition, phenomenological analysis arguably highlights certain conditions for any viable philosophy of mind to take place. Although this claim is controversial, it is not radically dissimilar to arguments that Frank Jackson (2003) and others offer for the indispensability of conceptual analysis, although the conceptual analysis in each case starts at a different place. Jackson asks how, without conceptual analysis of one's starting points (the ordinary concepts of belief, desire and so on) one could ever be clear about the success of any explanation or reduction of such matters. The phenomenologist Eduard Marbach suggests that non-conscious mental processing (if it is not a misnomer for brain activities) will be understandable only as belonging to a realm of the mental if phenomenological analyses of conscious mental life have given us the basic conceptual categories. Without such clarification, he says, "my suspicion will not go away that some kind of 'intrinsic' or 'magical connection' between putative vehicles of representation and what they stand for, so brilliantly discussed by Putnam, will be introduced willy-nilly in order (allegedly) to explain how reference is possible" (1993: 9).

The philosophical landscape on this topic has also begun to change recently, with developments in "post-analytic philosophy" and an increasing pluralism in analytic philosophy. The stronger forms of physicalism and reductivism in analytic philosophy of mind seem to be in partial abeyance, the computational model of the mind has encountered empirical and philosophical problems, and well-developed alternative models (such as connectionism, or the dynamic systems approach) have now appeared. Such developments might suggest to the optimistic among us that the "determined deafness of the mid-century has now given way to healthy curiosity" (Kelly 2008: 8). Sean Kelly adds that:

> what is notable today, by contrast, is the desire to appropriate phenomenology, to forage amongst its branches for the tastiest fruit; and along with this desire, the belief – or at least a resolute openness to the possibility – that the phenomenological fruit might offer philosophical nourishment. (*Ibid*.: 8–9)

On such a view, there has been a genuine meeting of minds between phenomenology and analytic philosophy of mind,[2] and in some respects we agree with this. The talking past each other that we have seen in earlier chapters is not as evident, and we can cite some philosophers who have brought the work of some major continental philosophers into dialogue with analytic philosophy of mind; we might think of Hubert Dreyfus's work on Heidegger and Merleau-Ponty, as well as his critique of the AI industry and associated models of the mind (see esp. Dreyfus 1992; Dreyfus & Dreyfus 1988), not to mention the work of many other philosophers connected with him, such as Kelly, Taylor Carman, John Haugeland and others, all of whom problematize the core presuppositions of traditional AI that the mind is (akin to) a symbol-processing machine. Francisco Varela, Evan Thompson and Eleanor Rosch's embodied enactive approach to perception and the mind in *The Embodied Mind* draws on Merleau-Ponty and other phenomenologists, and has been influential both within philosophy and to some extent in the neurosciences (Varela went on to do work that he called "neuro-phenomenology"). Others who are doing important crossover work in this respect include Maxine Sheets-Johnstone, José Bermudez, Shaun Gallagher, Dan Zahavi, Michael Wheeler and John Sutton. These philosophers are all typically indebted to at least one of three major continental philosophers: Husserl, Merleau-Ponty or Heidegger. It would hence be an overstatement to say today, as the editors of a book on Merleau-Ponty claimed in 1995 (when it was probably correct), that:

> contemporary philosophy of mind (and cognitive science) has proceeded with stunning disregard for Merleau-Ponty's work in this domain. Post-Cartesian philosophy of mind ... starts from a distinction between mind and body, and then 1. attempts to establish their connection (or parity), or 2. aims, in some fashion, to reduce one to the other, mind to body, mind to brain, mind to brain to computer. (Olkowski & Haas 1995: 15)

The scene is certainly more pluralistic than this, and engagements with phenomenology have become more plausible in the wake of the difficulties afflicting philosophy of mind in relation to phenomenal consciousness, difficulties that were partly heralded by Chalmers's *The Conscious Mind* (1996). Finally, there has simply been far more interaction between analytic philosophy of mind and phenomenology than there has been between the analytic tradition and poststructuralist philosophers, or say Badiou, Slavoj Žižek and Deleuze. The planets do come at least relatively close to one another on this topic. Indeed, one might argue that to the extent that phenomenologists and analytic philosophers of mind seem to have achieved explicit disagreement on substantive issues involving representation, the divide here is closing; there has been at least partial agreement in the conceptual framework to bring to the problem, and the debate here is no more a marker of the divide than any other debate within the philosophy of mind.[3]

Nonetheless, it would also be very hard to claim that there has been a wholesale rapprochement of these traditions in philosophy of mind. The work of Husserl, Heidegger and Merleau-Ponty has played a role only at the margins of analytic philosophy of mind. To take Dreyfus, one well-known philosopher sometimes thought to succeed in breaching the divide through the work of these philosophers, Terry Winograd notes that: "it would be an exaggeration to claim that the challenges posed by Dreyfus have been taken to heart by most AI researchers or cognitive scientists, even today. There are large chasms between the world of phenomenology and the world of symbolic programming" (2000: viii). And despite some important philosophical points in common, analytic philosophers inclined to contextualism also do not seem to seriously read or engage with Dreyfus (presumably because of his allegiance to existential phenomenology). Moreover, Husserl, Heidegger and Merleau-Ponty are still infrequently discussed in the major philosophy of mind journals, just as phenomenology journals (with the exception of *Phenomenology and the Cognitive Sciences*) rarely discuss analytic philosophers who have defended qualia epiphenomenalism (such as Chalmers and Jackson), let alone empirical functionalists such as Fodor or Ruth Millikan, eliminativists such as Paul Churchland, Patricia Churchland and Stich, or neo-behaviourists (or instrumentalists) such as Dennett, and so on. While Chalmers's work did reinvigorate interest in consciousness in the analytic tradition, there is little evidence that this has induced analytics to forage in phenomenological fields (*pace* Kelly). The divide in the philosophy of mind hence remains significant, even if it is slowly being complicated. In addition to the methodological issues discussed earlier in the book, there are perhaps three major philosophical difficulties that are all bound up with each other that explain this residual distrust: the broad analytic commitment to the language of representationalism in setting out the problem landscape (even for projects that end in some form of anti-representationalism); the analytic concern for liaison with the relevant sciences (or, alternatively, with clearly demarcating the conceptual and the scientific questions here); and ontology more generally (the issue is whether the desire to avoid dualisms, which is a shared desire, results in a radical narrowing of the available possibilities for conceptualizing the relation between mind and nature).

We shall focus on representationalism about the mind here, since it seems to us that the fundamental issue of contention between analytic and continental philosophers in relation to mind (and subjectivity, consciousness, etc.) pertains to representation: are there mental states or entities that "stand for", or refer to, things in the world, or that represent things to be a certain way? Few continental philosophers would maintain that the mind is fundamentally

representational, whereas representationalism of some kind, although challenged, unquestionably has default status on the analytic side of the fence.
Many cognitive scientists go even further; Steven Pinker, for instance, holds
that the package deal of representationalism and computationalism is "as
fundamental to cognitive science as the cell doctrine is to biology and plate
tectonics is to geology" (1994: 73). That representationalism is key to the
divide is not a new idea; Rorty (1999) makes much the same claim, and
Williamson (at one time) points to a representational turn in the analytic
tradition.[4] Trying to get clear on precisely what this difference amounts to
raises some difficult exegetical issues, since the sense of representation in
play here is not the same as that in play in epistemological debates in the
eighteenth century; representationalism, in the analytic tradition, need not
involve the positing of an *intermediary* between mind and world (mental
images, sense data, etc.), which is one of the enduring concerns of continental philosophers. Indeed, sometimes analytic philosophers identify representations in reverse, so to speak, wherever intentionality is detected; this is,
roughly, the big idea behind Dennett's account:

> It is not that we attribute (or should attribute) beliefs and desires
> only to things in which we find internal representations, but rather
> that when we discover some object for which the intentional strat-
> egy works, we endeavour to interpret some of its internal states or
> processes as internal representations. What makes some internal
> feature of a thing a representation could only be its role in regulat-
> ing the behavior of an intentional system.   (1987: 32)

More generally, analytic philosophers who adopt instrumentalist, non-
cognitivist, reductive, anti-realist or other non-literal approaches to the reality
of the denizens of the mind are quite capable of talking the representationalist talk without necessarily being committed to the straightforward positing
of representations. So it is not yet at all clear what is at stake in the pro-
representationalism versus anti-representationalism debate, or indeed the
extent to which this means there are conceptual presuppositions in common
here between the traditions. But let us try to make this typology plausible,
before then venturing to undertake some of the more difficult comparative
and evaluative questions.

ANALYTIC REPRESENTATIONALISM

Many analytic philosophers maintain that most or all mental states are *representational* states, in the sense that they carry representational content,

and that mental processes are in the business of processing information (and misinformation) carried by these representations; perceptual systems receive environmental information and modify it for use elsewhere in the mind; memory is an information store; motor control is a matter of information-sending and responding to; and so on. As Kim Sterelny (1990: 19–22) notes, the idea that the mind represents the world has sources in both our self-image as creatures continuous with the natural world, and our folk psychology. Our behaviour, like that of many other animals, is flexible, in the sense that we are sensitive to new requirements the environment places on us, and can learn from experience. Moreover, what we are sensitive to is the information in a physical stimulus rather than the physical format of the stimulus; we do not simply exhibit reflexive behaviour when presented with a stimulus. But if our intelligent, adaptable behaviour is information-sensitive, a natural view is that we are forming representations of the world, drawing inferences from them, guiding our behaviour in the light of these inferences and so on.

Again, our folk psychology is heavily and explicitly representational, relying as it does on a rich language of propositional attitudes (beliefs, desires, hopes, fears and so on). This representational approach naturally carries over to those positions that amount to philosophical tweakings of folk psychology. Consider, for instance, Dennett's advocation of an intentional stance in *The Intentional Stance*, *Consciousness Explained* and other works. Dennett points out that we use a variety of strategies to correctly predict what will happen in the world around us: what cars, rain clouds, warming saucepans of milk, angry dogs and so forth are likely to do. On some occasions, we can get by in taking a "physical stance" to the relevant object: that is, by treating it as a physical entity and using our knowledge of the workings of physics. On other occasions (confronted by a television remote, say), treating the thing purely as a physical item is likely to be unhelpful; here I take the "design stance", treating the thing as the product of a process of design, predictable in that it will carry out the designer's goals. Finally, for some objects it is profitable to take the "intentional stance"; here I treat the object as an agent, attributing representations (in the form of beliefs and desires) to it, and predicting its behaviour in accordance with the platitudes of folk psychology. Here, although representations are certainly posited, they are thought of as to some extent theoretical, instrumentally useful, entities. In similar, although slightly more realist, vein, David Lewis's analytic functionalism involves a "map" account of intentional states, on which the contentful unit is the whole mind, single representations being distinctly secondary entities, to be read off the whole in much the same way that representational facts are read off a street map (see Lewis 1999). On the other hand, philosophical invocations of folk psychology can be much more realist in their treatment of representation; for empirical functionalists such as Fodor, for instance, beliefs, desires and the other propositional attitudes are generally individuated as states in which the very same representation is capable of playing different functional roles.

For these (admittedly not final) reasons, some commitment to the existence of representations has been standard in the analytic philosophy of mind. The classical programme within cognitive science reflects this; at its core, it consists of an assertion of this kind, together with a computational account of the way in which representations are used in the mind. On this further view, our inner representations are built up out of symbols in some way, and mental processing involves operations of symbolic manipulation that happen to satisfy the relevant semantic relations the contents of the representations exhibit. (For example, we can specify a manipulation that removes pairs of As from the front of a string of letters, if they begin that way, and this specification, although entirely symbolic, might well satisfy a *semantic* rule, such as the rule of double negation, which allows us to deduce a string of the form X from a string of the form not-not-X.) A particular form of computationalism, in turn, has been influential, in which these representations are language-like in respecting grammatical rules: this is Fodor's "language of thought" hypothesis (see Fodor 1975). All these combinations have on occasion been called "representationalism", as their co-involvement was at first thought to be nearly immediate; it has taken some time for non-linguistic computationalism to emerge as a rival to Fodor's view, or for non-computationalist representationalism to become a serious view within the tradition. And within the analytic tradition, quite apart from the differing takes on folk psychology evinced by Dennett, Lewis and Fodor, there are disagreements about how far to posit representations of particular kinds in explaining particular faculties. On the one hand, Ryle's *Concept of Mind* famously argues against the "intellectualist" view that knowing how to do something is primarily a matter of contemplating internal rules or propositions, and a whole tradition of non-linguistic representation takes off from here. In the other direction, analytic philosophy of mind contains numerous suggestions on which the role of mental imagery, say, is to be largely taken over by linguistic representations, or on which know-how – such as riding a bike – is to be analysed as a species of propositional knowledge, as in Jason Stanley and Timothy Williamson's recent essay (2001).

Unsurprisingly, the representational account of the mind firmly commits its practitioners to an intentionality claim. But where Brentano claimed that intentionality was an essentially irreducible feature of mental states, this thesis is not open to contemporary materialists who have eschewed dualism and who are appropriately worried about the positing of any kind of "ghost in the machine" that is not naturalistically explainable. Hence representationalism gives rise to a "psychosemantic" research project within analytic philosophy of mind: the project of explaining how mental states can have meanings. Given the constraints of naturalism and materialism, not to mention the influence of Kripkean and Putnamian arguments for content externalism, this task is generally taken to be equivalent to explaining intentionality through the connections that mental representations have with the non-semantic environment external to the agent; moreover, to carrying this task out for all and only those creatures for which representations are posited. The analytic literature here is large, and includes consideration of such matters as the causal/historical origins of mental state types (Devitt & Sterelny 1987), patterns of covariation between tokens of a mental state type and the external environment (Dretske 1981; Fodor 1990), and appeal to facts about the evolutionary history of the species of the agent (Millikan 1984; see also Millikan 1989). Typically, theories must steer between over-generation concerns (why does my concept mean "dog" instead of "dog skull", if both are among the causes of its tokening?), under-generation concerns (why does my concept mean "dog" in a way that extends to dogs I have not encountered?), and misrepresentation concerns (it is all too easy for a psychosemantic theory to accidentally rule out the possibility of error).

This has proved an extremely difficult task. As a result, there is at least some pressure within the less behaviourist end of the analytic tradition to reconsider strong representationalism, however natural it might be as a first port of call in developing the cognitive sciences. Fodor puts the worry this way:

> A naturalistic psychology ... remains a sort of ideal of pure reason; there must *be* such a psychology since, presumably, we do sometimes think of Venus and, presumably, we do so in virtue of a causal relation between it and us. But there's no practical hope of making science out of this relation. And, of course, for methodology, practical hope is *everything.*　　　　(1981: 252)

A second pressure on representationalism comes from the eliminativist tendencies within analytic philosophy of mind. For instance, Stich (1978: 575) employs variants of the Twin Earth thought experiment to argue for the view that the mind is essentially a "syntactic", contentless engine, and the syntactic states that it shifts between are states that are individuated by their causal relations to other such states and to behaviour and perceptual inputs. We overlay this, for our own reasons, with a folk-psychological interpretation, but the content attributions that we therefore come up with should be kept completely distinct from (proper) psychological work. Stich and others have more recently developed the further claim that connectionist (non-computational, in a certain way) accounts of the mind have no place for the notion of a contentful representation as that notion arises in folk psychology. For instance, folk psychology contains the truism that our beliefs have differential causal powers: on a particular occasion it is my belief that the car keys are on the hook, and not any of my background beliefs about Venezuela, Schubert or mathematics, that causes me to act the way I do. Yet if my representations are distributed through the weightings of something like a connectionist network, it is not immediately apparent how one can genuinely cause my actions without others also being involved (Ramsey *et al.* 1990).

Analytic representationalists are, however, not merely engaged with these theoretical challenges. There is a further debate, of potential relevance to continental philosophy, about the extent to which representations explain the qualitative aspects of experience as well as the intentional content of mental states. This is a major battleground in contemporary analytic philosophy of mind. In Jackson's terms:

> Minimal representationalism, as we might call it, holds that experience is *essentially* representational while being silent on whether an experience's representing that things are thus and so, for some suitable thus and so, exhausts its nature in the sense of settling it without remainder. Strong representationalism adds the exhaustion claim to minimal representationalism ... it is hard to make sense of a phenomenal "overflow" from the representational content. Such an overflow would appear to be something with feel but without representational content, but once we have feel, we have, it seems, representation.   (2008: 323–4)

We cannot go further into this debate at present. The fact that such views are mainstream in analytic but not continental philosophy is, however, a clear indication of the differing trust in representation in each tradition.

CONTINENTAL ANTI-REPRESENTATIONALISM ABOUT THE MIND

We think that an anti-representationalism about the mind (and this includes what we today call computational and functionalist models) is one of the key family resemblance features of continental philosophy. Before attempting to show this, however, we need to note that rather than exclusively pursue philosophy of mind, what tends to take place, as David Morris observes, is a preliminary meta-philosophy: all philosophy begins by scrutinizing the philosophizing subject, philosophical method and the conceptual prejudices of philosophy. This means that "study of what amounts to mind becomes inseparable from ontology, epistemology, and other areas" (2007: 533), and that there is always an eye on what a certain way of confronting a problem betrays, say in regard to dualism, or residual Cartesianism. The hard problem of consciousness, for example, may be viewed as a false problem, or at least a problem that is made too hard by presuppositions in its framing. As Morris suggests, consciousness is world-embedded, "actively involved and manifest in a publicly accessible external world, and is opaque to itself in virtue of its situation" (*ibid.*). The focus is then not on lateral difficulties with relations between consciousness and world, mind and matter, but on examining the layers or strata within the mind–world complex, the relation between pre-reflective and reflective consciousness, or non-conceptual content and conceptual awareness.

We can begin to get a feel for this tendency by looking at Derrida's essay "Envoi" (or "Sendings – On Representations"), which focuses on historical issues to do with the word representation, in its German, French and English varieties, and its conceptual deployment in the Franco-German traditions. Derrida's essay addresses philosophy of mind, along with issues to do with political representation and philosophy of language, as well as Heidegger's conception of modernity as constituting an epoch of representation. Derrida also notes that at a conference on the borders of various European countries at the start of the twentieth century, Bergson tried to ban the term "representation" from being used at all, on account of its Germanic connotations; we are alerted immediately to an important divide within continental philosophy – between France and Germany. Bergson, of course, also had philosophical worries with representationalism beyond its German inheritance. His *Matter and Memory* involves an account of the brain (emphasizing it as centre of action rather than organ of representation) that has been influential. Indeed, Derrida makes the following claim about the prevailing philosophical landscape on the continent:

> Today many people set their thinking against representation. In a more or less articulated or rigorous way, this thinking gives in facilely to an evaluation: representation is bad. And this without being able to assign, in the final analysis, the place and necessity of the evaluation. (2007: 102)

Derrida is referring here to philosophy of mind and the Heidegger-influenced trajectory within European philosophy, in which a philosophy of representation is bound up with the assumption of a Cartesian subject with privileged access to their own minds. For Heidegger, representational thinking is characteristic of our technological epoch and Rorty has made similar claims more recently in *Philosophy and the Mirror of Nature*. Derrida also suggests that both Nietzsche and Hegel were likewise against representation; for Nietzsche in *The Birth of Tragedy*, the Apollonian order pertains to representation and is contrasted unfavourably with the Dionysian order. Derrida's analysis of representation touches on concerns about the metaphysics involved, suggesting that it is committed to the idea that the content that is represented is thought to be a presence that is not itself a representation. If this is so, representationalism is bound up with a metaphysics of presence, and a view of language as a representation or mirror of reality, something that few continental philosophers endorse as the *raison d'être* of language. In the course of engaging with Frege in *The Logic of Sense*, Deleuze, for example, contends that the model of language as a representational medium results in the "circle of the proposition" (1990a: 17), and that there is nothing in such a model (which he calls the model of resemblance) to account for the practical generation of sense prior to the proposition (*ibid.*: 123). Language is hence not understood primarily in terms of representing, or mirroring, a non-linguistic reality. This is generally considered to be a naive metaphysical view of language for many continental philosophers, something that is belied by the complexity of communication evidenced by the task of translation (there is no single literal translation, but always also interpretation) and intersubjective communication more generally. While it is true that "postmodern" philosophers frequently talk about discourse and representational systems, in arguably the defining philosophical discourse on postmodernism, *The Postmodern Condition*, Lyotard defines postmodernism as a "crisis in representation" induced because language comes to constitute reality rather than to reflect it. Moreover, despite the apparently deterministic implications of this statement, Lyotard's enduring interest in desire and libidinal philosophy, as well as his philosophy of art, revolves around precisely that which exceeds these representations, and in *Difference and Repetition* Deleuze contends that representation "is a site of transcendental illusion" (1994: 265).

Husserl and other phenomenologists often distinguish re-presentation (in memory, imagination, etc.) from presentation in perception. The former is, however, frequently understood to be derivative of the latter, and with existential phenomenology, for example, the fundamental move is to situate representational accounts of the mind within an allegedly more basic framework of bodily intentionality and coping with an environment that is claimed to be the condition of possibility of representations. This resistance to representationalism also stems from the insistence on understanding mind and body as one, rather than separate, with the lived-body an "agent" that is only ambiguously aware of itself. As Merleau-Ponty states in *The Structure of Behaviour*, "consciousness is lived rather than known, and the possession of a representation or the exercise of a judgment is not coextensive with the life of consciousness" (1983: 173). Merleau-Ponty also names an essay "The Primacy of Perception", and the focus here is on the presentation of phenomena, not the mind as internally representing that which presents itself. This distinction is itself thought to be a falsification of many phenomenological experiences and we shall shortly turn to the question of its empirical adequacy.

In Heidegger's work, representational thinking is again a secondary rather than primary phenomenon. While it might be alleged that he does not simply reject the correspondence theory of truth, which typically holds that truth is a relation between mental (or other) representations and non-mental things (and is rightly characteristic of the present-at-hand attitude), he does want to account for such a view via something that is again alleged to be more basic (the ready-to-hand). As Heidegger states:

> when Dasein directs itself towards something and grasps it, it does not somehow first get out of an inner sphere in which it has been proximally encapsulated, but its primary kind of Being is such that it is always "outside" alongside entities which it encounters and which belong to a world already discovered.   (1962: §13)

Whether this entails a rejection of representationalism is a subject of some debate in Heidegger scholarship, but much of this dispute stems from just how one is to understand the famous distinction (and perhaps priority) between the ready-to-hand and the present-at-hand, since one of Heidegger's claims is that it is when Dasein has withdrawn from the world in a theoretical attitude that the mind represents objects as present-at-hand. On Wheeler's Heidegger-inspired account, this means that: "Smooth coping is a process of real-time environmental interaction involving the subtle generation of fluid and flexible context-specific responses to incoming stimuli. Crucially, those responses are not the product of representation-based or reason-based control" (2005: 134). In a related vein Haugeland contends:

> Until recently ... research has retained the assumption that the relevant "furniture of information" is ... complex symbol structures ... internal to the individual agent ... but since the significant complexity of intelligent behaviour depends intimately on the concrete details of the agent's embodiment and worldly situation ... intelligence as such should be understood as characteristic, in the first instance, of some more complex structure than an internal, disembodied "mind".   (2000: 211)

The meaningful is not a model – that is, it's not representational – but is instead concepts embedded in the context of references.

> And we do not store the meaningful inside of ourselves, but rather live and are at home in it … The meaningful is the world itself.
>
> (*Ibid.*: 231)

But it is Dreyfus who continues to pose one of the most oft-repeated rejoinders to representationalism, in a view that synthesizes aspects of the work of Merleau-Ponty and Heidegger. For him, basic everyday coping, or real-time adaptive responses to stimuli, does not necessarily involve representations. If it did, and if these representations were codifiable in symbolic form, Dreyfus argues, AI would have had far more success than it has. In *Mind Over Machine*, Dreyfus and his brother Stuart declared:

> Current AI is based on the idea, prominent in philosophy since Descartes, that all understanding consists in forming and using appropriate representations. Given the nature of inference engines, AI's representations must be formal ones, and so common-sense understanding must be understood as some vast body of precise propositions, beliefs, rules, and procedures. Thus formulated, the problem has so far resisted solution. We predict it will continue to do so. (Dreyfus & Dreyfus 1988: 99)

Intelligence does not consist, on this view, in the manipulation of physical symbols according to formal rules, and practical engagement with the world is not, at its most basic level, mediated by mental representations or intentional content that is abstractable from the material setting of what one is doing. Hubert Dreyfus's emphasis on the necessity of the body to learning and intelligence is shared by some psychologists in the embodied psychology (Lakoff & Johnson 1999) and distributed cognition traditions (see e.g. Clark 1997). In response to accounts of the mind that maintain that we are processing information, representations of states of affairs (beliefs about this state of affairs, desires for another state of affairs), Dreyfus suggests that the kind of "if–then" principles that we might be alleged to be using are philosophical reconstructions that are implausible; even if we had a tremendously long and elaborate list of all the relevant rules and principles, to apply these myriad principles and rules requires good judgement about when to apply them. This kind of practical wisdom is precisely what Dreyfus says computers cannot have, since they do not have this background knowledge that is grounded in the embodied manner that we learn things in a given culture.

In *The Embodied Mind*, Varela *et al.* (1992) also offer an anti-representationalist account of the mind–world relation that is indebted to various continental philosophers (mainly Husserl, Heidegger and Merleau-

Ponty). They also allege that cognitive representationalism has three problematic assumptions:

> the first is that we inhabit a world with particular properties, such
> as length, colour, movement, sound, etc. The second is that we
> pick up or recover these properties by internally representing
> them. The third is that there is a separate subjective "we" who does
> these things. These three assumptions amount to a strong, often
> tacit and unquestioned, commitment to realism or objectivism/
> subjectivism about the way the world is, what we are, and how we
> can come to know the world.   (*Ibid.*: 9)

For the enactive approach, on the other hand, cognition is not a representation of a pre-given world by a pre-given mind, but "the enactment of a world
and a mind on the basis of the history of the variety of actions that a being in
the world performs" (*ibid.*). Cognitive structures are hence claimed to emerge
from the recurrent sensorimotor patterns that enable action to be perceptu-
ally guided. In many respects, this is a contemporary development of the
phenomenological ontology of Heidegger and Merleau-Ponty, and Gallagher
and Zahavi capture well the reigning continental suspicion of representation
in *The Phenomenological Mind*:

> It has been customary to say that perception has representational
> or conceptual content. But perhaps such a way of talking fails to
> fully capture the situated nature of perceptual experience. Rather
> than saying that I represent the car as drivable, it is better to say
> that – given the design of the car, the shape of my body and its
> action possibilities, and the state of the environment – the car is
> drivable and I perceive it as such.   (2008a: 8)

A CONVERSATION

It seems that there is a strong contrast between theoretical accounts of the
mind that emphasize the mind as something like an inference engine (and as
primarily motivated by inferential relations between beliefs and desires) and
more anti-theoretical accounts of the mind that see instrumental rationality as part of subjectivity, but as a derivative part. It is clear, of course, that
intelligent, adaptable behaviour of the kind found in humans, apes and some
other animals is information sensitive. The question then is: how do we
best explain this? Must we conclude that we are forming representations
of the world, drawing inferences from them, guiding our behaviour in the

light of these inferences and so on, as is suggested by the representational theory of the mind? Certainly in the parts of analytic philosophy of mind closely associated with the cognitive sciences, until recently the idea that one should explain intelligent behaviour – that is informational sensitivity – by appeal to internal representations had the status of received truth. On this view, which tries to understand the brain in isolation from the organism as a whole, the wellsprings of intelligence are fundamentally inner mechanisms of inference and discrimination in the brain (Wheeler 2001). Even the more behaviourist aspects of analytic philosophy of mind exhibit something of the same tendency; on most such views, for instance, something like the token–token identity theory is taken to hold between *brain* states and mental states (indeed, this is often taken to be the basic claim any materialist is committed to in this area).

As would be apparent, the contrast between Dreyfus's views and those of, say, Frank Jackson is quite stark (although there are other views in the analytic tradition, such as Wittgenstein's, where the contrast is nowhere near as great). Dreyfus argues that propositional attitudes (belief, desire) are not needed for skilled and intelligent activity of various sorts. In an essay written with Kelly, he states:

> Consider an example of someone walking out of a room. We can observe him marching confidently toward and through the door. If we want to make sense of his behavior, we might imagine him having the desire that he leave the room and, among many other beliefs, the belief that one does that by using the door. Furthermore, if asked to reflect on his experience and given a forced choice as to whether or not he believed the floor extended beyond the room, he might well have to conclude he believed that the floor, not a chasm, was on the other side of the door. But, if we trained him to report his experience as he left the room, we would discover, as Sartre and the psychologist J. J. Gibson would have predicted, that he just responded to the "to-go-out" without giving a thought to the door or to the floor on the other side. In fact, no beliefs at all need be involved. (Dreyfus & Kelly 2007: 49)

Jackson and David Braddon-Mitchell interpret this "mindless coping" very differently, however, emphasizing the sense in which actions depend on something like dispositional propositional beliefs:

> The very beliefs and desires which guide our behaviour are over-whelmingly non-occurrent. When we go to the refrigerator to get a bottle of mineral water, beliefs about the spatial layout of

the kitchen, desires to minimise the effort involved in covering the distance, and countless others are all contributing to this process.   (1996: 137)

They go on:

> We cannot write down in full detail the rules we follow ... but there must be rules that we are following (in part implicitly ...) when we make these judgments. The alternative is the incredible one that we make the judgments by miracle. Thus, although it may be true that all that is possible for us here and now is a partial codifying of rationality, there is a full codifying to be had.
>
> (*Ibid.*: 156)

Standing up, on this view, might be said to presuppose a belief that the ground is solid, that we have two legs and so on. Of course, the degree to which this account is "intellectualist" depends in large part on the associated theory of belief and desire that Jackson and Braddon-Mitchell offer; on something like Lewis's map account (which both broadly endorse) the individual beliefs being identified here are in some sense abstractions from an overall belief-state. On such a view, the belief-state acquires its content precisely through the nexus between belief, desire and behaviour; it has as its content that set of possible worlds that is such that, were each to be actual, the agent's behaviour would tend to further his or her desires.[5] Hence the attribution of implicit background beliefs turns out to be rather less committal than it might seem at first; indeed, the account shares a great deal with instrumentalist accounts of the mind such as Dennett's. Nonetheless, and notwithstanding this caveat, our suggestion is that few continental philosophers would accept such an intellectualist view. An alternative perspective, sketched out here in a rudimentary way, would be the model of embodied understanding and know-how, endorsed by existential phenomenologists and cognitive scientists indebted to them. It seems that for Jackson and Braddon-Mitchell's rule-governed account, bodily intentionality is derivative of minded belief-desire intentionality, while it is the other way around for Dreyfus and other continental philosophers. Jackson holds that we think with representations that are like maps and pictures; Merleau-Ponty says that perception of depth presupposes movement and action first (being-in-the-world and dwelling for Heidegger), not a map or picture first and then action within it.

There are similar worries at the heart of the series of debates over the past thirty years between the sometimes antagonistic colleagues Dreyfus and John Searle. Do we need to represent a goal beforehand for success or failure to be assigned in relation to a given action, as Searle argues, against Dreyfus's view? Searle holds that the conditions of satisfaction for a given activity must be a goal in the actor's mind, or, if unconscious, the sort of goal that one *could* consciously entertain. For Dreyfus, on the other hand, Searle's account presupposes that the experience of acting has a mind-to-world direction of causation, but this is not what happens in skilful coping for Dreyfus; it is more like structural coupling with the environment that also involves world-to-mind causation.[6] Of course, the risk of the Dreyfusian account is that our being-in-the-world seems to be primarily one of mind-less coping as Searle has alleged, and perhaps we should hence consider Jackson's common-sense rejoinder to some related views: those who doubt that thought is representational should consider the map they had in their pocket that got them to a particular conference venue. While this is a fair reminder, the reverse risk is that a theoretical attitude, the philosopher's atti-tude, can be retroactively imposed on forms of existence where it manifestly will not fit, and hence that insufficient attention is given to the conditions of possibility (ontogenetic, phenomenological, childhood development, etc.) for the theoretical attitude. This problem is perhaps particularly pressing for higher-order representationalists. An important question, then, the answer to which separates many analytic and continental philosophers, is: what is the relation between embodied know-how and knowledge-that? While Ryle, Brian O'Shaughnessy, Michael Martin, Susan Hurley, Ned Block and some other well-known analytic philosophers share a verdict on this issue that links their work with that of some continental philosophers, they remain unusual in their tradition. Moreover their answer to this question does not (usually) preclude the claim that the mind is representational, at least in some attenuated sense. Where the representational baby is wholeheartedly thrown out with the bathwater, say in McDowell's *Mind and World* or in the work of Taylor, Rorty and (in places) Davidson,[7] it is perhaps no accident that such philosophers are labelled post-analytic. In many ways, Dreyfus, Merleau-Ponty and others in the continental anti-representationalist trad-ition are making a simple point that had earlier been made by Hume. How do children learn to dance, or even learn a language? Usually, not by rule-following but by embodied imitation. (Contrast this answer with the kind of answer given by Kripke's Wittgenstein to the related question as to how it is that we can follow one rule rather than another: there is no fact as to what rule is being followed; nonetheless, our ascriptions of rule-governed behav-iour here serve a function for us.) Of course, more can be said in support of the positing of implicit rules in explaining intelligent action and cognition; a pure empiricism in language acquisition, for instance, faces difficulties, given Chomsky's poverty of the stimulus argument. Does the conjunction of these worries present us with a forced alternative as Jackson and Braddon-Mitchell suggest: either implicit rules undergird the mind or we must invoke an explanation that is akin to magic? Or does the thematization of bodily intentionality offer a middle way that is naturalistically respectable, yet not subject to Chomskyian-style worries about empiricism? Without being able to resolve this here, there are reasons to think that the continental views that we have been discussing and analytic representationalism could arrive at the status of mature opponents, each alive to the prospects and problems of the other. Whether such a dialogue will happen, given the enduring analytic resistance to the idea of cognition as embodied understanding (rather than simply embrained understanding), and continental concern with the centrality of the idea of representation, remains to be seen.

19. ETHICS AND POLITICS

THEORETICAL AND ANTI-THEORETICAL APPROACHES

For much of its history in the twentieth century, analytic philosophy retreated from ethical and political engagement into meta-ethics, at least before the resurgence of interest in applied and normative ethics of the early 1970s: the influential journal *Philosophy and Public Affairs* was first published in 1971, as was Rawls's landmark *A Theory of Justice*, and Peter Singer's *Animal Liberation* was published in 1975. Some have seen this abdication as a partial explanation for the success of analytic philosophy in the United States during McCarthyism (see John McCumber's *Time in the Ditch*), although it is worth noting that, despite or because of their rather coercive theories of meaning, the logical positivists were leftist and often politically engaged in their personal lives. On the continental side, philosophers have perhaps more regularly got their hands dirty in sociopolitical matters, often co-imbricating philosophical and sociopolitical reflections, whether it be with Nazism (in Heidegger's case), or with a generally critical relation to totalitarianism, modernity and capitalism. Bergson, Beauvoir, Sartre, Merleau-Ponty (the latter three set up *Les temps modernes*), Althusser, Deleuze, Derrida, Foucault and others have all been heavily involved in ethico-political matters, continuing a certain French tradition of the engaged public intellectual that derives from Voltaire and Zola, among others.

It seems to us that enshrined in analytic and continental political philosophy are two (perhaps more) competing ways of treating the political. Ethico-political reflection in the continental tradition tends to conceive of the political very broadly and such that philosophical interventions, even artistic and stylistic innovations, are always also political interventions (see, for example, Rancière's influential book *The Politics of Aesthetics*). It is also generally oriented around the problem of violence, in regard to both conceptual and empirical orders, and also has an overarching concern with big picture issues such as capitalism, modernity and so on. Badiou captures some of this when he states that post-1940s French philosophy is distinctive for wanting to:

situate philosophy directly within the political arena, without making the detour via political philosophy; to invent what I would call the "philosophical militant", to make philosophy into a militant practice in its presence, in its way of being: not simply a reflection upon politics, but a real political intervention.   (2005: 76)

Such ambitions are perhaps behind the continued worries about continental fascism or absolutism expressed by analytic philosophers. Certainly in contrast to such ambitions much analytic political philosophy conceives of the political far more narrowly, as the contingent realm in which we make (and justify) claims in public in a pluralist society (hence analytic philosophy's default liberalism). In *A Theory of Justice*, for example, Rawls claimed to have established the distributive principles that must hold for a just society but also to give us clear guidelines as to how they might be implemented. His intention is also expressly to find principles to secure democracy's stability: hardly a focus of continental political philosophy, given its utopian and critical impetus. Analytic political philosophers are not usually interested in offering a "critique of modernity", for example, but many continental philosophers including Nietzsche, critical theorists, Deleuze, Derrida and others want to produce the new, that which is "to come", or invoke the "people who are missing" (Deleuze & Guattari 1994: 99). A political philosophy without this element threatens to be merely that which codifies existing arrangements, the reshuffling of the pack of intuitions and "everybody knows" formulations on which our social life is, admittedly, partly predicated, but without leaving a space for the new.

In this chapter, we begin with the utilitarian and liberal treatments of the ethico-political, neither of which has a strong presence in the continental tradition. We also consider, with Rawls as an example, continental concerns about the focus on distributive justice, the role of intuitions in political theory, and the role of (unconscious) emotions and desire in political philosophy. We then turn to a partial absence on the analytic side, that of virtue ethics. We argue that a number of continental philosophers can be seen as falling within an anti-theoretical virtue ethical school, and we assess the divide by looking at the different reception of virtue ethics in analytic philosophy.

LIBERALISM AND UTILITARIANISM

Contemporary analytic philosophy is markedly more tolerant of liberalism than continental philosophy; like utilitarianism, this is an obvious inheritance from Mill, but it also has well-known roots in Locke and Kant. Although there are influential earlier analytic discussions of liberalism by Berlin and H. L. A.

Hart, analytic discussion of questions of distributive justice was enlivened by Rawls's liberal manifesto, *A Theory of Justice*. The book seeks to show that the civil society of a kind of egalitarian liberalism is just. Rawls insists on the overarching distributive requirement of "justice as fairness", a state of affairs in which social institutions avoid moral arbitrariness in allocating resources. The procedure through which we are to locate appropriate institutions – decision-making under the veil of ignorance – is intended to distance us not only from our knowledge of our own social circumstances, abilities, religion, sex and race, but also from our own personal conception of the good life. Under such circumstances, Rawls argues, we will prefer maximin principles, which pro-tect both the economic interests and the autonomy of those at the bottom of the social order. Rawls goes further, arguing that, in a Kantian sense, agents who act by the maximin principle are acting autonomously, since "they are acting from principles that they would acknowledge under conditions that best express their nature as free and equal rational beings" (2005: 515). That one's situation under the veil of ignorance would best express one's nature as a free and equal rational being, of course, indicates a kind of impartiality here, in which decisions about social organization are to be settled by relatively contextless, disinterested rational agents.

Utilitarianism and its consequentialist descendants are also influential within analytic philosophy, as Rawls acknowledges, although most utilitar-ians adopt versions of the view designed to bring it more into line with our everyday moral intuitions. The most straightforward version of the view is act utilitarianism, which holds that the right act to perform is that act the consequences of which maximize value. Since the consequences of my act will often be difficult to determine, acting rightly somewhat loses its action-guiding force, in favour of avoiding blameworthiness. The act utilitarian points out, in reply, that a theory's decision procedure can diverge from its criterion of rightness; if time is short, one is permitted to satisfice, by choos-ing the first good enough option that comes along, or to choose the best option of those you have time to consider, or simply to follow rules of thumb. The rule utilitarian, by contrast, takes the view that the right set of rules (indexed perhaps to an agent or a community) is that set of rules compliance with which will have the best consequences, where the best consequences are again those that maximize value. At least some rule utilitarians at this point take care to ensure that the problem of epistemic access to rightness is at least lessened; for instance, Brad Hooker suggests the following method:

> Find a code of rules such that there is no other code whose inter-nalization by the overwhelming majority of everyone *could rea-sonably be expected* to produce better consequences. Two or more codes may pass this test. Of these codes with unsurpassed

> expected value, the one closest to conventional morality deter-
> mines which kinds of act are wrong. An agent is blameworthy
> if she or he does a wrong act, unless this results from legitimate
> ignorance. (1998: 21–2)

A side consequence of this view is that rule utilitarianism tends to dampen the act utilitarian's extreme commitment to impartiality, which can have counter-intuitive consequences in downplaying agent-relative attachment or matters of justice. Nonetheless, utilitarianism of both kinds does have something of a natural tilt towards agent neutrality, such that impartialist views retain a voice in ongoing analytic debates.

There is a structural similarity, as many have noticed, between some modern forms of utilitarianism, and the formal systems used to model rational behaviour in economics and other fields.[1] A claimed direct connection between rationality and utilitarianism goes back to Henry Sidgwick's case for the position; in contemporary philosophy, John Harsanyi (1978) and John Broome (1991) have presented a contractarian justification for the view, relying on a variation of Rawls's original position case, but endorsing the use of a principle of insufficient reason (rather than maximin) in a situation of decision under ignorance. Indeed, decision theory does look very much like a subjectivized version of an individualist utilitarianism, right down to the language of "utility maximization".

Now, as far as we can ascertain, no well-known continental philosopher has ever subscribed to utilitarianism, and surprisingly few have unambiguously subscribed to liberalism. This is a significant anomaly. Historical facts partly explain this situation, including the prevalence of German idealism and Romanticism, which made utilitarianism unlikely to gain a significant foothold in Germany during the nineteenth century, at least given the feeling that Coleridge was roughly right to claim that Bentham's utilitarianism was the product of a rationalistic "mechanico-corpuscular" philosophy originating from Locke and Newton.

However, this history is not sufficient to explain the continued neglect in the twentieth century and beyond. One possible reason for the neglect of liberalism is the continental preoccupation with thematizing intersubjectivity and situation, notwithstanding that certain manifestations of existentialism insist on the importance of the individual and Husserlian phenomenology might seem to be premised on a methodological subjectivism. While Kierkegaard, Nietzsche, Sartre and others do have a focus on the individual, in those cases the radical singularity involved precludes the possibility of general prescriptions (including the negative liberty advocated by many liberals since Berlin) beyond the often stifling norms of *das Man*, the herd, the crowd and so on, which these philosophers all rail against. Somewhat paradoxically, given these existential sentiments, it is also arguable that phenomenology lends itself to forms of communitarianism. Dreyfus explicitly argues for this, as we shall see, but he is not the only phenomenologist whose work alludes to this connection. Consider the work of "neo-phenomenologists", or hermeneutic phenomenologists, such as Charles Taylor, Ricoeur and others, all of whom have been influenced by Heidegger. It is also worth recalling the early explicit critiques of liberalism advanced by existential phenomenologists such as Merleau-Ponty and Beauvoir.[2] They are essentially communitarian in their focus on the difficulties inherent in liberalism's atomistic conception of the subject; they will not accept the supposition of a rational disengaged agent, even as a regulative ideal, or as a heuristic device that captures our alleged intuitive assent to the idea that justice is fairness (as with Rawls).

DISTRIBUTIVE JUSTICE IN ANALYTIC POLITICAL PHILOSOPHY

A major focus (if not *the* major focus) of analytic political philosophy is distributive justice, a topic that has moved to the centre of analytic philosophical work on liberalism since *A Theory of Justice*. Much has been said about this preoccupation with distributive justice by Michael Walzer, William Connolly, Bonnie Honig and Iris Marion Young (see esp. Walzer 1984; Honig 1993; Young 1990), the last three of whom all draw substantially on continental philosophers to mount their criticisms and might be considered as such themselves. Connolly, Honig, Young and the German theorist of recognition Axel Honneth have also sought to supplant the preoccupation with distributive justice with a return to what they consider to be the more fundamental concerns of justice, such as domination, oppression and power. These themes were, of course, all foregrounded by Hegel's "struggle for recognition", and Marx also criticized any focus on distributive justice as inevitably neglecting the more important issue of the inequality in the forces of production. More significantly, from all these diverse perspectives the feeling is that the contemporary analytic focus on distributive justice is itself a kind of reification of capitalist relations in that, as Young (1990: 8) puts it, it is preoccupied with having (i.e. possessing) more than doing. For her, this bias precludes adequate engagement with issues to do with domination and oppression, and the problem is compounded by the fact that moral and political theories in the analytic tradition focus on deliberate and conscious action – i.e. on the agent's present aims and preferences (*ibid.*: 11). As such, she suggests that these kinds of calculable rationalisms, whether of liberal or utilitarian varieties, will find it difficult to comprehend that people often act in ways contrary to their present preferences: the more irrational forms of politics become hard to explain. Those agents or groups perpetuating them can only be treated as extraneous to the system in question: as accidents, abnormalities, outlaws and rogues.

Of course, most Anglo-American political philosophers will point out that a focus on distributive justice hardly exhausts all the dimensions of justice, let alone political philosophy *per se*. Indeed, some bring more intangible matters into the distributive framework, considering, for instance, the distribution of socially constituted phenomena such as self-respect, rights, power and so on. Young complains that this extension treats such political values as a static commodity that one either possesses or does not, rather than as a social and temporal process (*ibid*.: 16). This kind of complaint about distortion also appears in the analytic literature. Nozick (1974: 198–9), for instance, argues against this kind of patterned view of distributive justice for its ahistoricism, and for acting, according to his memorable phrase, as if goods and resources descended from the gods like "manna from heaven".

INTUITIONS AND THE UNCONSCIOUS

A methodological reliance on one's intuitive judgements is also, obviously, presupposed by much post-Rawlsian moral and political philosophy, since it leans heavily on reflective equilibrium methods (and, in so doing, on thought experiments designed to elicit particular intuitions). In various different essays and his book *Ideal Code, Real World*, Hooker explicitly argues that the first two conditions of any adequate moral theory are that it: (i) "have implications that cohere with the moral convictions that we share"; and (ii) that "moral theories should start from attractive general beliefs about morality" (2003a: 12). These are not unusual moves in the analytic tradition and they return us to issues we have addressed earlier: does the use of thought experiments in moral and political matters, for example, involve simplifications that hide the complexity of problems? Does their narrowness preclude their extension into the realm of prescriptive philosophy and questions of what one should do? From many continental perspective(s), seeking such a match between theory and moral intuitions obscures the question of the genesis of the intuitions in question, and forgets about the unconscious and the possibility of various Marxian notions that have been influential even in passing out of fashion, including false-consciousness, ideology and so on.

As an example, let us return to Rawls's "veil of ignorance" supposition. We are to imagine ourselves in a position of equality in which we do not know most of the socially significant facts about ourselves – for example race, sex, religion, economic class, social standing and natural abilities (2005: 12) – and this thought experiment is supposed both to exemplify our intuitive association of "justice with fairness" and to tease out its implications. Under this veil of ignorance, we are to decide what principles we can agree to, in order to further our own interests, whatever they may be. Not knowing our position in society, Rawls argues that we are driven by this fact to prioritize those with the worst life prospects and make their situation as bearable as possible, as it is possible that we are the poor or oppressed. Rawls also argues that we would choose to allow social and economic inequalities, if they increase the social goods (such as liberty, opportunity, income, etc.) of the least advantaged in a society. Sometimes referred to as the difference principle, this allows unequal abilities to produce differential rewards if, and only if, it is to the benefit of the least fortunate.

Of course, many in both traditions have felt that it is by no means obvious that we would maximin in these circumstances. A Marxist might choose absolute social and economic equality for every person, or perhaps even the distribution of goods purely according to need, as is suggested by Marx and Engels's famous principle in *The Communist Manifesto*: "from each according to ability, to each according to need". Rawls, however, contends that such choices would be irrational if it is granted that allowing certain kinds of inequalities would actually improve the quality of life (understood in terms of social goods) of those worst off, perhaps because of the greater incentives and productivity built into a system that allows for differential wealth accrual. Others respond that under the veil, they might also choose the utilitarian principle of maximizing the overall *aggregate* happiness of all people (or even sentient beings), and not worry about fairness and relatively equal levels of happiness between the different people concerned. Rawls, however, suggests that risking one's welfare being sacrificed for the greater good of everyone else is *prudentially* irrational, because behind the veil we also do not know the probability of whether or not these utilitarian calculations are likely to legitimate some, or many, people being forced into slavery to provide for the overall happiness of the rest of a society.[3]

It has been a major communitarian criticism of Rawlsian liberalism that it presupposes an imaginable subject who can somehow decide under the veil, despite being divorced from all of their positive attributes and their social situation. There seems to be an unargued-for conception of personal identity, as if, at bottom, we are unencumbered individuals divested of all social influences. The communitarians ask: what is left of the self when we exclude our past, our social situation, our vision of the good life, when behind the veil? Could we even really decide anything in this situation at all? This is a part of Michael Sandel's (1982; 1996: 3–35) generally perceptive critique of Rawls, as well as one that various Marxists have endorsed; most continental philosophers would follow suit. Rawls later comes to maintain that the "veil" is merely a heuristic device to draw out the implications and theoretical consequences of our conception of justice as fairness. In other words, it is an expository device that represents equality between human beings as moral people and sums up the meaning of our supposed acquiescence to the principle of impartiality. If that is so, however, then there is not actually anything like a fair bargain taking place in this situation, as the possibility of substantive differences has been precluded from the beginning by the details of the original position.

Another aspect of continental concern with intuition can also be brought out here. While Rawls acknowledges that ordinary moral thought and intuitions may sometimes be deeply divided, even contradictory, the unconscious has no place in his analysis. From a continental perspective, this is highly significant. Even if the metaphysical reification of the concept is frequently unhelpful, both psychoanalysts and poststructuralists typically emphasize that we must not disassociate questions of desire and pleasure (which are often not fully conscious) from the political. Indeed, if there is consensus on anything in continental philosophy since Husserl, it would be that a pure epistemology is impossible, and that what is required is instead theoretical adumbrations of the interconnections between knowledge, power and desire. Foucault, and Deleuze and Guattari, are enjoined in this respect, and the latter pairing contend, for example, that "the question of desire's involvement in its own involuntary servitude is the fundamental problem of political philosophy" (1987: 29). If our "unconscious" desires are at least partly determinative of our intuitions, and if both the desires and the ways they might be satisfied are multiple and in conflict with one another, what kind of consensus on this intuitive level might there be?

Consider again Hooker's rule utilitarianism. While Hooker's view does not postulate absolute consensus about people internalizing society's rules, a certain level of acquiescence is nonetheless required for the rules he is advocating to be functional and efficacious. Hooker suggests that this means "internalization by the overwhelming majority, everywhere, in each new generation", and he also settles on a figure: 90 per cent (2003a: 80–81). Of the 90 per cent who internalize the given rules that are thought to maximize well-being, not all are thought to comply, but Hooker nevertheless presupposes that it will result in "general" compliance. This claim seems contentious, resting on his tacit conception of the subject as rational and self-interested. Against this position, continental philosophers would typically maintain that psychoanalysis shows us that internalizing a rule does not entail complying with it (consider, for example, the phenomena of sadism and masochism, among numerous other symptoms). On the contrary, what becomes clear is that there will always be forms of resistance, conscious or otherwise – we might even suggest that laws and rules create resistance and non-compliance – and Hooker, from this perspective, does not spend enough time exploring the gap between internalized rules and behaviour. This "gap" or "between" is something that continental philosophers continually thematize in different ways. In fact, for them it is the condition of possibility of ethics (of responsibility), and any theory predicated on the absence of such a gap is "anethical", merely about the judicial application of rules and law.

One might worry, as Putnam (1992: 197) and many other analytic philosophers do, that such continental philosophies constitute a form of "parapolitics", a politicized philosophy that sees itself primarily in social and political terms. On the other hand, the continental reproach here is that seeing oneself *not* primarily in such terms involves ignoring important background considerations (including the historical) and avoiding the affective dimensions of the problem being considered. We appear to be reaching another of the many impasses in this work.[4]

VIRTUE ETHICS AND ANTI-THEORY IN CONTINENTAL PHILOSOPHY

Much continental discussion of ethical matters can be loosely situated within the virtue ethical tradition (and, we think, without the myriad problems that crop up if they are labelled anti-realist, for example). Many continental philosophers have thought that Greek morality – including the focus on character rather than acts – was preferable to their own in various ways (although also worse in other ways, given the sexism and aristocratic aspects of Athens), and a positive emphasis on character generally plays a significant role in "continental ethics". We might think of Nietzsche, Heidegger and Foucault here, the last of whom certainly thought that the "care of the self" emphasized in Greek society, its "aesthetics of existence", was more promising than the morality and modes of subjectivity of contemporary disciplinary society, even though no simple return to the Greeks is possible (see e.g. Foucault 1990b; Nietzsche 1999). Indeed, it is Foucault whose late work also revisits and valorizes the ancient ideal of *parrhēsia*, of fearlessly speaking the truth (see, unsurprisingly, *Fearless Speech*). Let us take a short tour through some important moments in continental ethics, to trace these connections.

First, while Nietzsche argues for some different and not always compatible interpretations of the eternal return, according to the account offered in *The Gay Science* ([1887] 2001), the idea poses a question of fundamental import for his entire revaluation of all values: what if a malevolent genie informed you that, whatever mode of action you choose now, it will recur indefinitely as you have once experienced it? Nietzsche intends this thought experiment to function as a test designed to intensify experience, and to ensure that we choose to do something that we are prepared to affirm over and over again. For any mode of action, we should act *as if* that particular action were to recur indefinitely, and Nietzsche's imperative would be something like: act in such a manner that you could never say "it just happened", but rather "I willed it thus". It is thus a means of promoting active and affirmative forces, rather than negative and resentful ones.

Second, in *The Logic of Sense*, Deleuze offers a subtle ethics that combines both Nietzschean sentiments (the distinction between active and reactive forces) and Stoicism. He offers the characteristically strong view: "either ethics makes no sense at all, or this is what it means and has nothing else to say: not to be unworthy of what happens to us" (1990a: 169). We cannot address his subsequent advocation of what he calls "counter-actualization" here, but it is clear that for Deleuze ethico-political principles and norms are too abstract to be much use in particular situations (hence his advocacy of "jurisprudence"), much as Aristotle suggested.

Third, Hubert Dreyfus, similarly, argues that there is not likely to be any overall theory or principle that can unify the behaviour of someone whom we consider to be morally mature; his further claim is that the search for rational principles that undergird any such activity in fact blocks further development beyond the stage of moral competence. While he admits that deliberation is sometimes necessary and helpful (and can even be a type of expertise), to read it as endemic to morality, or the *telos* of morality, is ultimately unjustifiable. Rather than see critical rationality as overriding our intuitive ethical comportment, Dreyfus advocates a reversal of this priority and sides with caring over justice in the age-old debate. On his view, considerations of justice tend to be part of the competent stage of skill acquisition, but something like practical wisdom is more typical of the phenomenology of expertise. He suggests that while one aspect of moral life, and most of moral philosophy, has been concerned with choice, responsibility and the justification of validity claims, we should instead take more seriously the idea that moral maturity is better understood in terms of a skilled ethical comportment, "which consists in unreflective, egoless responses to the current interpersonal situation" (1990: 2).[5] He suggests three general methodological precautions for all moral philosophy:

1. We should begin by describing our everyday, ongoing ethical coping.
2. We should then seek to determine under which conditions deliberation and choice occur.
3. We should beware of making the typical philosophical mistake of reading the structure of deliberation and choice back into our account of everyday coping.

Fourth, another dominant tradition in continental reflections on ethics and politics is to point to paradoxes and dilemmas that afflict ethical life, and which defy any lexical ordering that would allow for their rule-

229

oriented resolution. Instead, any resolution will consist in a practical leap of faith (Kierkegaard), or a moment of madness precipitated by undecidability (Derrida). Drawing on the work of Kierkegaard, in multiple different texts Derrida argues that the instant of the decision must be mad, provocatively telling us that a decision requires an undecidable leap beyond all prior preparations and rational calculations for that decision (see Derrida 1995a: 77). According to him, this applies to all decisions, and not just those regarding the conversion to religious faith that preoccupies Kierkegaard. A decision is never simply about weighing up pros and cons (or hedons, or interests), and reckoning to a solution. We may, for example, work out that it is definitely in our best interests to leave our current lover, or to use the knight in order to best facilitate a checkmate. However, the decision itself does not automatically follow from this. It still needs to be taken, and that requires a leap beyond any prior preparations for that decision. Kierkegaard, Derrida and Sartre (and many other continental theorists) all come together in their rejection of the Kantian categorical imperative and the claim that all decisions can and should be based on reason (again, Habermas's "discourse ethics" looms as a notable exception).

Fifth, Sartre and Beauvoir offer a philosophy of authenticity, which primarily depends on certain internal attributes: not taking one's value as given by certain external factors (occupation, wealth, social status, etc.), and not lying to oneself and being in the state of duality or contradiction that they call bad faith. While Beauvoir's work offers the best and perhaps the only sustained example of an existentialist ethics, she retains the existential insistence on avoiding any kind of moral prescription or a single monistic theory of what is valuable. As she comments:

> It will be said that these considerations remain quite abstract. What must be done, practically? Which action is good? Which action is bad? To ask such a question is also to fall into a naive abstraction ... Ethics does not furnish recipes any more than do science and art. One can merely propose methods.   (1976: 134)

Finally, Stan van Hooft (2005) has tied the tradition of virtue ethics to the work of Emmanuel Levinas, who famously suggests that ethics is first philosophy (see Levinas 1969). Levinas argues for the metaphysical priority of the other. We need to note, however, that Levinas has little to say about ethics traditionally conceived: that is, with prescribing moral norms, justifying them, or meta-ethical analysis of ethical discourse. Rather, his work offers a continual reminder of the way otherness interrupts and conditions our totalizing explanations. This "other" orientation might help to open up a tradition of virtue ethics that is less about prudential concern for oneself and more about an account of our obligations to the other that cannot be fleshed out in rule-following terms. We have, of course, only touched on the work of a few continental philosophers here, but the analogy with virtue ethics seems reasonably strong.

ANALYTIC VIRTUE ETHICS

If there is a virtue ethical thread within the continental tradition, it is anti-theoretical. This is not to intimate that it is bereft of theory *tout court*, but simply to indicate that there is widespread scepticism about the possibility of articulating ethical and political rules, principles or formal systems, which will allow for the codification of morality and prescriptive norms regarding it. However, there is also a tradition of virtue ethics in analytic philosophy. While she played a major role in applying analytic methods to ancient and medieval philosophy, this tradition seems to have begun with G. E. Anscombe's 1958 essay "Modern Moral Philosophy", and received more sustained treatment in Alisdair MacIntyre's *After Virtue* (1981) and Philippa Foot's *Virtues and Vices and Other Essays in Moral Philosophy* (1978). As such, it is not a simple opposition that we will be intimating here between analytic and continental philosophy. Indeed, there is something of a case for the anti-theoretical nature of analytic virtue ethics in turn.

In Anscombe's seminal essay, she points out that the conception of morality in the dominant Anglo-American moral philosophies was legalistic, preoccupied with obligations and duties: for Kantians, we must respect the moral law as revealed by reason; for utilitarians, we must act so as to maximize welfare, happiness, informed preference satisfaction and so on. Given that humans must be obedient in both of these cases to the moral law, they thus might be said to be rule-following understandings of morality. Such views seem to tacitly presuppose that our practical lives ought to become the logical expression of a system of rational principles. While it is acknowledged that agents cannot decide on such a basis all of the time, decisions are only just or morally right if such a logical reconstruction could be made. For Anscombe, however, this notion of morality as consisting in obedience to rules makes no sense without the supposition of a divine law-giver. Moreover, what is invariably not considered in the duty-ethics tradition is the moral significance of character, something that had been a central part of moral enquiry for the ancient Greeks. As we have seen, Nietzsche's *On the Genealogy of Morals* makes many similar points, and it is no coincidence that Nietzsche has also been quite frequently interpreted as a virtue ethicist, albeit by reversing many of the typical character traits that are usually considered to be the virtues (certainly, piety, modesty

231

and chastity are clearly not virtues for Nietzsche, but self-love, audacity and *parrhēsia* might be).

This framework induces a kind of anti-theoretical attitude that is also to be found in Aristotle. In his *Nichomachean Ethics*, Aristotle holds that ethics cannot be rule-bound, since one always needs to exercise practical judgement – *phronēsis* – about when to employ given rules, which requires moral sensitivity, perception, imagination and so on, all of which are argued not to be codifiable. Aristotle's ethics is hence not prescriptive. Rather than directly answer the question "what should I do?", he focuses on the question "what should I be?" His moral philosophy nonetheless provides some practical guidance; he suggests that we look to moral exemplars for guidance rather than to principles or rules, and he suggests that we need to attempt to find the golden mean between excess and deficiency of each virtue. Analytic virtue ethics is similarly anti-theoretical in that it shuns any focus on the rightness of a particular act as a basic category, and so resists discussion of first-personal or third-personal rules or principles, let alone standard devices for eliciting them. As such, a large part of what most analytics take to be the ethical project is rejected, and generally on contextual or particularist grounds. We might also say that virtue ethics resists a purely representational framework for moral reasoning or practical deliberation. Robert Louden puts the contrast well when he suggests that "virtue ethicists emphasise know-how over know-that", and adds that "these skills of moral perception and practical reason are not completely routinisable, and so cannot be transferred from agent to agent as any sort of decision procedure 'package deal'". As he puts it:

> Act-centred ethics, because they focus on discrete acts and moral quandaries, are naturally very interested in formulating decision procedures for making practical choices … Agent-centred ethics, on the other hand, focus on long-term characteristic patterns of action, intentionally downplaying atomic acts and particular choice situations in the process. (1998: 204)

On Louden's view, then, act-centred ethics is atemporal in the sense that it shifts attention to abstract decision procedures, whereas virtue ethics, or agent-centred ethics, is concerned with patterns of action over long periods of time.

As well as recalling our earlier claims about a temporal turn in twentieth-century continental philosophy, this also touches on the issue of whether norms are grounded primarily in reason, or in a more holistic account that involves the body and the emotions. For Kant (and for some utilitarian and liberal traditions) decisions must be made on the basis of *a priori* reason, devoid of emotion and interest: at the very least, they need to be able to be reconstructed in accord with impartial reason. As Michael Stocker (1998) has observed, one problem with the utilitarian and Kantian accounts is that they create a "schizophrenic self", a disjunction between reasons/justifications and our motives/feelings. By contrast, virtue ethics applauds positive emotions and denigrates negative ones such as resentment and envy (cf. Nietzsche); there is no reason–emotion (and mind–body) cleavage of this sort in virtue ethics. Of course, many people, philosophers and otherwise, think that impartiality must be part of ethics. While virtue ethicists might agree that there is a moral importance to impartiality, especially in certain situations, they are committed to maintaining that it should not be understood as the foundation for a set of rules and principles. For them, both utilitarianism and Kantianism are impersonal and abstract, and involve a counter-intuitive conception of morality that depends on the assumption of a rational, autonomous person.

Is this kind of anti-theoretical attitude justified? It is certainly controversial within analytic philosophy. Brad Hooker, Elinor Mason and Dale Miller (2000: 1) argue that two key ideas are fundamental to morality: that it ought to contain certain rules or principles that we can follow; and that consequences matter. On such a view, the task of ethical theory is to come up with a code of rules or principles, that, ideally, (i) would allow a decision procedure for determining right action in a particular case, and (ii) could be stated in such terms that any non-virtuous person could understand it and apply it correctly. Likewise, Thomas Hurka rebukes Wittgenstein, McDowell and Bernard Williams, for their anti-theoretical positions in regard to ethics: "an anti-theoretical position is properly open only to those who have made a serious effort to theorise a given domain and found that it cannot succeed" (2004: 251). It is worth noting again the manner in which many alleged post-analytic philosophers are thus drummed from the regiment. Without this initial effort, Hurka suggests that anti-theoretical philosophers are just being lazy. While it is not entirely clear what would count as sufficient effort for Hurka, should we thus conclude that almost all continental philosophers are lazy, given that many have an anti-theoretical position in regard to ethics and politics?

Of course, an explanatory agenda immediately opens up; most notably, why was analytic virtue ethics such a late starter in that tradition, despite considerable analytic access to, and familiarity with, the key Aristotelian texts? A partial answer lies in the peculiar nature of early-twentieth-century analytic ethics; the focus on meta-ethical questions at the expense of substantive ethics itself meant that there was effectively no tradition of the major analytic figures publicly working through concrete ethical situations. Again, it is clear from the reception of Anscombe that many analytics felt that the inability to codify virtues in terms of rules or principles meant virtue ethics would not be very helpful for action guidance. Because it is about "know-how", Louden suggests that virtue ethics cannot be prescriptive or solve moral dilemmas, and merely leads to the silent appreciation of the sage: "its derivative oughts are too vague and unhelpful for persons who have not yet acquired the requisite moral insight" (1998: 206). Next, a concern about relativism was expressed; if different cultures embody different virtues does this mean that right and wrong will be relative to a particular culture, and thus that virtue ethicists are relativists (MacIntyre 1981)? Perhaps this is a consequence, but there are stronger and weaker forms of relativism and it might be maintained that virtue ethicists are only committed to a plausibly weak version of relativism; indeed, some (such as Martha Nussbaum [1988]) argue that it is no more relativist than any other account that takes seriously the data of cultural relativism. This is, of course, for the continental tradition a point of departure rather than a point of criticism. There is a sense in which ethics are socially constructed for both virtue ethicists and many continental philosophers; culture, training and enculturation, habitus for Pierre Bourdieu, are very important. Indeed, part of the force behind genealogical analyses is their claim to exhibit the lack of necessity for certain moralities, conceptions of subjectivity and so on.

While philosophers such as Derrida and Deleuze, for example, acknowledge the necessity of political calculation, it is also the case that such calculations are generally not engaged in, with the aim often being to situate the necessity for such decisions against a background of other concerns and to indicate what such views presuppose. Utilitarianism and liberalism offer two sustained and important attempts at providing such a calculation and it seems to us that a rapprochement of these traditions is possible, fleshing out the kinds of political calculations that might better respect the significant moral insights, and psychoanalytic complications, that are the home ground of continental political philosophy. On the other side, the analytic virtue ethicists already provide that tradition with an internal critique (MacIntyre's *After Virtue* most obviously playing this role), and there is something of an engagement on this matter, which may well extend to consider some of the continental themes we have touched on. Can the theoretical and anti-theoretical perspectives of analytic and continental philosophy be mutually enlightening? Although this generally has not happened, as yet, we think they can potentially serve as constraints of a kind, reminding each other of the difficulties of both particularism and abstraction in these fields.

20. PROBLEM(S) OF OTHER MINDS

SOLUTIONS AND DISSOLUTIONS IN ANALYTIC AND CONTINENTAL PHILOSOPHY

Given its resonance in both traditions, the problem of other minds seems to us especially suitable as a case-study, or a symptom, in order to make clear some of the different methodological and meta-philosophical commitments of the two traditions. Although there is no canonical account of the problem(s) of other minds that can be baldly stated and that is exhaustive of both traditions, several aspects of the problem can be set out. It seems to have: (i) an epistemological dimension (How do we know that others exist? Can we justifiably claim to know that they do?); (ii) an ontological dimension incorporating issues to do with personal identity (What is the structure of our world such that intersubjectivity is possible? What are the fundamental aspects of our relations to others and how do they impact upon/constitute our self-identity?); and (iii) some involvement with one's conception of the nature of mind (How does the mind – or the concept of "mind" – relate to the brain, the body, and the world?). While these three issues are co-imbricated, analytic engagements with the problem of other minds generally treat it as a straightforward sceptical problem, of much the same kind as Hume's problem of induction, Descartes' arguments for global scepticism, Russell's scepticism about the past and so on. Hence in the analytic tradition the focus is on epistemic matters primarily, although conceptual issues to do with "mindedness" also arise. By contrast, continental philosophers focus far more on the ontological dimension, on the ways in which reflection on other minds can allow us to reach conclusions about the structure or nature of our world; the aim is to ground our relations with others in a pre-reflective manner of inhabiting the world that is said to be the condition of reflection and knowledge. At this point, it should be obvious that we are in the presence of familiar oppositions, arguably brought about by the completely differing attitudes to empiricism in each tradition; recall the analytic concern with the ineffectiveness of transcendental reasoning in sceptical contexts, and the continental bafflement with this (apparently narrow) focus; recall also the continental willingness to draw ontological conclusions from phenomenological investigations, and the analytic bafflement with this (apparently wilful) approach.

AN EPISTEMOLOGICAL PROBLEM

Analytic philosophy and the problem of other minds

Analytic philosophy's interest in the problem of other minds is typically posed in epistemic terms. The core problem is that we have two competing intuitions about our knowledge of the existence of the other that both have some *prima facie* plausibility: a behaviourist intuition that in our daily life we do in fact know others with reliability; and a Cartesian one that insists that there is something about the other (their mental life) that necessarily remains unknowable (Overgaard 2005: 250). These then induce a global sceptical concern (How could I know that you have a mind?), but also a series of particular sceptical challenges (Even if I know you have a mind, how could I be justified in attributing particular mental states to you on particular occasions?). Very often, as Ryle and others have noted, our knowledge of others is not only reliable but seems to be apprehended by us with non-inferential immediacy, and this appears to generate further puzzles for those who seek to ground such knowledge in induction, analogy or the like.

Ryle's own solution in *The Concept of Mind* is that the conception of minds as potentially private is a relic of Cartesian dualism; our mentalist language includes action terms as much as such canonically private states as beliefs and desires, and our understanding of others as minded agents is largely, and entirely properly, grounded in their actual and potential behaviour. To be intelligent is to be disposed to solve certain kinds of problems relatively quickly, to know how to ride a bicycle is to be able to do so more or less on command, and so on. For many, however, the issue of subjectivity (and hence intersubjectivity) has been too quickly dispensed with by Ryle; not every mental state has the implicative relations to behaviour that intelligence has, and in some cases (as with the qualitative aspects of experience, pain and so on), the behaviourist account simply looks implausible. Analytic philosophy hence contains few pure behaviourists (even Ryle admits to being "only one arm and a leg a behaviourist"; see Byrne 1994: 135), but the idea that there is a conceptual, and not merely causal, link between behaviour and mentation has been of great influence. In differing ways, many contemporary accounts of mind within analytic philosophy can be read as following Ryle on this point. However, this part of the Rylean heritage does not by itself guarantee a solution to the problem of other minds; analytic functionalists, for instance, face the problem. Without the behaviourist's entailment relation between pain behaviour and pain, it seems that the best we can do is to return to the traditional arguments, and here things become difficult. We might, for instance, argue by analogy from our own experiences of the relation between us having mental states and behaving in certain ways, as was suggested by Mill (1962: 191) and later defended in a more sophisticated form by Ayer (1954). Arguments by analogy are, however, at best probabilistic, and probabilistic claims (or indeed inductive generalizations) based on a single experience seem rather irresponsible, as Wittgenstein suggests in *Philosophical Investigations* (1997: §293). Moreover, they do not capture the judgements of common-sense/folk psychology on this issue, nor our pre-reflective relation with others that phenomenology aims to describe and disclose.

Faced with the inductive problem of arguments by analogy (the fact that one case is not sufficient), as Stern (2004: 220) suggests, we have two choices. We can try to improve the argument from analogy, and/or supplement it with other inductive or quasi-inductive arguments; alternatively, we can give up the inferential problematic and seek another way to show how belief can be justified. Most continental philosophers pursue some version of the second alternative. For instance, some norms are said to be grounded in perception rather than inference, and there is often claimed to be a transcendental conception of normativity, whether it be the structure of our perceptual being-in the-world, or Apel and Habermas on so-called "transcendental pragmatics" and the claim that everyday conversation and argument presupposes certain regulative ideals that we should endeavour to live up to. Direct, or "local", analytic attempts to pursue this strategy are much rarer, confined to the post-Wittgensteinian tradition of conceptual and criteria-based solutions to the problem. (The analytic tradition also contains a number of "off-the-shelf" solutions to the problem, each dependent in some way on an externalist account of knowledge or justification, but these involve no particular reflection on the special features of this sceptical problem, and will not be explored here.[1]) The claim made by Wittgenstein, Norman Malcolm and Peter Strawson, in different ways, is that the required link between the observed behaviour of the other and the attribution of mental states to them is neither an inductive inference nor a direct entailment (as in behaviourism); rather, the relation between certain mental states and pieces of behaviour is claimed to be criterial – that is, a relation of near-complete justification but not entailment, arising from our decision to use language in a certain way. This remains, however, a comparatively marginal position within analytic philosophy, perhaps in part because the notion of criterion in play (and related notions, such as that of a "hinge proposition"), and its use to resolve a sceptical issue, is suspiciously reminiscent of the conventionalism of the logical positivists and its anti-sceptical use, the ordinary-language attempt to factor out the analytic and empirical components of sceptical concerns, and other such devices.

More contemporary analytic responses to the problem of other minds hence attempt the first option: to reconstrue the argument by analogy as a stage within a larger inference to the best explanation. My experience of other people is consistent with a range of hypotheses about their mindfulness or non-mindfulness; I am justified in accepting that hypothesis that is simplest, most general, most falsifiable, most consistent with past belief, or some trade-off of these or other indicia; the traditional argument from analogy now drops into place as part of a case for the mindfulness of others being the simplest hypothesis, and it is backed by considerations of conservatism (we do actually attribute minds to others) and generality, if not falsifiability.

The invocation of conservatism here is also a reminder that the problem of other minds has at least an explanatory connection to folk psychology. The folk, of course, have a faith that other people exist; they also evince an everyday ability to attribute desires, beliefs and intentionality to other people despite the possibility of them being but cloaks and springs. The task for the analytic philosopher who takes this datum seriously (not all do) becomes one of explaining how this common-sense folk psychology about the other might have come about, how it functions, and what roles it plays in regard to the ascription of psychological states to others or to the way we are to conceive of those states. Two main answers to such questions have emerged in analytic philosophy and related parts of the cognitive sciences: "theory theory" (see Lewis 1970) and "simulation theory" (see Goldman 1989, 1993). As we shall see, at this descriptive rather than justificatory end of the problem of other minds, there is something of a meeting place between the analytic and continental traditions.

On the standard "theory" theory view, it is because we have an implicit theory that we are able to identify other minds and predict their behaviour. Hence "theory" theory is inferential and quasi-scientific, in that the mental states of others are thought to be akin to theoretical entities that we use to explain observed behaviour. While the mental states of others are themselves unobservable, for "theory" theory we can nonetheless say that "a theory about unobservables can be belief worthy if it allows us to explain and to predict some domain of observable phenomena better than any competing theory" (Churchland 1988: 71). *Prima facie*, however, "theory" theory is confronted with an obvious problem. Given that infants seem to lack a *theory* of mind, being without the required inferential abilities (and especially the awareness of others as mental agents with beliefs different from their own), "theory" theory seems committed to the view that there is no genuine understanding of self and other until roughly four years of age. This is not only counter-intuitive, but it is also a difficult position to maintain given certain empirical facts concerning early infant perception.

For simulation theory, on the other hand, we represent the mental activities of others by mentally simulating them, or by simulating similar activities and processes (for some versions of simulation theory this is said to happen at the subconscious level). The explicit version of simulation theory remains within the argument by analogy paradigm. Rather than maintaining that we have some general information (or theory) that makes understanding of others possible, we use our own mind (and behavioural processes) as a model of what the other's mind might be like, mainly through imagination. For Alvin Goldman, we have a privileged understanding of our own mind through introspection, and using these resources we then attempt to put ourselves in the other's shoes. Newborn infants are not able to reason by analogy in this way but still evidence an understanding of others, picking out human faces and selectively imitating them, and perceiving bodily movement and voices as expressive of emotions (see e.g. Gallagher & Meltzoff 1996; Gopnik & Meltzoff 1997; Meltzoff & Moore 1994; Scholl & Tremoulet 2000).

To try to consciously put ourselves in the other's shoes presupposes that we already have some understanding that they are in fact others, and it thus at least begs the question about how this may have come about; from this point of view, simulation theory offers an answer to local questions about mentalist attribution, but not to the global practice of attributing a mind in the first place. Another problem is that there seems to be little phenomenological evidence of the indispensability of such introspective and imaginative simulations to our everyday dealings with others, even in an average adult life. Finally, as is well known, a major problem with the argument from analogy is its heavy reliance on my intimate knowledge of *my own* mental life, which does not license inferences to other cases. While "theory" theory's best explanation argument avoids that problem, it shares an intellectualist commitment with simulation theory to the indispensability of the requirement of inference for social cognition, given the unobservability of other's mental states.

One solution to this problem with simulation theory is to abandon any insistence on the importance of introspection and the imagination, and to maintain that the simulations are sub-personal. It is frequently claimed that recent evidence from neurology and cognitive sciences supports this view, in particular the "firing" of mirror neurons, neurons that fire both when the agent performs an act and when the agent observes the act being performed by another. While mirror neurons have as yet only been found in macaques, coupled with other well-known findings in developmental psychology (the newborn imitation of tongue protuberance, the recognition of basic emotions and so on) they provide some (probabilistic) evidence for the claim that the human brain has systems that may be activated either "endogenously – for example, by the output of one's own decision-making, emotion-formation, or pain perception systems – or exogenously, directly fed by the sight of other human faces and bodies" (Gordon 2009). At least as "implicit simulation theory" interprets such data, this suggests that one perceives the other and there is then an activation of mirror neurons that represent/replicate the experience that is being perceived. But why should these sub-personal processes be characterized as *simulations* (or inferences for that matter), when "simulations" on the usual understanding involves reference to either pretence, with an agent who does the pretending/simulating, or to an instrumental model that we can use to understand some other thing? Neither of these definitions seems to be involved in the use that *implicit* simulation theory makes of the term "simulation", as Gallagher and Zahavi suggest in *The Phenomenological Mind* (2008a: 179). Without a clear answer to this conceptual issue, it is not clear that these neural resonance processes are not better understood as *part of* perception, rather than something that comes *after* perception (as implicit simulation theory contends). To put it another way, are there internal replicas or representations of the other involved here, or are they directly part of the perceptual apprehension without intermediary, in the manner that Merleau-Ponty and Max Scheler have maintained? The scientific findings have not ruled out either interpretation, and it might be argued that we can in fact make better sense of the evidence if we think of our understanding of other minds as something that we can explain in terms of perception, rather than in terms of inference and simulation.[2] Such an approach may be better able to explain the sense in which neonates do exhibit an embodied comprehension of self and other from birth, based in proprioception, and prior to them possessing any kind of theoretical knowledge about beliefs, desires and agency more generally.

Continental responses: creating a dialogue

It seems to us that virtually all continental philosophers would resist understanding our competence in interacting with others in terms of either "theory" theory or simulation theory (see Hutto & Ratcliffe 2007). Where they concede that we do have such competence, the explanatory preference would be for a combination of narrative models of how children learn to attribute intentionality to others, as well as a variety of differing philosophical arguments for a fundamental expressivism of the other that is more basic than the attribution to them of belief/desire intentionality. Freud and psychoanalysis are again in the background here. Even if we are "always already" with others ontologically, as we shall shortly see is almost universally maintained, many continental philosophers would also contend that to the extent that we do understand others, most of the time it is on an unconscious (or affective) rather than a conscious, reflective level. Our expressive relations with others are hence frequently envisaged to exceed what we can know of them, or what we can rationally represent of them.

Having suggested that epistemology is central to the way that the problem of other minds is traditionally formulated in analytic philosophy, and having suggested that there is a background analytic concern to integrate (or cohere) with the knowledge claims from the various brain sciences, both of these foci are *comparatively* absent from continental reflections on intersubjectivity. Instead, philosophers such as Heidegger, Merleau-Ponty and Hegel (and arguably also the later Wittgenstein; see Overgaard 2007) seek to establish a new outlook on the world and our (social) place within it, precisely by overturning the modern conception of knowledge and the various paradoxes bound up with it, with the problem of other minds being envisaged as an exemplary case (see Taylor 1995a: 8). The problem for the above philosophers is the focus on epistemology *and* the particular paradoxical understanding of epistemology that we have inherited. The worry is that the modern conception of knowledge might serve to disguise from the fly a way out of the bottle. In a related vein, Rorty suggests in *Philosophy and the Mirror of Nature* that epistemic scepticism about the external world or other minds depends on the mirror of nature conception of the mind, in which the mind is assumed to be ontologically distinct from its environment. But even without accepting this kind of general diagnosis of analytic philosophy as tacitly dualist, based on the foregoing account of other minds (which resembles the thing-in-itself) it seems fair to suggest that analytic philosophy's epistemic and justificatory focus reflects its broadly empiricist heritage, and consequent engagement with the sceptical problematic. Things are very different in continental philosophy, however, where the task is more to explicate our place in the world and there is an abiding attempt to establish that the other is of a different ontological order to things: that the perception of other people is radically different to the perception of external objects. This is evinced in the various discussions of intersubjectivity, alterity, the other, being-with (*Mitsein*) and so on that have been central to continental philosophy, occurring in virtually all the canonical texts.[3] While Wittgenstein arguably also wanted to dissolve the problem, the important question about the problem of other minds *vis-à-vis* the "divide" hence becomes the following: is it an epistemological problem that might be solved (even if only probabilistically), or is it an ontological one that needs to be dissolved and/or shown to be untenable via phenomenological descriptions and transcendental arguments?

An aversion to epistemologically inflected accounts of the existence of the other is manifest internally within continental philosophy, despite the fact that Husserl's *Cartesian Meditations* contains a modified version of an argument by analogy (see Meditation 5). When Heidegger criticizes Kant for suggesting that it is a scandal that the problem of the external world (including other minds) has not been solved, and when he instead insists that that scandal is actually the attempt to solve it, he continues the Hegelian efforts to move beyond epistemology (1962: §43). Although in *Being and Nothingness* Sartre (1993: 230) praises Hegel, Husserl and Heidegger for installing the other at the heart of consciousness and hence contributing to the over-turning of a dualistic worldview, they are also simultaneously criticized for remaining too epistemological and hence for labouring under versions of the problem of other minds bequeathed to us by Descartes. Likewise, when Levinas in *Totality and Infinity* critiques Western philosophy's "imperialism of the same" – that is, its epistemological focus that unerringly aims at reducing the unknown object to the understanding of the knowing subject – he is also careful to distance himself from contemporaries such as Merleau-Ponty, because, on his view, Merleau-Ponty's philosophy of touch remained too epistemological in its relation with the other (see Levinas 1990). This gesture, in which epistemology becomes a dirty word, is a common one in continental philosophy in the twentieth century and especially so in regard to reflections on intersubjectivity. But what, from this perspective, is wrong with this epistemological focus?

One problem would be that it functions on the basis of certain philosophical presuppositions, most notably the existence of a knowing subject with privileged epistemic access in relation to their own thoughts/feelings and a more speculative or theoretical relation in the case of other people. The difficult task is then one of explaining how it is that we might have justified knowledge of other minds (and external things more generally). This, of course, is roughly the predicament that Descartes faced in his *Meditations*, but for many continental philosophers this suggests that something has already gone wrong and that the premises that lead to such a dilemma – other minds as hypothesized entities – need to be rejected. Ontological re-descriptions are hence given to explain aspects of the phenomena in question – such as desire, shame and so on, which are claimed to presuppose the difference of the other – but which simultaneously avoid the problematic consequences that are thought to ensue if we understand that difference as one pertaining to epistemic access between the first- and second-person perspectives. The uncanny and surprising nature of our relations with others is generally not to be explained by, or understood in terms of, the possibility of misunderstanding and failure in relation to our knowledge of the other (see McGinn 1998: 50). For Merleau-Ponty, Heidegger and the other existential phenomenologists, this level of judgement – of knowing consciousness – is not our fundamental relation to the world, which is, rather, pre-reflective. If it can be shown that the latter precedes and is the condition of possibility of the former, then reflective and sceptical judgements are undermined. It is for such reasons that most continental philosophers will not accept the Cartesian premise that we have privileged epistemic access to ourselves, and nor will they accept that accounting for our relations with others via knowledge (or probability) can be adequate, since our connection with others is first (in both a developmental and transcendental sense) non-inferential, grounded in perception, affection, intensity and so on. Moreover, for those continental philosophers indebted to Hegel, self-consciousness (and self-knowledge) are thought to be possible only following an encounter with others. To summarize then, continental philosophers tend to respond in at least one of the two following ways to the problem of other minds: (i) maintain that expression in some cases gives constitutive evidence of mentality (although this need not preclude ambiguity); and/or (ii) argue that we have certain capacities (thought, shame, meaningful expression, self-consciousness, awareness, etc.) for which the existence of others is a necessary condition.

INVOLVEMENT WITH THE MENTAL

Continental philosophy, the mind–body problem and expressivism

As many philosophers have noted, from Strawson to Merleau-Ponty, there is a clear link between the mind–body problem and the problem of other minds. Certainly, if we consider the mind (or the mental) as transcending the body, or as radically different from the body, then we are immediately in a difficult position in trying to establish that other people do in fact exist. On the other hand, any strategy of dissolving the problem by pointing to a mind–body unity, perhaps by insisting that the mental must stretch out into our body and even our environment (cf. Clark's extended mind), must not deny the perspectival asymmetry between first and second persons, nor the fact that communicative expressivity is a matter of degrees. It seems difficult to dispute, for example, that the facially expressive nature of emotions such as anger or any of the other purportedly universal facial expressions (joy, disgust, surprise, sadness, fear) is more transparent than in the case of a complex state such as nostalgia, say, and than is the case with regard to the knowledge that one might have of something specific. In this respect, Overgaard points to an important distinction in expression between "occurrent mental phenomena, which have a beginning and an end (e.g. sensations, perceptions, and emotions) and phenomena that seem to be dispositional in nature" (2005: 258), including beliefs and knowledge. Again, if a philosopher can convincingly show that this latter relation is not basic then we have the beginnings of an argument for intersubjective expressionism. Roughly speaking, this is the argumentative strategy that the existential phenomenologists pursue in thematizing in great detail the lived body as locus of agency rather than the mind; "mind" does not reduce to body in the manner suggested by behaviourists, but the body is enlarged and made intelligent, and also claimed to be the condition of reflective thinking.

Such views tend to be accompanied by a denial of the necessity of intermediate entities (e.g. representations, judgements, the Kantian "I think", etc.) in everyday intersubjectivity. According to one of Merleau-Ponty's examples, a friend's consent or refusal of a request for them to move nearer is immediately understood through bodily interaction. Moreover, this does not involve a perception, followed by an interpretation, and then a behavioural response. Rather:

> both form a system which varies as a whole. If, for example, realising that I am not going to be obeyed, I vary my gesture, we have here, not two acts of consciousness. What happens is that I see my partner's unwillingness, and my gesture of impatience emerges from this situation without any intervening thought. (2002: 111)

The interpretation is thus built into the perception itself, rather than something secondary that is added to the raw perception of sense data, in a manner related to some of Heidegger's thematizations of "seeing-as" in *Being and Time*. In the perception of the other, a certain gesture does not make me think of anger, or read anger behind the expression, but that it is anger in-itself (*ibid.*: 184). Likewise, Merleau-Ponty consistently draws attention to the way in which newborn babies are able to imitate the facial expression of others (see Merleau-Ponty 1964), something that provides the basis for our relations to others thereafter. As Thomas Fuchs notes in regard to the imitative capacities of children, "by the mimetic capacity of their body, they transpose the seen gestures and mimics of others into their own proprioception and movement" (2005: 98). On this Merleau-Pontyian inspired view, our body-schema responds immediately to the other's expressions, and elicits a non-inferential process of what might be called "empathic perception" that involves some kind of transfer of corporeal-schema.

While this kind of turn to the body is typical of phenomenology from the later Husserl on, it does not exhaust continental philosophy *per se*. The notion of the body "proper" has been contested by many recent theorists (especially poststructuralists), sometimes in the name of the vast differences between bodies that are occluded in the general deployment of the term, as well as because of the claim that the necessary relation between the body and technology (e.g. prostheses and supplements) renders problematic some phenomenological accounts of the lived body. Nonetheless, virtually all continental philosophers dispute the view of the mind as pre-dominantly representational, and, to put it more positively, there is a cor-responding advocation of forms of expressivism. Expressivism defends the semantic priority of expression over representation, and thus links in with claims to the genesis of theoretical knowledge from practical experience/ knowledge in many continental philosophers. Rather than committing its advocates to forms of irrationalism, it involves a disciplining of rationality (or the propositional) as the dominant mode of interacting with the world, and expressive behaviour is viewed as meaning-saturated, often in such a manner as to deny the need for inference.

Sartre is also committed to a form of expressivism regarding others when he states that nothing is hidden in principle. Modes of conduct of bad faith are nothing separate from the way they are enacted in the world: style, manner-isms and comportment. In a very different way, Deleuze also advocates a form of expressivism, and this is one of the reasons why Spinoza and Nietzsche are increasingly popular in continental circles. In the last two chapters of *Difference and Repetition* and *Spinoza: Expressionism in Philosophy*, Deleuze insists that expression has a power that exceeds that which we can represent, and that also exceeds that which we can be self-aware of. Levinas's philoso-phy likewise attempts to negotiate that difficult balance between respecting the alterity of the other and yet nonetheless insisting on the immediate com-municability of bodily expressivism. Levinas is famous for his discussion of the face-to-face in which in an encounter with the other we experience the other as an ungraspable infinity, rather than as a graspable totality as in our appropriative relation with other objects. On Levinas's view in *Totality and Infinity*, what the face expresses is precisely the other's transcendence (1969: 198). As such, expression does not give us the other's interiority, but nor does it hide this realm (*ibid.*: 202). Another's mental life is not waiting to be encountered and known in the manner of an object; rather, it expresses itself in an unfolding dynamic that does not have me at its source (Overgaard 2005: 262). Transformation and unpredictability are thus built into the expressivity of the face. As Overgaard argues, the "notion of expression is both intended to convey something more than a merely contingent relation between mind and body, and to reflect a certain inaccessibility of the mental lives of others" (*ibid.*: 256). As he goes on to suggest, "the Cartesian thinks the counterpart to my possible uncertainty regarding the mental states of another is her cer-tainty, but this is precisely wrong" (*ibid.*: 267), since even if I were certain about the other's mental states (and surely we sometimes are), there would still be a difference between the perspectives. Focusing on epistemic access thus seems a misleading way to explain this, and what becomes clear in the work of all of these philosophers is that expression is not a representation of an inner realm. It is an *entre nous* (between us) that is differently experienced by the expressive face and the apprehension of it by another expressive face. Expressivism of this kind, however, remains a marginal view within analytic philosophy, a position that is more commonly associated with so-called "post-analytic" philosophers: Taylor, McDowell and, to a lesser extent, Brandom (see e.g. Taylor 1985). Both Taylor and Brandom trace expressivism back to its roots in Romanticism, suggesting that the historical contestation between Romanticism and more reason-oriented views of the Enlightenment heritage is an important precursor to the analytic–continental divide.

Analytic responses

Many analytic philosophers would have at least two responses to this, concerning not only the putative immediacy of relations with others, but also any priority that is accorded to this mode of comportment. First, it might be suggested that such a position threatens to make deception and misinterpretation in our relations with others impossible, which is perhaps another way of saying that the asymmetry of perspectives is thereby occluded (although we suggested earlier that phenomenologists are not committed to incorrigibility claims). Second, analytic philosophers often maintain that these kinds of phenomenological descriptions do not foreclose on the possibility that representations or simulations undergird such experiences. Phenomenology has little to say about the sub-personal and associated brain processes, for example, and some would hence maintain that these phenomenological descriptions may simply be wrong (in some sense). A variant of this might be the response that it is psychologically necessary that we *think* that we know and interact with others, as Ayer (1982: 221) says against Merleau-Ponty and Heidegger's analyses of intersubjectivity, but that this does not provide any kind of access to the other's mind or more general reason for thinking that they do in fact exist. We are thus returned to the background issue of the mind and how it works. Is intentionality predominantly to be understood as involving representational content, such that we represent the other as having beliefs and desires? The answer is no for most continental philosophers, and we have already seen some background reasons why this might be so: it is partly because of this general reluctance to resolve such matters by positing sophisticated judgements of this kind, however implicit (at least if they fail to take account of our primary immersion in a life-world [*Lebenswelt*] or social milieu). The concern is that if one hypostasizes a reasoned relation to the world that is dependent on a more practical one (genetically, developmentally, etc.), then one will never be able to reconstruct what Merleau-Ponty calls the "perceptual faith", and the way in which this necessarily opens on perspectives other than our own.

INTERSUBJECTIVITY

Transcendental arguments regarding intersubjectivity in continental philosophy

Of course, analytic philosophers are likely to be unconvinced. The simple assertion of our embodied and lived relationship with others can certainly amount to a dogmatic foreclosure on scepticism.[4] What, to continental eyes, avoids the dogmatic manoeuvre here is the additional critical question: how is the lived position possible? In this respect, it is perhaps unsurprising that the various continental arguments for intersubjectivity all the way down are inevitably buttressed by a multiplicity of variants on transcendental arguments. Such arguments are used to show that perception presupposes the existence of others (in Merleau-Ponty), that our ready-to-hand way of relating to the world involves an equipmental totality that again presupposes alternative perspectives and others (in Heidegger), or that the experience of shame offers the possibility of a phenomenological "proof" of the other (in Sartre). Often, as we have seen, such a position is supplemented by a transcendental argument that claims that relations of knowledge are not basic to our encounter with others, and that doubting this derivative relationship of knowledge in fact presupposes a more basic relation with others that remains intact. It might be claimed, for instance, that the epistemic focus on our relation with other minds presupposes a first- and second-person differentiation, without noting that the very idea of a "person" or "ego" can be understood as itself a response to, and thus dependent on, the Other. These are precisely the kinds of arguments that various continental philosophers do raise, whether the priority is given to perception, intensity, sensibility, mood, affect, desire, the unconscious and so on over the knowledge relation. If the transcendental claim of priority could be made good, this would seem convincing: the problem of other minds occurs only for a reflective human who has adopted (or tried to adopt) the view from nowhere, what Merleau-Ponty calls "high-altitude thinking", and if a condition of possibility of such reflection/knowing is social learning, imitation and interconnectedness (or desire and the unconscious, to gesture towards another trajectory), then the sceptical problem seems alleviated. Yet to the analytic philosopher, the appeals to the transcendental here are a sign that sceptical arguments have been evaded, not eliminated; such "skyhook" methods (to use Dennett's phrase) are the philosophical equivalent of the penny dreadful cliché "With one bound Jack was free".

Of course, one need not reject transcendental reasoning to feel that such arguments are not all equally successful. It is thus worth briefly recounting Sartre's famous argument in order to again consider some of the strengths and limitations of transcendental reasoning. In *Being and Nothingness*, Sartre describes a person peering through a keyhole at something on the other side of the closed door, captivated by whatever is going on. All of this occurs on the level of pre-reflective consciousness; the person is peering through the keyhole, entirely caught up in their activity, absorbed in the world. Suddenly, they hear footsteps in the corridor and they are aware that somebody is now watching them. No longer concerned with what is going on behind the door, they are conscious of their identity as escaping them in ways that they cannot control and they are ashamed of this fact. According to Sartre, the experience of shame recognizes both that we are that object which the Other is looking at and judging, and that we have our foundation outside ourselves: the Other sees an aspect of us that we cannot control and that requires their mediation. As Sartre suggests, "pure shame is not a feeling of being this or that guilty object, but in general of being an object" (1993: 288). In this experience of the look we apprehend our embodiment in a manner that is irreducible to the body as point of view around which a perceptual field is organized (since our being embodied is revealed to us in a manner that is very different from the way it is presupposed in our absorbed coping), and also as irreducible to the brute physicalist understanding of the body (Sacks 2005b). For Sartre, the important philosophical point to take away from this example is that the Other who catches the person peeping and causes them to feel shame cannot just be another object, but rather must be induced by a subject. In other words, Sartre argues that this experience of shame, and of feeling like an object, could not happen if other people did not exist. It might be felt that such an ontological conclusion is too strong, but for our purposes the point is that this feeling of shame is impossible to resist; it overwhelms us and there is no room for inference. The other who perceives us may not necessarily unambiguously apprehend all our higher-order psychological states, or at least not in the way that we experience this pre-reflectively, but they immediately apprehend us nonetheless.

Now it is possible that the person caught peering through the keyhole might be mistaken when they think that they have been caught in this precarious position (the footfall sounds may be resonating from elsewhere in the building, for instance). It is hence clear that another person does not actually have to be present for an individual to experience the look. This seems to suggest that perhaps Sartre has not refuted solipsism and the epistemological scepticism that engenders it. Sartre's response to this is to say that while there may not be someone literally there at a particular time and place in which we feel shame, at least one other person must exist – or, more minimally, must have existed – for the experience of shame to be comprehensible at all (1993: 280). Sartre also points out that it is significant that upon realizing that our shame was initially "mistaken", in the sense that there was actually nobody observing us, our feeling of vulnerability before the look of the

Other is actually far from dissipated; on the contrary, it is more likely that we will experience ourselves as an object all the more intensely. As Sacks notes:

> what I am experiencing, despite there being no actual person in the room behind me, is that the world contains some such persons ... to experience their absence is just to be committed to them existing elsewhere. That is just what it is for something to be absent rather than non-existent. (2005b: 292)

While I can be mistaken in particular cases, what is necessary is that some such other exists (or has existed) for such an experience to be possible. To put it another way, Sartre seeks to overcome the epistemological gap between self and world (self and other) by finding the other at the centre of our phenomenological experiences and thus indubitable in a certain sense.

Analytic responses

Recall the general critique of transcendental reasoning within the analytic tradition. On the one hand, it is maintained that transcendental arguments fail to establish the claimed necessity, in so far as they ignore other alternative explanations; hence they amount to a form of dogmatism (Körner 1966). On the other hand, the sceptic can always maintain that the necessity is only that we *believe* there are extra-mental facts (Stroud 1968), since this is sufficient to account for the mental experience in question; hence such an argument cannot establish the putative extra-mental facts. Partly because of these repeatedly expressed reservations regarding transcendental arguments, they have not been at centre stage in the analytic literature on other minds.[5] However, there is an analytic tradition of this kind, including Davidson's well-known invocation of the principle of charity and, most famously, Peter Strawson's modest transcendental arguments in *Individuals*. Strawson argues that the concept of person is basic to our understanding of "mind", and if we can meaningfully attribute mind to ourselves (which he says we can) then we necessarily have some logically adequate criteria for this that can also be applied in other cases, including to identify the minds of others (1959: 109–12). Against the argument from analogy, Strawson points out that such an argument depends on my being able to identify my own experiences, which he thinks itself logically depends on the concept of other perspectives. While there is a difference between self-ascription of mental states and other-ascription of mental states, both are nonetheless bound up in the same language-game surrounding the more basic concept of "person". By showing that the concept of "person" is more primitive than the abstraction from it that is the concept of "mind",

249

Strawson is thus able to provide an answer to the conceptual problem of other minds; for example, how do we know that it is a single concept of mind that persists throughout these two different uses, rather than involving two (or more) different concepts, a first-person and second-person concept? On his view, once this descriptive work regarding the connection between "person" and "mind" has been done, there is no coherent problem of other minds that requires an inference.

As many have pointed out, however, Strawson's argument does not seem to show that the world must actually contain others, but merely that we must have criteria for identifying them if they do in fact exist (see Sacks 2005b: 295). However, Sartre's argument – if one accepts the phenomenological description of being objectified by another person that functions as its core premise – seems to take us further than Strawson's, in that it is necessary that we construe the world as involving others, even if we remain agnostic about any stronger metaphysical conclusion. However, here we run up against a further analytic criticism of transcendental reasoning: Stroud's well-known point that in contexts where transcendental arguments are acceptable (i.e. within the scope of a verificationist, idealist or more generally anti-realist position), they become entirely unnecessary. In effect, Sartre has carried out much the same manoeuvre, and so the issue simply devolves to that of the plausibility of Sartre's non-naturalism about the mental and consciousness. Sacks's essay comparing Strawson and Sartre makes this explicit: "a disruption of the static order of the objective world is left optional in Strawson, rendered necessary in Sartre" (*ibid.*: 296). So, at least with respect to this case, Stroud is arguably correct in holding there to be a question-begging assumption of anti-realism in play in the discussion. However, the rejoinder can also be made that the criticism equally presupposes a hard realism and a subject-independent conception of the real. As Anita Avramides (2001) notes, the Stroudian position supposes a logical and metaphysical gap between me and everything else, and it also presupposes that knowledge has primacy over action. From a pragmatic or action-oriented picture, however, this idea of a separated Cartesian subject attempting to know things seems peculiar, as does the co-implicated idea of an objective reality that is independent of subjectivity. Indeed, it might be said that such a perspective is itself precariously poised next to scepticism, and it is certainly very different from the dominant holism in continental philosophy in which the subject is co-implicated with the real.

As such, we seem to be left with a rather stark alternative between analytic and continental philosophy on two major questions that often also overlap: (i) whether or not there are experiential norms of philosophical (as opposed to psychological) import, or whether beliefs are merely justified by other beliefs *ad infinitum*; and (ii) the question regarding transcendental arguments and their committal relation to the realism–anti-realism debate. It is clear, then, that their respective treatments of intersubjectivity and the problem of other minds have taken very different directions: one that is invested in the epistemological problematic and seeks to maintain close integration with the cognitive sciences; the other which seems to discredit pure epistemology on the basis of an overarching assessment that it is a dead end and is inextricably bound up with a problematically atomistic worldview. Given some of the various problems and lacunae evident in analytic philosophy on other minds, it might be maintained (as Rorty, Taylor and others hold) that this lends some inductive support (or at least support through inference to the best explanation) to the ostensibly non-inductive method of transcendental argumentation, as well as to a more constructivist remit for the philosopher. From this perspective, the epistemological attempt to establish the existence of the other seems insufficient on its own, bracketing away so much of what is central to social life and overstating the difficulty of relating to others in making their mental states hypothesized entities. Against this, it might be protested that transcendental arguments are, at best, risky, and that we have reached no dead end in relation to analytic philosophy of other minds; all we have seen is the need for more hybrid and pluralist accounts that incorporate the best features of simulation theory and "theory" theory, and deploy additional resources, as Nichols and Stich (2003) argue. If the typology presented here is generally accurate, then we have seen in some detail the manner in which the methods and background norms of each tradition have significant consequences for their respective views regarding intersubjectivity. As such, we have seen the importance of methodological factors to the institution of the analytic–continental "divide". Any project of rapprochement will have to grapple with some of these rather stark meta-philosophical differences.

CONCLUSION

Glendinning ends *The Idea of Continental Philosophy* by leaving philosophers with an existential predicament of sorts: whether we are to be "enders" or "benders" in relation to the perceived divide between analytic and continental philosophy.

The ender is "the one who knows that (what is in any case obvious) the very idea of a Continental tradition is contentious or even perverse and so will be inclined to work with a certain lack of interest in securing or maintaining the idea of the analytic/Continental distinction". The bender, on the other hand:

> demands that we acknowledge the *de facto*, real-world gulf or, at the very least, real-world gulf-effects, holding apart many whose work is marked by a serious interest in (among others) the usual suspects and many analytic philosophers. And the bender is (at least on occasion) willing to appropriate the title "continental philosophy" in order to do so. (2007: 119–20)

Some so-called "continental philosophers" based in Anglo-American countries are deflationary; they are "enders". They read work from each tradition seriously, and are very reluctant to proffer any kind of more general enquiry into each. This is the programme that Glendinning recommends more generally in his book, but we are not sure it is the way to go in philosophy as a whole. Frankly, we still do not understand enough about the divide to put it strategically in abeyance: to work as if it did not exist philosophically. We do know that the divide is marked by very different patterns of attention and citation, very different distributions of truth and authority, and these are not simply social facts; they reflect methodological norms on each side that make crossing the divide difficult, to say the least. In these circumstances, we feel that it is best to map what is going on in the spirit of a non-essentialist bender, looking at the methodologies and understandings of the value of philosophy exemplified in each tradition, and at how they come into play in different philosophical topics.

The results of such exercises can be piecemeal, but we feel that in turn the pieces can be built up into something of a coherent picture.

First, the results of this book confirm the broadly family resemblance account of each tradition that we have put forward. The continental tradition exhibits a greater degree of looseness, but it does seem to be organized around recurrent commitments to transcendental reasoning in philosophy, a "temporal turn" that not only affirms our historicity but argues for its philosophical primacy, a wariness of the philosophical value of common sense, the resistance to mechanistic or homuncular explanations (say, in regard to science and philosophy of mind) and anti-theoretical approaches to ethico-political matters. Each of these particular indicators (whatever the disagreements about precisely how to construe them) has clear methodological implications.

Moreover, it is not only the two traditions but the divide between them that is real. It is very difficult, in looking at the series of topical impasses here, not to be struck by the extent to which an analytic commitment to intuition-based methods and common sense regularly runs up against continental historicity and genealogy, and the continental investment in the transcendental regularly runs up against analytic logic-based scruples and empiricist leanings. In the philosophy of religion, a "weak agnostic" is one who holds that, given the state of the evidence, there exist no good reasons for a non-theist to become a theist, or a non-atheist to become an atheist. We are, in effect, weak agnostics about the divide wherever methodological commitments preclude both analytic–continental crossover work and the taking seriously of criticisms raised in the other tradition; that is, we hold that continental concerns about analytic work and methodology are (by analytic standards) difficult to regard as final, and that analytic concerns about continental work and methodology are (by continental standards) equally provisional. It seems to us that this is broadly the case with respect to most of the topics we have discussed, the major exceptions perhaps being a possible rapprochement within the cognitive sciences (to the extent that phenomenological results are absorbed within the relevant cognitive sciences, the analytic attitude of deference to the sciences at least means that some dialogue is necessary), and a partial overlap in those parts of the ethical literature that focus on practice (most obviously, virtue ethics). That said, such rapprochement (thus far) typically takes place at the margins of each field, or is extremely limited.

However, the divide is not necessarily insuperable. One point that comes out of our historical survey (in Part I) very clearly is the extent to which famous encounters are put to polemical use on both sides of the divide: that is, the extent to which there has been rather more potential, historically, for discussion than is often acknowledged. True, some interactions have been sterile (Royaumont, Popper and Habermas), but in other cases it is not so much the original encounter as the later invocation of it that comes across as uncomprehending. Again, there have been several missed opportunities for potentially fruitful overlap between the traditions; consider Reinach's apparent prefiguring of speech act theory, or the recent reading of the Frege–Husserl debate. Other possible missed opportunities have been suggested: for instance, Friedman (2000) suggests that Cassirer represents something of a missing "middle way" figure and Overgaard (2010) suggests that the ordinary-language philosophers who attended Royaumont had much more in common with the phenomenologists than they recognized at the time.

Our project has been largely descriptive rather than prescriptive (acknowledging that the terms themselves have a meta-philosophical and hence prescriptive register throughout much of the twentieth century); not much has been offered by way of a positive account of the future(s) for philosophy. However, weak meta-philosophical agnosticism is compatible with seeing value in at least some regular dialogue and/or disputation. For one thing, a kind of trust is possible across such divides; engagement with the other tradition can induce respect of at least some aspects of the work that tradition carries out, even if it is not at all clear how to bring that work into relation with one's own tradition. And often it does seem possible; consider, for instance, the "Pittsburgh Hegelians" such as McDowell (certainly pre-1995) and Brandom within the analytic tradition. Again, dialogue has the useful effect of keeping the role played by basic methodological commitments in each tradition highly salient. Without regular re-examination of these commitments, philosophy of both kinds can become insular and overconfident, and although each tradition certainly examines its own methods from the inside, the disconcerting or provocative voices of those who are completely unconvinced has obvious gadfly potential. Finally, the acceptance of weak meta-philosophical agnosticism itself can have value for a tradition. It is not unduly relativistic to believe that the pre-existing philosophical beliefs and commitments of a person might rationally preclude them from seeing philosophy the same way as oneself, and to admit, in fallibilist spirit, that the same holds in the converse direction. As Socrates said, let us know that we do not know, which, in the context of this book, might amount to saying let us hope that more philosophers can identify the bets that they (and their forebears) have placed, and are reliant on.

NOTES

INTRODUCTION

1. Although, of course, a great deal can be gleaned from both the terms and who tends to describe the distinction this way. The term "continental", in particular, is taken to have pejorative overtones (and certainly has something of a pejorative origin); the term "analytic" has been taken as self-commending. We recognize that there is no neutral ground here, but given that our view is that the "two traditions" theory is not mistaken and has particular methodological significance, we have stuck with these terms here.
2. For further remarks along these lines, see Prado (2003: 9), Priest (2003b: 237) and Wrathall (1999: 306).
3. For instance: in *The Dialogue of Reason*, Jonathan Cohen argues that analytic philosophy is characterized both by a kind of connectivity and by a common concern with rationality (cf. Cohen 1986: 49–50); in *What is Analytic Philosophy?*, Hans-Johann Glock opts for a characterization of analytic philosophy in terms of connectivity of this kind, together with a family resemblance claim (cf. Glock 2008: 222–3).
4. For a study of analytic citation patterns with respect to four alleged figures of this kind – Wittgenstein, Davidson, Rorty and McDowell – see Duke *et al.* (2010).
5. The situation is a little like that involved in cases of normative self-application; some normative systems approve of themselves, as it were, and others do not, and this can be worth knowing as an indicator of internal coherence. For instance, it is illuminatory that, by David Hume's own standards of knowledge, his theory of knowledge is apparently unknowable.
6. See, for example, Glendinning (2007: 115), Glock (2008: 151–78) and Mullarkey (2006). In some respects, however, Neil Levy's essay "Analytic and Continental: Explaining the Differences" (2003) offers support for the analyses offered here, in that he looks at their divergent research practices (with some reflection on their respective methodologies) by way of an analogy with Thomas Kuhn's account of scientific methodology. For Levy, analytic philosophy is paradigmatic, and functions in the manner of a normal science (with research clusters, methodological canons, technical training, etc.), whereas continental philosophy exhibits the features of what Kuhn called pre-science (lack of agreement on methods, no unifying work, etc.). Although we agree that continental philosophy is not paradigmatic in the manner of analytic philosophy, the "pre-science" characterization seems to us to underplay the communal norms and common philosophical and methodological features genuinely present in that tradition.

PART I. FORMATIVE ENCOUNTERS: A SHORT HISTORY OF THE DIVIDE

1. There is a haze of such usages in the modern sense around 1935; for instance, the term is used throughout A. C. Ewing's "Two Kinds of Analysis" (1935), and in John Wisdom's *Problems of Mind and Matter* (1934). Hacker (1998) contends that the term really caught on with Arthur Pap's *Elements of Analytic Philosophy* (1949).
2. For more on this, see Cutrofello (2000: ch. 1).

1. FREGE AND HUSSERL

1. See Monk (1996: 116). Russell's late 1890s Hegelianism was very strongly influenced by McTaggart's *Studies in the Hegelian Dialectic* (1896).
2. "Über Sinn und Bedeutung", perhaps the most influential of Frege's papers on the later analytic tradition, was first translated into English in 1948 (by Max Black; cf. Frege 1948) and 1949 (by Herbert Feigl; cf. Frege 1949).
3. The full review was first seen in English in the translation by E. W. Kluge (Frege 1972).
4. For a vigorous presentation of this view, see Hill & Haddock (2000).
5. At the time of Frege's work, no satisfactory set of axioms for arithmetic had been identified; the first version of what we now call the Peano postulates was put forward by Dedekind in 1888 (cf. Dedekind 1963: 31–115). Frege's *Foundations* contains the work required to show that from his definitions and logic these axioms can be proved, on the assumption that every concept has an extension; establishing this in turn became the next goal of the logicist programme. For a discussion of this, see George & Velleman (2002: ch. 2).

2. RUSSELL VERSUS BERGSON

1. Apparently Bergson held that Russell's later review of his work was "revenge" for this episode (see Monk 1996: 238).
2. That the concern is with Bergson's method as much as his conclusions can be seen when Russell expresses concern at the *gratuitousness* of Bergson's metaphysical conclusions; cf. Russell's remarks on Bergson's way of constructing a time-series in his unpublished 1913 "Theory of Knowledge": "There is no *logical* error in [Bergson's] procedure, but there is a greater accumulation of questionable metaphysics than is suitable for our purposes" (Russell 1984: 75).

3. CARNAP VERSUS HEIDEGGER

1. These are remarks made by Wittgenstein to the Vienna Circle at Moritz Schlick's house, 30 December 1929, recorded by Waismann (1979: 68).

4. THE FRANKFURT SCHOOL, THE POSITIVISTS AND POPPER

1. Both Glock and Cohen undertake a defence of analytic philosophy against the charge of irrelevancy, and Glock also considers the broader charge of political conservatism; cf. Cohen (1986: 57–63) and Glock (2008: 182–95).
2. Charles Taylor, for example, argues that although Popper's comments about many

of these important continental philosophers were largely baseless, they have been received with attention and respect because of his fame as an epistemologist. See Taylor (1995a: 1).

5. ROYAUMONT: RYLE AND HARE VERSUS FRENCH AND GERMAN PHILOSOPHY

1. Remarkably enough there is no agreement between commentators on when Royaumont actually took place, with different sources alleging anywhere between 1958 and 1962, and Peter Strawson (a participant!) even suggesting the early 1950s. We think that 1958 is the most probable date. For a discussion of these issues, see S. Overgaard (2010).
2. See *ibid.*, which draws heavily on the work of Stanley Cavell.

6. DERRIDA VERSUS SEARLE AND BEYOND

1. Wheeler draws further conclusions: "Among the distinctions that abandoning the logos/clothing distinction undermines are the use/mention distinction and the token/ type distinction ... If no principled distinctions separate facts from meaning, facts from value, rhetoric from logic, or sentences from other meaningful items (that is, if these are not natural dichotomies), a critique must be a critique of a discourse or concrete text. And ... considerations that would be 'irrelevant to the argument' in a standard philosophical discussion may well be relevant to showing a discourse to be incoherent" (Wheeler 2000: 221, 224).
2. Thanks to Ricky Sebold for this observation.
3. In this respect, also see Descombes (1982).
4. There have been a few different journals that have devoted issues to this topic in recent times, including *International Journal of Philosophical Studies* (2001), *Metaphilosophy* (2003) and *Monist* (1999), as well as Prado (2003).
5. This is not an entirely new phenomenon; the *Southern Journal of Philosophy* has been pluralist in its publication tendencies since its inception in 1963, and *Inquiry* since it began in 1958.

7. INTRODUCTION TO PHILOSOPHICAL METHOD

1. See Dummett (1978), in particular the essays "Truth" (1–24) and "The Philosophical Basis of Intuitionistic Logic" (215–47).
2. In his classic *Epistemology and Cognition* (1986), Goldman develops his process relia-bilist account of justification by reference to accounts of the deliberative processes we actually follow in this way.
3. In the main, this methodological precept turns into the Quinean commitment to global revisability.
4. This is John McDowell's characterization of a critical remark on his *Mind and World* by Crispin Wright; the phrase is apparently Richard Rorty's description of a fairly regular occurrence in his own career. See McDowell (2002: 291, 304).
5. James Williams explains the Deleuzian account of this well in *The Transversal Thought of Gilles Deleuze* (2005). For Deleuze, analysis presupposes the discrete nature of possibilities, and denies context/background, as well as the connectedness and rela-

tionality of all problems to one another. In particular, the association of clarity and distinctness falsely abstracts from the process of genesis and the future evolutions that are always at work in the present, interrupting it.

6. Priest (2003b) makes a similar claim.

8. ANALYTIC PHILOSOPHY AND THE INTUITION PUMP: THE USES AND ABUSES OF THOUGHT EXPERIMENTS

1. This is a standard characterization of intuition in the literature; for objections to this approach to intuition see Weinberg (2007).
2. Particularly important in this literature have been Gendler (2000), Sorensen (1992) and many of the papers in DePaul & Ramsey (2002).
3. Other clear examples would be John Harris's complication of the killing/letting die debate with his "The Survival Lottery" (1975), and Daniel Dennett's recurrent attempts to express his dissatisfaction with qualia theories through the Chase–Sanborn thought experiment (cf. his "Quining Qualia" [1988]).
4. Peter Unger presents an impressive array of biasing agents in the case of ethical thought experiments in his *Living High and Letting Die* (1996).
5. Alvin Plantinga does this as part of the development of a virtue reliabilist account of justification; the idea is to demonstrate that our allegedly deontological intuitions about justification are a relatively recent and theoretically biased state of affairs. See Plantinga (1992).
6. For details, see Witt-Hansen (2003). Christiane Schildknecht has apparently (according to Witt-Hansen) pointed out the earlier use of a related term in Lichtenberg's common-place book (cf. Schildknecht 1990).
7. The subsequent discussion (Bradley 1922: 86–7) suggests that Bradley's supposition is best seen as a form of thought experiment in which we acquire knowledge about our concepts, rather than the world.
8. Russell's thought experiment has been given a new lease of life in several more recent debates, most notably by Unger in opposing the causal theory of reference. In these cases, it takes on more of the qualities of a thought experiment, in the sense that it more clearly elicits intuitions that are intended to point to a particular conclusion.
9. "Modern logic … has the effect of enlarging our abstract imagination, and providing an infinite number of possible hypotheses to be applied in the analysis of any complex fact" (Russell 1914: 68).
10. Consider Russell's well-known remark "it is a wholesome plan, in thinking about logic, to stock the mind with as many puzzles as possible, since these serve much the same purpose as is served by experiments in physical science" (1905: 484–5). The puzzles that Russell discusses are arguments to false conclusions, and although two of them make use of display sentences requiring some empirical knowledge of the world to see their point (George IV, the present king of France), in neither case are the characteristic features of a thought experiment present. In passing, there is at least some evidence of a continuing tradition of opposing analysis to imagination; cf. G. J. Warnock (1956).
11. This view may, however, be a misjudgement. As Mary Warnock points out, Prichard and Ross appear to be generally ignorant of the similarities between their views and those of the last two chapters of *Principia Ethica*. Cf. M. Warnock (1960: 58–9).
12. Ross does believe that our moral convictions can be illusory, but when the act of intuiting is successfully performed, it brings with it a kind of warrant that one is tracking a genuine property in the world. See Ross (1930: 39–40). Ross's views on the balancing

act required in taking account of moral convictions bring a further element into play – that of the attitude of analytic philosophy to common sense – which we consider in Chapter 9.

13. Daniel Stoljar and Yujin Nagasawa (2004) find earlier instances of the "knowledge intuition" (the intuition elicited by Frank Jackson's Mary example, in which someone who knows all physical facts concerning colour perception perceives red for the first time) in Russell, J. W. Dunne and C. D. Broad, and in the latter two (non-analytic) cases the intuition is explicitly elicited by thought experiment using an omniscient being in the tradition of Laplace's demon.

14. The 1930s also see a shift within the field of philosophy of science to a more positive attitude to *scientific* thought experiments, largely under the influence of Karl Popper, although we can find no evidence that he influenced the growth of thought experiment within analytic philosophy. See Popper (1959: appendix xi).

15. Sorensen (1992: 45–6) nicely makes this point.

16. An example of the shift under way occurs in a pair of papers given together at the 1962 annual meeting of the Eastern Division of the American Philosophical Association. Keith Donnellan raises doubts about alleged criteria of necessity in his "Necessity and Criteria" (1962), and does so by considering a range of non-actual but very ordinary imagined cases: a child who knows about fathers but not about the facts of life, and so on. The cases are not especially distinctive; indeed, they could just as easily be taken to be illustrations of an argument that could be made generally and without examples. Putnam's reply "It Ain't Necessarily So" (1962) kicks over the traces by introducing the "Martian robot cat" thought experiment, which is at once more bizarre and more essential to the surrounding argument than Donnellan's examples, and which gained a secondary literature of its own. As Putnam later acknowledged, this thought experiment was an early instance of a pattern used more fully in his later "The Meaning of 'Meaning'" (1975).

17. Gettier's original examples do not fit this characterization particularly well, since they secured a great deal of acceptance almost immediately. However, since they also inspired an entire literature rich with further variant thought experiments – and so structured the discussion of knowledge in analytic epistemology for twenty years or so – the general point here still holds.

18. Deleuze's essay on Michel Tournier's rewriting of the Robinson Crusoe tale, *Friday*, *seems* to be a prolonged thought experiment (see his appendix essay, "Michel Tournier and the World Without Others" [1990b]). However, one of the defining features of analytic thought experiments is that they are short and pithy, something that cannot be said of Deleuze's essay. For Sorensen (1992: ch. 1), when the thought experiment becomes a story, and one that refuses to be translated into a deductive argument, we are in the realm of literature rather than philosophy. Another way of putting this might be to say that the Deleuzian preoccupation with Crusoe is not a consistency test or tool of any kind. It is not engaged with to sharpen distinctions. Rather, it is preoccupied with broader issues: what is our place in the world? How might we think of it otherwise? What does this show us about our normal commitments? How might we exist otherwise?

19. Sider is here making a case for the methods of analytic metaphysics in general, whatever they might be.

20. This is, in effect, Hare's reason for rejecting anti-consequentialist thought experiments; it is also in effect the ground for Goldman's virtue reliabilism, as we discussed in Chapter 7.

9. REFLECTIVE EQUILIBRIUM: COMMON SENSE OR CONSERVATISM?

1. Brad Hooker claims this also applies to moral particularists (which we might take the poststructuralists to be) because the theoretical position that there are no overarching moral or political principles that unify our various judgements must nonetheless stand or fall as a claim in relation to the diversity (or otherwise) of our intuitive commitments. In that minimal sense, reflective equilibria can still be said to obtain.
2. See Daniels (1979). It is an influential argument that wide reflective equilibrium should be standard in analytic ethics.
3. Russell is regularly to be found outside the empiricist fence, since (for instance) his solution to the problem of induction relies on a kind of synthetic *a priori* knowledge, but empiricism remains a methodologically important doctrine for him – empiricist scruples are only to be flouted as a very last resort. See Russell (1948: ch. 10).
4. The difficulties with finessing foundational worries with convention were well displayed by Quine (1966).
5. "Bootstrapping" is a way of getting a process up and running, in which a small starting process is begun that in turn starts up the remainder of the process (this is what "booting" a computer means). The idea has appeared sporadically in the analytic literature as a way of avoiding apparently vicious circularity; cf. also Glymour (1980).
6. Perhaps the most well-known employment of critical cognitivism is its application to Descartes' foundational difficulties in Van Cleve (1979).
7. In such systems, there is often a mechanism to ensure that coherence demands responsivity to occurrent experiential beliefs. For an example, cf. BonJour (1985).
8. A fairly bald example, from David Lewis: "Modal realism is fruitful; that gives us good reason to believe that it is true" (1986: 4).

10. THE FATE OF TRANSCENDENTAL REASONING

1. Analytic philosophers do occasionally use the term for arguments from a state of affairs to its presuppositions; the fact "transcendental argument" has been given such a thin reading is itself an interesting fact about the analytic attitude to the transcendental.
2. Davidson's reflections on triangulation and his later formulations of the principle of charity are commonly thought to involve them, and it is perhaps not a coincidence that shortly after this became apparent his work was far less discussed in some of the central journals of analytic philosophy. The most cited papers in *Mind* and the *Journal of Philosophy* are the ones before Davidson's project clearly becomes a transcendental one: "Actions, Reasons and Causes", "Truth and Meaning" and "Mental Events". In more "cross-over" journals, such as *European Journal of Philosophy* and *Southern Journal of Philosophy*, it is essays after "On the Very Idea of a Conceptual Scheme" that are more frequently cited. For these citational details, see Duke *et al.* (2010).
3. We saw earlier that Crispin Wright outed McDowell from the analytic tradition ostensibly for his lack of clarity, rather than use of transcendental arguments, but the issues seem interwoven since what is at stake in McDowell's post-Sellarsian worries about empiricism is precisely this dimension.
4. Many contemporary analytic rationalists maintain that synthetic *a priori* knowable truths exist, but shun transcendental argument as a way of establishing this. BonJour's *In Defense of Pure Reason* (1998), for instance, sets out an influential case for rationalism, and for the synthetic *a priori*, without making use of transcendental argument. Rather, BonJour appeals to the "pre-critical" notion of rational insight.

5. Kant does use the term ("*transzendentalen Argumente*") in the *Critique of Pure Reason* at A627/B655, but in a different sense. The connection between transcendental exposition and transcendental argument is somewhat controversial.

6. Allison (1986) gives an influential criticism of the traditional anglophone reading of Kant.

7. In an interview, Stiegler says "I think one must pass through the transcendental in order to get beyond the transcendental. The misunderstanding between continental philosophy and Anglo-Saxon philosophy relates to this point, for one cannot short-circuit transcendental experience; it is impossible" (2007: 340). Thanks to Daniel Ross for pointing this out.

8. To note one of the most obvious differences, Gallagher and Zahavi point out that "Husserl's emphasis on intuition makes him far less inclined than Kant to appeal to and employ inferences to best explanation. Indeed, for Husserl transcendental conditions of possibility must be experientially accessible – otherwise the very idea of a phenomenological transcendental philosophy would have to be abandoned" (Gallagher & Zahavi 2008b: 88).

9. Cases of people without proprioception complicate this view, but do not necessarily refute it. See the discussion of Ian Waterman by Gallagher (2006) and Bermudez (1995).

10. Every figure has an optimal context in which to view it, for example. In this respect, see Kelly (2005).

11. The suggestion that phenomenological arguments are committed to infallibility or incorrigibility is convincingly disputed in Taylor Carman's "On the Inescapability of Phenomenology" (2005).

12. For Merleau-Ponty, Humean association of ideas takes for granted the kind of perceptual coherence that it is meant to explain. The mind is said to combine ideas according to three principles for Hume: resemblance, contiguity and causality. But to which ideas do we apply these principles, and how do we do so? What qualities in the ideas motivate us to combine them as we do? They can only be contextualized features: baseballs, basketballs, things that have a significance for us. It is hard to see how mere sensations or atomic qualities, such as red or hot, would be associated or disassociated. In other words, Merleau-Ponty claims that empiricism's explanatory atomism is not made good on; it is aborted, and a descriptive phenomenology is (necessarily) presupposed. See Carman (2008).

13. Derrida notes that he is an "ultra-transcendentalist or quasi-transcendentalist" and explains this in terms of his concern to avoid reductive empiricism. See Glendinning (2001: 107).

11. PHENOMENOLOGY: RETURNING TO THE THINGS THEMSELVES

1. Karl Schumann and Barry Smith (1987) point out that the Munich phenomenologists were influenced by the British empiricist tradition.

2. Glendinning (2007) notes the following comments as salutary in this regard. Austin said, "I think it might be better to use, for this way of doing philosophy, some less misleading name than those given above – for instance 'linguistic phenomenology', only that is rather a mouthful" (1961: 130); Ryle said, "Though it is entitled *The Concept of Mind*, the book could be described as a sustained essay in phenomenology, if you are at home with that label" (1971: vol. 1, 188); and Wittgenstein also remarked, "You could say of my work that it is 'phenomenology'" (1984: 116). As has often been noted when analytic engagements with phenomenology are discussed, Wilfrid Sellars has

also declared that, "for longer than I care to remember, I have conceived of philosophical analysis (and synthesis) as akin to phenomenology" (1978: 170).

3. See Thompson (2007) on this point.

4. Libet's experiments seem to show that our conscious experience of making decisions is actually misleading. When we are conscious of having made a decision, in actual fact the decision was made (judging by neural activity) about 300 milliseconds earlier. What do such findings mean for phenomenology? Such data would be taken by most phenomenologists to support (rather than falsify) their view, in that embodied intentionality is shown to operate at a different level from conscious reflective decision-making (roughly the know-how/know-that distinction), and the manner in which the former kind of pre-reflective motor intentionality is always-already at work. See Libet (1999).

5. Beata Stawarska suggests that for Merleau-Ponty "psychoanalysis helps to thicken and deepen the meaning of human existence by transcending the classical subject-act-object structure of pure consciousness" (2008: 58).

12. GENEALOGY, HERMENEUTICS AND DECONSTRUCTION

1. While Foucault comments in an interview that he attempts to "historicise to the utmost in order to leave as little space as possible to the transcendental", this statement indicates that it is an effort that in his view can never totally succeed. See Foucault (1996: 99).

2. Gary Shapiro (1990) makes some of these points.

15. ONTOLOGY AND METAPHYSICS

1. Davidson also argues that events are required as the relata of causal relations.

16. TRUTH, OBJECTIVITY AND REALISM

1. For an early version, see Russell (1912b: ch. 12).

2. A recursive, as opposed to "straight", definition captures the entities falling under a concept by a repeatable procedure. For instance, a straight definition, within the non-negative integers (0, 1, 2, …), of "even number" might be "number divisible by 2 without remainder". A recursive definition of the same concept might be as follows: (i) 0 is an even number; (ii) if x is an even number, so is $x + 2$, (iii) nothing else is an even number.

3. See Dummett (1978: esp. papers 1, 10, 13, 14 and 21); for the background view of the relation between metaphysics and language, see Dummett (1991).

4. See Goodman's essays in the collection *Star-Making: Realism, Anti-realism, and Irrealism* (McCormick 1996) and Goodman (1978).

17. TIME: A CONTRETEMPS

1. This chapter conjoins and develops several articles published by Jack Reynolds: see Reynolds (2009a,b; 2010a).

2. It also challenges the "growing universe" theory, which holds that both the present

and the past are real (the name deriving from the idea that any list of entities that are real necessarily increases over time as things that are present become past), but we cannot consider this position here.

3. McTaggart also discusses a C-series, in which temporal events are simply considered as ordered in a particular way. As with the B-series ordering, McTaggart suggests that this is incomplete, in so far as it does not allow for the succession of time.

4. This is not an entirely satisfactory term for Reichenbach, whose preferred self-description was that of "logical empiricist". On these issues, however, the two are much the same.

5. A *differend* seems closely akin to what Miranda Fricker (2003) calls a hermeneutic injustice, where a vocabulary is not even available in which to state a given injustice.

6. Because of its synchronic focus, structuralism is difficult to accommodate within such a "temporal turn".

7. While Levinas's philosophy of time is more commonly associated with an emphasis on an irrecoverable past that obliges us to respond to it, even though we cannot represent it or know it, he also suggests that "anticipation of the future and projection of the future, sanctioned as essential to time from Bergson to Sartre, are but the present of the future and not the authentic future; the future which is not grasped, which befalls us and lays hold of us. The Other is the future" (1987: 76–7). This is also a key aspect of the work of Antonio Negri; see Negri (2005).

8. As John McCumber points out in *Reshaping Reason*, "An assertion must be simultaneous with whatever it is that justifies it, whether that justifying factor is a state of affairs in the world or other assertions from which it follows … The perceptual evidence for beauty of Cleopatra lies irretrievably in the past; all that can justify belief in it today is the surviving testimony" (2007: 69).

9. Hugh Mellor, however, deplores thought experiments that use "fantasy arguments" about time. He writes, "it presumes to show something possible by describing an imaginary world in which we should apparently be inclined to believe the possibility actual" (1982: 66). For Mellor, though, showing plausibility is not enough to show possibility.

10. See Dolev (2007). Dolev suggests they both share an "ontological assumption" and he intimates that a return to phenomenology might be worthwhile.

18. MIND, BODY AND REPRESENTATIONALISM

1. Ferdinand de Saussure himself provides an interesting potential (missed) point of overlap between the traditions. His structural linguistics was highly influential in the United States, but at a time when philosophical engagement with linguistics was attenuated. By the time philosophers and linguists did interact actively in the nascent project of cognitive science (from around 1960), the Chomskian revolution had seen Saussure's influence decline. (It is also interesting to note that references to Chomsky by continental philosophers continue to be scarce; on the other hand, Saussure's influence within continental philosophy has continued: consider for instance Merleau-Ponty, Lacan or Derrida.) This is something of a missed opportunity for connection between the traditions. For another, see the discussion of Adolf Reinach in Chapter 11.

2. This sentiment is endorsed in Wheeler & Cappuccio (2010).

3. This point has been made to us by Søren Overgaard.

4. While Williamson (2005) also argues that there is something like a "representationalist turn" in analytic philosophy, whether it be construed as mental or linguistic (about

thought or language), he contends that this does not suffice to distinguish what is analytic from philosophy that is non-analytic, because he claims that phenomenologists and postmodernists also take this representationalist turn. We shall argue that he is mistaken in the latter regard. We note that, in his later *The Philosophy of Philosophy* (2008), Williamson prefers to characterize this as the "conceptual turn".

5. A similar account is then given for desire. That such circularity is not vicious is not entirely uncontroversial, but highly plausible given the availability of well-known devices for generating network definitions.

6. See, for example, the exchange between Dreyfus and Searle in Wrathall & Malpas (2000).

7. For Davidson's representationalism or anti-representationalism, see Rorty (1988).

19. ETHICS AND POLITICS: THEORETICAL AND ANTI-THEORETICAL APPROACHES

1. Given the origins of utilitarianism – Bentham's emphasis on calculation of utility, Mill's interest in economics as much as ethics – this is not at all surprising.

2. See Merleau-Ponty (1969a), and Beauvoir (1976). It is only the persistence in their work of a version of the master–slave dialectic that precludes their political philosophy from being a form of communitarianism.

3. These are aspects of Rawls's main argument for adopting maximin; other considerations he stresses are the uniqueness and gravity of the situation and the irrevocability of the choice. A curious point is that these considerations are much like those that, in "The Will to Believe", William James uses to characterize "genuine" option: that is, that it be live, momentous and forced. James, of course, famously argues that under such circumstances, when decision on intellectual grounds is impossible, one is not irrational in setting one's level of risk as one likes.

4. One example of work being done to overcome this impasse is that of Linda Alcoff, who attempts to steer a middle way between analytic and continental philosophies in her book *Real Knowing* (2008).

5. See Dreyfus & Dreyfus (2004). See also Dreyfus's website, http://socrates.berkeley.edu/~hdreyfus/html/papers.html (accessed September 2010).

20. PROBLEM(S) OF OTHER MINDS: SOLUTIONS AND DISSOLUTIONS IN ANALYTIC AND CONTINENTAL PHILOSOPHY

1. See, for instance, Goldman (1986) for a process reliabilist account of justification.

2. See Gallagher (2006, 2008). Thanks to Edoardo Zamuner for conversations about this.

3. In addition to the philosophers cited in this regard elsewhere in this book, think also of Riceour's *Oneself as Another* (1992), and Jean-Luc Nancy's *Being Singular Plural* (2000) and *Inoperative Community* (1991).

4. Avramides (2001: 236) makes this claim in relation to the transcendental arguments of Davidson and Strawson, rather than any continental philosopher, but the point holds in this regard as well.

5. Hyslop's *Other Minds* (1995) does not mention transcendental arguments at all, and Avramides's *Other Minds* (2001) ignores the entire phenomenological and continental tradition, although she at least acknowledges this exclusion.

BIBLIOGRAPHY

Adorno, T. 2000. *The Adorno Reader*, B. O'Connor (ed.). London: Blackwell.

Adorno, T. *et al.* (eds) 1976. *The Positivist Dispute in German Sociology*. London: Heinemann.

Akehurst, T. 2008. "The Nazi Tradition: The Analytic Critique of Continental Philosophy in Mid-century Britain". *History of European Ideas* **34**: 548–57.

Alcoff, L. 2008. *Real Knowing*. Ithaca, NY: Cornell University Press.

Alliez, É. 1995. *Capital Times*. Minneapolis, MN: University of Minnesota Press.

Alliez, É. 1997. "Questionnaire on Deleuze", P. Goodchild & N. Millett (trans.). *Theory, Culture & Society* **14**(2): 81–7.

Allison, H. 1986. *Kant's Transcendental Idealism*. New Haven, CT: Yale University Press.

Ameriks, K. 2006. *Kant and the Historical Turn*. New York, Oxford University Press.

Anscombe, G. E. 1958. "Modern Moral Philosophy". *Philosophy* **33**(124): 1–19.

Ansell-Pearson, K. 2002. *Philosophy and the Adventure of the Virtual*. London: Routledge.

Antiseri, D. 1996. *The Weak Thought and its Strength*. Aldershot: Ashgate.

Apel, K. 1987. "The Problem of Philosophical Foundations in Light of a Transcendental Pragmatics of Language". In *After Philosophy: End or Transformation?*, K. Baynes, J. Bohman & T. McCarthy (eds), 250–90. Cambridge, MA: MIT Press.

Arendt, H. 1978. *The Life of the Mind*. New York: Harcourt.

Aristotle 1980. *The Nicomachean Ethics*, D. Ross (trans.). New York: Oxford University Press.

Aristotle 1993. *Posterior Analytics*, J. Barnes (trans.). New York: Oxford University Press.

Armstrong, D. M. 1978. *Universals and Scientific Realism, Volume 2: A Theory of Universals*. Cambridge: Cambridge University Press.

Austin, J. L. 1961. *Philosophical Papers*, J. O. Urmson & G. J. Warnock (eds). Oxford: Oxford University Press.

Austin, J. L. 1962. *Sense and Sensibilia*. Oxford: Clarendon Press.

Austin, J. L. 1979. "Truth". In *Philosophical Papers*, 2nd edn, J. O. Urmson & G. J. Warnock (eds), 117–133. Oxford: Oxford University Press.

Avramides, A. 2001. *Other Minds*. London: Routledge.

Ayer, A. J. 1952. *Language, Truth and Logic*. London: Dover.

Ayer, A. J. 1954. "One's Knowledge of Other Minds". In *Philosophical Essays*, 191–214. London: Macmillan.

Ayer, A. J. 1982. *Philosophy in the Twentieth Century*. London: Random House.

Ayer, A. J. 1986. *More of my Life*. Oxford: Oxford University Press.

Badiou, A. 1999. *Manifesto for Philosophy*, N. Madarasz (trans.). Albany, NY: SUNY Press.

Badiou, A. 2001. *Ethics*, P. Hallward (trans.). London: Verso.

Badiou, A. 2005. "The Adventure of French Philosophy". *New Left Review* **35**: 67–77.

Badiou, A. 2007. *Being and Event*, O. Feltham (trans.). London: Continuum.

Baggini, J. & J. Stangroom 2002. *New British Philosophy: the Interviews*. London: Routledge.

Barbaras, R. 2003. *The Being of the Phenomenon*, T. Toadvine & L. Lawlor (trans.). Indianapolis, IN: Indiana University Press.

Barrett, W. 1979. *The Illusion of Technique*. New York: Anchor.

Bataille, G. 2004. *The Unfinished System of Non-Knowledge*, S. Kendall (trans.). Minneapolis, MN: University of Minnesota Press.

Beaney, M. (ed.) 2007. *The Analytic Turn*. London: Routledge.

Beaney, M. 2009. "Conceptions of Analysis in Analytic Philosophy". *Stanford Encyclopaedia of Philosophy*. http://stanford.library.usyd.edu.au/entries/analysis/s6.html#9 [accessed September 2010].

Beauvoir, S. de 1976. *The Ethics of Ambiguity*, B. Frechtman (trans.). New York: Kensington Publishing.

Bergson, H. 1944. *Creative Evolution*, A. Mitchell (trans.). New York: Modern Library.

Bergson, H. 1968. *The Creative Mind*, M. Andison (trans.). Westport, CN: Greenwood Press.

Bergson, H. 2008. *Matter and Memory*, N. M. Paul & W. S. Palmer (trans.). New York: Zone Books.

Bermudez, J. 1995. "Transcendental Arguments and Psychology". *Metaphilosophy* **26**(4): 379–401.

Bermudez, J. 2006. "The Phenomenology of Bodily Awareness". In *Phenomenology and Philosophy of Mind*, D. Smith & A. Thomasson (eds), 295–316. Oxford: Oxford University Press.

Blackburn, S. 1984. *Spreading the Word*. Oxford: Clarendon Press.

Blanshard, B. 2002. *The Nature of Thought, Volume 2*. London: Routledge.

BonJour, L. 1985. *The Structure of Empirical Knowledge*. Cambridge, MA: Harvard University Press.

BonJour, L. 1998. *In Defense of Pure Reason*. Cambridge: Cambridge University Press.

Bordwell, D. & N. Carroll 1996. *Post-Theory: Reconstructing Film Studies*. Madison, WI: University of Wisconsin Press.

Bradley, F. H. 1922. *Principles of Logic, Vol. I*. Oxford: Oxford University Press.

Bradley, J. 2003. "Transformations in Speculative Philosophy". In *The Cambridge History of Philosophy 1870–1945, Vol. I*, T. Baldwin (ed.), 436–46. Cambridge: Cambridge University Press.

Brandom, R. 2002. *Tales of the Mighty Dead*. Cambridge, MA: Harvard University Press.

Braver, L. 2007. *A Thing of This World: A History of Continental Anti-Realism*. Evanston, IL: Northwestern University Press.

Broome, J. 1991. *Weighing Goods*. Oxford: Blackwell.

Brown, J. R. 1991. *The Laboratory of the Mind*. London: Routledge.

Byrne, A. 1994. "Behaviourism". In *A Companion to the Philosophy of Mind*, S. Guttenplan (ed.), 132–40. Oxford: Blackwell.

Campbell, R. 2001. "The Covert Metaphysics of the Clash Between 'Analytic' and 'Continental' Philosophy". *British Journal for the History of Philosophy* **9**(2): 341–59.

Canguilhem, G. 1988. *Ideology and Rationality in the History of the Life Sciences*, A. Goldhammer (trans.). Cambridge, MA: MIT Press.

Carman, T. 2002. *Heidegger's Analytic*. Cambridge: Cambridge University Press.

Carman, T. 2005. "On the Inescapability of Phenomenology". In *Phenomenology and Philosophy of Mind*, D. W. Smith & A. L. Thomasson (eds), 67–91. Oxford: Oxford University Press.

Carman, T. 2008. "Between Intellectualism and Empiricism". In *Merleau-Ponty: Key Concepts*, R. Diprose & J. Reynolds (eds), 44–56. Stocksfield: Acumen.

Carnap, R. 1934. *Logical Syntax of Language*, A. Smeaton (trans.). London: Kegan Paul.

Carnap, R. [1947] 1988. "Empiricism, Semantics, and Ontology". In *Meaning and Necessity*, 205–21. Chicago, IL: University of Chicago Press.

Carnap, R. 1996. "The Elimination of Metaphysics Through Logical Analysis of Language". In *Logical Empiricism at its Peak: Schlick, Carnap and Neurath*, S. Sarkar (ed), 10–31. New York: Garland.

Cassam, Q. 2009. *The Possibility of Knowledge*. New York: Oxford University Press.

Catalano, J. 1985. *A Commentary on Jean-Paul Sartre's Being and Nothingness*. Chicago, IL: University of Chicago Press.

Chalmers, D. 1996. *The Conscious Mind: In Search of a Fundamental Theory*. Oxford: Oxford University Press.

Chalmers, D. 2002. "Does Conceivability Entail Possibility?" In *Conceivability and Possibility*, T. S. Gendler & J. Hawthorn (eds), 145–200. New York: Oxford University Press, 2002.

Chase, J. 2010. "Analytic Philosophy and Dialogic Conservatism". In Reynolds *et al.* (2010), 85–104.

Chisholm, R. 1982. "The Problem of the Criterion". In *The Foundations of Knowing*, 61–75. Brighton: Harvester.

Chisholm, R. 1989. "States and Events". In *On Metaphysics*, R. Chisholm (ed.), 150–55. Minneapolis, MN: University of Minnesota Press.

Churchland, P. 1981. "Eliminative Materialism and the Propositional Attitudes". *Journal of Philosophy* **78**: 67–90.

Churchland, P. 1988. *Matter and Consciousness*. Cambridge, MA: MIT Press.

Clark, A. 1997. *Being There: Putting Brain, Body, and World Together Again*. Cambridge, MA: MIT Press.

Cobb-Stevens, R. 1990. *Husserl and Analytic Philosophy*. Dordrecht: Kluwer.

Cohen, J. 1986. *The Dialogue of Reason*. New York: Oxford University Press.

Cooke, M. 2002. "Meaning and Truth in Habermas's Pragmatics". *European Journal of Philosophy* **9**(1): 1–23.

Cooper, D. 2003. "Nietzsche and the Analytic Ambition". *Journal of Nietzsche Studies* **26**(1): 1–11.

Critchley, S. 2001. *Continental Philosophy: A Very Short Introduction*. Oxford: Oxford University Press.

Cutrofello, A. 2000. *Continental Philosophy*. London: Routledge.

Daniels, N. 1979. "Wide Reflective Equilibrium and Theory Acceptance in Ethics". *Journal of Philosophy* **76**: 256–82.

Davey, N. 1995. "Beyond the Mannered: The Question of Style in Philosophy or Questionable Styles of Philosophy". In *The Question of Style in Philosophy and the Arts*, C. Van Eck, J. McAllister & R. Van de Vall (eds), 177–200. Cambridge: Cambridge University Press.

Davidson, D. 2001a. *Essays on Actions and Events*. Oxford: Clarendon Press.

Davidson, D. 2001b. "Actions, Reasons and Causes". In Davidson (2001a), 3–20.

Davidson, D. 2001c. "The Individuation of Events". In Davidson (2001a), 163–80.

Davidson, D. 2001d. "Mental Events". In Davidson (2001a), 207–24.

Davidson, D. 2001e. *Inquiries into Truth and Interpretation*. Oxford: Clarendon Press.

Davidson, D. 2001f. "Truth and Meaning". In Davidson (2001e), 17–42.

Davidson, D. 2001g. "On the Very Idea of a Conceptual Scheme". In Davidson (2001e), 183–98.

Dedekind, R. 1963. *Essays on the Theory of Numbers*, W. W. Beman (trans.). New York: Dover.

Deleuze, G. 1990a. *The Logic of Sense*, M. Lester & C. Stivale (trans.). London: Athlone.

Deleuze, G. 1990b. "Michel Tournier and the World Without Others". In *The Logic of Sense*, M. Lester & C. Stivale (trans.), 301–21. London: Athlone.

Deleuze, G. 1992. *Spinoza: Expressionism in Philosophy*, M. Joughin (trans.). New York: Zone Books.

Deleuze, G. 1994. *Difference and Repetition*, P. Patton (trans.). New York: Columbia University Press.

Deleuze, G. 2003. *Francis Bacon: The Logic of Sensation*, D. W. Smith (trans.). London: Continuum.

Deleuze, G. & F. Guattari 1977. *Anti-Oedipus*, R. Hurley, M. Seem & H. Lane (trans.). New York: Viking.

Deleuze, G. & F. Guattari 1987. *A Thousand Plateaus: Capitalism and Schizophrenia*, B. Massumi (trans.). Minneapolis, MN: University of Minnesota Press.

Deleuze, G. & F. Guattari. 1994. *What is Philosophy?*, H. Tomlinson & G. Burchell (trans.). New York: Columbia University Press.

Dennett, D. 1981. "Reflections". In *The Mind's I: Fantasies and Reflections on Self and Soul*, 457–60. Harmondsworth: Penguin.

Dennett, D. 1987. *The Intentional Stance*. Cambridge, MA: MIT Press.

Dennett, D. 1988. "Quining Qualia". In *Consciousness in Contemporary Science*, A. Marcel & E. Bisiach (eds), 42–77. Oxford: Oxford University Press.

Dennett, D. 1992. *Consciousness Explained*. New York: Bay Back Books.

Dennett, D. 2001. "The Fantasy of First-Person Science". http://ase.tufts.edu/cogstud/papers/chalmersdeb3dft.htm (accessed September 2010).

Dennett, D. 2007. "Heterophenomenology Reconsidered". *Phenomenology and the Cognitive Sciences* **6**(1–2): 247–70.

Dennett, D. 2008. "Autobiography (Part 2)". *Philosophy Now* **69**: 21–5.

DePaul, M. 2006. "Intuitions in Moral Inquiry". In *The Oxford Handbook of Ethical Theory*, D. Copp (ed.), 595–623. Oxford: Oxford University Press.

DePaul, M. and W. Ramsey (eds). 2002. *Rethinking Intuition*. Lanham, MD: Rowman & Littlefield.

Derrida, J. 1978a. "Cogito and the History of Madness". In *Writing and Difference*, A. Bass (trans.), 36–76. London: Routledge.

Derrida, J. 1978b. *Edmund Husserl's Origin of Geometry: An Introduction*, J. P. Leavey (trans.). New York: Harvester.

Derrida, J. 1979. *Speech and Phenomena: and Other Essays on Husserl's Theory of Signs*, D. Allison (trans.). Evanston, IL: Northwestern University Press.

Derrida, J. 1982a. "Signature Event Context". In *Margins of Philosophy*, Alan Bass (trans.), 307–30. Chicago, IL: University of Chicago Press.

Derrida, J. 1982b. "White Mythology: Metaphor in the Text of Philosophy". In *Margins of Philosophy*, A. Bass (trans.), 207–72. Chicago, IL: University Of Chicago Press.

Derrida, J. 1983. *Dissemination*, B. Johnson (trans.). Chicago, IL: University Of Chicago Press.

Derrida, J. 1988. *Limited Inc*, G. Graff (ed.). Evanston, IL: Northwestern University Press.

Derrida, J. 1990. *Glas*, J. P. Leavey Jr. & R. Rand (trans.). Lincoln, NE: University of Nebraska Press.

Derrida, J. 1993a. *Aporias*, T. Dutoit (trans.). Stanford, CA: Stanford University Press.

Derrida, J. 1993b. *Memoirs of the Blind: the Self-Portrait and Other Ruins*, P. Brault & M. Naas (trans.). Chicago, IL: University Of Chicago Press.

Derrida, J. 1995a. *The Gift of Death*, D. Wills (trans.). Chicago, IL: University of Chicago Press.

Derrida, J. 1995b. *Points ... Interviews 1974–94*, E. Weber (ed. & trans.). Stanford, CA: Stanford University Press.

Derrida, J. 2001. *A Taste for the Secret*, G. Donis (trans.). Cambridge: Polity.

Derrida, J. 2005. *On Touching – Jean Luc Nancy*, C. Irizarry (trans.). Stanford, CA: Stanford University Press.

Derrida, J. 2007. "Envoi". In *Psyche: Inventions of the Other, Vol. 1*, P. Kamuf & E. Rottenberg (eds), 94–128. Stanford, CA: Stanford University Press.

Descartes, R. 1984. *Meditations on First Philosophy*. In *The Philosophical Writings of*

Descartes, Vol. 2, J. Cottingham, R. Stoothoff & D. Murdoch (trans.), 1–61. Cambridge: Cambridge University Press.

Descombes, V. 1982. *Objects of All Sorts: A Philosophical Grammar*. Baltimore, MD: Johns Hopkins University Press.

Deutscher, M. 2009. "Being Paul Edwards". *Crossroads* **4**(1): 33–42.

Devitt, M. 1997. *Realism and Truth*. Princeton, NJ: Princeton University Press.

Devitt, M. & K. Sterelny 1987. *Language and Reality*. Oxford: Blackwell.

Diamond, C. 1996. *The Realistic Spirit*. Cambridge, MA: MIT Press.

Dillon, M. 1988. *Merleau-Ponty's Ontology*. Evanston, IL: Northwestern University Press.

Dolev, Y. 2007. *Time and Realism*. Cambridge, MA: MIT Press.

Dombrowski, D. 2006. *Rethinking the Ontological Argument*. Cambridge: Cambridge University Press.

Donellan, K. 1962. "Necessity and Criteria". *Journal of Philosophy* **59**: 647–58.

Dowden, B. 2010. "Time". *Internet Encyclopedia of Philosophy*. www.iep.utm.edu/time/ (accessed September 2010).

Dretske, F. 1981. *Knowledge and the Flow of Information*. Oxford: Blackwell.

Dreyfus, H. 1990. "What is Moral Maturity? A Phenomenological Account of the Development of Ethical Expertise". http://socrates.berkeley.edu/~hdreyfus/rtf/Moral_Maturity_8_90.rtf (accessed September 2010).

Dreyfus, H. 1992. *What Computers Still Can't Do*. Cambridge, MA: MIT Press.

Dreyfus, H. & S. Dreyfus 1988. *Mind Over Machine*. New York: Free Press.

Dreyfus, H. & S. Dreyfus 2004. "The Ethical Implications of the Five-Stage Skill-Acquisition Model". *Bulletin of Science, Technology, and Society* **24**: 251–74.

Dreyfus, H. & S. Kelly 2007. "Heterophenomenology". *Phenomenology and Cognitive Sciences* **6**(1): 45–55.

Duke, G., E. Walsh, J. Chase & J. Reynolds 2010. "Postanalytic Philosophy: Overcoming the Divide?" In Reynolds *et al.* (2010), 7–24.

Dummett, M. 1978. *Truth and Other Enigmas*. London: Duckworth.

Dummett, M. 1991. *The Logical Basis of Metaphysics*. Cambridge, MA: Harvard University Press.

Dummett, M. 1993. *Origins of Analytical Philosophy*. London: Duckworth.

Dummett, M. 1996. "Frege and the Paradox of Analysis". In *Frege and Other Philosophers*, 24–48. New York: Oxford University Press.

Dummett, M. 2010. *The Nature and Future of Philosophy*. New York: Columbia University Press.

Duncan-Jones, A. E. 1933. "Statement of Policy", *Analysis* **1**: 1.

Edwards, P. 2004. *Heidegger's Confusions*. Amherst, NY: Prometheus.

Egginton, W. & M. Sandbothe (eds) 2004. *The Pragmatic Turn in Philosophy: Contemporary Engagements Between Analytic and Continental Thought*. Albany, NY: SUNY Press.

Engel, P. 1989. "Continental Insularity: Contemporary French Analytical Philosophy". In *Contemporary French Philosophy*, A. Griffiths (ed.), 1–20. Cambridge: Cambridge University Press.

Engel, P. 1991. "Interpretation Without Hermeneutics: A Plea Against Ecumenism". *Topoi* **10**: 137–46.

Engel, P. 1999. "Analytic Philosophy and Cognitive Norms". *Monist* **82**(2): 218–32.

Everitt, N. 2004. *The Non-Existence of God*. Oxford: Blackwell.

Ewing, A. C. 1935. "Two Kinds of Analysis". *Analysis* **2**: 60–64.

Farber, M. 1940. "Edmund Husserl and the Background of his Philosophy". *Philosophy and Phenomenological Research* **1**: 1–20.

Feigl, H. & W. Sellars (eds) 1949. *Readings in Philosophical Analysis*. New York: Appleton-Century-Crofts.

Ferrell, R. 1993. "Why Bother? Defending Derrida and the Significance of Writing". *Australasian Journal of Philosophy* **71**(2): 121–31.

Fodor, J. 1975. *The Language of Thought*. Cambridge, MA: Harvard University Press.

Fodor, J. 1981. "Methodological Solipsism Considered as a Research Strategy in Cognitive Psychology". In *Representations*, 225–53. Cambridge, MA: MIT Press.

Fodor, J. 1990. "A Theory of Content II: the Theory". In *A Theory of Content and Other Essays*, 89–136. Cambridge, MA: MIT Press.

Foley, R. 1983. "Epistemic Conservatism". *Philosophical Studies* **43**: 165–82.

Føllesdal, D. 1958. *Husserl und Frege*. Oslo: Ashehoug.

Føllesdal, D. 1996. "Analytic Philosophy: What is it and Why Should One Engage In It?" *Ratio* **9**(3): 193–208.

Foot, P. 1978. *Virtues and Vices and Other Essays in Moral Philosophy*. Oxford: Oxford University Press.

Foucault, M. 1972. *The Archeology of Knowledge and The Discourse on Language*, A. M. Sheridan (trans.). New York: Harper Colophon.

Foucault, M. 1977. *Discipline and Punish*, A. Sheridan (trans.). Harmondsworth: Penguin.

Foucault, M. 1984. "Nietzsche, Genealogy, History". In *The Foucault Reader*, P. Rabinow (ed.), 76–100. New York: Pantheon.

Foucault, M. 1990a. *The History of Sexuality*, R. Hurley (trans.). Harmondsworth: Penguin.

Foucault, M. 1990b. *The Use of Pleasure*, R. Hurley (trans.). New York: Vintage.

Foucault, M. 1994. "The Art of Telling the Truth", A. Sheridan (trans.). In *Critique and Power*, M. Kelly (ed.), 139–56. Cambridge, MA: MIT Press.

Foucault, M. 1996. *Foucault Live*, S. Lotringer (ed.), L. Hochroth & J. Johnston (trans.). New York: Semiotext(e).

Foucault, M. 2001a. *Fearless Speech*, J. Pearson (trans.). New York: Semiotext(e).

Foucault, M. 2001b. *The Order of Things: An Archeology of the Human Sciences*, A. M. Sheridan (trans.). New York: Routledge.

Foucault, M. 2005. *The Hermeneutics of the Subject*, F. Gros (ed.), G. Burchell (trans.). New York: Palgrave Macmillan.

Foucault, M. 2006. *The History of Madness*, J. Murphy & J. Khalfa (trans.). London: Routledge.

Frege, G. 1948. "Sense and Reference", H. Feigl (trans.). *Philosophical Review* **57**: 207–30.

Frege, G. 1949. "On Sense and Nominatum", H. Feigl (trans.). In *Readings in Philosophical Analysis*, H. Feigl & W. Sellars (eds), 85–102. New York: Appleton-Century-Crofts.

Frege, G. 1953. *The Foundations of Arithmetic*, 2nd edn, J. L. Austin (trans.). Oxford: Blackwell.

Frege, G. 1972. "Review of Dr. E. Husserl's Philosophy of Arithmetic", E. W. Kluge (trans.). *Mind* **81**: 321–37.

Fricker, M. 2003. "Epistemic Injustice and a Role for Virtue in the Politics of Knowing", *Metaphilosophy* **34**(1–2): 154–73.

Friedman, M. 2000. *A Parting of the Ways: Carnap, Cassirer and Heidegger*. La Salle, IL: Open Court.

Fuchs, T. 2005. "Corporealized and Disembodied Minds". *Philosophy, Psychiatry, Psychology* **12**(2): 95–107.

Fuller, S. 2006. "Karl Popper and the Reconstitution of the Rationalist Left". In *Karl Popper: A Centenary Assessment, Vol. 3, Science*, I. Jarvie, D. Miller & K. Milford (eds), 181–96. London: Ashgate.

Gadamer, H. 1984. "The Hermeneutics of Suspicion". In *Hermeneutics: Questions and Prospects*, G. Shapiro & A. Sica (eds), 73–84. Amherst, MA: University of Massachusetts Press.

Gadamer, H. 2005. *Truth and Method*, J. Weinsheimer & D. G. Marshall (trans.). London: Continuum.

Gaita, R. 1999. *A Common Humanity*. Melbourne: Text Publishing.

Gallagher, S. 2006. *How The Body Shapes the Mind*. Oxford: Oxford University Press.

Gallagher, S. 2008. "Cognitive Science". In *Merleau-Ponty: Key Concepts*, R. Diprose & J. Reynolds (eds), 207–17. Stocksfield: Acumen.

Gallagher, S. & A. Meltzoff 1996. "The Earliest Sense of Self and Others". *Philosophical Psychology* **9**: 213–36.

Gallagher, S. & D. Zahavi 2008a. *The Phenomenological Mind*. New York: Routledge.

Gallagher, S. & D. Zahavi 2008b. "Reply: A Phenomenology with Legs and Brains". *Abstracta*, Special Issue **2**: 86–107.

Gaut, B. 2003. "Justifying Moral Pluralism". In *Ethical Intuitionism*, P. Stratton-Lake (ed.), 137–60. Oxford: Oxford University Press.

Gendler, T. S. 1998. "Galileo and the Indispensability of Scientific Thought Experiments". *British Journal for the Philosophy of Science* **49**: 397–424.

Gendler, T. S. 2000. *Thought Experiment: On the Powers and Limits of Imaginary Cases*. New York: Garland.

George, A. & D. J. Velleman 2002. *Philosophies of Mathematics*. Oxford: Blackwell.

Glendinning, S. (ed.) 2001. *Arguing With Derrida*. Oxford: Blackwell.

Glendinning, S. 2007. *The Idea of Continental Philosophy*. Edinburgh: Edinburgh University Press.

Glendinning, S. 2010. "Argument All the Way Down: The Demanding Discipline of Non-Argumentocentric Modes of Philosophy". In Reynolds *et al*. (2010), 71–84.

Glock, H. 2008. *What is Analytic Philosophy?* Cambridge: Cambridge University Press.

Glymour, C. 1980. *Theory and Evidence*. Princeton, NJ: Princeton University Press.

Goldman, A. I. 1986. *Epistemology and Cognition*. Cambridge, MA: Harvard University Press.

Goldman, A. I. 1989. "Interpretation Psychologized". *Mind and Language* **4**: 161–85.

Goldman, A. I. 1992. "Epistemic Folkways and Scientific Epistemology". In *Liaisons: Philosophy Meets the Cognitive and Social Sciences*, 155–75. Cambridge, MA: MIT Press.

Goldman, A. I. 1993. "The Psychology of Folk Psychology". *Behavioural and Brain Sciences* **16**: 15–28.

Goodman, N. 1978. *Ways of Worldmaking*. New York: Hackett.

Goodman, N. 1983. *Fact, Fiction, and Forecast*. Cambridge, MA: Harvard University Press.

Gopnik, A. & A. Meltzoff 1997. *Words, Thoughts and Theories*. Cambridge, MA: MIT Press.

Gordon, R. 2009. "Folk Psychology as Mental Simulation". *Stanford Encyclopedia of Philosophy*. http://stanford.library.usyd.edu.au/entries/folkpsych-simulation/ (accessed September 2010).

Habermas, J. 1986. "Taking Aim at the Heart of the Present". In *Foucault: A Critical Reader*, D. Hoy (ed.), 103–8. Oxford: Blackwell.

Habermas, J. 1990. *The Philosophical Discourse of Modernity*, F. Lawrence (trans.). Cambridge, MA: MIT Press.

Hacker, P. M. S. 1998. "Analytic Philosophy: What, Whence and Whither?" In *The Story of Analytic Philosophy*, A. Biletzki & A. Matar (eds), 3–36. London: Routledge.

Hanna, R. 2001. *Kant and the Foundations of Analytic Philosophy*. New York: Oxford University Press.

Hare, R. M. 1960. "A School for Philosophers". *Ratio* **2**(2): 107–20.

Hare, R. M. 1979. "What is Wrong with Slavery?" *Policy and Public Affairs* **8**(2): 103–21.

Hare, R. M. 1981. *Moral Thinking*. Oxford: Oxford University Press.

Harman, G. 1965. "The Inference to the Best Explanation". *Philosophical Review* **74**: 88–95.

Harman, G. 1968. "Knowledge, Inference, and Explanation". *American Philosophical Quarterly* **5**: 164–73.

Harris, J. 1975. "The Survival Lottery". *Philosophy* **50**: 81–7.

Harsanyi, J. 1978. "Bayesian Decision Theory and Utilitarian Ethics". *American Economic Review* **68**: 223–8.

Haugeland, J. 2000. *Having Thought*. Cambridge, MA: Harvard University Press.

Hegel, G. W. F. 1979. *Phenomenology of Spirit*, A. V. Miller (trans.). New York: Oxford University Press.

Heidegger, M. 1962. *Being and Time*, J. Macquarrie & E. Robison (trans.). Oxford: Blackwell.

Heidegger, M. 1996a. "What is Metaphysics?" In *Basic Writings*, D. Krell (ed.), 89–110. London: Routledge.

Heidegger, M. 1996b. "The Origin of the Work of Art". In *Basic Writings*, D. Krell (ed.), 139–212. London: Routledge.

Heidegger, M. 1998a. *Parmenides*, A. Schuwer (trans.). Indianapolis, IN: Indiana University Press.

Heidegger, M. 1998b. *Pathmarks*, W. McNeill (ed.). Cambridge: Cambridge University Press.

Heinemann, F. H. 1953. *Existentialism and the Modern Predicament*. New York: Harper.

Hempel, C. 1965. "Aspects of Scientific Explanation". In *Aspects of Scientific Explanation and other Essays*, 331–498. New York: Free Press.

Hill, C. O. & G. E. R. Haddock 2000. *Husserl or Frege? Meaning, Objectivity, and Mathematics*. La Salle, IL: Open Court.

Honig, B. 1993. *Political Theory and the Displacement of Politics*. Ithaca, NY: Cornell University Press.

Hooker, B. 1998. "Rule-Consequentialism and Obligations Toward the Needy". *Pacific Philosophical Quarterly* **79**: 19–33.

Hooker, B. 2003a. *Ideal Code, Real World*. Oxford: Oxford University Press.

Hooker, B. 2003b. "Intuitions and Moral Theorising". In *Ethical Intuitionism*, P. Stratton-Lake (ed.), 161–83. Oxford: Oxford University Press.

Hooker, B., E. Mason & D. Miller (eds) 2000. *Morality, Rules and Consequences: A Critical Reader*. Lanham, MD: Rowman & Littlefield.

Horkheimer, M. 1975. *Critical Theory*, M. J. O'Connell (trans.). London: Continuum.

Hoy, D. 2009. *The Time of Our Lives*. Cambridge, MA: MIT Press.

Hume, D. 2000. *A Treatise of Human Nature*. Oxford: Oxford University Press.

Hurka, T. 2004. "Normative Ethics: Back to the Future". In *The Future for Philosophy*, B. Leiter (ed.), 246–64. Oxford: Oxford University Press.

Husserl, E. 1950. *Cartesian Meditations: An Introduction to Phenomenology*. D. Cairns (trans.). Dordrecht: Martinus Nijhoff.

Husserl, E. 2001. *Logical Investigations*, 2 vols, D. Moran (ed.), J. Findlay (trans.). London: Routledge.

Husserl, E. 2003. *Philosophy of Arithmetic*, D. Willard (trans.). New York: Springer.

Husserl, E. 2004. *Ideas*, U. Melle & S. Spileers (trans.). New York: Routledge.

Hutto, D. & M. Ratcliffe (eds) 2007. *Folk Psychology Reassessed*. New York: Springer.

Hyslop, A. 1995. *Other Minds*. Dordrecht: Kluwer.

Jackson, F. 2003. *From Metaphysics to Ethics: A Defence of Conceptual Analysis*. Oxford: Oxford University Press.

Jackson, F. 2008. "Consciousness". In *Oxford Handbook of Contemporary Philosophy*, 310–33. Oxford: Oxford University Press.

Jackson, F. & D. Braddon-Mitchell 1996. *The Philosophy of Mind and Cognition*. Oxford: Blackwell.

James, W. 1956. *The Will to Believe and Other Essays in Popular Philosophy*. New York: Dover.

Kant, I. 1929. *Critique of Pure Reason*, N. Kemp Smith (trans.). London: Macmillan.

Kelly, S. 2005. "Seeing Things in Merleau-Ponty". In *Cambridge Companion to Merleau-Ponty*, T. Carman & M. Hansen (eds), 74–110. Cambridge: Cambridge University Press.

Kelly, S. 2008. "Husserl's Phenomenology", *Times Literary Supplement* **5482** (25 April): 8–9.

Kenaan, H. 2002. "Language, Philosophy and the Risk of Failure: Rereading the Debate between Searle and Derrida". *Continental Philosophy Review* **35**(2): 117–33.

Kierkegaard, S. 2009. *Concluding Unscientific Postscript to the Philosophical Crumbs*, A. Hannay (trans.). Cambridge: Cambridge University Press.

Knight, C. 2006. "The Method of Reflective Equilibrium: Wide, Radical, Fallible, Plausible". *Philosophical Papers* **35**(2): 205–29.

Kornblith, H. 2002. *Knowledge and its Place in Nature*. Oxford: Clarendon Press.

Körner, S. 1966. "Transcendental Tendencies in Recent Philosophy". *Journal of Philosophy* **63**: 551–61.

Körner, S. 1967. "The Impossibility of Transcendental Deductions". *Monist* **51**(3): 317–31.

Korsgaard, C. 1996. "Reflective Endorsement". In *The Sources of Normativity*, O. O'Neill (ed.), 49–89. Cambridge: Cambridge University Press.

Kripke, S. 1981. *Naming and Necessity*. Oxford: Blackwell.

Kuhn, T. 1977. "A Function for Thought Experiments". In *The Essential Tension*, 240–65. Chicago, IL: University of Chicago Press.

Lakoff, G. & M. Johnson 1999. *Philosophy in the Flesh*. New York: Basic Books.

Lecercle, J. 1987. "The Misprision of Pragmatics: Conceptions of Language in Contemporary French Philosophy". In *Contemporary French Philosophy*, A. P. Griffiths (ed.), 21–41. Cambridge: Cambridge University Press.

Lecercle, J. 2002. *Deleuze and Language*. New York: Palgrave Macmillan.

Leiter, B. 2002. *Routledge Philosophical Guidebook to Nietzsche on Morality*. London: Routledge.

Le Poidevin, R. & M. Macbeath 1993. "Introduction". In *The Philosophy of Time*, R. Le Poidevin & M. MacBeath (eds), 1–20. Oxford: Oxford University Press.

Levinas, E. 1969. *Totality and Infinity*, A. Lingis (trans.). Pittsburgh, PA: Duquesne University Press.

Levinas, E. 1987. *Time and the Other*, R. Cohen (trans.). Pittsburgh, PA: Duquesne University Press.

Levinas, E. 1990. "Intersubjectivity: Notes on Merleau-Ponty". In *Ontology and Alterity in Merleau-Ponty*, G. Johnson & M. Smith (eds), 55–60. Evanston, IL: Northwestern University Press.

Levinas, E. 1998. *Otherwise than Being or Beyond Essence*, A. Lingis (trans.). Pittsburgh, PA: Duquesne University Press.

Levy, N. 2003. "Analytic and Continental: Explaining the Differences". *Metaphilosophy* **34**(3): 284–304.

Lewis, C. I. & C. H. Langford 1932. *Symbolic Logic*. New York: Appleton-Century.

Lewis, D. 1970. "How to Define Theoretical Terms". *Journal of Philosophy* **67**: 17–25.

Lewis, D. 1973. *Counterfactuals*. Cambridge, MA: Harvard University Press.

Lewis, D. 1986. *On the Plurality of Worlds*. Oxford: Blackwell.

Lewis, D. 1999. "Reduction of Mind". In *Papers in Metaphysics and Epistemology*, 291–324. Cambridge: Cambridge University Press.

Libet, B. 1999. "Do We Have Free Will?" In *The Volitional Brain: Towards a Neuroscience of Free Will*, B. Libet, A. Freeman & K. Sunderland (eds), 45–55. Thorverton: Imprint Academic.

Louden, R. 1998. "On Some Vices of Virtue Ethics". In *Virtue Ethics*, R. Crisp & M. Slote (eds), 201–16. New York: Oxford University Press.

Loux, M. J. & D. W. Zimmerman 2003. "Introduction". In *The Oxford Handbook of Metaphysics*, M. J. Loux & D. W. Zimmerman (eds), 1–9. Oxford: Oxford University Press.

Lowe, V. 1985. *Alfred North Whitehead: The Man and His Work, Volume 1, 1861–1910*. Baltimore, MD: Johns Hopkins University Press.

Luchte, J. 2007. "Martin Heidegger and Rudolph Carnap: Radical Phenomenology, Logical Positivism, and the Roots of the Continental/Analytic Divide". *Philosophy Today* **51**(3): 241–60.

Lycan, W. 2001. "Moore against the New Skeptics". *Philosophical Studies* **103**: 35–53.

Lyotard, J.-F. 1984. *The Postmodern Condition*, G. Bennington & B. Massumi (trans.). Minneapolis, MN: University of Minnesota Press.

Lyotard, J.-F. 1989. *The Differend: Phrases in Dispute*, G. Van Den Abbeele (trans.). Minneapolis, MN: University of Minnesota Press.

Lyotard, J.-F. 1991. *The Inhuman: Reflections on Time*. Stanford, CA: Stanford University Press.

Mach, E. 1976. "On Thought Experiments". In *Knowledge and Error: Sketches on the Philosophy of Enquiry*, J. McCormack (trans.), 134–47. Dordrecht: D. Reidel.

MacIntyre, A. 1981. *After Virtue*. Notre Dame, IN: University of Notre Dame Press.

Mackie, J. 1983. *The Miracle of Theism*. New York: Oxford University Press.

Malpas, J. 1997. "The Transcendental Circle". *Australasian Journal of Philosophy* **75**(1): 1–20.

Malpas, J. 2003. *From Kant to Davidson: Philosophy and the Idea of the Transcendental*. Cambridge: Cambridge University Press.

Mandelbaum, M. 1962. "Philosophy, Science, and Sense Perception". *Proceedings and Addresses of the American Philosophical Association* **36**: 5–20.

Marbach, E. 1993. *Mental Representation and Consciousness*. Dordrecht: Kluwer.

Marcel, G. 1973. *Tragic Wisdom and Beyond*, S. Jolin & P. McCormick (trans.). Evanston, IL: Northwestern University Press.

Marcuse, H. 1991. *One Dimensional Man*. Boston, MA: Beacon Press.

Marx, K. & F. Engels 1999. *The Communist Manifesto*, J. E. Toews (ed.). Boston, MA: St Martin's Press.

McCormick, P. (ed.) 1996. *Star-Making: Realism, Anti-realism, and Irrealism*. Cambridge, MA: MIT Press.

McCumber, J. 2001. *Time in the Ditch*. Evanston, IL: Northwestern University Press.

McCumber, J. 2007. *Reshaping Reason*. Indianapolis, IN: Indiana University Press.

McDowell, J. 1996. *Mind and World*. Cambridge, MA: Harvard University Press.

McDowell, J. 2002. "Responses". In *Reading McDowell: On Mind and World*, N. Smith (ed.), 269–305. London: Routledge.

McGinn, M. 1998. "The Real Problem of Others". *European Journal of Philosophy* **6**(1): 45–58.

McTaggart, J. 1896. *Studies in the Hegelian Dialectic*. Cambridge: Cambridge University Press.

McTaggart, J. [1908] 1993. "The Unreality of Time". In *The Philosophy of Time*, R. Le Poidevin & M. MacBeath (eds), 23–34. Oxford: Oxford University Press.

Meillassoux, Q. 2008. *After Finitude*, R. Brassier (trans.). London: Continuum.

Mellor, D. H. 1982. "Theoretically Structured Time". *Philosophical Books* **23**: 65–9.

Meltzoff, A. & M. Moore 1994. "Imitation, Memory, and the Representation of Persons". *Infant Behaviour and Development* **17**: 83–99.

Merleau-Ponty, M. 1964. "The Child's Relations with Others", W. Cobb (trans.). In *The Primacy of Perception and Other Essays*, J. Edie (ed.), 96–158. Evanston, IL: Northwestern University Press.

Merleau-Ponty, M. 1969a. *Humanism and Terror*, J. O'Neill (trans.). Boston, MA: Beacon Press.

Merleau-Ponty, M. 1969b. *The Visible and the Invisible*, A. Lingis (trans.). Evanston, IL: Northwestern University Press.

Merleau-Ponty, M. 1983. *The Structure of Behaviour*, A. Fisher (trans.). Pittsburgh, PA: Duquesne University Press.

Merleau-Ponty, M. 2002. *The Phenomenology of Perception*, C. Smith (trans.). New York: Routledge.

Mill, J. S. 1843. *System of Logic*. London: Longmans.

Mill, J. S. 1962. *Collected Works of John Stuart Mill, Vol. ix*, J. M. Robson (ed.). London: Routledge.

Millikan, R. 1984. *Language, Thought, and Other Biological Categories*. Cambridge, MA: MIT Press.

Millikan, R. 1989. "Biosemantics". *Journal of Philosophy* **86**: 281–97.

Minkowski, H. 1952. "Space and Time". In H. A. Lorentz, A. Einstein, H. Minkowski & H. Weyl, *The Principle of Relativity*, 73–91. New York: Dover.

Mohanty, J. N. 1977. "Husserl and Frege: A New Look at Their Relationship". In *Readings on Edmund Husserl's Logical Investigations*, J. Mohanty (ed.), 22–42. Dordrecht: Springer.

Mohanty, J. N. 1982. *Husserl and Frege*. Bloomington, IN: Indiana University Press.

Mohanty, J. N. 1991. "Method of Imaginative Variation in Phenomenology". In *Thought Experiments in Science and Philosophy*, T. Horowitz & G. Massey (eds), 261–72. Lanham, MD: Rowman & Littlefield.

Monk, R. 1996. *Bertrand Russell*. London: Jonathan Cape.

Moore, G. E. 1989. *Principia Ethica*. Cambridge: Cambridge University Press.

Morris, D. 2007. "Continental Philosophy of Mind". In *Columbia Companion to Twentieth Century Philosophies*, C. Boundas (ed.), 531–44. New York: Columbia University Press.

Mullarkey, J. 2006. *Postcontinental Philosophy*. London: Continuum.

Murray, A. 2002. "Philosophy and the Anteriority Complex". *Phenomenology and the Cognitive Sciences* **1**: 27–47.

Nancy, J.-L. 1991. *Inoperative Community*, P. Connor (ed.), P. Connor, L. Garbus, M. Holland & S. Sawhney (trans.). Minneapolis, MN: University of Minnesota Press.

Nancy, J.-L. 2000. *Being Singular Plural*, R. Richardson & A. O'Byrne (trans.). Stanford, CA: Stanford University Press.

Negri, A. 2005. *Time for Revolution*, M. Mandarini (trans.). London: Continuum.

Newton-Smith, W. 1980. *The Structure of Time*. London: Routledge.

Nichols, S. & S. Stich. 2003. *Mindreading*. Oxford: Oxford University Press.

Nietzsche, F. 1968. *The Will to Power*, W. Kaufmann (ed. & trans.). New York: Vingate.

Nietzsche, F. 1989. *On the Genealogy of Morals and Ecce Homo*, W. Kaufman (ed. & trans.). New York: Vintage.

Nietzsche, F. 1999. *The Birth of Tragedy*, R. Spears (trans.). Cambridge: Cambridge University Press.

Nietzsche, F. 2001. *The Gay Science*, B. Williams (ed.), J. Nauckhoff (trans.). Cambridge: Cambridge University Press.

Norris, C. 2000. *Minding the Gap: Epistemology and Philosophy of Science in the Two Traditions*. Amherst, MA: University of Massachusetts Press.

Norton, J. 1996. "Are Thought Experiments Just What You Thought?" *Canadian Journal of Philosophy* **26**: 333–66.

Nozick, R. 1974. *Anarchy, State, and Utopia*. New York: Basic Books.

Nussbaum, M. 1988. "Non-Relative Virtues: An Aristotelian Approach". In *Midwest Studies in Philosophy Vol. XIII Ethical Theory: Character and Virtue*, P. Uehling & H. Wettstein (eds), 32–5. Notre Dame, IN: University of Notre Dame Press.

Olkowski, D. & L. Haas 1995. *Rereading Merleau-Ponty*. New York: Humanity Press.

Ophir, A. 2001. "How to Take Aim at the Heart of the Present and Remain Analytic". *International Journal of Philosophical Studies* **9**(3): 401–15.

Oppy, G. 1995. *Ontological Arguments and Belief in God*. Cambridge: Cambridge University Press.

Overgaard, S. 2005. "Rethinking Other Minds: Wittgenstein and Levinas on Expression". *Inquiry* **48**(3): 249–74.

Overgaard, S. 2007. *Wittgenstein and Other Minds*. London: Routledge.

Overgaard, S. 2010. "Royaumont Revisited". *British Journal for the History of Philosophy* **18**(5): 899–924.

Pap, A. 1949. *Elements of Analytic Philosophy*. London: Macmillan.

Passmore, J. 1978. *A Hundred Years of Philosophy*. New York: Penguin.

Patton, P. 1989. "Taylor and Foucault on Power and Freedom", *Political Studies* **37**: 260–76.

Petitot, J., F. J. Varela, B. Pachoud & J.-M. Roy (eds) 2000. *Naturalising Phenomenology: Issues in Contemporary Phenomenology and Cognitive Science*. Stanford, CA: Stanford University Press.

Pihlstrom, S. 2003. *Naturalising the Transcendental*. Amherst, NY: Prometheus.

Pinkard, T. 1999. "Analytics, Continentals, and Modern Skepticism". *Monist* **82**(2): 189–217.

Pinker, S. 1994. *The Language Instinct*. Harmondsworth: Penguin.

Pippin, R. 1991. *Modernism as a Philosophical Problem*. Oxford: Blackwell.

Plantinga, A. 1992. "Justification in the 20th Century". In *Philosophical Issues 2, Rationality in Epistemology*, E. Villanueva (ed.), 43–77. Atascadero, CA: Ridgeview.

Popper, K. 1959. "On the Use and Misuse of Imaginary Experiments". In *The Logic of Scientific Discovery*, 464–80. New York: Routledge.

Popper, K. [1945] 2002a. *The Open Society and its Enemies*. New York: Routledge.

Popper, K. 2002b. *Conjectures and Refutations*. New York: Routledge.

Prado, C. G. 2003. *A House Divided*. Amherst, NY: Humanity Books.

Prado, C. G. 2005. *Searle and Foucault on Truth*. Cambridge: Cambridge University Press.

Price, H. 1996. *Time's Arrow and Archimedes' Point*. Oxford: Oxford University Press.

Prichard, H. A. 1968. "Does Moral Philosophy Rest on a Mistake?" In *Moral Obligation and Duty & Interest*, 1–17. Oxford: Oxford University Press.

Priest, G. 2003a. *Beyond the Limits of Thought*. Oxford: Oxford University Press.

Priest, G. 2003b. "Where is Philosophy at the Start of the Twenty-First Century?" *Proceedings of the Aristotelean Soci*ety **103**: 85–99.

Putnam, H. 1962. "It Ain't Necessarily So". *Journal of Philosophy* **59**: 658–71.

Putnam, H. 1974. "The 'Corroboration' of Theories". In *The Philosophy of Karl R. Popper*, P. A. Schilpp (ed.), 221–40. LaSalle, IL: Open Court.

Putnam, H. 1975. "The Meaning of 'Meaning'". In *Mind, Language and Reality: Philosophical Papers Volume 2*, 215–71. Cambridge: Cambridge University Press.

Putnam, H. 1981. *Reason, Truth, and History*. Cambridge: Cambridge University Press.

Putnam, H. 1992. *Renewing Philosophy*. Cambridge, MA: Harvard University Press.

Putnam, H. 1997. "A Half Century of Philosophy". *Daedalus* **12**: 175–208.

Putnam, H. 2005. *Ethics Without Ontology*. Cambridge, MA: Harvard University Press.

Quine, W. V. 1953a. "On What There Is". In *From a Logical Point of View*, 1–19. New York: Harper.

Quine, W. V. 1953b. "Two Dogmas of Empiricism". In *From a Logical Point of View*, 20–46. New York: Harper.

Quine, W. V. [1936] 1966. "Truth by Convention". In *The Ways of Paradox*, 77–106. New York: Random House.

Quine, W. V. 1977. "Epistemology Naturalized". In *Ontological Relativity*, 69–90. New York: Columbia University Press.

Quine, W. V. & J. Ullian 1978. *The Web of Belief*. New York: Random House.

Rachjman, J. and C. West (eds) 1985. *Postanalytic Philosophy*. New York: Columbia University Press.

Ramberg, B. & K. Gjesdal 2005. "Hermeneutics". *Stanford Encyclopedia of Philosophy*, http://plato.stanford.edu/entries/hermeneutics/ (accessed September 2010).

Ramsey, F. 1990. "General Propositions and Causality". In *Philosophical Papers*, D. H. Mellor (ed.), 145–63. Cambridge: Cambridge University Press.

Ramsey, W., S. Stich & J. Garon 1990. "Connectionism, Eliminativism, and the Future of Folk Psychology". *Philosophical Perspectives* **4**: 499–533.

Rancière, J. 2006. *The Politics of Aesthetics*, G. Rockhill (trans.). London: Continuum.

Rawls, J. 2005. *A Theory of Justice*. Cambridge, MA: Harvard University Press.

Redding, P. 2007. *Analytic Philosophy and the Return of Hegelian Thought*. Cambridge: Cambridge University Press.

Reynolds, J. 2006a. "Sadism and Masochism – A Symptomatology of Analytic and Continental Philosophy". *Parrhesia* **1**(1): 88–111.

Reynolds, J. 2006b. "Negotiating the Non-negotiable: Rawls, Derrida, and the Intertwining of Political Calculation and 'Ultra-Politics'". *Theory and Event* **9**(3).

Reynolds, J. 2009a. "Chickening Out and the Idea of Continental Philosophy". *International Journal of Philosophical Studies* **17**(2): 255–72.

Reynolds, J. 2009b. "Reply to Glendinning". *International Journal of Philosophical Studies* **17**(2): 281–7.

Reynolds, J. 2010a. "The Analytic/Continental Divide: A Contretemps?" In *The Antipodean Philosopher, Vol. 2: Public Lectures in Australia and New Zealand*, G. Oppy & N. Trakakis (eds). Lanham, MD: Lexington Books.

Reynolds, J. 2010b. "Common-sense and Philosophical Methodology: Some Metaphilosophical Reflections on Analytic Philosophy and Deleuze". *Philosophical Forum* **41**(3): 231–58.

Reynolds, J. 2010c. "Problem(s) of Other Minds: Solutions and Dissolutions in Analytic and Continental Philosophy". *Philosophy Compass* **4**(1): 1–10.

Reynolds, J., J. Chase, J. Williams & E. Mares (eds) 2010. *Postanalytic and Metacontinental: Crossing Philosophical Divides*. London: Continuum.

Ricoeur, P. 1981. *The Rule of Metaphor*, R. Czerny (trans.). Toronto: University of Toronto Press.

Ricoeur, P. 1992. *Oneself as Another*, K. Blamey (trans.). Chicago, IL: University of Chicago Press.

Ricoeur, P. 2004. *The Conflict of Interpretations: Essays in Hermeneutics*, B. Dauenhauer (trans.). London: Continuum.

Rifkin, J. 1987. *Time Wars*. New York: Touchstone.

Rorty, R. 1981. *Philosophy and the Mirror of Nature*. Princeton, NJ: Princeton University Press.

Rorty, R. 1988. "Representation, Social Practice, and Truth". Philosophical Studies **54**: 215–28.

Rorty, R. 1999. "A Pragmatist View of Contemporary Analytic Philosophy". http://evans-experientialism.freewebspace.com/rorty04.htm (accessed September 2010).

Rosch, E. 1973. "On the Internal Structure of Perceptual and Semantic Categories". In *Cognitive Development and the Acquisition of Language*, T. Moore (ed.), 111–44. New York: Academic Press.

Rosch, E. 1999. "Principles of Categorization". In *Concepts: Core Readings*, S. Laurence & E. Margolis (trans.), 189–206. Cambridge, MA: MIT Press.

Ross, W. D. 1930. *The Right and the Good*. Oxford: Clarendon Press.

Roy, J. M. 2007. "Hetero-Phenomenology and Phenomenological Skepticism". *Phenomenology and the Cognitive Sciences* **6**(1): 1–20.

Russell, B. 1905. "On Denoting". *Mind* **24**(4): 479–93.

Russell, B. 1912a. "The Philosophy of Bergson". *Monist* **22**: 321–47.

Russell, B. 1912b. *The Problems of Philosophy*. Oxford: Oxford University Press.

Russell, B. 1914. *Our Knowledge of the External World*. London: Allen & Unwin.

Russell, B. 1917a. "Mysticism and Logic". In *Mysticism and Logic*, B. Russell (ed), 1–32. London: Allen & Unwin.

Russell, B. 1917b. "On Scientific Method in Philosophy". In *Mysticism and Logic*, B. Russell (ed.), 97–124. London: Allen & Unwin.

Russell, B. 1948. *Human Knowledge: Its Scope and Limits*. London: Allen & Unwin.

Russell, B. 1953. "The Cult of 'Common Usage'". *British Journal for the Philosophy of Science* **3**: 303–7.

Russell, B. 1956. "The Philosophy of Logical Atomism". In *Logic and Knowledge*, R. C. Marsh (ed.), 177–282. London: Allen & Unwin.

Russell, B. 1984. *Theory of Knowledge: the 1913 Manuscript, volume 7 of the Collected Papers of Bertrand Russell*, E. R. Eames (ed.). London: Allen & Unwin.

Russell, B. [1903] 2005. *The Principles of Mathematics*. Ann Arbor, MI: University of Michigan Press.

Russell, B. 2007. *History of Western Philosophy*. New York: Touchstone.

Ryle, G. 1949. *The Concept of Mind*. London: Hutchinson.

Ryle, G. 1952. "Systematically Misleading Expressions". In *Essays on Logic and Language*, A. Flew (ed.), 11–36. Oxford: Blackwell.

Ryle, G. 1971. *Collected Papers*. London: Hutchinson.

Sacks, M. 2005a. "The Nature of Transcendental Arguments". *International Journal of Philosophical Studies* **13**(4): 439–60.

Sacks, M. 2005b. "Sartre, Strawson and Others". *Inquiry* **48**(3): 275–99.

Sacks, M. 2006. "Naturalism and the Transcendental Turn". *Ratio* **19**: 92–106.

Sandel, M. 1982. *Liberalism and the Limits of Justice*. Cambridge: Cambridge University Press.

Sandel, M. 1996. *Democracy's Discontents*. Cambridge, MA: Harvard University Press.

Sartre, J.-P. 1991. *The Transcendence of the Ego: An Existentialist Theory of Consciousness*, B. Frechtman (trans.). New York: Hill & Wang.

Sartre, J.-P. 1993. *Being and Nothingness: An Essay in Phenomenological Ontology*, H. Barnes (trans.). London: Routledge.

Scarre, G. 2007. *Death*. Stocksfield: Acumen.

Schildknecht, C. 1990. *Philosophische Masken: Literarische Formen der Philosophie bei Platon, Descartes, Wolff und Lichtenberg*. Stuttgart: Metzler.

Schiller, F. C. S. 1921. "Novelty: The Presidential Address". *Proceedings of the Aristotelian Society* **22**: 1–22.

Scholl, B. & P. Tremoulet 2000. "Perceptual Causality and Animacy". *Trends in Cognitive Sciences* **4**(8): 299–309.

Schumann, K. & B. Smith 1987. "Adolf Reinach: An Intellectual Biography". In *Speech Act and Sachverhalt: Reinach and the Foundations of Realist Phenomenology*, K. Mulligan (ed.), 1–27. Dordrecht: Nijhoff.

Searle, J. 1970. *Speech Acts*. Cambridge: Cambridge University Press.

Searle, J. 1999. "Neither Phenomenological Description Nor Rational Reconstruction: Reply to Dreyfus". http://socrates.berkeley.edu/~jsearle/articles.html (accessed September 2010).

Searle, J. 2008. *Expression and Meaning*. Cambridge: Cambridge University Press.

Sellars, W. 1978. "Some Reflections on Perceptual Consciousness". In *Crosscurrents in Phenomenology*, R. Bruzina & B. Wilshire (eds), 169–85. The Hague: Martinus Nijhoff.

Shapiro, G. 1990. "Translating, Repeating, Naming: Foucault, Derrida, and the *Genealogy of Morals*". In *Nietzsche as Postmodernist*, C. Koelb (ed.), 39–56. Albany, NY: SUNY Press.

Shoemaker, S. 1969. "Time Without Change". *Journal of Philosophy* **66**(12): 363–81.

Sider, T. 2001. *Four Dimensionalism*. Oxford: Clarendon Press.

Singer, P. 2009. *Animal Liberation*. London: Harper.

Sinnerbrink, R. 2010. "Disenfranching Film? On the Analytic-Cognitivist Turn in Film Theory". In Reynolds *et al.* (2010), 173–90.

Smith, B. *et al.* 1992. "Open Letter Against Derrida Receiving an Honorary Doctorate from Cambridge University". *The Times*, Saturday 9 May.

Soames, S. 2003a. *Philosophical Analysis in the Twentieth Century, Volume I: The Dawn of Analysis*. Princeton, NJ: Princeton University Press.

Soames, S. 2003b. *Philosophical Analysis in the Twentieth Century, Volume II: The Age of Meaning*. Princeton, NJ: Princeton University Press.

Sobel, J. 2004. *Logic and Theism*. New York: Cambridge University Press.

Sokal, A. & J. Bricmont 1999. *Fashionable Nonsense*. New York: Picador.

Sorensen, R. 1992. *Thought Experiments*. Oxford: Oxford University Press.

Sosa, E. 1983. "Consciousness of the Self and of the Present". In *Agent, Language and the Structure of the World*, J. Tomberlin (ed.), 131–43. Indianapolis, IN: Hackett.

Stanley, J. & T. Williamson 2001. "Knowing How". *Journal of Philosophy* **98**: 441–4.

Stawarska, B. 2008. "Psychoanalysis". In *Merleau-Ponty: Key Concepts*, R. Diprose & J. Reynolds (eds), 57–69. Stocksfield: Acumen.

Sterelny, K. 1990. *The Representational Theory of Mind*. Oxford: Blackwell.

Stern, R. 2004. *Transcendental Arguments and Scepticism*. Oxford: Clarendon Press.

Stich, S. 1978. "Autonomous Psychology and the Belief-Desire Thesis". *Monist* **61**: 573–91.

Stich, S. 1993. *The Fragmentation of Reason*. Cambridge, MA: MIT Press.

Stiegler, B. 1998. *Technics and Time, 1*, R. Beardsworth & G. Collins (trans.). Stanford, CA: Stanford University Press.

Stiegler, B. 2007. "Technics, Media, Teleology: An Interview with Bernard Stiegler". *Theory, Culture and Society* **24**(7–8): 334–41.

Stocker, M. 1998. "The Schizophrenia of Modern Ethical Theories". In *Virtue Ethics*, R. Crisp & M. Slote (eds), 66–78. New York: Oxford University Press.

Stoljar, D. and Y. Nagasawa 2004. "Introduction". In *There's Something About Mary*, P. Ludlow, Y. Nagasawa & D. Stoljar (eds), 1–36. Cambridge, MA: MIT Press.

Strawson, P. F. 1952. *Introduction to Logical Theory*. London: Methuen.

Strawson, P. F. 1959. *Individuals*. London: Methuen.

Strawson, P. F. 1966. *The Bounds of Sense*. London: Methuen.

Strawson, P. F. 1985. *Skepticism and Naturalism*. New York: Columbia University Press.

Stroll, A. 2001. *Twentieth-Century Analytic Philosophy*. New York: Columbia University Press.

Stroud, B. 1968. "Transcendental Arguments". *Journal of Philosophy* **65**: 241–56.

Sunstein, C. 2005. "Moral Heuristics", *Behavioral and Brain Sciences* **28**: 531–73.

Swinburne, R. 1990. "Tensed Facts", *American Philosophical Quarterly* **27**: 117–30.

Tarski, A. 1956. "The Concept of Truth in Formalized Languages". In *Logic, Semantics, Meta-Mathematics*, 152–278. Oxford: Clarendon Press.

Taylor, C. 1984a. "Foucault on Freedom and Truth". *Political Theory* **12**(2): 152–83.

Taylor, C. 1984b. "Philosophy and its History". In *Philosophy in History*, R. Rorty, J. B. Schneewind & Q. Skinner (eds), 17–30. Cambridge: Cambridge University Press.

Taylor, C. 1985. *Philosophical Papers I*. Cambridge: Cambridge University Press.

Taylor, C. 1995a. "Overcoming Epistemology". In *Philosophical Arguments*, 1–19. Cambridge, MA: Harvard University Press.

Taylor, C. 1995b. "The Validity of Transcendental Arguments". In *Philosophical Arguments*, 20–33. Cambridge, MA: Harvard University Press.

Thompson, E. 2007. *Mind in Life*. Cambridge, MA: Harvard University Press.

Thomson, J. J. 1971. "A Defence of Abortion". *Philosophy and Public Affairs* **1**(1): 47–66.

Toadvine, T. 2008. "Phenomenology and Hyper-reflection". In *Merleau-Ponty: Key Concepts*, R. Diprose & J. Reynolds (eds), 17–29. Stocksfield: Acumen.

Tugendhat, E. 1976. *Traditional and Analytical Philosophy*. Cambridge: Cambridge University Press.

Tversky, A. & D. Kahneman 1982. "Judgment Under Uncertainty: Heuristics and Biases". In *Judgment under Uncertainty: Heuristics and Biases*, D. Kahneman, P. Slovic & A. Tversky (eds), 3–20. Cambridge: Cambridge University Press.

Unger, P. 1996. *Living High and Letting Die*. New York: Oxford University Press.

Van Cleve, J. 1979. "Foundationalism, Epistemic Principles and the Cartesian Circle". *Philosophical Review* **88**: 55–91.

Van Hooft, S. 2005. *Understanding Virtue Ethics*. Chesham: Acumen.

281

Van Inwagen, P. 2009. "Being, Existence and Ontological Commitment". In *Metametaphysics*, D. Chalmers, G. Manley & L. Wasserman (eds), 472–506. Oxford: Oxford University Press.

Varela, F., E. Thompson & E. Rosch 1992. *The Embodied Mind*. Cambridge, MA: MIT Press.

Waismann, F. 1979. *Ludwig Wittgenstein and the Vienna Circle*. Oxford: Blackwell.

Walzer, M. 1984. *Spheres of Justice*. New York: Basic Books.

Warnock, G. J. 1956. "Analysis and Imagination". In *The Revolution in Philosophy*, A. J. Ayer (ed.), 111–26. London: Macmillan.

Warnock, M. 1960. *Ethics Since 1900*. Oxford: Oxford University Press.

Weinberg, J. 2007. "How to Challenge Intuitions Empirically Without Risking Skepticism". *Midwest Studies in Philosophy* **31**: 318–43.

Weinberg, J., S. Stich & S. Nichols 2001. "Normativity and Epistemic Intuitions". *Philosophical Topics* **29**: 429–60.

Weitz, M. 1950. "Analysis and Real Definition". *Philosophical Studies* **1**: 1–8.

Wheeler, S. 2000. *Deconstruction as Analytic Philosophy*. Stanford, CA: Stanford University Press.

Wheeler, M. 2001. "Two Threats to Representationalism", *Synthese* **129**(2): 211–31.

Wheeler, M. 2005. *Reconstructing the Cognitive World*. Cambridge, MA: MIT Press.

Wheeler, M. & M. Cappuccio 2010. "Can the Philosophy of Mind be a Meeting of Minds?" In Reynolds *et al.* (2010), 25–44.

Whewell, W. 1840. *The Philosophy of the Inductive Sciences*. London: John Parker.

Whitehead, A. N. 2009. *Treatise on Universal Algebra*. Cambridge: Cambridge University Press.

Williams, B. 1973. "The Self and the Future". In *Problems of the Self*, 46–63. Cambridge: Cambridge University Press.

Williams, B. 1976. *Utilitarianism: For and Against*. Cambridge: Cambridge University Press.

Williams, B. 1996. "Contemporary Philosophy: A Second Look". In *The Blackwell Companion to Philosophy*, N. Bunnin and E. P. Tsui-James (eds), 23–33. Oxford: Blackwell.

Williams, B. 2002. *Truth and Truthfulness: An Essay in Genealogy*. Princeton, NJ: Princeton University Press.

Williams, J. 2005. *The Transversal Thought of Gilles Deleuze*. Manchester: Clinamen Press.

Williamson, T. 2005. "Past The Linguistic Turn?" In *The Future For Philosophy*, B. Leiter (ed.), 106–28. Oxford: Oxford University Press.

Williamson, T. 2008. *The Philosophy of Philosophy*. London: Wiley-Blackwell.

Winograd, T. 2000. "Foreword". In *Heidegger, Coping and Cognitive Science*, M. Wrathall & J. Malpas (eds), vii–x. Cambridge, MA: MIT Press.

Wisdom, J. 1934. *Problems of Mind and Matter*. Cambridge: Cambridge University Press.

Witt-Hansen, J. 2003. "H. C. Ørsted: Immanuel Kant and the Thought Experiment". In *Kierkegaard and his Contemporaries: the Culture of Golden Age Denmark*, J. Stewart (ed.), 62–77. Berlin: de Gruyter.

Wittgenstein, L. 1984. *Culture and Value*, G. E. M. Anscombe (ed.), L. McAlister (trans.). Chicago, IL: University of Chicago Press.

Wittgenstein, L. 1997. *Philosophical Investigations*, G. E. M. Anscombe (ed.). New York: Blackwell.

Wittgenstein, L. 2003. *Tractatus Logico-Philosophicus*, D. F. Pears & B. F. McGuinness (trans.). New York: Routledge.

Wittgenstein, L. 2007. *Zettel*, G. E. M. Anscombe (trans.). Oxford: Blackwell.

Woodward, A. 2008. "The Status of Transcendental Arguments". Paper presented at Analytic–Continental conference, Melbourne, July.

Wrathall, M. 1999. "The Conditions of Truth in Heidegger and Davidson". *Monist* **82**: 304–23.

Wrathall, M. & J. Malpas (eds) 2000. *Heidegger, Coping and Cognitive Science*. Cambridge, MA: MIT Press.

Wright, C. 1992. *Truth and Objectivity*. Cambridge, MA: Harvard University Press.
Young, I. M. 1990. *Justice and the Politics of Difference*. Princeton, NJ: Princeton University Press.
Zahavi, D. 2007. "Killing the Straw Man: Dennett and Phenomenology". *Phenomenology and Cognitive Sciences* **6**(1): 21–43.

INDEX

285